T0373471

THE
PUBLICATIONS

OF THE

Lincoln Record Society,

ESTABLISHED IN THE YEAR

1910.

VOLUME I.

FOR THE YEAR ENDING 30TH SEPTEMBER, 1911.

Fenestres.

G. 3. Keyes Or.
B. 3. Crosses portate Arg.
Lozengy Or. & G. — Crown.
Lozengy Sa. & Ermyne — Patten.
Empaled {Quarterly France, & England
         {G. 2. Barres betw. 6. martlets Or.
G. 3. Crosses botony.
G. a Crosse Patonce Or — Latymer.
G. Crosse Crusilly fitchy a Lyon rampant Arg. — La Warre.
G. a Bende & 2. Bendlets above — Grelle.
Lozengy Or. & G. — Crown.
Or. a Saltier engrayled Sa. — Botetorte.
Quarterly {Arg. a cheife G. over all a Bend. B. — Cromwell.
          {Chequy Or. & G. a Cheife Ermine — Tateshale.
Barry of 6. peices Arg. & B. in cheife 3 Lozenges}
          G. a mullet difference. — Fleming.
B. a Bend or. — Scrope.
Arg. a Felse G. in Cheife 3 Torteauxes — Deverux.
Arg. a chevron betw. 3. Martlets Sa. —
Sa. a Frett Arg. — Harington.
Quarterly {Sa. a Crosse engrayled Or. — Willughby.
          {G. a Crosse Molyn Arg. —
Arg. a Crosse Molin Sa. —
Arg. a Saltier G. —
B. a Saltier Arg. —
Quarterly {Arg. a Crosse engrayled. G. betw. 4.}
          {   waterbougets Sa. — Bourchier.
          {G. Billetty Or. a Felse Arg. — Louaine.
Quarterly G. & Or. a Mullet on y first Quter Arg. — Vere.
B. an Estoyle Arg. —
Empaled {B. an Estoyle Arg.
        {Verry Or. & G. — Ferrers.
Or. a Chevron. G. on a Border B. 8. Myters Or. — Stafford Epus.
Arg. a Felse G. betw. 3. Popinjayes Vert — Lumley.
B. a Chevron betw. 3. Garbes Or. —
G. a Saltier Arg. — Neuile.
Quarterly {Bourchier.}
          {Louaine. —} Bourchier Earle of
                      Essex.
Quarterly France semy. & England a Border Arg.
Quarterly France semy. & England a Label of 3. Ermyne —
Quarterly France semy. & England a Label of 3 Arg. —
Quarterly France semy. & England, on a Border B.}
          8. Fleures. de Lize Or. —
Arg. a chevron betw. 3. Gryphons heads erased. B. — Tilney.
G. 3. waterbougets Ermyne — Roos.
Arg. 2. Barres & a Canton. —
G. a Crosse Patonce Or. a Border Arg. —

Croyland.

**Facsimile of page 239 of Harleian Manuscript 6829 in the
British Museum** (*see pages* 180·1).

LINCOLNSHIRE
CHURCH NOTES

MADE BY

GERVASE HOLLES,

A.D. 1634 TO A.D. 1642.

AND EDITED FROM HARLEIAN MANUSCRIPT 6829, IN THE BRITISH
MUSEUM, BY

R. E. G. COLE, M.A.

———

LINCOLN :

PRINTED FOR THE LINCOLN RECORD SOCIETY BY
W. K. MORTON & SONS, 290 HIGH STREET, LINCOLN.

———

1911.

First published 1911

Reprinted 2010
Transferred to digital printing

A Lincoln Record Society Publication
published by The Boydell Press
PO Box 9, Woodbridge, Suffolk IP12 3DF, UK
and of Boydell & Brewer Inc.
668 Mt. Hope Avenue, Rochester NY 14620, USA
website: www.boydellandbrewer.com

ISBN 978-0-901503-90-9

A catalogue record for this title is available
from the British Library

This publication is printed on acid-free paper

Printed in Great Britain by
CPI Antony Rowe Ltd, Chippenham, and Eastbourne

Introduction.

GERVASE HOLLES, M.A. & M.P., royalist Colonel
of Foot, and above all "a learned and judicious
Antiquary," to whom we are indebted for the following Notes on our Lincolnshire Churches as they
were before the Great Rebellion, was born at Great
Grimsby in this county on 9 March, 1606-7, his
baptism, as "Gervis ye sonne of Fretchwell Hollis,
gent.," being entered in the Register of St. James' Church on March
13th of that year.   He was the representative of a younger branch of
the noble family of Holles, which by marriage had acquired property at
Grimsby, and had settled there early in the 17th century.   Like many
other noble families, that of Holles owed its rise to an ancestor who
had made a fortune in trade, its virtual founder being Sir William
Holles, knt., who lived in the reigns of Henry VII and Henry VIII.
He was made free of the Mercers' Company in London in 1499. rose
to be Master of that Company in 1519, and after becoming Sheriff and
Alderman of London in 1527, and holding the office of Lord Mayor
in 1539, he died in 1542.   His two sons, Sir Thomas and Sir William
Holles, were knighted at the coronation of Edward VI, but while the
elder son, Sir Thomas, wasted his patrimony so that his descendants
fell into obscurity, the second son, Sir William Holles, bought from
the Stanhope family the estate of Haughton near Tuxford, and built or
added to the hall there (now destroyed) which, as his descendant tells
us, bore carved in stone on either side of the entrance his initials,
W.H., with the date 1545, and his device of a holly-branch with clusters
of berries.   Here he resided in great state, Thoroton telling us that he
began his Christmas-tide at All-Hallows, and continued it till Candle-
mas, during which time any man might stay three days at Haughton
without being asked who he was or whence he came.*   His lavish
hospitality gained him the title of the good Sir William ; and in spite
of it, when he died in 1591, at the age of 87, he is said to have left an
estate of £10,000 a year to his heir.   He had, however, outlived his
natural heir, his eldest son, Denzil Holles, who had resided at Irby
near Grimsby, and who, dying on 12th April, 1590, was buried in Irby

---

* Thoroton's *Notts.*, vol. iii, p. 360.

church. He was succeeded therefore at Haughton by his grandson, Denzil's eldest son, John Holles, created by James I Baron of Haughton in 1616, and Earl of Clare in 1624, who was the father of John Holles, second Earl of Clare, and Denzil Holles, who took so prominent a part in the House of Commons against the king, but who later was created by Charles II Baron Holles of Ifield.

A second son of the good Sir William was Gervase Holles—Sir Gervase Holles, of Burgh, co. Linc., knt.—as his grandson and namesake styles him. He was born at Haughton in 1547, taking his name from his godfather, Sir Gervase Clifton, of Clifton, knt., with whose family he formed subsequently a closer connection by his marriage to Sir Gervase Clifton's grand-daughter, Frances, daughter and coheiress of Peter Frescheville, of Staveley, co. Derby, esq. Sir Gervase Holles died, aged 80, in 1628, and was buried in St. James' Church, Great Grimsby, his burial being entered in the Parish Register in capital letters on 7 March, 1627-8, as "Sr Gervis Hollis, Knight."* He left two sons, Frescheville and Francis, of whom the elder Frescheville had become resident in Grimsby through his marriage there in 1600 with Elizabeth, daughter and heiress of John Kingston of that town. Here Gervase Holles, the author of the following notes, was born, as has been said, on 9th March, 1607. The next year his mother died, and his father married, secondly, at West Keale in 1613 Dorothy, daughter of Herbert Lacon, and widow of Francis Tyrwhit. She only survived till 1619. when she was buried at Humberston, having had two children who both died young. Frescheville Holles himself was Mayor of Grimsby in 1627, but died 10 May, 1630, and was buried with his first wife and others of his family in St. James' Church, as recorded in the following notes.

Gervase Holles, the only surviving son. had been admitted to the Middle Temple in 1628, but on his father's death and his succession to the family estates he returned to Grimsby. Shortly after, on 17th June, 1630, he married Dorothy, daughter of John Kirkton of that town, and here he spent the next four years, occupying himself in altering and rebuilding his house,† and in gathering materials, "Records, Charters, and Church Monuments," for a history of "the County of Lincoln, the place where I received my birth, and have had my habitation," as he himself relates.‡ In Sept., 1634, he removed for a while to Mansfield, co. Notts., near Haughton. "in the centre of his principal kindred and relations." Here four months later his wife, Dorothy, died in childbirth, and she and her infant daughter were buried in Mansfield church

---

* The Register of St. James' Church, Great Grimsby, has been edited and privately printed by G. S. Stephenson, M.D.

† This was "the old stone house on the west side of Haven Street, which has recently been taken down," says Dr. G. Oliver, Curate of Grimsby, 1829, in his *Hist. & Ant. of St. James', Grimsby*.

‡ Collins' *Noble Families*, p. 51.

in January, 1635. Another child, George, died at Grimsby the following August, leaving him with one only daughter, Elizabeth, born at
Grimsby in 1631. At Michaelmas he returned to the Middle Temple,
where he was chosen Comptroller of that society, and contributed
largely towards the expenses of their Christmas Masque. In 1636 he
was elected Mayor of Grimsby, as he was again in 1638. and in
December, 1637, there is an entry in the State Papers of a sum of £15
having been paid on his behalf for Ship-money collected by him in
Grimsby during the first year of his mayoralty.* About this time too
he married as his second wife, Elizabeth, daughter of Col. William
Molesworth, who like himself had been born at Grimsby, though the
marriage took place on 4th December, 1637, at St. Andrew's, Holborn.

In 1640 Gervase Holles was chosen as M.P. for Grimsby at the two
elections of that year, in March and in October. The latter was the
beginning of the Long Parliament, in which in opposition to his kinsman Denzil Holles, he was a strenuous defender of the royal prerogative, with the result that on 26th April, 1641, he was suspended from
the service of the House. and finally was disabled from sitting in it, a
new writ being issued for Grimsby, 22nd August, 1642. On 27th
August of that year the king raised his standard at Nottingham, and
Gervase Holles proceeded to join him there with 117 men. Subsequently he raised a regiment of infantry at his own cost, which he
commanded as Colonel at Edgehill and elsewhere for a space of 13
months.† At Edgehill he was again opposed to his kinsman Denzil
Holles who, on the Parliamentary side, commanded a regiment of
Cockney red-coats, so called from the place of their recruitment and
the colour of their coats. Later he attended the King to Oxford,
where he received the degree of M.A. from that loyal university on 1st
Nov., 1642, being then described as "Serjeant-Major of the army," and
he took his seat as Member for Grimsby in the Parliament which
assembled at Oxford the following year.‡ For some portion of this
time he formed part of the royalist garrison at Newark where. it seems,
his wife had already taken refuge, as his son Frescheville Holles was
born there on 8th June, 1642. Here he had to deplore the loss of his
first cousin William Holles, only child of his uncle Francis, who had
been closely associated with him in his antiquarian researches, but who
was killed at the age of 23, on the 6th March, 1643, while serving as
Captain under his command in a fight with the rebels near Muskham
bridge.§ In December, 1645, when the king's cause was hopeless, he

* *Cal. of State Papers*, 1637-8, p. 2.

† *Cal. of State Papers*, 1660-1, p. 112.

‡ Wood's *Fasti Oxon*, v. ii, p. 29.

§ *Addit. MSS.* 6118 ; at the close of which Gervase Holles after recording that
the last 100 pp. of the MS. had been transcribed for him by his cousin William
Holles, pays a touching tribute to his memory, and relates the manner of his death.

attempted to compound with the Parliamentary Commissioners for his
so-called delinquency, pleading that he had voluntarily laid down his
commission two years since and surrendered to the Earl of Manchester.
He was fined £738, reckoned as one-third of his estate, which he was
unable to pay.* In 1648 he took part in that royalist rising which
ended in the siege and surrender of Colchester in the August of that
year. More fortunate than the two commanders, Sir Charles Lucas
and Sir George Lisle, who were shot in cold blood, he escaped with a
long imprisonment, and after Charles I's death was allowed to retire in
banishment to France. The young king admitted him to his Council,
and it is said, would have created him a Baronet had he cared to
accept that honour. No doubt it must have appealed to his love of
heraldry that Charles II granted him a honorary augmentation of his
Coat of Arms, authorizing him to bear *Or, two Piles, Gules*, quartered
with his paternal coat, *Erm. two Piles, Sable.*† The Sign Manual
making him the grant, dated at Jersey, 4th Dec., 1649, sets forth that it
was in consideration of his descent and services, that in Parliament he
strenuously defended the king's prerogative, and being Colonel of a
Regiment in the time of the Rebellion behaved with exemplary valour
against the rebels in the several battles of Kenton (Edgehill), Banbury,
Brentford, Newark, Atherton, Bradford and Newbury, as well as in the
siege of Colchester, and had suffered divers imprisonments, with the
loss of all his inheritance in the royal cause.‡

On 25th February, 1652, his wife Elizabeth, with two children and
two servants, had a warrant to join him in France,§ but her stay there
could have been but temporary, as on 20th May of that year she was
petitioning the Parliamentary Commissioners for the arrears of her
allowance of one-fifth of her husband's confiscated estate, of which she
had received nothing. This request was granted, and a little later, on
26th Oct., 1653, Gervase Holles succeeded in compounding with
Parliament for his forfeited estates on payment of a fine of £860.‖ In
1657 he was still in exile in Holland, engaged in forwarding the interests
of the king, but personally so impoverished that in July, 1659, he writes
to Sir Edward Nicholas from Rotterdam that he could not quit that
city for want of money, and that for the last three years he had been
dependent on the hospitality of a good woman, who had kept him from

---

* *Cases for Compounding*, pt. ii, p. 1056.

† Most of the many representations of G. Holles' Coat of Arms in his MSS.
are of earlier date than this, and have *Erm. 2 piles Sable*, in their first quarter. One
only (*Addit. MS.* 6118) has *Or, 2 piles, Gules*, as the first quartering, instead of, not
in addition to, his paternal coat It is the first of 12 quarterings and impales
Molesworth, quarterly of four.

‡ Collins' *Noble Families*, p. 73.

§ *Cal. of State Papers*, 1652, p. 552.

‖ *Cases for Compounding.* p. 1056.

starving.* With the Restoration naturally his prospects changed. He returned to England, and before July, 1660, was made Master of Requests to the king, and in the following January an annuity of £100 a year was settled upon him.† On 3rd April, 1661, his townsfolk at Grimsby returned him as their representative to Parliament ; he continued to represent the borough until his death, and held the office of Mayor for the third time in 1663.

By his second wife Elizabeth, who died at Chelsea, 21st March, 1661, Gervase Holles had one only surviving son, Sir Frescheville Holles, born in 1642, a naval captain who was knighted after the sea fight with the Dutch off Lowestoft in 1665. He was M.P. for Grimsby with his father in 1667, and Mayor of Grimsby in 1669 ; but was killed while in the command of the *Cambridge* man-of-war at the Battle of Sole-bay on 28th May, 1672. He was buried, as his relative Sir George Holles had been, in St. Edmund's Chapel in Westminster Abbey. At his death a debt of £1500 was found to be due from his estate to the king, this was ultimately remitted in consideration of Col. Gervase Holles' own sufferings and services, and the loss of his only son, and of the fact that his son's widow, Dame Jane Holles, had brought him a marriage portion of £5000, but was now left without provision for her support.‡ By Sir Frescheville's death without issue, the male line of Gervase Holles' family became extinct, but his daughter Elizabeth, who was married to Edward Berkeley, Esq., was living in 1670, and had a son, Gervase Berkeley, born 29th March, 1665.§

" Coll. Jervais Hollis, Master of Requests, died 10th Feb., 1674-5, and was buried at Mansfield, co. Notts." So writes Mr. Ashmole in his Diary,∥ and his burial at Mansfield is entered thus in the Register there, " 1674, March 13, Gervice Hollis, Esq., bur." He was aged 68, and by an irony of fate he who has been the means of preserving the memorials of so many other men, has remained without any memorial to himself.

When Holles' house at Grimsby was plundered by the Parliamentarians, a great part of his treasured collections were lost. " The remainder of the wreck," as he calls it, he contrived to have transported over to him in the Low Countries, but though there he had abundance of leisure, he found it impossible to continue his history of Lincolnshire with such imperfect materials. All he could do was to compile an account of his own family, which has been printed in Collins' *Noble Families*. Of his manuscripts which have been preserved, the best

---

* *Cal. of State Papers*, 1659, p. 22.
† *Cal. of State Papers*, 1660-1, p. 496.
‡ *Cal. of State Papers*, 1673, p. 434.
§ *Lansdowne MSS.*, 207 D.
∥ Wood's *Fasti Oxonienses*, v. II, p. 29.

known and most valuable is the present Harleian MS. 6829, now in the British Museum. This is a folio volume of 349 pp., 16 inches by 11 inches, enriched on either margin by nearly 1,900 coloured shields of the coats of arms blazoned in the text, which were gathered by him out of some 290 churches in this county. The work has never before been printed as a whole, probably owing to the cost and difficulty of reproducing these illustrations; but copious extracts have been made from it, no local history being complete unless it included G. Holles' account of the church and its monuments as they were before the time of the Commonwealth. Manuscript copies of course exist; special mention must here be made of the beautiful manuscript reproduction of the volume, with its many coats of arms illuminated in a style far surpassing that of the original. This was made for the late Mr. J. L. ffytche, of Thorpe Hall, Louth, at a cost it is said of £250, a sum which may readily be believed. Subsequently it was purchased by Miss Ruston, of Monks' Manor, Lincoln, and by her was generously presented to the Cathedral Library, where the present editor has been allowed to make use of it. It must be confessed however that the accuracy of its text is by no means equal to the beauty of its illustrations. Far more accurate as regards the text is a manuscript copy made for his own use by the late Rev. Frederick Pyndar Lowe, rector of Salt-fleetby, and one of the earliest and most prominent members of the *Lincolnshire & Notts. Architectural Society.* This has been placed by his daughter, Miss Helen Lowe, at the editor's disposal, and has been collated by him with the original, to which also any subsequent difficul-. ties have been referred, chiefly by the kind intervention of the Rev. Canon Foster.

The volume commences with a full account of his native town of Grimsby and the adjoining parishes of Little Cotes and Humberstone. This was written in 1634, and is a sample probably of what his history of Lincolnshire would have been like had it ever been completed. Grimsby was then in a state of decay. The two parishes, St. James' and St. Mary's, had been united in 1586* on account of the poverty and paucity of their inhabitants, and the church of St. Mary's had since then been pulled down, as G. Holles regretfully records. Contrasting its low estate in his day when the town owned but one poor coal-ship and could scarcely provide mariners for that, with its flourishing condition in Edward III's time when it sent 11 ships with 171 mariners to

---

* An Act Book in the Registry at Lincoln records that this union was effected by John, Archbishop of Canterbury, and William, Bishop of Lincoln, with the consent of Si. George Heneage, Knt., as patron, on 30th May, 1586, on the petition of Robert Hundlebie, Vicar of St. James, and the parishioners of both parishes, who represented that the revenues of St. James' not exceeding £7, did not suffice for the maintenance of a vicar, that there were few houses in the parishes, and that the churches were not more than half-a-mile apart, so that the people of St. Mary's could without inconvenience attend St. James' Church. *Episcopal Act Book*, Lincoln, f. 71-72^b.—*Ed.*

the siege of Calais, he concludes his account with the Virgilian dirge, *Fuit Ilium.* He little foresaw its marvellous growth in our day, when a dozen churches are all too few for its teeming population, and when its trade rivals that of its neighbour Hull, and its fishing fleet and harbour have no equals in the world.

Following this description there comes (on pages 17 and 18), rather irrelevantly, the *Chronicon de Allerdale post Conquest' Anglie*, relating to Cumberland, probably introduced by Holles to illustrate the descent of the families of Multon and Percy. The document is taken from the *Register of the Priory of Wetherhal*,* where its title is given as *Distributio Cumberlandiæ ad Conquestum Angliæ.* It is printed by Dr. Prescott, Archdeacon of Carlisle. in his scholarly edition of the *Register* (London, Elliot Stock; Kendal, T. Wilson; 1897), and also in Dugdale's *Monasticon* (ed. 1821, vol. iii, pages 584, 585). The text given by Gervase Holles is hopelessly corrupt, and it has not seemed worth while to print in an appendix, as was at first proposed, a better text with notes, since the document is historically inaccurate and misleading.† Moreover the *Chronicon* does not relate to Lincolnshire, and it is unnecessary to traverse ground which has been covered by Dr. Prescott. The names in the *Chronicon* have not been included in the index to this volume, since in very many cases they are given in an inaccurate form in the text.

Holles next gives a long series of documents—deeds, charters and extracts from public records‡—illustrating the history of the ancient family of Clifton, of Clifton, Notts., from which he himself was descended and derived his christian name. The remainder of the volume is taken up with his main subject, which has made it so valuable to us to-day, and records the monuments and coats of arms which were found by him as then existing in some 290 of our Lincolnshire churches which were visited by him either in person or by deputy. He only diverges from the county to include Mansfield, Haughton and Tuxford in Nottinghamshire on account of their connection with the Holles family, and Staveley in Derbyshire, with which also he had family ties. He was at

---

* The original *Register*, which is now lost, was at one time in possession of the Dean and Chapter of Carlisle. There are several copies, complete or partial, which have been used by Dr. Prescott. The Rev. James Wilson, Rector of Dalston, Cumberland, gave valuable help in tracing the *Chronicon* to its source.

† Dr. Prescott speaks of it as "the ridiculous addition to the *Register* . . . . which is quite at variance with the early charters." (*Register*, pp v, vi.)

‡ In printing these Deeds, &c., it has been thought well to extend the contracted Latin. These contractions were adopted to save the time and labour of the mediæval scribe, but for the modern compositor they have the opposite effect ; the searching out the unfamiliar types is an addition to his time and trouble, while there is no question which is the more pleasing to the eye and more convenient to the modern reader. With this exception the text and spelling of the original MS. have been carefully retained throughout.—*Ed.*

Mansfield we know in 1634, and the latest date subsequently mentioned is 1640, so we may suppose that his notes were compiled during the years from 1634 to 1642, when the Civil War put a stop to them. We might have wished indeed that he had given us more notes on the architecture and condition of the many churches which he visited, but his love of heraldry led him to make special record of the coats of arms depicted in their windows and on their monuments. Of the many monuments described by him in St. James' Church, Grimsby, but three now remain, and of the many hundred coats of arms seen by him in the windows of our churches scarcely any now exist. Many, such as those in the Cathedral and the Bishop's Palace, were destroyed within a few years of his description of them. No doubt his intention was to use these heraldic records in order to trace the connection of the families who bore them with the places where they were found. For this purpose they are of service still. Many genealogical notes might have been founded on them, and a considerable number of such notes are in the editor's hands; but it has been thought better, and more in accordance with the object of the Record Society, to print the text alone, with only such short notes as are appended by G. Holles himself, or as may seem required to give some needful explanation.

Eight other manuscript volumes of Gervase Holles' collection have been preserved in the British Museum. Of these Lansdowne MSS. 207 A., B., C. & E. and Addit. MS. 6118 are thick quarto volumes, fancifully distinguished by him as 1. Darcy; 2. Gant; 3. Croun; 4. Deyncourt; 5. Trusbut. They were compiled by him during the years 1638-9 and 1643-4, and are filled with extracts relating to Lincolnshire taken from public records, such as Domesday Book, Patent and Close Rolls, Placita and Originalia, Monastic Cartularies, and the like. These must have been sought out and transcribed by him with infinite industry and pains, but they have for the most part since been printed and made readily accessible. Lansdowne MS. 207D. is of the same character, but of later date, containing mention of himself as "superstes, 1670," and of his daughter Elizabeth Berkeley and his grandson as then alive. To Addit. MS. 6118, 'Trusbut,' we are indebted for his signature, a fac-simile of which is given on page xiii. It is appended to the Memorandum in which he relates and laments the death of his cousin, William Holles, killed in a skirmish with the rebels outside Newark on 6th March, 1643. The two other volumes, Lansdowne MS. 207 F, and Addit. MS. 5531, are of smaller size and contain pedigrees of the Holles, Denzil, Frescheville and a few Lincolnshire families.

An excellent summary of Gervase Holles' life is given in the *Nat. Dictionary of Biography*, from which many of the facts given above have been derived; and no one can treat of any matter of Lincolnshire Genealogy without being indebted to the four volumes of *Lincolnshire Pedigrees*, edited by Canon Maddison for the Harleian Society. Above

INTRODUCTION. xiii

all the Editor desires gratefully to acknowledge the valuable and ever-ready help received by him throughout from the Rev. Canon Foster, who has spared neither time nor trouble to ensure the accuracy and completeness of the present volume.

Lincoln,   R.E.G.C.

    29th September, 1911.

[Signature of Gervase Holles from Additional Manuscript 6118, British Museum].

Grimsby Magna.

THIS is as Auncient a corporation as most are in England, and consists of a Mayor, twelve Aldermen, and thirty-six Burgesses. Out of ye Aldermen are yearely chosen (ye Tuesday foureteene night before ye feast of S^t. Michaell the Archangell) the Mayor and two Justices and two Coroners, whereof ye old Mayor is alwayes one. Out of the 36 Burgesses are chosen two Baylyffes, being elected out of the twelve who onely (of ye Burgesses) have voyces in electing of two Aldermen to goe upon the Leete, out of which two by the voyces of the whole Corporation the Mayor is chosen :—the other Bayliffe is elected onely by and oute of the foure and twenty, as ye head baylyffe is by the Aldermen and ye twelve. These keepe their weekely courts upon Friday, as ye Mayor doeth his upon Tuesday. There be likewise two Chamberlaynes chosen yearely for gathering the Townes rents, and for discharging ye Kings Fee-farme. The Mayor yearely keeps two Court-leetes, where always ye Recorder is present to assist the Mayor with his counsell when he sitts upon matters Criminall, which in these Court Leetes are determinable. There belonge to the Corporation three Maces, wch by as many Serjeantes are borne before the Mayor and Bayliffes on their days of solemnity, ye chiefe of which is Midsommer Day, when also ye Mayor makes his cheife Feast. They were incorporate by King John, who by his charter granted them many immunityes and privyledges, wch were from tyme to tyme confirmed, and sometymes enlarged by ye succeeding princes—amongst others this, that they should every Parliament send forth two Burgesses to advyse of the great affayres of the Kingdome.

Grimsby heretofore hath bin fortyfyed wth two Blockhouses (though now not so much as ye Ruines remain to testify that they were), and beautifyed with two Churches (of wch ye Church of S^t. Mary, a hand-

some peice and a good Sea marke was sacrilegiously pulled down and
quite demolish'd within yᵉ memory of some late living ; yᵉ other of Sᵗ.
James yet stands ill repayred, being a Church large and spacious, but
nothing beautifyed), an Abbey, a Nunnery, two Frieryes, a Chauntrey,
and a House of Hospitaliers of Sᵗ. John of Jerusalem. The Haven
hath bin heretofore commodious, now decayèd ; yᵉ traffique good, now
gone : yᵉ place rich and populous, yᵉ Houses now meane and stragling
by reason of depopulation, and the Towne very poore. In yᵉ days of
Edward yᵉ third Grimsby furnisht out to yᵉ seige of Calais (as appears
by a record now in my hands*) eleaven shipps, 171 marriners, where
now she hath but one poore Coale ship belonging to it and scarce
marriners in yᵉ Towne to man it. So will we leave it venerable for
Antiquity, and write over yᵉ Gate—*Fuit Ilium.*

And it will not be amiss to say something concerning yᵉ common
tradition of her first founder Grime, as yᵉ inhabitants (with a Catho-
lique faith) name him. The tradition is thus—Grime (say they) a
poore fisherman (as he was launching into yᵉ River for fish in his little
Boate upon humber) espyed not far from him another little Boate
empty (as he might conceave) which by yᵉ favour of yᵉ wynde and
tyde still approached nearer and nearer unto him ; he betakes himself
to his oares and meetes itt, wherein he found onely a Childe wrapt in
Swathing Clothes, purposely exposed (as it should seeme) to the pity-
lesse of yᵉ wilde and wide ocean. He moved with pitty takes it home,
and like a good foster-father carefully nourisht itt, and endeavoured
to nourishe it in his owne occupation ; but yᵉ childe contrarily was
wholy devoted to exercises of Activity, and when he began to write man
to Martyall sports, and at length by his Signall Valour obtained such
renoune, yᵗ he marryed yᵉ King of Englands daughter, and last of all,
founde [p. 2] who was his true Father, and that he was sonne to yᵉ
King of Denmarke, and for the Comicke close of all, that Haveloke
(for such was his name) exceedingly advanced and enriched his foster-
father Grime, who thus enriched builded a fayre Towne near the place
where Haveloke was founde, and named it Grimesby. Thus say
some—others differ a little in yᵉ circumstances, as namely, that Grime
was not a Fisherman, but a Merchant, and that Haveloke should be
preferred to ye King's Kitchen and there live long time as a Scullion ;
but however the circumstances differ, they all agree in the consequence
as concerning yᵉ Towne's foundation, to which (sayth the storey) Haveloke yᵉ Danish Prince afterwards granted many immunityes. This is
the famous tradition concerning Grimsby wᶜʰ learned Mʳ. Cambden
gives so little creditt to that he thinks it only *Illis dignissima qui
anilibus fabulis noctem solent protrudere* † ; yet under favour of so
reverent an Antiquary I doe not think it deserves " utterly to be ex-
ploded for false and fabulous " : my reasons are these, First, yᵉ etimology of yᵉ word (Grimesby) will carry a probability, yᵉ Termination

---

* Ex Archivis Gerv. Holles.　　　† Camden's Brit. in Lincs.

(by) signifying in yᵉ Danish Tongue *Habitatio*, a dwelling; so as I know noe reason why Grimsby should not import yᵉ dwelling of Grime, and receave this denomination from him, as well as Ormesby from Orme, and Ketelsby from Ketell two Danish Captaines under Canute in yᵉ dayes of King Ethelred, which Captaine Henry Skipwith (a valiant Gentleman, and judicious Antiquary) affirmed unto me, and that he could prove itt, not onely out of yᵉ Legend of Nun-Ormesby, but from other good and unquestionable Records. Secondly, that there was such a Prince as Havelocke, take old Robert of Gloucester for proofe, who speakes him yᵉ sonne of Gunter, or Gurthrum, Gutron or Gurmond (for all these foure names I fynde given him) Kinge of Denmarke.

> Than Gunter, that fader was of Haveloke,
> King of Denmarke, was than of myckle myght
> Arevyd so than in Ingylond with his floke, &c.

Thirdly, that Havelocke did some tyme reside in Grimsby may be gathered from a great blew Boundry-Stone lying at yᵉ East-ende of Briggow-gate, which retaines yᵉ name of Havelocks Stone to this day. Agayne yᵉ great priviledges and Immunityes that this Towne hath in Denmarke above any other in England (as freedom from Toll and yᵉ rest) may fairly induce a Beliefe, that some preceding favour or good turne called on this remuneration. But lastly (which proofe I take to be *instar omnium*), the Common Seal of yᵉ Towne, and that a most auncient one for yᵉ circumscription is thus in old Saxon letters *SIGILLUM COMUNITATIS* (not *MAIORITATIS*) *GRI-MEBY*.* The antiquity of which Seale cannot be far remote from yᵉ Saxon tymes (it being their Seale before they were incorporate) takes away all objection and gives us, as it were, an Epitome of yᵉ whole story, for there wee may see yᵉ Effigies of a tall growne man brandishing a drawn Sword in his right hande, his left Arme advancing before him a broad Target, over him in Saxon letters *GRYEM ;* on his right hand yᵉ effigies of a stripling holding in his left hand a Halberd, a Crowne a little distance from his head, and near him this written *HABLOC.* On yᵉ left hande of Grime stands a young virgin in a longe Vestment with a crowne over her heade, holding a Scepter in her left hande, about her this, *GOLDE BVRGH.* But least I pusle you with an untoward description, take here yᵉ Draught of it in yᵉ Margent.

Thus much for yᵉ Tradition, wᶜʰ notwithstanding I may not beleave to be true in all circumstances (for rare it is to have any Tradition without yᵉ mixture of something fabulous), yet that yᵉ Founders name was *GRIME*, I easily incline to beleave, but neither *GRIME* yᵉ Marchant, nor *GRIME* yᵉ Fisherman : I can name a third, who (if my judgment may passe) shall be yᵉ man. You shall finde him in

* Engraved in Lewis's Topographical Dict.

yᵉ Chronicle of Isaac Pontanus to have bin a Norwegean Pyrate about yᵉ tyme .of Frotho King of Denmarke ; wᶜʰ Grimus (by Pontanus' relation) was a man of vast stature, that attempting yᵉ marriage of Thorilda yᵉ Kinge of . . . . daughter, he was slaine in single combat by Haldanus, a Danish prince. The Stories have some resemblance. Haldanus and Havelocus are in sound [p. 3] not extreamly distant, and not unlikely is it that a Maritime Towne in Lincolnshire should be built by a Norway Pyrate.

But noe more, least I be thought *Conamine magno nugas agere ;* Onely thus much for yᵉ support of decrepid Antiquity. He that is not satisfyed with this, let him repayre to Dicke Jackson's famous Manuscript concerning this matter, where he shall fynde a great deale more to as little (if not lesse) purpose.

Monuments in yᵉ Church of great Grimsby.

In yᵉ uppermost part of yᵗ North Isle is a fayre Monumᵗ of free stone carved, and arched, under wᶜʰ Arch-worke are divers fayre Sheildes cut in Stone, on wᶜʰ are these Armes, vizt : On a Bende 3 Heartes between yᵉ Roman W, and an Annulett, *Wele:* divers escocheons of yᵉ same bordured about yᵉ top ; yᵉ Inscription thus :

Hic jacet Walterus de Wele, qui obiit
undecimo die Februarii, Año dñi Mᵒ
CCCᵒLXXXᵒVIIJᵒ. Cuius animæ propitietʳ dominus.

Over agaynst this Monument close adjoyning to the North Isle Wall are two Monuments made of Free-stone ; yᵉ uppermost covered wᵗʰ a Blew Marble, whereon yet is noe Inscription ; underneath lye both in one grave Freschevile Holles, Esq. sonne and heyre of Sʳ Gervas Holles, Kt. who dyed yᵉ tenth of May Año dñi 1630, and Elizabeth his wyfe sole daughter and heyre of John Kingston of great Grimsby, Esq. who dyed in childbed at Grimsby yᵉ last of October, 1608.

Under yᵗ other lyes Sʳ Gervas Holles, Kt. father of yᵉ sayd Freschevile Holles, who dyed yᵗ fifth day of March, 1627.

At yᵉ feete of yᵉ Tombe of Freschevile Holles lye two of his Children wᶜʰ he had by his wife Elizabeth, of whom yᵉ sonne named John lyes under a flatt freestone ; the Daughter named Anne lyes within him, having her Brothers grave on yᵉ South, yᵗ Church Wall North, yᵉ partition-wall betweene yᵉ North Isle and yᵉ Bell-house East, and their Fathers Tombe West. John Holles departed this life iiᵒ Aprilis, 1607 ; Anne Holles dyed xxvᵒ Octobris, 1608. In yᵉ same grave lye George, William, and another sonne not christened, all Children of Gervas Holles, Esqʳ. sonne and heyre of Freschevile Holles, Esqʳ.

Close by yᵉ side of yᵉ Tombe of Freschevile Holles and his wyfe lye buryed her Father and Mother, John Kingston of great Grimsby, Esqʳ. and Katherine daughter of Henry Gaynsford of Carshalton in the County of Surrey, Esq. wyfe of yᵉ sayd John Kingston. He departed to Heaven xxvjᵒ Maii 1617 : Shee iijᵒ Martii, 1628.

South from yᵉ Monumᵗ of Walter Wele lyes yᵉ body of John Kings ton, Father of yᵉ fore-named John, whose Grave-stone once had his Picture and Epitaph insculpt in Brasse, but now with divers others defaced and stolne (torne) away. He dyed Año ij and iij Phil. and Mar. and was buryed xv° Maii, 1555. He dyed xij" ejusdem Mens'.*

Upon a Pillar on yᵉ left hand as you enter into the Quire this Inscription :—Orate pro anima Johannis Kingston, qui hanc | Columnam fecit, Año Dñi M°CCC°LXV°.

It appears by this Inscription that yᵉ Kingstons have bin auncient Inhabitants of this Towne and Benefactors to this Church. They bore for their Armes, B. a plaine Crosse, Gold, between 4 Leopards faces, Silver. *Kingston.*

One of this family named Richard Kingston was Abbott of Wellow juxta Grimsby, as appeares by some Court Rolls of Swallow, which Courts were held for him there Año x°, xj°, xij° Henr. 8.†

On another Gravestone in yᵉ North Isle are yᵉ pourtraytures of a man and his wyfe : he with a Collar of SS. about his necke, and his sworde by his side ; the Inscription thus :—

Hac sunt in Fossa Wilhelmi Wele, Miliscentæ
Corpora suffossa Christo . . . . .
. . . .
Anno Caleno‡ Iuliique die quasi seno.

[**p. 4.**] In yᵉ same Isle lyes buryed Eden Kingston wife of John Kingston, who was buryed 7° die Aprilis, Año 1543.

On another gravestone :

Hic jacet Dña Elizabetha Fundatrix istius loci
Filia et heres Wilhelmi Francke, Militis, quondam
Uxor Richardi Tunstall, Militis, et Camerarii Hen-
-rici sexti Anglie, que obiit . . Mensis . . A° Dñi
M°CCCC° . . et Thomas filius ejvs, qui obiit VIJ die
Mensis Maii M°CCCC°XCIIJ°, cujus aïabus propiti-
-etur Dñs. Amen.

Upon yᵉ stone engraven are she and her sonne in their winding sheetes, about yᵉ middle of yᵉ stone 2 Escocheons— Tunstalls Coate within yᵉ Garter, and her owne paternall coate by itt.

S. 3 Combes, Argent—*Tunstall.*
Vert, a Saltier engrayled Or—*Franke.*

(Fundatrix istius domus) she was yᵉ Foundresse of ye . . . . . Friers in Grimsby, where it seems she was buryed, and from whence att yᵉ Dissolution of Monasteries this stone (likely) was removed.

In Fotherbyes Isle on a faire thicke Marble, whereon is engraven a sword length-wayes, this Inscription in Saxon characters.

*ICI GIST SIR PIERS DE GOUSELL LE FRERE
SIR GILES.*

---

* Ex Registro de Grimsby.   ‡ So in MS.—*Ed.*
† Ex Archivis Gerv. Holles.

A man on another wth a Belt about his necke, and a Sword hanging
in it, both his handes elevated, on either of them a Gauntlett : about
ye Stone this :—

> Hic jacet Galfridus Pedde, qui obiit XXIJ° die
> Mensis Decembris Anno Dñi M°CCCC°VIIJ°. cu-
> -jus animæ propitietur Deus.   Amen.

Over his head written thus—In God is all quoth Pedde.

On another—

> Hic jacet Wilhelmus Banningholme, Capel-
> -lanus, qui obiit Mense Novembris Año Dñi
> M°CCC°LXXXVIII°.   Cujus aïæ propitietur, &c.

On another—

> Hic jacet Johannes Keleby, Capellanus,
> qui obiit sexto die Mensis Septembris Año
> Dñi M°CCCC°XLIIJ°, cujus aniñæ, &c.

On another —

> Hic jacet Dominus Johannes Binbroke.   .   .

On another—

> Obitus Wilhelmi Duffeld primo die Martii
> Año Dñi Millesimo CCCC° vicesimo primo,
> et Margaretæ ux'ris suæ .   .   Año Dñi M°CCCC°.

In ye Quire under ye Communion Table lye ye bodyes of William
Kirkton and John Kirkton, Sonnes of John Kirkton of great Grimsby,
Gent. of which William dyed x° Februarii MDCIII°, and John dyed
xiij° Octobr. Año Dñi MDCX°.

In ye North ende of ye uppermost Isle uppon a playne free-Stone
lyes the Statue of a Chevalier of free stone artificially wrought in full
proportion and Stature, and compleate Armour, guilded at ye first as
yett may appeare in some places ; he hath upon him a shirt of Mayle,
and over that a Surcoat, upon which are 6 Lyons rampant, crowned,
2.2.2., His Sword in a belt buckled about his belly, his Dagger by
his side, His Head (as likewise his feete) resting upon a couchant
Lyon : No Inscription.

This (say ye Townesmen) is ye Monument of Grime their Founder,
but indeed it is ye very Monument of Sr Thomas Haselerton, first
Founder or Re-edifier of ye Nunnery of St. Leonards in Grimsby, as
appeares evidently by these ensuing circumstances : vizt.—First, ye 6
Lyons rampant crowned, wch are upon his Surcoat, have relation (wthout
all doubt) [p. 5] unto a fayre Coate of Armes in ye window over y^e
Bayliffes Seate, wch Coate is *Haselertons*, who bore Gules, 6 Lyoncelles
ramp. Arg. crowned Gold, 3.2.1.

Now he being a Founder, or (wch I rather think) a Benefactor, or
Re-edifyer (for this Nunnery hath bin severall tymes ruyned by fire) it
is most likely he was enterred in his owne new foundation, and his
monum^t removed hither att ye dissolution of Monasteryes, and though

it be a Northern family. yet that they had landes hereabouts, appeares by a Record I have seene, which sayth that Euphemia de Haselerton *tenuit unam medietatem in Alesby pro termino vite sue*, wch Alesby is within three myles of Grymsby, and likely they were neare hande seated.

But it shall not be amisse here to rectify an Errour wch I fynde currant in Authours about ye Foundation of this Nunnery. Bishop Godwine (in his Catalogue of Bishops) makes Robert Grosstest, Bp. of Lincolne ye first Founder; and Speede (in his Catalogue of Religious Houses)* names ye s^d Robert Grosstest and this Sr Thomas Haselerton for ye men, and this in ye dayes of Henry ye 3^d, in ye 37th yeare of whose reigne indeed Robert Grosstest died, Año Dñi 1253, and therefore could be noe Founder. For above 70 yeares before that had this Nunnery a being, as fully appears by a Bull of Pope Lucius ye 3^d, who lived Año Dñi 1181, sate 4 yeares 2 moneths and 24 dayes, and died at Verona (whence this Bull was dated) Año Dñi 1185 (after they had put out his eyes for endeavouring to putt downe ye Consulls of Rome, and banish't him to Verona) in the Cathedrall Church of wch he lyes buryed. The Bull runs thus :—

Lucius Episcopus Servus servorum Dei, Dilectis Filiis Abbati de Neusam et de Kima et de Elesham Prioribus Salutem et Apostolicam benediccionem—conquestionem Monialium Sancti Leonardi de Grymesbi ad nos transmissam accepimus—Quod enim Fratrum S. Augustini de Grymesbi provisioni sint commissæ, iidem quendam de Fratribus suis G. nomine Monasterio præfeceruut, qui possessiones quasdam de quibus Moniales sustentacionem habebant in territorio de Ravendale, Monachis de Parco Lude temeritatis ausu distraxit, et quasdam ex ipsis minis et contumeliis afflixit, ut venditioni secum pariter assentarent—Quin . . . . eisdem Monialibus tanto fortius debemus adesse quanto minus sua jura possunt pro sexus fragilitate tueri, discretioni vestræ per Apostolica scripta mandamus, quatenus . . . . . propter hoc fueritis requisiti, partes ad vestram presentiam convocetis, et veritate diligentius indagata, si vobis constiterit ita esse, predictam venditionem, contradictione et appellatione cessante, in irritum revocetis, predictos Fratres de Parco ad restitucionem earundem possessionum ea, quæ convenit, severitate cogentes. Verum si aliter res se habet, eam audiatis, et mediante justitia terminetis, Nullis literis obstantibus, si quæ apparuerint a sede Apostolica impetratæ, Quod si omnes his exequendis nequiveritis interesse, duo vestrum ea nichilominus exequantur. Datum Veronæ iij° Id. Januarii.†

The Seal is of lead in a hempen label, on one side of wch is stamped a Crosse betw: two faces, and above them written in great Roman letters S.PA.-S.PE, wch I take is as much as Scus Paulus, Scus Petrus ; on ye other side this, LVCIVS PP. III.

---

* Speedes Chron. 630, 1377^b.   † Ex Archivis Gerv. Holles.

And yet I have extant a more auncient Bull of his Predecessor
Alexander y⁵ 3ᵈ directed to the Abbots of Thorneton and Neusam
about yᵉ same business : Vizt.—

Alexander Episcopus servus servorum Dei dilectis Filiis de Torn-
entun et de Newsam Abbatibus Salutem et Apostolicam benedicionem,
Dilectæ in Christo filiæ nostræ, Priorıssa et Moniales de Grimesbi
transmissa nobis [**p. 6.**] conquestione monstraverunt quod G. eiusdem
Monasterii quondam procurator terram de Ravendala dilectis filiis
nostris Abbati et Fratribus de Luda sine ipsarum assensu vendidit, et pro
sua voluntate distraxit, quum quidem indempnitati eiusdem Monasterii
tanto fortius precavere debemus quanto minus eædem sorores pro
imbellicitate sui sexus, sufficiunt sua jura tueri, discrecioni vestræ per
Apostolica Scripta mandamus quatenus prefatum Abbatem et Fratres
de Luda diligentius moneatis, Ut recepta summa pecuniæ a prescriptis
Priorissa et Sororibus quam pro iam dicta terra dederunt, ipsam
eisdem Priorissæ et Sororibus sine difficultate restituant et in pace
dimittant, aut sub vestræ discrecionis examine plenam eis justitiam
facere non morentur. Si vero ad commonitionem vestram neutrum
horum facere forte voluerint, ipsos ad alterum exequendnm, nostra
freti auctoritate, contradicione et appellacione cessante, cogatis. Datum
Tusculan', xiiij Kl. Sept.*

By these two records it plainely appeares that this Nunnery was
founded before yᵉ tyme of Bp. Grosstest, and that he and Sʳ Thomas
Haselerton were only Benefactors, or happily (as I said before) re-
edifyed it.

In yᵉ top of yᵉ Steeple this—Pray for the soule of John Empringham. This family of the Empringhams hath bin very auncient and
eminent in this Corporation. To one of this name (happily yᵉ man
above mentioned who its seems was a Benefactour to this Church), yᵉ
Prioresse of St. Leonards granted a Messuage in Briggowgate in
Grimsby Año . . Hen. 4ᵗʰ.*

Richard Empringham (who lived in the dayes of Hen. 8, and Edw.
6.) had a daughter named Margaret marryed to John Kingston, Esq.,
by whom he had John Kingston, whose sole heire Elizabeth was
marryed to Freschevile Holles, Esq. by whom he had Gervas Holles
now living, Año dñi 1634. The Armes of *Empringham* were—
Argent, a Bordure Vert, en-aluron of Martlets, Gold.

Michael Empringham sonne of yᵉ afore-named Richard and
Margaret his wife sister of Sʳ Richard Thimelby, of Irnham, Kt. dyed
boeth in one houre, and were buryed boeth in one grave in yᵉ Church-
porch of Grimsby under a blew marble stone ; they were buryed yᵉ
sixth day of October, 1578.†

These two Familyes of Empringham and Kingston, with De la See,
Fotherby and Cooke have bin of longest continuance in this Corpor-

---

* Ex Archivis Gerv. Holles.   † Ex Registro de Grimsby.

ation.   Cooke and Fotherby yet continue boeth Aldermen at this present (the first having bin three tymes Mayor); ye male line of ye rest being quite gone out, unlesse Arnold Empringham live and have children, of which I am ignorant.   I have in my hands a letter of K. Henr. 8 directed to John Kingston (ye Father of ye last John) sealed with his seale and signed with his stampe; ye contents are as followeth :—

By ye Kinge, Henry :

Trusty & welbeloved, wee greete you well, Lating you wit, that for as much as by ye manifold Injuryes, wronges & displeasures doone unto us, our Realme & Subjects by ye Scotts, wee have bin enforced lately to enter into open Warr and Hostility with ye same, which wee Intende & purpose (God willing) oonlesse ye Nobles of Scotland shall conforme themselves to reason, to prosecute in such sorte as shall redounde to o^r honour & to ye Commonwealth of our Realme & Subjects.   To th'intent wee may ye better know ye forces of o^r said Realme & thereby put the same in such order & areadynesse as they may serve us in this enterprice as ye cace shall require.   We have thought meet & necessary to have speciall Musters taken of all our pepull, and therein to have also such plaine & perfect certificate made, as shall declare what may be trusted to in that behalfe.   Wherefore o^r pleasure & commandm^t is that you, by virtue & authority thereof, shall with all convenient diligence take ye Musters of all th'able men, as well horsemen as foote-men, which you can make & furnish, boeth of o^r Tennants inhabiting upon Fermes, Feildes & Tenures within any Office whereof you have the Stewardship under us (if you have any such).   And also of yor owne Servants & Tenants dwelling upon yor owne Tenures, And ye same so taken, to certify in writing to o^r right trusty & right entirely beloved Cosen & Counsellour the Duke of Suffolk our Lieutenant General in ye North partyes with all possible diligence with a special Note & Declaration to be expressed in ye s^d Certificate [p. 7], how many of the sayd persons be furnished with horses, hable trapin, a speare or a javelin. How many be Archers, & how many bee Billmen, & how many prin-cipall men may be pyked out of every sorte of thole number.   Fore-seing that in these Musters & Certificate you medle not in any wise with any Marriners, Forasmuch as we purpose to reserve ye same for o^r furniture by Sea, And that you putt all ye same in such areadynesse as they sett forth upon oone houres warning, whensoever you shall receave commandment from o^r s^d Cosin in that behalfe, And these o^r Lers shall be yor sufficient Warrant & discharge herein accordingly.   Given under o^r Signett at o^r Honnour of Hampton Court ye xxij day of January in ye xxxiiij^o yeare of o^r Reigne.

Superscribed—To o^r Trusty & Welbeloved Subject John Kingston, Esq.*

---

* Ex Archivis Gerv. Holles.

This Towne hath bin honoured with ye presence of this Prince H. 8, who lodged in it three nights, and wth ye birth of John Whitgift, Archbp. of Canterbury, Martin Fotherby, Bp. of Salisbury, and his Brother, John Fotherby, Deane of Canterbury. Likewise John Welsh, or Walleis, that overcame Mortileto de Villenos, a Navarrois, in single combate in ye presence of K. Richard ye 2^d, "qui (sayth Walsingham) ad spectaculum duelli cum principibus sui regni consederat," was an Inhabitant, and most likely native of this place.*

Coates of Armes in ye Church of St. James, in Great Grimsby. In ye windows of ye North Isle.

First Window.

1. Or, 2 Barrs Gules, in cheife 3 Torteauxes . . . *Wake*
2. Or, a Lyon rampant, Azure . , . . . *Percy*
3. Defaced, but seemes to have bin 3 Lyons passants gardants, with a labell . . . . [*Lancaster ?*]

Second Window.

1. Gules, 3 water bougets, Silver . . . . . *Ros*
2. Chequy, happily Arg. & Gules, for Vaux of Gillesland, but hid wth playster . . . . *Vaux*
3. A Fesse betweene divers Roundles, ye colours not to be discerned for ye playster, but I take it to be ye Coate of ye Barons Engaine, wch is G. Crosse crusily a Fesse Or . *Engaine*

Third Window.

1. G. a Chevron betweene xj Crosseletts Or, 4. 2. in chiefe, and 5 in base . . . . *Kyme*
2. Azure, Billetty, a Fesse Dauncetty, d'Or. . . *Deyncourt*
3. Defaced.

Fourth Window.

1. G. a Crosse sarcely d'Argent. . . . . . *Beke*
2. Verry, Argent and B. . . . . . . *Beauchamp*
3. Defaced.

Fifth Window.

1. Gules, a Saltier Argent. . . . . . . *Neville*
2. Defaced. 3. Argent, a Saltier, Gules.

All these Coates above-mentioned are fayre and large Escocheons, and seeme to have bin set up longe synce ; every one of them is encompassed with a roundle or hoope of Iron. These Nobles, it seemes, were principall Benefactors to this Church.

The West ende window of this North Isle is a very faire one, wherein are the pictures of all ye Kings of Judah, Jesse making ye Root, and ye rest branching from him. This Church hath bin of larger extent ; for a great part of ye Quire fell downe some forty yeares agoe ; ye Roofe also hath bin twice stricken.

---

* Walsingham, 7 Ric. II. fol. 311.

Other Armories in Houses about the Towne, in likelyhood taken from yᵉ demolished Church of St. Mary, and yᵉ other Religious Houses.

1. G. a playne Crosse, Argent,
2. Verry, Arg. and B. a Fesse, Gules . . . *Marmion*
3. Argent, 2 Barrs engrayled, Sables . . . . *Stayne*
4. Sable, 3 pik-axes within a Bordure, Argent . . [*Pigot*]
5. Argent, a Saltier engrayled, Vert. . . . [*Franke*]

[p. 8.]

6. B. a Fesse nebuly d'Ermine betw. 6 Crosselettes Botony d'Argent . . . . . [*Barnardiston*]
7. B. a Bend betweene 6 Martletts, Argent . . . *Lutterell*
8. G. a Crosse Botony, Golde.
9. Lozengy, Ermine and Gules . . . . . *Rokeley*
10. B. 2 Barrs Nebuly Erm. a Bordure d'Or semy of Saltoires, Sables.
11. Or, 3 Piles, Sable, a Canton Ermine . . . [*Bassett*]
12. The Armes of England empaled with yᵉ Lady Catherine Howards honorary Atchievemᵗ, viz. B. 3 Flowers de Lize in pale d'Or, on 2 Flanches, Ermine, as many Roses Lancastrian.
13. The Armes of yᵉ Archbishoppricke of Canterbury * empaled with Argent, a Pale lozengy Sables.

In yᵉ Walls of my house these 3 fayre and large Escocheons cutt in Stone :

1. Nebuly, or 3 Barrs Nebuly . . . . . [*Del See*]
2. An Inescocheon within an Orle of Roses.
3. A Saltier engrayled . . . . [*Franke*]

If yᵉ last coate be for Francke, as I take it, it is then without doubt they were taken from yᵉ . . . Fryars.

On the outside of a Stone Window in yᵉ Dining Chamber—John Kynston, And Hedon his wyfe. This John Kyngston was father of the last John Kyngston.

COTES PARVA.

[p. 9].

Cotes Parva (distant about a mile from Grimsby to yᵉ west) hath aunciently belonged to a Knightly Family that were there settled, and from itt tooke their denomination. The name signifys (according to Verstegan†) in yᵉ singular number a little slightly built countrey house, and from yᵉ plurality of these Cotes it is likely this village got hir

---

* A mistake for the old Arms of York which bore a Pall till Cardinal Wolsey introduced the present coat : the Arms impaled are those of Savage, Archbp. of York, 1501-7.—*Ed.*

† Rest: of Decayed Antiquity, 214

name. I have seen y⁰ Testament of one of this family, which runs
thus :—

In Dei nomine, Amen—Die Dominica in festo S. Matthei Apostoli,
A.D. mccccxxi, Ego, Johannes Cotes de parva Cotes, Armiger, compos
mentis et sanæ memoriæ condo Testamentum meum in hunc modum.
In primis commendo animam meam Omnipotenti Deo et beatæ Mariæ
Virgini et omnibus Sanctis eius, et corpus meum ad sepeliendum in
Ecclesia Fratrum Ordinis S. Augustini de Grimesby. Et lego duos
bonos boves Conventui domus dictorum Fratrum pro Sepultura mea,
Et lego cuilibet fratri ejusdem domus quatuor denarios, et cuilibet
Sacerdoti existenti ad exequias et ad missam die Sepulturæ meæ
quatuor denarios, Et lego summo Altari Ecclesiæ Sci. Michaelis de
parva Cotes vjˢ viijᵈ. Et lego summo Altari matricis Ecclesiæ Lincoln
unum annulum aureum. Et lego Roberto Batelay de Grimesby unam
novam et nigram togam cum furrara nigra de Boge.* Et lego Johanni
Attehall de parva Cotes unam vaccam flekkit. Et lego Elizabethæ
uxori dicti Johannis Attehall unum bonum Porcum. Et lego Dominæ
Beatricæ Moniali de Grimesby unam vaccam cum uno vitulo. Et lego
Willelmo Brigham de Grimesby clerico unam bonam ovem et unum
bonum porcum. Et lego Domino Johanni West Rectori Ecclesiæ de
Bradley xiijˢ iiijᵈ. Et lego Domino Johanni Cromthorpe Vicario
Ecclesiæ de parva Cotes xiijˢ iiijᵈ ad adjuvandum et fortificandum
Executricem meam subscriptam. Item volo quod Feoffati mei in terris
et tenementis meis cum suis pertinentiis in Villa et Campis de Teuelby
post decessum meum feoffent Elizabetham uxorem meam in eisdem
terris et tenementis cum suis pertinentiis pro termino vitæ suæ, et post
ejus decessum Volo quod omnia predicta terræ et tenementa cum suis
pertinentiis ibidem revertantur Petro filio meo et heredi de corpore suo
legitime procreato, Et si contingat predictum Petrum obire sine herede,
Tunc volo quod omnia predicta terræ et tenementa cum suis pertinentiis revertantur rectis heredibus meis. Item volo quod illa messuagia
terræ et tenementa mea cum pertinentiis in Imyngham Haburgh et
Gowsill que nuper habui ex perquisitione diversorum hominum
vendantur per Executricem meam et ejus coadjutores ad acquietanda
debita mea cum pecunia inde recepta, et pro anima mea in operibus
charitatis expendenda. Residuum vero bonorum meorum non
legatorum do et lego Executrici meæ subscriptæ ad disponendum
fideliter cum eisdem bonis pro anima mea. Hujus autem Testamenti
mei facio et constituo Executricem meam, vizᵗ Elizabetham Cotes
uxorem meam, et D. Johannem West Rectorem Ecclesiæ de Bradley,
et D. Johannem Cromthorpe Vicarium Ecclesiæ de parva Cotes
coadjutores dictæ Executricis meæ, et Johannem Barnaby de Barton
juniorem Supervisorem, ut ipsi præ oculis Deum habentes meam ultim
-am voluntatem impleant cum effectu. In cujus rei testimonium

*Boge, i.e. Budge, lamb's-wool.—Ed.

Sigillum meum apposui. Datum apud parva Cotes die et anno Dñi supradicto.

The Seale to this Testament was a very fayre Seale and curiously cutt, and noe inscription about it, as commonly is seene in old Seales. It carryed in an Escocheon a playne Crosse engrayled, wch is not ye paternall Coate of this Family ; for they bore Argent, a Crosse sarcely engrayled Sables. But this Coate of Armes wch I fynde in litle Cotes Church-windows, and is G. a Crosse engrayled Argent, belongs to ye Family of Inglethorpe, whose heyr Cotes marryed.

Sr James Cotes, knt. (as I fynde in Records) lived Año . . .

The inheritance came after by marriage to Del See, and from Del See to Hildyard by marryage likewise. Sr Christopher Hildyard now enjoyeth it, Año 1634. The Parsonage is impropriate, and now 'tis owned by ye Lord Culpepper.

In ye Windows of Little Cotes Church.

1. Gules, a plaine Crosse engrayled Argent . . . . *Cotes*
[p. 10.]
2. B. 2 Barrs nebuly Argent . . . . . . *Del See*
3. B. 3 Barrs nebuly Argent . . . . . . *Del See*
4. G. a Crosse sarcely d'Or empaled with [*blank*].
5. B. 2 Barrs nebuly d'Argent . . . . . . *Del See*

Out of Doomesday Book—Lincolnescire.

Terra Ivonis de Taillgebose :—In Tatenai habuerunt Turgisle et Swen iiii carucatas terre ad geldam. Terra ad viii carucatas. In Soca i carucata et ii bovate et tercia pars ii bovatarum de hac terra. Nunc Ivo Taillebosc habet ibi in dominico vi carucatas et xxv villanos et unum bordarium, et xii Sochmannos habentes vj carucatas. Ibi i molendinum xvj solidorum, et xiij saline xij solidorum, et cxl acre prati. T.R.E. valuit x libras, nunc xx libras. Tailla xx^l.

In Holtone Soca hujus Manerii ij carucate terre ad geldam. Terra ad iiij carucatas. Ibi xiiij Sochmanni habent iij carucatas. Valet xl sol.

M. Ibidem habet Esbern i carucatam terre ad geldam. Terra ad ii carucatas. Ibi Hermer, homo Ivonis habet v villanos et ij bordarios arantes v bobus. Ibi scitus Molendini et xiiij acre prati. T.R.E. et nunc valet xl sol.

In Humbrestone, Soca de Tatenai, vj carucate terre ad geldam. Terra ad xij carucatas. Ibi lxvij Sochmanni habent xviij carucas et cc acras prati.

HUMBERSTAINE.

This now is written Humberston, but in divers old Records it is written Humbrestayne and Umberstan. The termination Stan or Staine being (as I conceave it) most proper ; for though Humberston (which is as much as to say Humberstowne) would seeme to carry a plaine and acceptable reason for ye Etimology, it being scituate upon ye very mouth of ye River Humber ; yet for ye credit of old Orthography let me rather thinke itt most truely compounded with Stane or Stan, which in old Saxon signifyes a Stone, and here upon ye Shoare lyes a great Boundry blew Stone just at ye place where Humber looseth himselfe in ye German Ocean. *Abundat quisque suo sensu.* This is mine, I leave other men to their better judgements.

At this place Rafe ye sonne of Drago, Drigo, or Drogo (for thus I do fynde his name varyed in Records), layd ye Foundation of an Abbey, which he dedicated to ye Virgin Mary and St Peter, *temp. Reg. Johis*, of ye Order of St Bennet which att ye Suppression was valued att £42 11 3.

Ranulph Earle of Chester, and Drigo ye Sonne of Rafe gave landes in Humberston to Henry Falconer as appeares by their Charters ensueing.

R. Comes Cestriæ, Constabularius, Dapifer, Baronibus, Vice-comitibus, Militibus, et Ministris, Ballivis et omnibus hominibus suis, Francis et Anglis, Salutem. Scitote me dedisse Henrico Falconario meo totam terram et tenuram Turoldi filii Bern de Hungrestain pro servicio suo, scil. x^l et i sol. terræ predictæ. Quia volo et firmiter precipio quod ipse Henricus et heredes sui de me et heredibus meis in feodo et hereditate teneant ita bene et honorifice per servicium ancipitrum meorum sicut melius teneo terram meam propriam,—In villa et extra, in foro et mercato, in bosco et plano, in pratis et pascuis, in viis et semitis, in stangnis et molendinis, in piscariis et salinis, et in omnibus locis aliis, cum saca et soca, et Tol et Theom et Infangthef, et cum omnibus aliis consuetudinibus et libertatibus. T . . . fil : Willi, et Hugone Bardolf, et Willo fil : Hac., et Hugone Officiario, et Berengario Falconario, et Gisleberto Neivill, et Radulfo fil : Drogonis, apud Lincoln.*

Drigo fil : Radulphi omnibus hominibus suis Francis et Anglicis tam presentibus quam futuris Salutem : Sciatis me dedisse et concessise Radulfo filio Henrici Falconarii et heredibus suis duas bovatas terre in Umbrestan que fuerunt Haudi fil : Anche et Helwini Welp, quas pater ejus Henricus tenuit de patre [p. 11] meo et de me in feodo et hereditate, Tenendum de me et de heredibus meis per idem servicium quo pater ejus tenuit, scil. reddendo annuatim inter duo festa Sanctæ Mariæ Nisum† ruffum, et faciendo forinsecum servicium. Testantibus—Achet Dridford : Jacobo Dribi : Hermero fil : Dreu : Willo de Bred': Thomas de Humbrestan ; Rolf ejusdem villæ : Picot de Houton : Rogero de Lesbi ; Ricardo ejusdem villæ ; Roberto de Bredula ; Gilberto capellano ; Clemente presbitero, et aliis.*

The Seales of boeth these Charters are perisht, that wch. belonged to the Earle of Chesters, lapt in wooll and sowed up in a linen bagge

---

* Ex Archivis Gerv. Holles.   † Nisus—a Fish-hawk.—*Ed.*

for yᵉ better preservation of it, yet when I opened it, I found it mowldred to dust.

H. Rex Angl : Dux Norm : et Aquit : et Comes Andeg : Justic-iariis, Vice-comitibus, et omnibus Ministris et omnibus fidelibus suis de Lincoln subditis Salutem—Precipio quod Columbæ Henrici Flamengs Falconerii mei habeant pacem, et prohibeo ne quis super hoc eas capere presumet cum retibus vel alio modo absque ejus licentia super x libr : forisfacturam. T. Alano de Neville, Hug : de Unnd'. Apud Clarendun.*

To Rafe yᵉ sonne of this Henry Falconer whose true name (as appeares by the fore-mencioned Charter of Henry the 2ⁿᵈ) was Flamengs, though it seemes he left that, and was after knowne by yᵉ name of his office onely Philip de Chancey gave a Rent in Halington in franke mariage wᵗʰ his daughter Hillary, as appeares by this ensue-ing Record :—

Sciant presentes et futuri quod ego Philippus de Chancey dedi, concessi, et hac presenti Carta mea confirmavi Radulfo filio Henrici Falconarii de Humbrestan in libero maritagio cum Hillaria filia mea, et heredibus suis qui de eis egredeantur, redditum duarum marcarum in Villa de Halington quem habui de dono Philippi de Kyma de heredibus Gilberti filii Beringh' de Tothwell annuatim ad festum Sĉi Botulphi percipiendum. Si autem contingat, quod absit, quod dicta Hillaria filia mea sine heredibus de corpore suo decedat, predictus redditus duarum marcarum michi et heredibus meis remanebit. Et ego, Philippus de Chancy, et heredes mei, waranti-zabunt, defendent et acquietabunt predictum annualem redditum duarum marcarum predicto Radulfo et Hillariæ filiæ meæ et heredibus suis qui de ipsis egredientur in omnibus et contra omnes homines in perpetuum. Et ut hoc meum donum ratum et stabile in posterum perseveret huic scripto sigillum meum apposui, Hiis Testibus—Dño Willo tunc Abbate de Humbrestayn, Dño Rico de Heyling, Philippo de Wivelsby, Rico Falconar', Gerlone fratre suo, Johe Malet, Eudone de Westmell, Rico de Hol', Rado fil' Sim' de Humbrestayn et aliis.*

To yᵉ same man did Henry de Fountney grant 2 Ox-ganges of lande in Hole for his services, as appeares by this following Charter :—

Sciant omnes tam presentes quam futuri quod ego Henricus de Funtenay concessi, et hac presenti carta mea comfirmavi Radulfo de Humbrestayn Falconario et Henrico filio suo, et heredibus eorum pro homagio et servicio suo de me et heredibus meis illas duas bovatas terræ cum duobus toftis in Hol que idem R. et pater ejus tenuerunt de patre meo et de antecessoribus meis in Hol, cum pratis pascuis et pasturis, et omnibus aisiamentis infra Villam et extra, Tenendum et habendum de me et heredibus meis in feodo et hereditate adeo libere et quiete, honorifice et in bono pacis sicut ego potui illas duas bovatas cum prenominatis pertinenciis liberius vel melius concedere et confirmare. Reddendo mihi et heredibus meis xxviij^d p^{er} ann., vij^d ad Natalem, vij^d ad Pascham, vij^d ad festum Sc̄i Botulfi, vij^d ad festum Sc̄i Michaelis, pro omne servicio et demanda et exaccione salvo forinseco ad tenentem terre pertinent'. Et ego dictus Henricus et heredes mei fideliter warantizabimus dicto R. et H. filio suo et heredibus eorum omnia prenominata versus omnes et in omnibus pro dicto servicio, salvo forinseco ad tenentem terre pertinent' imperpetuum. Hiis Testibus— W. fil. Drogonis, R. fil. ejus, R. de Heyling, W. fratre ejus, W. fil. W. de Belesby, R. Majore de Grimesby, R. H. . . Steph. B . . fratre ejus, W. de Hadeclive, Norman de Hol, et aliis. Anno Dn̄i M°CC° vicesimo.*

Obiit Radulphus Falconarius de Humbrestan A° Dn̄i m°cc°lxxiij°.

---

* Ex Aichivis Gerv. Holles.

Chronic' de Allerdale.

[p. 12.]

Rex Willelmus cognomine Bastardus Dux Normanniæ Conquestor Angliæ, dedit totam terram de Comitatu Cumbriæ Ranulpho de Meschine, et Galfrido fratri suo ejusdem Ranulphi totum Comitatum Cestriæ, Et Willelmo fratri eorumdem totam terram de Cowpland inter Duden et Derwent. Ranulphus de Meschine feoffavit Hubbertum Vaux de Baronia de Gillesland, et Ranulphum fratrem ejus de Soureby, Carlaton, Hubbrightby, et Robertum fratrem eorundem de Baronia de Dalston. Et feoffavit Robertum D'Estomers de Baronia de Burgo, Et Richerum de Boyvill de Baronia de Loungton, Et Oderdum de Logis de Baronia de Staynton. Et feoffavit Waldenum filium Gospatricii de Dunbar Comitis in Scotia de tota Baronia de Allerdale inter Wathenpole et Derwent. Predictus Willelmus de Meschine Dñus de Cowpeland feoffavit Waldenum filium Gospatricii de Dunbar Comitis in Scotia de tota terra inter Coker et Derwent simul cum quinque Villis, scilicet Brightm, Eglesfeld, Dene, Brainthayt, Gisothen, et duo Clifton et Stainburn. Et feoffavit Oderdum le Clerke de quarta parte de Crosthayt pro custodia Asturcorum* suorum. Galfridus Meschine Comes Cestriæ obiit sine heredibus de corpore suo, et Ranulphus de Meschyne fuit Comes Cestriæ, et reddidit Dño Regi totum Com: Cumbriæ tali condicione, ut singuli feoffati sui tenuissent terras suas de Dño Rege in capite.

Predictus Waldonus fil: Comitis Gospatricii feoffavit Oderdum de Logis de Baronia de Wigton, Doudegat, Waverton, Bleucogo, et Kirkebride, qui fundavit Ecclesiam de Wigton, et dedit Oderdo fil: Lyolfe Talentir et Castelryg cum Foresta inter Caltre et Greta, Et Priori et Conventui de Gisburn Appulton et Bricekirke cum Advocacione ejusdem Ecclesiæ, Et dedit Ade fil: Lyolfe Uldale Gitatle. Et dedit Gamello fil: Brun Bothill. Et dedit Waldeno fil: Gilemun' cum Ethereda sorore sua Broghton, Ribton, et Broghton parva, et duo Waldefe ad unam logeam. Et dedit Ormo fil: Ketelli Seton, Comberton, Femyngby, Craiksothen, cum Gurmella sorore sua. Et Dolphino fil: Alwardi cum Matillia sorore sua, Applelwath et parva Crosseby, Langryg et Brigham cum Advocacione

---

* Asturcus, or Austurcus—a Goshawk.—*Ed.*

ejusdem Ecclesiæ. Et dedit Melbech' medico suo Villam de Brom-
feld salva sibi advocacione ejusdem Ecclesiæ. Alanus fil : et
heres ejusdem Waldeni dedit Ranulpho de Lyndsey Blewhayset
et Ukmanby cum Ethereda sorore sua. Et dedit Vitredo fil :
Fergi Dño Galwidiæ cum Gurmella sorore sua Torpenhow cum
advocacione Ecclesiæ. Et dedit Catello de Spenser Threpeland.
Et dedit . . . . Villam de Thoresby pro tercia parte unius
Villæ. Et dedit Gospatricio fil : Orm Altham, Ireby, pro tercia
parte unius villæ. Et dedit Gamello le Brun Rugthayt pro tercia
parte unius villæ. Et dedit Radulpho . . . yne Ilsall cum
pertinenciis, Bleucake cum Averico de Newton. Et idem Alanus
habuit unum fratrem bastardum nomine Cospatricium, cui dedit
Bolton, Bastinthayt, et Estholm. Et dedit Oderdo Newton cum
pertinentiis. Et dedit tribus Venatoribus suis, vizt Seth et sociis suis
Hayton, Et dedit Vitredo unam carucatam terræ in Aspatrick ut
esset summonitor in Allerdale, Et Dolfino sex bovatas terræ in alta
Crossby, ut esset serviens Dñi Regis in Allerdale. Et dedit Simoni
de Shestlyngs medietatem de Derem, et Dolphino filio Cospatricii
aliam medietatem. Et dedit Waldeno filio Dolfini Brakenthayt.
Et dedit Prioratui Scæ Begæ Stambrun. Et dedit Prioratui Carlioli
cum corpore Waldeni filii sui Crucem sanctam, quam adhuc possident,
et Crosseby cum advocacione ejusdem Ecclesiæ, et cum servicio
Vitredi, et advocacione Ecclesiæ de Aspatrick cum servicio Alani de
Brayten, cum advocacione Ecclesiæ de Irby cum servicio Waldeni de
Longthayt. Idem Alanus filius Waldeni dedit Dño. H. Regi landas
Forestæ de Allerdale, Et Abbati de Holme una cum venacione ap[d]
Coltram, Cui Alano successit Willelmus filius Doncani Comes de
Murrey, nepos ipsius Alani et heres, procreatus ex Ectreila sorore
Waldeni patris sui. Idem Willelmus filius Doncani desponsavit Ali-
ciam filiam Roberti de Romney, Dñi de Skypton in Cravyn, qui
Robertus quondam desponsavit filiam de Meschyne, Dñi de Cowpe-
land. Idem Willelmus procreavit ex predicta Alicia uxore sua Willelmum
puerum de Egremond, qui infra ætatem obiit, Et tres filias quarum
prima, nomine Cicilia, maritata fuit cum honore de Skypton Willelmo
Grosso Comiti Albi Marliæ per Dñum H. Regem Angliæ. Item
secunda, nomine Amabilla, maritata fuit Reginaldo de Lucy cum
honore de Egremond per eundem Regem. Et tertia, nomine
Alicia de Romney, maritata fuit Gilberto Pypard cum Aspatrik et
Baronia de Allerdale, et libertate de Cokermouth per eundem Regem,
et iterum per Reginam Roberto de Courtney, et obiit sine heredibus
de se. Willelmus Grossus, Comes Albi Marliæ, genuit ex ea Cicilia
Hawisiam, cui successit Willelmus de Fortibus, Comes Albi-Marliæ,
cui successit alter Willelmus de [p. 13] Fortibus, cui successit Avelina
quæ fuit desponsata Dño Edmundo fratri Dñi Regis E. et obiit
sine herede. Et idem Reginaldus de Lucy genuit ex Amabilla,
Amabillam et Aliciam, et successit Amabillæ Lambertus de Multon,
cui successit Thomas de Multon, et successit Aliciæ Thomas de Lucy.

Clifton.

Recordes & monuments concerning the Family of Clyfton,
Lords of yᵉ Mannor of Clyfton juxta Nottingham.

Ex libro censuali, vulgo Domesday, composito Anno Vicesimo
Gulielmi Conquestoris Angliæ. Cap. 1⁰.

Super socam que jacet ad Cliftune, debet habere comes tertiam
partem omnium consuetudinum et operum.

Ibidem, Cap. 9⁰. Terra Willelmi Peverell.

In Clifton habet Gode comitissa duas carucatas terræ et dimidium
ad geldam. Terra qninque carucatæ. Ibi habet Willelmus duas
carucatas in dominio, et quatuor sochemannos et viginti novem
villanos et octo bordarios habentes novem carucatas. Ibi presbiter et
Ecclesia et unum molendinum viginti denariorum, et duodecim acre
prati. Tempore R. Edwardi valuit xvi libras, modo ix libras.

In Willesford soca tres acræ prati ad geldam. Terra sex carucatæ.
Ibidem viginti tres sochemanni habent septem carucatas. Ibi presbiter
et octodecim acræ prati et dimidium piscariæ.

Terra Radulphi filii Huberti. Cap. 13⁰.

In Cliftune duæ bovatæ terræ ad geldam ad Bartone pertinentes,
valent xx⁸.

Risceliue Wapentakium.

Terra Tainorum. Cap. 30⁰.

In Clifton habet Ulchel de Rege unam bovatam terræ ad geldam.
Ibi habet unum villanum cum duobus bobus arantem, et unam acram
prati.

Terra Alani Comitis. Cap. 6ᵗᵒ.

In Clifton ad geldam tres carucatæ et duo carucæ possunt esse. Ibi
habeat Cnut manerium. Nunc habet Donemuald. Ibi una carucata
et tres villani cum una caruca et dimidio. Totum dimidium leucæ
longitudine, et dimidium latitudine. Tempore R. Edwardi valuit viii⁸,
modo v⁸.

Ex antiquo Manuscripto :—Memorandum quod quidam Aluaredus
Clifton, miles, Dominus Manerii Wilford cum pertinenciis in dominico

suo, ut de feodo, fuit Gardianus Castelli Nottinghamie tempore Willelmi Peverell ; post cujus mortem quidam Robertus Clifton, miles, filius et heres predicti Aluaredi, Dominus Manerii predicti, fuit Gardianus Castelli predicti ; et post ejus mortem quidam Gervasius Clifton, miles, filius et heres predicti Roberti, fuit Dominus Manerii predicti et Gardianus Castelli Nottinghamie ; et post obitum suum quidam alius Gervasius Clifton, miles, filius et heres predicti Gervasii, et dominus Manerii predicti fuit Custos Castelli predicti totis diebus vitæ suæ. Idem Gervasius fecit unum wardum Castelli predicti vocatum le Utter Ward, fecitque molendinum ejusdem Castelli. Idem predictus Gervasius fecit unam trencheam ab aqua Trentæ usque molendinum predictum per propriam suam terram dominicalem usque quoddam pratum vocatum Kyngis-meddowe. Idem dictus Gervasius fecit unum Gurgustum* in sua aqua de Trent predicta ad dictam aquam ponendum molendinis predictis per medium trencheæ predictæ.

Nota quod Gulielmus Peverell filius fuit nothus Regis Gulielmi Conquestoris.

Hæc est Finalis Concordia facta in curia Domini Regis apud Legr : die Sabbathi proximo ante festum Sancti Egidii, Anno Regni R. Johannis 5to, coram Domino G. filio Petri Comitis Essex, Hugoni Bard : Willelmo de Cantelupe, tunc Justiciariis, et aliis fidelibus Domini Regis ibidem tunc presentibus, inter Gervasium de Clyfton et Ismaniam sororem ejus petentes, et Robertum de Aluidelegh tenentem, de placito terræ et convencionis quod fuit inter eos in [**p. 14**] predicta curia :—Scilicet, quod predicti Gervasius et Ismania reddiderunt et quietum-clamaverunt chartas factas inter ipsum Gervasium et predictum Robertum de convencione maritagii filii ipsius Gervasii et filiæ ipsius Roberti, et omnes alias chartas cujuscunque convencionis inter ipsos Gervasium et Robertum, et preterea omnes chartas de hereditate ipsius Roberti quietas predicto Roberto et heredibus suis de predictis Gervasio et Ismania et heredibus suis in perpetuum. Et pro hac quietum-clamacione, fine. et concordia predictus Robertus concessit predictæ Ismaniæ totam terram quæ fuit Ricardi Barioneis, quondam avunculi ipsius Roberti, in Gedling et in Stoke, tenendum predictæ Ismaniæ ut dotem rationabilem de predicto Roberto et heredibus suis omnibus diebus vitæ ipsius Ismaniæ. Et post mortem ipsius Ismaniæ redibit tota predicta terra de Gedling et de Stoke quieta ipsi Roberto et heredibus suis, ut jus suum hereditarium de predicta Ismania et heredibus suis in perpetuum.

In antiquo rotulo sic inseritur :—Hæc sunt exigenda in Nottinghamscire et Derbysire pro Essartis et Vastis, et purpresturis et placitis

---

* *Gurgustum*—Gurgitum, a Weir.—*Ed.*

Forrestæ, per Galfridum filium Petri, Anno 33° regni Henrici Regis 2^{di}, in crastino Ascensionis :—

De Gervasio de Cliftune dimidiam marcam pro bissa* a manupastu† suo occisa in meta Forestæ.

Ex carta sine data penes Gabrielem Armestrong de Thorpe, Arm : in com : Nott :—

Ricardus filius Gulielmi de Trowell in Staneford dedit Gervasio filio Gervasii de Ciiftone terras in Staneford.

Hæc est Finalis Concordia facta in curia Dñi Regis apud West-monasterium, a die Paschæ in unum mensem, anno regni R. Edwardi filii R. Henrici sexto [1277-8] coram Magistro Rogero de Seyton, Magistro Johanne de Fremingham, Thomas Welond, Johanne de Luvetot, et Rogero de Leycestre, Justiciariis, et aliis Dñi Regis fidelibus tunc ibidem presentibus, inter Gervasium filium Gervasii de Clifton querentem, et Johannem filium Alfredi de Sullny, deforcientem, de octo virgatis terræ cum pertinentiis in Brocton, quam terram Adam de Sancto Laudo et Sibilla uxor ejus tenent in dotem ipsius Sibillæ de hereditate ipsius Johannis. Et unde placitum convencionis summon-itum fuit inter eos in eadem curia, Scilicet, quod predictus Johannes recognovit predictam terram cum pertinenciis, scilicet, unam virgatam terræ quam Simon de Rakedale, unam virgatam terræ quam Ricardus le Blund, unam virgatam terræ quam Thurgis de Brocton, unam virgatam terræ quam Alicia de Thorlaston, unam &c. quam Ricardus de Oxthon, unam &c. quam Willelmus de Rakedale, unam &c. quam Hugo de Westreys, et unam &c. quam Elyas de Oxthon, tenuerunt de predictis Ada et Sibilla ad voluntatem eorundem Adæ et Sibillæ die quo hæc concordia facta fuit, esse jus ipsius Gervasii, ut illam quam idem Johannes concessit predicto Gervasio post mortem predictæ Sibillæ. Ita quod predicti Adam et Sibylla de cetero tenebant predicta tene-menta cum pertinenciis, una cum predictis tenentibus, de predicto Gervasio et heredibus suis per servicia quæ ad illa tenementa pertinent. Et post decessum ipsius Sibillæ omnia predicta tenementa cum pertinenciis, simul cum predictis tenentibus, quæ ad predictum Johannem vel heredes suos post mortem ipsius Sibyllæ reverti deberent, integre remaneant predicto Gervasio et heredibus suis absque contradictione vel impedimento predicti Johannis vel heredum suorum, tenenda de capitalibus Dominis feodorum illorum per servitia quæ ad illa tenementa pertinent in perpetuum.

Et pro hac recognicione fine et concordia idem Gervasius dedit predicto Johanni unum spervarium sorum, et hæc concordia, present-

---

* *Bissa*—a Hind.   † *Manupastus*—a domestic servant.

ibus Ada et Sibylla et cognoscentibus, se nihil juris clamare in predicta terra et tenentibus quæ tenent, sicut predictum est, nisi nomine dotis, Et similiter presentibus predictis Simone, Ricardo le Blund, Thurgis, Alicia, Ricardo de Oxthon, Wfllelmo, Hugone et Elia, et cognoscent, ibus, se nihil juris clamare in predictis tenementis quæ tenent, sicut predictum est, nisi ad voluntatem predictorum Adæ et Sibillæ.

[p. 15.]

Finalis Concordia facta apud Nottingham a die S. Martini in unum mensem, Anno regni R. Edwardi filii R. Henrici 9° [1280-1], coram Johanne de Vallibus, Willelmo de Saham, Johanne de Metingham, et Magistro Thoma de Sudington, Justiciariis itinerantibus &c. Inter Gervasinm filium Gervasii de Clifton querentem, et Ricardum de Eynolf et Isoldam uxorem impedientes, de una bovata terræ cum pertinenciis, excepta medietate unius acræ terræ, in Wileford : Unde placitum Warrant' Chartæ summonitum fuit inter eos in eadem curia, Scilicet, quod predicti Ricardus et Isolda recognoverunt predictam bovatam terræ, &c.

Finalis Concordia &c. inter Rogerum de S. Andrea et Agnetem uxorem ejus querentes per Gervasium de Wilford positum in loco ad lucrandum vel perdendum, et Johannem de Clyfton deforcientem, de decem libratis redditus in Gotham, &c. Rogerus recognovit predictum redditum cum pertinenciis esse jus ipsius Johannis ut illum quem idem Johannes habet de dono ipsius Rogeri, &c. Habendum et tenendum iisdem Rogero et Agneti et heredibus suis, &c. Facta apud Eboracum in curia Dñi Regis a die S. Martini in quindecim dies, &c. Anno regni R. Edwardi filii R. Henrici 31° (1302-3). Coram Radulpho de Hengham, Willelmo de Bereford, Elia de Bekingham, Petro Mallore, Willelmo Howard, et Lamberto de Trikingham, Justiciariis, &c.

Notingh':—Finalis Concordia facta in curia Regis apud Notingham, a die S. Michaelis in quindecim dies, Anno regni R. Henrici filii R. Johannis 20° (1235-6) coram Willelmo de Eboraco, Willelmo de Insula, Radulpho de Norwic', Roberto de Dun, et Willelmo de Heriz, Justiciariis itinerantibus, &c. Inter Gervasium de Clyfton petentem, et Hugonem de Bel tenentem, de duabus bovatis terræ cum pertinenciis in Wileford &c. Tenendum eidem Hugoni et heredibus suis &c. reddendo inde annuatim duos solidos sterlingorum, &c. Et postea idem Hugo dedit predicto Gervasio viginti solidos sterlingorum.

Finalis Concordia facta in curia Dñi Regis apud Westm : in crastino S. Johannis Baptistæ, Anno regni R. Edwardi filii R. Edwardi 18° (1324-5), coram Willelmo de Bereford, Johanne de Mulford, Willelmo de Hale, Johanne de Stonore, et Johanne de Bonper, Justiciariis et aliis, &c. Inter Robertum de Clyfton et Gervasium filium ejus, et Margaretam uxorem ejusdem Gervasii, querentes, et Johannem de Shirewode custodem ipsorum Gervasii et Margaretæ per breve Dñi Regis ad lucrandum, et Thomam personam Ecclesiæ de Wileford, et Robertum Shipman de Wileford capellanum, deforcientes, de maneriis de Clyfton et Wileford cum pertinenciis, et de advocacionibus Ecclesi arum ejusdem *(sic)* villarum, &c. Robertus de Clyfton recognovit predicta Maneria cum pertinenciis et advocaciones predictas esse jus ipsius Thomæ, ut illa quæ idem Thomas et Robertus Shipman habent de dono predicti Roberti ; et pro hac recognicione fine et concordia iidem Thomas et Robertus conceperunt predicto Roberto predicta Maneria, &c.

Extractum Finium Cancellarie, A° 52 Hen. III (1267-8) :—
Gervasius filius Gervasii de Clifton dat dimidiam Marcam pro uno brevi : Noting'.

Escaetria de A° 7 Edw. I. no. 25 (1278-9) :—
Per inquisicionem post mortem Roberti le Bretun de Walton in com : Derb : constat quod Gervasius de Clifton fuit Vice-comes comitatum Nottingham' et Derb', A° 7 Edw. I.

[p. 16.]
Communia de termino Pasche, A° 9 Edw. I. (1280-1) :—
Recognitio Galfridi de Clifton (Lego Gervasii), Viee-comitis Com : Nott : facta Roberto Abbati Westmonasteriensi, Thesaurario Regis, de decem libris.

Clausi de A° 11 Edw. I. m. 2 (1282-3) :—
Gervasius de Clifton Vice-comes comitatum Nottingh' et Derbie.

Escaetria de A° 15 Edw. I. no. 6 (1286-7) :—
Robertus de Rabiriey tenuit unam bovatam terræ in Clapton in com : Nott : de herede Gulielmi Boyne, de feodo Gervasii de Clifton, per servicium trium solidorum.

Communia de termino Trinitatis, A° 15 Edw. I. rot. 12 :—
Recognitio Gervasii de Clifton, vice-comitis com : Ebor, de termino Michaelis, A° 15 Edw. I. Irrotulata predicto termino Trinitatis.

Communia de termino Michaelis A° 16 finiente, incipiente
17 Edw. I, rot 3 in dorso (1288) :—
De exonerando Gervasium de Clifton vice-comitem Derbie, A° 10 R. Edwardi primi (1281-2), per inquisicionem per eum factam, &c.

Communia de termino Hillarii, A° 19 Edw. I. rot. 4 in dorso (1291):—
Gervasius de Clifton, vice-comes com : Ebor : amerciatus.

Brevia de termino Pasche, A° 20 Edw. I. rot. 35 (1292) :—
Mandatum est Vice-comiti Nott : et Derb : quod attachiet Gervasium
de Clyfton ad reddendum compotum suum a die Paschæ in tres
septimanas de tempore quo fuit Vice-comes com : Ebor : ad quam
diem venit et computavit.

Communia de termino Pasche, A° 20 Edw. I. rot. 15 in dorso (1292):—
Gervasius de Clifton quondam Vice-comes com : Ebor : habet
allocacionem diversorum denariorum quos per preceptum Regis
posuit A° 19 Edw. I. Teste Rege apud Hereford 18 die Octobris, A°
19 Edw. I.

Ex libro inquisicionum in Scaccario de feodis Militum et eorum
tenentium honoris Peverelli in com : Nott : A° 21 Edw. I. (1292-3) :—
Robertus de Tibetot tenet manerium de Langar cum membris,
Videlicet, cum homagio Gervasii de Clyfton pro manerio de Clifton de
Dño Rege in capite pro feodo unius militis, et cum homagio Roberti
Lutterall pro manerio de Gameleston : Pro quibus quidem Maneriis
unica sit secta ad curiam Peverelli apud Nott : de tribus septimanis
per Henricum filium Gervasii de Wileford, qui terram suam de
Wileford tenet pro secta facienda.

Ibidem :—Clifton cum soca est eschaeta Dñi Regis, et est de honore
Peverelli de Nott : et valet per annum 40li, et Radulphus de Rodis
tenet eam per Dñum Regem per servicium dimidii feodi Militis.

Ibidem :—Gerardus de Rodes tenet Langare et Clyfton quæ sunt de
honore Peverelli, et quæ fuerunt dominica Willelmi Peverelli de dono
R. Johannis pro servicio unius Militis de novo feoffamento.*

[p. 17.]
Ex libro Feodorum in Scaccario de com : Nott : et Derb : secundum Inquisicionem inde factam coram Philippo de Wileby, Cancellario
de Scaccario, A° 24 Edw. I. (1295-6) :—

Wapp : de Riseclive. Gervasius de Clifton tenet manerium de
Clifton cum membris de honore Peverelli, sed non fit mentio per quod
servicinm.

Compotus Walteri Goushell Collectoris Scutagii in com : Nott : et
Derb : de exercitibus Scociæ, A° 28 Edw. I. fol. 90b (1299-300):—

* *Testa de Nevill*, 13, 17, 19.

CLIFTON.

Wapp : de Risclive : De Gervasio de Clifton pro dimidio feodo in Clifton, Wilford, Briggeford, et Staunton quod tenet de honore Peverelli.

Ibidem :—A° 31 Edw. I. fol. 94 (1302-3) :—

Wapp : de Risclive : De Gervasio de Clyfton pro dimidio feodo in Clyfton, Wilford, Briggeford, et Staunton quod tenet de honore Peverelli, 20ˢ.

Extracta Finium de Cancellaria, A° 25 Edw. I. in 22 Warr. (1296-7):—

Gervasius de Clyfton et Amflisia uxor ejus dant dimidiam marcam pro uno brevi.

Essonia de A° 9 Edw. I., rot. 4 (1280-1) :—

Gervasius de Clyfton, Vice comes Nott: in misericordia pro contemptu, et amerciatus ad decem libras &c. pardonatur per Johannem de Vallibus et Will: de Ingham.

In quodam placito Assisæ de A° 9 Edw. III. rot. 11, Nott.(1334) :—

Gervasius de Clyfton scribitur etiam Gervasius de Wileford, et ibidem placitatur utrum consuetudo villæ de Nott: talis sit quod si aliquis homo habens terras de hereditate vel perquisito ducat aliquam mulierem terram non habentem in uxorem, et vir terram illam in necessitate vendat, et pecuniam pro terra illa receptam simul cum uxore sua expendat, uxor sua quocunque fuit post obitum viri sui nihil juris nomine dotis in predictis tenementis clamare potest.

Placita coram Auditore querelarum apud Westmon : A° 18 Edw. I, no. 6 in dorso, Ebor. (1289-90) :—

Gervasius de Clifton, Vice-comes Ebor : de quo Johannes de Carleton queritur pro falso returno literis facto. Pro quo idem Vice-comes committitur gaolæ, &c.

Nomina Villarum in com : Nott : et earum Domini, A° 9 Edw. II. (1315-6) :—

Wapentach de Bingham —Hikeling et Brocton respondent pro villa integra. Dñs Ricardus de Grey infra ætatem, et in custodia Comitis Lancastriæ, et Gervasii de Clyfton. Clyfton cum membris respondet pro una villa integra. Dominus, Gervasius de Clyfton.

Originale de A° 17 Edw. II, no. 12, Nott: (1323-4) :—

Rex cepit homagium Roberti de Clyfton consanguinei et heredis Gervasii de Clyfton defuncti de omnibus terris et tenementis que idem [p. 18] Gervasius tenuit de Rege in capite die quo obiit, et ei terras illas et tenementa reddidit. Inde mandatum est Magistro Johanni Wayleman, Escaetori ultra Trentam, quod eidem Roberto seisinam habere faciat &c. Salvo jure cujuscunque. Teste Rege apud Castrum Barnardi, 11° die Septembris.

Notingh: Finalis Concordia facta apud Westmon: in crastino S. Martini, A° regni R. Edwardi filii R. Edwardi 20° (1326), coram Henrico de Staunton &c. Justiciariis :—Inter Rogerum de Clyfton et Basiliam de Neketon querentes, et Ricardum de Wowe de Bromfield et Amabillam uxorem ejus deforcientes, de octo acris terræ et octo denariis (denariatis) terræ redditus cum pertinenciis in Parva Waltham.

Essonia capta apud Justiciarios &c. die Mercurii proximo post festum S. Hillarii, A° 18 Edw. II, rot. 1 in dorso (1324) :—

Radulphus filius Gervasii de Clyfton tulit assisam novæ disseisinæ versus Robertum de Clyfton de tenementis in Broughton Sulney, &c. A° 18 Edw. II.

Placita apud Notingh: die Veneris proximo post festum S. Bartholomei, A° 20 Edw. II, rot. 1, in dorso (1326) :—

Radulphus filius Gervasii de Clyfton op-tulit &c. versus Johannem de Clyfton personam Ecclesiæ de Clyfton de placito trangressionis &c. A° 20 Edw. II.

Originale de A° 19 Edw. III (1345) :—

Gervasius de Clyfton Vice-comes Nott: et Derb: A° 19 Edw. III. Gervasius de Clyfton Escaetor Regis in com: Nott: et Derb: 20 Edw. III.

Charta de A° 10 Edw. III, No. 54 (1337) :—

Libera warenna concessa Gervasio de Clyfton in omnibus dominicis terris suis de Broughton Sulney &c. in com: Nott:—Ita quod nullus intret terras illas ad fugandum &c. sine licencia ipsius &c. sub pena forisfacturæ decem librarum. Testibus J. Archiepiscopo Cantuar: et Cancellario nostro. H. Lincoln: Episcopo Thesaurario nostro. Johanne Comite Cornubiæ, fratre nostro charissimo. Henrico de Percy, Willelmo de Monte-acuto, Roberto de Ufford, Radulpho de Nevill, Seneschallo hospitii nostri, &c. Datum apud Berewicum super Twedam 11o die Januarii. Per breve privati sigilli.

Notingh :—Finalis Concordia facta apud Westmon : a die S. Michaelis in tres septimanas, A° R. Edwardi Anglie III a conquestu 18° et
regni ejusdem R. Franciæ 5° (1344) :—Coram Johanne de Stonore,
Rogero Hillarii, Ricardo de Kelleshull, et Ricardo de Willughby,
Justiciariis &c.—Inter Gervasium de Clyfton, Chevalier, querentem, et
Robertum de Vaus et Amfeliciam uxorem ejus deforcientes, de manerio
de Normanton super Sore cum pertinenciis &c. Concesserunt pro se
et heredibus ipsius Roberti, quod ipsi warrantizabunt predicto Gervasio
et heredibus suis duas partes manerii predicti cum suis pertinenciis &c.
Et pro hac recognicione, remissione, et quieta-clamantia idem Gervasius concessit pro se et heredibus suis quod ipsi reddent singulis
annis predicto Roberto et Amflisiæ sexdecim libras sterlingorum.

Notingh : Finalis Concordia facta apud Westmon : a die Paschæ
A° regni Edwardi R. Angliæ III post conquestum 19°, et regni ejusdem
R. Franciæ 6° (1345), coram Johanne Stonore, ut supra, et recordatur
coram predictis et Johanne de Stanford, Justiciariis :—Inter Robertum
filium Gervasii de Clyfton et Isabellam uxorem ejus querentes, et
Gervasium de Clyfton, Chevalier, deforcientem, de manerio de Broughton cum pertinenciis, et de advocacione Ecclesiæ ejusdem manerii &c.
Predictus Gervasius concessit predictis Roberto et Isabellæ predictum
[p. 19] manerium cum pertinenciis et advocacionen predictam, et duas
partes predicti manerii cum pertinencis eis reddidit in eadem curia,
tenendas eidem Roberto et Isabellæ et heredibus de corporibus ipsorum
exeuntibus de predicto Gervasio in perpetuum. Reddendo inde per
annum unam Rosam ad festum Nativitatis S. Johannis Baptiste pro
omni servitio, &c. Et predictus Gervasius warrantizabit &c. Et pro
hac concordia &c., dederunt predicto Gervasio centum marcas sterlingorum.

Notingh : Finalis Concordia &c. A° 30° Edw. (1356); coram Rogero
Hillarii, Ricardo de Willughby, Johanne de Stanford, Henrico Grene,
et Thoma de Seton, Justiciariis et aliis, &c. :—Inter Gervasium de
Clyfton, Chevalier, et Isabellam uxorem ejus, et Robertum filium ejus
dem Gervasii, querentes, et Henricum de Raddeford, capellanum, et
Willelmum Julian, capellanum, deforcientes, de manerio de Wilford
cum pertinenciis &c. Idem Henricus et Willelmus pro hac recognicione
&c., concesserunt predictis Gervasio et Isabellæ predictum manerium
&c. Et illa eis reddiderunt.

Si aliquis captus fuerit cum manuopere* infra manerium de Clyfton
de latrocinio vel roberia factis infra idem manerium Domini tenentes
ejusdem manerii arrennare solebant talem captum pro hujusmodi

---

* *Manu-opus, Manuopera*, stolen goods taken on a thief.—Ed.

felonia ad sectam sequentis, Et si ipse se ponere voluisset de bono et malo, facere de ipso judicium secundum quod compertum fuisset de eo : Et si nollet se ponere, mittere eum ad gaolam Regis, &c.

Radulphus filius Gervasii de Clyfton et Isabella uxor ejus tulerunt assisam novæ disseisinæ versus Gervasium de Clyfton et Margaretam uxorem ejus, et alios in brevi, de tenementis in Clifton, Gnapton, Wilford et Broughton, &c.

Radulphus filius Gervasii de Clifton injuste disseisivit Matildam quæ fuit uxor Henrici de Wilford'de libero tenemento in Wilford, &c., post primam, &c. Et inde queritur quod disseisivit eam de duobus solidatis et sex denariatis redditus, duobus quarteriis ordei, et uno quarterio pisarum, et duobus quarteriis frumenti cum pertinenciis. Et profert quoddam scriptum sub nomine ipsius Radulphi quod testatur quod idem Radulphus concessit predictæ Matildæ predictos redditus. Dicta Matilda recuperat. Et predictus Radulphus. quia cognovit disseisinam contra factum suum proprium, ideo committitur gaolæ. Postea finem fecit cum Rege pro xx solidis.

Charta de Aº 9 Edw. I, No. 102, m. 17 (1280) :

Rex Archiepiscopis Episcopis Abbatibus Prioribus Comitibus Baronibus, &c.—Salutem. Inspeximus chartam quam Gerardus de Rodes fecit Gervasio de Clyfton in hæc verba, Sciant presentes et futuri quod ego Gerardus de Rhodes dedi concessi et hac presenti charta mea confirmavi Dño Gervasio de Clyfton omnes terras et tenementa de Clifton et Willesford cum omnibus pertinenciis et omnimoda homagia et servicia liberorum hominum et villanorum meorum de Clifton Willesford et Brocton, &c., Habendum et tenendum eidem Gervasio, &c. Reddendo inde annuatim mihi xxx libras, &c. Nos autem predictas donaciones ratas habentes, eas pro nobis et heredibus nostris concedimus, &c. Hiis testibus—Ven : patribus R. Bathon : et Wellens : et Thoma Menevens : Episcopis. Edmundo Comite Cornubiæ. Rogero de Mortuo Mari, Rogero de Clifford, Johanne de Vescy, Roberto Tibetot, Patricio de Cadurcis, Hugone fil : Ottonis, Tho : de Weyland, Roberto fil : Johannis, [p. 20] Johanni de Lovetot, Petro de Huntingfield, et aliis. Datum apud Westmon : 24 Nov. Aº regni nostri nono.

Patentes de Aº 51, Edw. III, m. 1, a. (1377) :

Rex omnibus Ballivis et fidelibus suis ad quos, &.—Salutem. Sciatis quod de gratia nostra speciali concessimus pro nobis et heredibus nostris dilecto et fideli nostro Gervasio de Clifton, Chivaler, quod ipse ad totam vitam suam habeat libertatem quod non ponatur in assisis juratis seu recognitionibus quibuscunque. Et quod non fiat Maior, Vice-comes, Escaetor, aut aliquis Ballivus seu Minister noster vel heredum nostrorum contra voluntatem suam. Et ideo vobis mandamus quod ipsum Gervasium contra concessionem nostram non molestetis in aliquo seu gravetis. In cujus, &c. Teste Rege, apud Manerium nostrum de Shene 5° die Junii.

Originale de A° 1 Hen. IV, bund. 2, rot. 24 (1400).

Rex pro bono servicio quod dilectus et fidelis Miles noster Johannes de Clifton nobis impendit, &c., concessimus ei XL marcas annuatim percipiendas per manus Vice-comitis com : Nott. 5° die Febr.

Idem Johannes Clifton, miles, duxit in uxorem Catharinam filiam Johannis Cressy, militis, et unam sororum et heredum Hugonis Cressy, filii et heredis ejusdem Johannis Cressy, militis, ut dilucide apparet per inquis : captam A° 9 Hen. IV, post mortem ejusdem Hugonis. Escaet : A° 9 Hen. IV, No. 30 (1407-8).

Johannes de Cressy, Chivaler.

Hugo de Cressy, ob. s.p. 9 Hen. IV.	Catharina, soror et co-h : nupta, 1° Johanni Clifton : postea Radulpho Makerell.	Elizabetha, altera sororum et heredum ; nupta Johanni Markham.

Inquis : No. 30.
        Braytoft Man. ⎫
        Risegate Man. ⎬ Lincs.
        Claypole Man. ⎭

In hac inquisicione de predictis terris et aliis predictis filiabus (pro defectu heredum masculorum de corpore predicti Johannis Cressy, Militis,) devolutis.

In ye rebellion of ye Percies in ye 4th yeare of the reign of King Henry ye 4th was slayne (among others) on the King's part Sir John Clifton, knt., who receaved the same morning ye order of Knight-hood. *Holinshead*, p. 1140.

Now that wee are come to this match with ye heyre of Cressy, it shall not be amisse to step a little aside out of ye way, & insert some records concerning the name & family.

Notingh :—Hæc est Finalis Concordia facta in curia D. Regis apud Clarendum die Lunæ proxima post mediam Quadragesimam, Aº R. Johannis 5º, (1204), coram Dño G. fil. Petri, Comitis Essex', Simone de Pateshull, Magistro Radulpho de Stoke, Magistro Jocelino de Well, Justiciariis, &c. Inter Ceciliam quæ fuit uxor Rogeri de Creissi, petentem, et Wilelmum de Creissi tenentem, de rationabili dote ipsius Ceciliæ quam ipsa clamavit versus ipsum Wilelmum de dono predicti Rogeri quondam viri sui in Hoddishac, Gedling, Kelum, Weston, Rampton, et Marcham. Unde placitum fuit inter eos in predicta curia, Scilicet, quod predictus Wilelmus concessit predictæ Ceciliæ feodum dimidii Militis cum pert : in Melton, et quinque acras prati in cum pert : in Lokingis Tenendam prefatæ Ceciliæ de prefato Wilelmo et heredibus suis omnibus diebus vitæ ipsius Ceciliæ nomine dotis. Et pro hac recognicione, &c., predicta Cecilia remisit et quietum clamavit predicto Wilelmo et heredibus suis totum jus et clameam quod habuit nomine dotis in residuo terrarum quæ fuerunt ipsius Rogeri ubicunque sint de se in perpetuum.

Placita de tempore R. Johannis, Aº incerto, rot : 4 : Nott :—

Gaufridus de Clifton, positus loco Ceciliæ de Cressi, optulit &c. quarto die versus Wilelmum de Cressi, de sex solidatis redditus in Hodesac et de tertia parte servicii feodi duorum militum et dimidii in Kelum, et in Gedling, et in Rampton & Weston [p. 21.] & Marcham, que clamat in dotem versus eundem Wilelmum. Et ipse non venit vel se essoniavit. Summoniti testes sint. Judicium—Redditus predictus et servicium capiantur in manum D. Regis : Et die captionis, &c. Et Wilelmus summoneatur adesse coram Rege ubicunque fuerit die Dominica in media Quadragesima inde responsurus, &c.

Finalis Concordia facta apud Ebor : &c. coram Radulpho de Hing-ham, Wilelmo de Bereford, Elia de Bekingham, Petro Malorre, Wilelmo Howard, et Lamberto de Trikingham, Justiciariis &c. in Octabis S. Martini, Aº regni R. Edwardi fil : R. Henrici 31º (1303)—Inter Richardum de Furness et Sibillam uxorem ejus querentes, et Wilelmum de Cressy et Johannam uxorem ejus impedientes, de Manerio de Carleton in Lyndryck &c. Notingh :

Placita de Quo Warranto coram Gulielmo de Hale et sociis suis, Justiciariis Itinerantibus in com : Nott : Aº 3 Edw. III. (1329). De Parco et Warrenna et aliis libertatibus apud Hodeshak. Ubi Edmundus de Cressy summonitus fuit ad respondendum D. Regi de placito quo warranto clamat habere in manerio suo de Hodesak Infangthef, furcas, parcum et warrennam in omnibus dominicis terris suis. Et dicit quod predictæ libertates sunt pertinentes ad terminum vitæ suæ de hereditate Wilelmi filii Rogeri de Cressy. Et Edmundus dicit quod a tempore de quo memoria non exstat, habuerunt libertates predictas tanquam manerio illi pertinentes &c.

Ex Registro quodam olim pertinente Monasteriolo de Haverholme in com : Linc.

Hugo Cressy, Vice-comes Nott: et Derb : 4 Hen. IV. (1402-3).

Inter Communia de Termino Trinitatis, A° 23 Hen. VI. rot: 9 (1445).

Gervasius Clifton locum tenens Humfridi Ducis Gloucestriæ Constabularii Castri R. Dover', 2° die Julii.

Originale de A° 30 Hen. VI. rot: 21 (1452).

Cales :—Kanc :—Rex dilecto sibi Gervasio Clifton, Arm. Thesaurario villæ suæ de Cales—Salutem. Sciatis quod de fidelitate et circumspectione vestra plenius confidentes assignavimus vos ad CCXL saccos Lanæ nostræ quibuscunque personis cujuscunque fuerint nationis ubicunque ad opus et utilitatem nostram melioribus modis et pretio quibus poteritis vendent, et singulas denariorum summas de lana predicta provenientes, ad in et circa operaciones apud Cales magis necessarias juxta discrecionem vestram, tredecim solidis et quatuor denariis de quolibet sacco lanæ predictæ, quos soldariis villæ predictæ per vos solvi volumus, duntaxat exceptis. Teste Rege apud Westmon : 26° Jan.

Ex originali predicto de A° 30 Hen. VI. rot : 16 (1452) :—

Lincoln.—Duæ partes maneriorum de Skirbecke, Wekes, et Frampton per Regem commissæ Gervasio Clifton, arm: et Johanni Scot, arm: ad [p. 22] finem XII annorum ; Et iterum custodia dictarum duarum partium iis commissa ad finem XI annorum ulterius, reddendo Regi et heredibus suis CXXII libras sterlingorum per ann. Teste Rege apud Westmon : 25 die Maii.

Ibidem, Rot. 28. Kanc :—

Rex omnibus &c. Sciatis quod per manucaptionem* Thomæ Barley de com : Hereford, arm : commisimus Gervasio de Clyfton, arm : &c. custodiam omnium temporalium Archiepiscopatus Cantuar : in manibus nostris post mortem Johannis nuper Archiepiscopi, quamdiu ea in manibus nostris contigerit &c.—Reddendo nobis prout inter Thesaurarium Angliæ et eosdem, &c.

---

* *Manucaptio*—Mainprise, Surety.—*Ed.*

Communia, A° 27 Hen. VI, termino Michaelis, rot. 16 in dorso (1448).

Rex per certam manucaptionem* commisit Johanni tunc S. Balbinæ Presbytero Cardinali, et Gervasio Clyfton, arm: custodiam omnium terrarum et tenementorum cum pertinenciis que fuerunt Gulielmi defuncti, &c. Teste &c. 2° die Novembris, A° regni 27°.

Per billam Thesaurarii, et de data predicta authoritate Parliamenti.

Precepta de termino Hillarii A° 2 Hen. VI, rot. 3 (1424).

Robertus Clyfton, Vice-comes Norf. et Suff. A° 1 Hen. VI.

Termino Michaelis, A° 19 Hen. VI (1440).

Gervasius Clyfton, nuper Vice-comes com: Kanc. a festo S. Michaelis ad eundem festum sequentem.

A° 29 Hen. VI (1450):

Gervasius Clyfton, Vice-comes com: Kanc. a festo S. Michaelis ad eundem festum sequentem.

Termino Michaelis A° 30 Hen. VI, rot. 3 (1451):

Robertus Clyfton, Vice-comes Nott. et Derb. A° 29 Hen. VI.

Termino Hillarii A° 38 Hen. VI, rot. 1 (1460):

Gervasius Clyfton, miles, Vice-comes com: Kanc. A° 37 Hen. VI.

Termino Michaelis, A° 39 Hen. VI, rot. 1 (1460):

Robertus Clyfton, Vice-comes com: Nott. et Derb. A° 38 Hen. VI.

Officium Thesaurarii de Cales datum Gervasio Clyfton, arm., cum Ricardus Vernoun, Miles, literas suas patentes pro eodem officio in Cancellariam restituit cancellandas, 24 Maii, A° 29 Hen. VI (1450): Hoc officium ei concessum a Rege (ut exprimitur) de gratia Regis speciali in recompensationem boni et gratuiti servitii quod dilectus nobis Gervasius Clyfton, arm., nobis impendit, et impendet in futurum. Inter billas signatas per Regem, temp. R. Hen. VI.

A Petition to y° King by Sr Gervase Clifton, Treasurer of Cales, to graunte his lettres of warrant to y° Treasurer Barons & Chamberlaines of the Exchequer, commanding them to take up his accounts from yeare to yeare duely upon his oathe, which without his warrant they will not doe, &c. Robert Whittingham, John Langton, & Richard Vernon were successively Treasurers before him.

---

* *Manucaptio*—Mainprise, Surety.—*Ed.*

Ex Originale de A° 36 Hen. VI, 23 (1458), Cales :

Fiat protectio cum clausula Volumus pro Ricardo Kyngesmelle, nuper de Crowley in com : Sussex, yeom. alias dicto Ricardo Kynsmille nuper de Crowley, &c., seu quocunqne alio nomine censeatur qui in obsequio D. nostri Regis in comitiva mea super salva custodia defensione et vitellatione villæ dictæ D. nostri Regis Cales in partibus Picardiæ moratur per unum annum duratura. Custodi privati Sigilli D. nostri Regis, Per Gervasium Clyfton, Militem, Thesaurar : Villæ de Cales. Dat : et ex : apud Westmon : 1° die Maii, A° 36 Hen. VI.

Diversæ consimiles protectiones per eundem Gervasium Clifton, mil : concessæ sub sigillo suo armorum, prout superius.

(A pen and ink drawing is here given of the Seal attached to the fore-going documents, representing a shield with the Clifton arms, Semée of cinquefoils, a lion rampant ; and on a helmet the Crest, a demi-Peacock, wings expanded.)

A Peticion made to ye Kinge by Sr Gervas Clifton, Kt., Treasurer of ye Towne of Calais, & of Sr John Cheney, Kt., victualler of ye said Towne. The Tenour of it is that—Forasmuch as they stand chargeable to y[e] King as by way of account for y[e] summe of ix^m ccc^l in his Exchequer to be employed by them upon y[e] workes of y[e] same towne, & especially upon y[e] making of y[e] getties of y[e] said towne, & upon y[e] banke called ye Ruisbanke ; & forasmuch as they be daily called upon in his Maties Court of Exchequer for accompt of y[e] said summe, they beying busyed there about y[e] Kinges affayres with y[e] Commissioners thither sent ; & forasmuch as ye bookes & writings of accompt cannot yet be made perfect for that part of y[u] summe is yett in employing upon ye said workes, & that therefore ye officers may be charged with no process against ye said Sr. Gervas & Sr. John, &c., untill ye optãs of S. Michaell next comming, &c.

T. Cant.   R. Warrewicke.   J. Worcester.

Dominus Sõti. Severini.   } Bourgcheor.
R. Sĉti. Johannis   }

A° 34 Hen. VI, 26° die Junii (1456), apud Westmon : Rex de advisamento concilii sui voluit et mandavit quod custos privati sigilli sui literas sub eodem sigillo fieri faceret secundum tenorem et formam predictam dominis se subscribentibus, ut patet :

By the Kinge. Right trusty & well-beloved, wee let you witt, That whereas there is due to divers & sundry creditors for Beefes & muttons purveyed for our household for y[e] time that Sr. Gervase Clifton, Kt., stood Treasurer of our said household, the summe of cccccLx^{li}, as by bills of debentures thereof it appeareth plainely, & noe payment thereof made to ye great hurt & undoeing of ye said creditors which we would in noe wise. Wherefore forasmuch as ye charge of ye abovesaid provision pertayneth to O^r well-beloved servant Philip Neele, esq., Sergeant of O^r Empcions, Wee will & charge you that under O^r privy Seale, beinge in your ward, you doe make yor Letters directed to ye Chamberlaynes of the receipte of [p. 24] ye Exchequer commanding them to make out & deliver to O^r said servant sufficient assignement for ye payment & contenting of ye summe of cccclx^li ; & this O^r Letters to be yor warrant. Yeoven under O^r Signet att . . . . Jan. 30 yeare of O^r Raigne.

To O^r Right Trusty & well-beloved Clerke, Mr. Robert Stillington, keeper of O^r Privy Seale. By the Kinge.

Trusty & well beloved, we thanke you hertely for all yor good kindnesse shewed unto us oft afore, doeing you to wite, y^t now late we have sent to our Broyer Th' Emperour in O^r Ambassiate O^r trusty & well beloved Robert Clifton, Kt. & Mr Stephen Wilton, Doctor of Decrees, to whom we pray you hertily to be assisting & councelling, with ye Wor^th Fadir in God ye Bp. of Seguen',* & with ye nobull & worthy Kt. Gasper Slygh, O^r Broyer th-Emperors Chancellour, to whom we have written O^r letters at this tyme for ye same in such matters as yei have to shew in O^r name to O^r said Broyer, for ye which we will con you right good yanke, & be more ready to doe such thinges as may be to yor profitt or worshipp, praying O^r Lord that he have you ever in his blessed keeping. Yeoven &c. at Westm, ye 23 day of January.

To Hertonk Van Clax: circa ann: 16 Hen. VI, ut patet in pagina prima sequente. Supradictus Hertonk van Clax fuit Alemannus, et eques ordinis Georgiani, temp. R. Hen. V.

Sir Gervase Clifton, Kt. left behind Captaine of Ponthoise, with Sir Nicholas Burdett, Henry Chandois, & others, A° 19 Hen. VI, (1440-1) *Hollinshead*, p. 1265—taken there p. 1265.

Privata Sigilla de A° 1, Edw. IV, (1460-1).

Per Regem. Sincere dilecte—Salutem. Vobis mandamus quod sub privato sigillo nostro in vestra custodia existente literas nostras Cancellario nostro Angliæ derigendas fieri faciatis, mandantes eidem sub magno sigillo nostro literas nostras patentes fieri facere in forma

---

* Probably the Spanish Bishop of Siguenza, Alfonso Carrillo, who was with the Emperor Sigismund and the Imperial Chancellor, Gaspar Schlicht, at the Council of Basle, and who died there in 1434.—*Ed.*

sequente :—Rex omnibus ad quos, &c.—Salutem. Sciatis quod de gratia nostra speciali ac ex certa scientia et mero motu nostris pardon-avimus, remisimus et relaxavimus Gervasio Clifton, militi, alias dicto Gerv. Clifton nuper de Biaborn in com : Kanc : mil., alias dicto Gerv : Clifton nuper de Clifton in com : Nott : mil., alias dicto Gerv : Clifton nuper de London, mil., alias dicto Gerv : Clifton, mil. nuper Thesaur-ario Villæ nostræ de Cales et marchiarum ibidem, alias dicto Gerv : Clifton, mil. nuper Thesaurario Villæ nostræ Cales, alias dicto Gerv : Clifton, mil. nuper Vice-comiti com : nostri Kanc., seu quocunque alio nomine censeatur, sectam pacis nostræ quæ ad nos versus ipsum pertinet pro omnimodis proditionibus murdris raptibus mulierum rebellionibus &c. In cujus rei &c. Et hæ literæ nostræ vobis erunt sufficientes in warrantum. Dat' nostro sub sigillo in Palatio nostro Westmon : 17° die Decemb : A° regni nostri primo.

Indorsatum sic., Sincere dilecto Clerico suo M^{ro} Roberto Stillington, Custodi privati Sigilli nostri.

[p. 26]
    Inter billas signatas per Regem, A° 20 Edw. IV (1480-1):

Edward by ye Grace of God, &c. To O^r trusty and wel-beloved Richard Shelden & John Cotton Greeting. Whereas we by O^r letters of privy signet bearing date of ye 29 day of August in ye 16 yeare of O^r Reigne made O^r trustie & welbeloved Squier Gervase Clifton O^r Generall Receaver of all ye Lordshipps of Nottingham, Arnall, Lindeby, Bulwell, Mansfield, Woodhus, Sutton, Retford, Darlington & Ragen-holl, Clipston in Shirewood, Edingstow, honour of Peverell, Bollsover, Horeston, Horseley, Chestrefeld, Whatton, Aslakton, Gedling, Shelford & Stoke-Bardolfe, onely ; & also our Styward of ye said Gedling, Shel-ford & Stoke-Bardolfe onely ; and also where wee by O^r letters patents bearing date ye 28 day of Februarie in ye 16 yeare of O^r Raigne ordeyned & made the said Gervase Clifton O^r Receaver of all O^r Castles, Mannors & Lordshipps & Fee Farms of Horestone, Bollesover, Chestrefeld, Mansfeld, Lindeby in Shirwood, Edingstow, Clipston in Shirwood, Bulwell, Darlington & Ragenhall, Arnall, Retford, Bayles-wike of ye honour of Peverell, the Milles of Retford & Nottingham, & ye Mannors & Lordshipps of Whatton, Aslokton, Gedling, Shelford & Stoke-bardolfe, with ye appurtenances in ye Countyes of Nottingham & Derby ; And also O^r Styward of O^r Mannors & Lordshipps of Gedling, Shelford & Stoke-Bardolfe, &c. To have, hold, & occupie ye afore-said offices unto ye aforesaid Gervase as long time as it pleased us, & for ye offices to be exercised we graunted unto ye same Gervase x^{li} yearly to be had of ye ishues, profitts &c., of ye said Mannors &c. And whereas also ye said Gervase, att O^r special desire & command-ment to him yeaven by O^r mouth ye said 29 day of August in ye said 16 year of O^r Reigne, hath bin & is surveyor of O^r workes & reparations in O[r] Castle of Nottingham, & upon y[e] new building in ye same O[r] Castle, & of repayring of O[r] Lodge in O[r] Parke of Beskwood & Clipston in O[r] co. of Nottingham, & hath also bought for ye same buildings & reparacions timber, stones &c., & paid also wages of Joyners, Glaysers, &c. Wee of certain knowledge & meere mocion will & charge you & give unto you full authoritie & power to take & heare y[e] yearely accompts of y[e] said Gervase &c. Yeaven y[e] 9 day of March in y[e] 20 yeare of O[r] Raigne. Signat' in fronte per Regem manu sua propria.

Indorsatum sic,—To the Reverend Fadyr in God, O[r] right Trusty & well-beloved y[e] Bpp. of Rochester, Keeper of O[r] Privy Seale.

Gervasius Clifton, Armiger, 6 Edw. IV : Robertus Clifton, Armiger, 6 Edw. IV (1466-7).

Prima parte Patentium de A° 16 Edw. IV, m. 6 (1476).

Rex omnibus ad quos &c.—Salutem. Sciatis quod nos de gratia nostra speciali concessimus et licentiam dedimus, ac per presentes concedimus et licentiam damus pro nobis et heredibus nostris dilectis et fidelibus nostris Roberto Clifton, militi, et Gervasio Clifton, Armigero, filio suo et eorum utrique et heredibus suis quod ipsi vel eorum alter aut heredes sui ad gloriam laudem et honorem Omnipotentis Dei, et gloriossimæ et intemeratæ Virginis Mariæ Matris Jesu Christi, quondam ('quoddam) collegium perpetuum de uno custode et duobus capellanis divina singulis diebus in Ecclesia parochiali Beatæ Mariæ de Clyfton juxta Nottingham [p. 27.] in quadam capella S. Trinitatis infra eandem Ecclesiam pro salubri statu nostro ac predilectissimæ consortis nostræ Elizabethæ Reginæ Angliæ dum vixerimus, et pro animabus nostris cum ab hac luce migraverimus. Necdum pro bono statu predicti Roberti et Gervasii fundatorum collegii predicti dum vixerint, et pro animabus suis cum ab hac luce migraverint : Et pro anima Reverendissimi in Christo Patris Domini Wilelmi Booth, nuper Archiepiscopi Eborum : Necnon pro animabus Dominæ Aliciæ Clifton nuper uxoris Roberti Clifton, et Seth Worsley, Armigeri : Ac etiam pro animabus omnium antecessorum et consanguineorum ipsorum Roberti et Gervasii, et pro animabus omnium fidelium defunctorum : Ac ad quædam et quæcunque alia facienda juxta ordinacionem predict', Roberti et Gervasii seu eorum alteri vel heredum suorum in hac parte faciendam inperpetuum celebraturis, facere, fundare, erigere, et stabilire possint et possit perpetuis futuris temporibus duratur'. Et quod custos et capellani predicti et successores sui, cum collegium sic factum fundatum erectum et stabilitum fuerit, Custos et Capellani Collegii S. Trinitatis in Ecclesia parochiali Beatæ Mariæ de Clifton juxta Nottingham in perpetuum nuncupentur. Et quod custos et capellani collegii illius et successores sui custodes et capellani ejusdem collegii sint unum corpus, habeantque unum sigillum commune, et successionem perpetuam, ac sint personæ abiles et capaces in lege. Et quod iidem custos et capellani ejusdem collegii et successores sui custodes et capellani predicti per nomen et sub nomine Custodis et Capellanorum Collegii S. Trinitatis in Eccl : parochiali Beatæ Mariæ de Clifton juxta Nottingham, terras, tenementa, redditus, annuitates, et alias possessiones quoscunque cum pertinenciis de quibuscunque personis perquirere possint, obtinere et recipere.—Habenda et tenenda sibi et successoribus suis inperpetuum &c. In cujus rei &c. Et hæ literæ nostræ vobis erunt sufficiens warrantum. Dat' sub signeto nostro apud Castellum nostrum de Nottingham, 22 die Julii, A° regni nostri 16°.

Scribitur sincere dilecto Clerico ac Consiliario Regis Magistro Johanni Russell, Custodi privati sigilli, quod faceret literas Cancellario Angliæ dirigendas, mandantes eidem quod sub magno sigillo fieri faciat literas Regis patentes in forma predicta.

(A sketch of a shield : Two bendlets and a crescent in dexter chief, with title, S. Nicholai de Clifton.)

Precepta de termino Michaelis A° 8 Edw. IV, rot. 6 (1468).

Robertus Clyfton, Miles, nuper Vice-comes com : Nott. et Derb., a festo S. Michaelis, A° 7 Regis nunc usque ad idem festum proxime sequent'.

Precepta de termino Michaelis, A° 12 Edw. IV, rot. 10 (1472).

Gervasius Clyfton, Vice-comes com : Nott. et Derb., a festo Michaelis A° 11° usque ad idem festum proxime sequent'.

Precepta de termino S. Hillarii (1477).

Gervasius Clifton, Arm., nuper Vice-comes com : Nott. et Derb. a festo S. Michaelis, A° 17 Regis nunc usque ad idem festum tunc proxime sequent'.

[p. 28].

Inter Warranta de A° 22 Edw. IV (1482).

By the Kinge. Endorsed thus.—To Oᵣ Rt. Reverend Father in God, Oᵣ right trusty & welbeloved yᵉ Bpp. of Lincolne, Keeper of Oᵣ privy seale.

Right Reverend Fader in God, &c. We greet you well, & woll & charge you that under Oᵣ Privy Seale in yoᵣ ward you make Oᵣ lettres in forme following : Edward, &c.—To yᵉ Treasurer & Chamberlains of Oᵣ Exchequer—Greeting. Forasmuch as wee by the advice of yᵉ Lords of Oᵣ Councill have named & ordeyned Oᵣ well beloved Squyer Gervase Clifton to be Sheriff of the counties of Nottingham & Derbie for this yeare now ensuinge, In yᵉ which occupation we understand well that he shall sustaine & beare great costs & charges to his hinderance & great hurt without O^r grace be shewed unto him in this behalfe, Wee in consideracion of ye premises for ye indemnity of ye said Gervase Clifton herein woll & charge you that you make an assignment unto ye said Gervase of C^{li} by Taille at ye receipt of O^r said Exchequer in due forme to be leavyed upon ye said Gervase Clifton as Sheriffe of O^r countyes for ye said Gervase of reward to be had of him of ye issues & profitts of his Baliewicke of ye Counties of Nottingham & Derby; & that Taille soe leavyed to deliver unto the s^d Gervase so leavyed without prest or any other charge upon him to be sett or leavyed in any wise. And we woll that theis O^r lettres be to you sufficient warrant against us at all time hereafter in this behalfe. Yeoven under O^r signet att O^r Palais att Westminster, ye 8th day of November in ye 22nd yeare of O^r Raigne.

Subscribed—Herbert.

Inter Fines de temp. Edw. IV.

Finalis Concordia apud Westmon: A° 17 Edw. IV (1477-8), coram Thoma Bryan, Ricardo Chikke, Thoma Littleton et Ricardo Neele, Justiciariis: Inter Thomam Poutrell, Radulphum Fitzherbert, et Wilelmum Poutrell, querentes, et Matill,' que fuit uxor Gervasii Clifton, Militis, consanguineam et unam heredum Radulphi Cromwell, nuper de Cromwell, Militis, et Robertum Ratcliffe et Johannam uxorem ejus, consanguineam et alteram heredum predicti Radulphi deforcientes, de manerio de West Halum cum pert., ac de uno messuagio, duabus bovatis terræ, quatuor acris prati, et quinquaginta acris pasturæ cum pert. in West Halom et Mapurley, ac de advocacione Ecclesiæ de West Halom; Unde &c. Scilicet, quod predicti Matill', et Robertus et Johanna recognoverunt predictum Manerium et tenementa cum pert: et advocacionem predictam esse jus ipsius Thomæ &c. Et pro hac recognicione, quieta clamacione, warrantia, fine et concordia iidem Thomas, Radulphus, et Wilelmus dederunt predictis Matill' et Roberto et Johannæ quadraginta marcas argenti.

Ex Warrantis signatis per manum Regis Edw. IV (1477).

By the Kinge. Reverend Fader in God, right trusty & welbeloved, wee greete you well & charge you that under O^r privy seale, being in yor warde, yee doe make O^r letters of warrant to be directed to O^r trusty & wel-beloved Squyer, Gervais Clifton, receyver of O^r counties of Nottingham & Derbie charging him by ye same that of such money as is or shall come to his hands by [p. 29] reason of his said office hee doe employ C markes upon O^r workes within O^r Castle of Nottingham: And O^r other letters to ye Executors of ye Testament of Thomas

Bingham, late receyvor of O.^r said Countyes, chardgeing them to pay & deliver to ye said Gervais all such summes of O.^r money as remayned in his handes for ye xvi yeare of O.^r reigne ; & these O.^r letters shall be y.^or warrant. Yeoven under O.^r signet att O.^r Castle of Wyndsore ye 18th day of Juyn, the xvij yeare of O.^r Raigne.

Indorsatur :—To the Reverend Fader in God, O.^r right trustie & well beloved, ye Bpp. of Rochester, Keeper of O.^r Privy Seale.

Quarta pars Patentium de A° 1° Regis Ricardi III, m. 11ª (1483-4). Rex omnibus ad quos &c.—Salutem. Cum non solum generis nobilitas sed et justitiæ equitas omnes provocent, & maxime Reges et Principes, homines de se bene meritos premiis condignis afficere, Sciatis igitur quod ob singulare et fidele servitium quod dilectus ligeus et serviens noster Gervasius Clifton, Miles, nobis pre-antea impendit, non solum favendo Juri et Titulo, pro cujus juris et tituli vigore jam nuper ad coronam hujus regni nostri Angliæ (Deo adjuvante) pervenimus, verum etiam reprimendo prodiciones et malitias rebellium et proditorum nostrorum, qui infra idem regnum nostrum perfidam jamdudum commotionem suscitaverunt, ac pro bono et fideli servitio nobis et heredibus nostris Regibus Angliæ per eundem Gervasium et heredes suos pro defensione nostra et regni nostri predicti contra quoscunque proditores, inimicos, et rebelles, quoties futuris temporibus opus erit, impendendo, de gratia nostra speciali dedimus et concessimus, ac per presentes damus et concedimus, prefato Gervasio Clifton Manerium sive dominium de Radcliffe super Sore cum pert : in com : Nott. ac omnia alia, terras, tenementa, redditus, possessiones et hereditamenta quæcunque, quæ fuerunt Henrici nuper Ducis Buckingham, seu aliquorum aliorum aut alicujus alterius, ad ejus usum in Radcliffe super Sore predicto :—Et Kinston in eodem com : Nott., et Kegworth in com : Leic., quæ nuper ad manus nostras devenerunt racione forisfacturæ ejusdem nuper Ducis —Habenda et tenenda eidem Gervasio et heredibus masculinis de corpore suo exeuntibus de nobis et heredibus nostris per servitium militare, et redditus XL sol. per ann. ad festa Paschæ et S. Michaelis Archangeli æquis porcionibus solvend'. Dedimus etiam et concessimus, et per presentes damus et concedimus eidem Gervasio Manerium sive dominium de Overton Longvile cum suis pert : in com : Hunt. una cum advocacione Ecclesiæ parochialis ejusdem. Necnon omnia alia, terras, tenementa, redditus, possessiones et hereditamenta quæcunque in Overton Longvile predicta, quæ nuper fuerunt Rogeri Tocotes, nuper de Bromham, Militis, seu aliquorum aliorum aut alicujus alterius, ad ejus usum, et quæ ad manus nostras devenerunt racione forisfacturæ [p. 30] ejusdem Rogeri—Habenda et tenenda eidem Gervasio et heredibus masculinis de corpore suo exeuntibus de nobis et heredibus nostris per servitium militare et redditum . . per ann. ad festa Paschæ et S. Michaelis Archangeli æquis porcionibus solvend'. Ac insuper dedimus et concessimus, ac per presentes damus et concedimus eidem Gervasio Manerium sive dominium de Dalbury et Dalbury Lees cum suis pert: in com: Derbie, una cum advocacione Ecclesiæ parochialis ejusdem, ac omnia alia, terras, tenementa, redditus, possess-iones, et hereditamenta quæcunque cum suis pert: in Dalbury et Dalbury Lees predictis, ac in Etwall et Wirkesworth, alias dicto Was-worth in eodem com: Derbie, quæ nuper fuerunt Henrici nuper Ducis Exon:—Habenda et tenenda eidem Gervasio et heredibus masculis de corpore suo exeuntibus de nobis et heredibus nostris per servitium militare et redditum xx^a per ann. ad festa Paschæ et S. Michaelis Archangeli æquis porcionibus solvend'. Ac insuper de uberiori gratia nostra concessimus eidem Gervasio omnia exitus et proficua de omnibus predictis Maneriis sive dominiis ac terris tenementis redditibus, poss-essionibus, et hereditamentis supradictis cum suis pert: a decimo octavo die Octobris ultimo preterito hucusque provenientia, percipienda eidem Gervasio per manus occupatorum predictorum Maneriorum et aliorum premissorum qui pro tempore fuerint, absque aliquo computo seu aliquo alio nobis inde reddendo seu faciendo : Et quod expressa mentio de vero valore Maneriorum seu dominiorum ac ceterorum pre-missorum, seu de aliis donis sive concessionibus eidem Gervasio per nos ante hæc tempora factis in presentibus minine facta existit, aut aliquo statuto actu ordinacione seu restriccione in contrarium factis non obstantibus. In cujus rei &c. Teste Rege apud Nottingham, 24° die Aprilis. Per Breve de Privato Sigillo, et de data &c.

Sir Gervase Clifton made Knight of the Bath at ye coronation of Richard III. *Holinshed*, p. 1387.

Communia de A° 3 Hen. VII, termino Pasche (1488).

Gervasius Clifton, Miles, Vice-comes com: Nott. et Derbie.

Originale de A° 3 Hen. VII, rot. 9, Nott. (1488).

Rex 12° die Julii commisit Gervasio Clifton, Militi, custodiam Maner. de Carleton in Linderike et Kingeston in Carleton cum omni-bus pert. in manibus Regis existentibus per mortem Henrici nuper Domini Fitz-hugh, ac racione minoris ætatis Georgii filii et heredis predicti Henrici &c.

[p. 31.]

Clausi de A° 10 Hen. VII (1494).

Rex predilecto et fideli suo Thomæ filio et heredi charissimi consan-guinei nostri Thomæ Marchionis Dorsett—Salutem. Cum nos de advisamento et assensu concilii nostri charissimum filium Henricum secundo-genitum nostrum ordinem Militiæ de Balneo suscipere ac in Ducem Ebor. in festo Omnium Sanctorum proxime futuro creare decrevimus, necnon vos et alios nonnullos hujus regni nostri proceres juxta antiquam consuetudinem in hujusmodi creacione usitatam ad ordinem Militiæ predictam una cum prefato secundo-genito suscipiendum nominaverimus et elexerimus—Vobis igitur precipimus et mandamus quatenus in propria persona vestra ad presentiam nostram in festo predicto accedatis, et vosmet ad ordinem predictum suscipiendum sine dilacione ordinetis et preparetis ; et hoc sub pena quingentarum librarum nullatenus omittatis. Teste Rege apud Westmon : 20° die Septembris.

Consimilia Brevia diriguntur personis subscriptis sub eadem data— Dilectis et fidelibus suis &c. et inter alios Gervasio Clifton.

Originale de A° 17 Hen. VII, rot. 1 (1502).

Gervasius Clifton, Miles, constitutus Vice-comes com : Nott. et Derbie, 30° die Januarii, A° 17 Hen. VII.

Robertus Wield dedit Gervasio Clifton, militi, et Johanni de S. Andrea, arm. omnes terras suas in Bovington juxta Sutton, quæ quondam fuerunt Johannis Mody. Testibus—Hugone Annesley, arm. Hugone Bary, arm. Thomas Armestronge, arm. Penultimo die Julii A° 14 Hen. VII.

Ex ipsa Charta originali de A° 28 Hen. VIII, rot. 53 (1537)

Nott. Derb. De speciali liberacione Gervasii Clifton filii et heredis Roberti, 6° die Martii.

Sexta parte Patentium de A° 33 Hen. VIII, m. 41 (1542).

King Henrie yᵉ Eight graunts to his servaunt Sʳ Gervas Clifton, Kt. his Mannor of Armyn in yᵉ County of Yorke, late belonging to yᵉ dissolved Monasterie of yᵉ Virgin Marie in Yorke, with yᵉ appurtenances, to him his heyres & assignes for ever. Teste Rege apud Westmon. 16° die Martii. Per breve de Privato Sigillo et de data &c. Pro summa DCLI libr. et V sol.

[p. 32.]

Secunda parte Patentium de A° 34 Hen. VIII (1543).

Rex 29° die Januarii concessit Gervasio Clifton, Militi, custodiam corporis et maritagium Gervasii Boswell.

Patentes de A° 38 Hen. VIII, p. 4° (1546).

Rex 23° die Octobris concessit Gervasio Clifton, Militi, custodiam corporis et maritagium Thomæ Fairfax.

Ex Monumentis,—In Ecclesia de Clifton juxta Nottingham, ex parte ejusdem Ecclesiæ Boreali.

Hic jacet Isabella filia Roberti Franceys de Formarke, Militis, uxor Gervasii Clifton, militis, filii Dñi Johannis Clifton, Militis, quæ obiit 18° Junii, 1457. In pale, *Clifton*, & a chevron between 3 Eagletts displayed, which is *Franceys* of Formarke in Derbyshire.

Hic jacet Dña Alicia Clifton filia Johannis Bothe, Arm. soror bonæ memoriæ Dñi Willī Bothe quondam Eborum Archiepiscopi, et uxor Dñi Roberti Clifton, Militis, quæ obiit 9° die Septembris, Anno Dñi 1470. Cujus &c.

Orate pro anima Roberti Clifton, Militis, fundatoris trium Capellanorum Collegii in hac Ecclesia, qui obiit 9° die Aprilis, Anno Dñi 1478

On a flatt marble : Orate pro anima Gervasii Clifton, Militis, filii et heredis Roberti Clifton, Militis, fundatoris Collegii de Clifton, finiti et stabiliti per Dñum Gervasium, qui obiit in domo Fratrum Predicatorum apud London : 12ᵘ die Maii, Anno Dñi 1491. Cujus corpus abinde per Agnetem filiam Roberti Constable de Flamburgh, Militis, secundam uxorem ejusdem Gervasii, et alios ejus Executores juxta voluntatem suam istuc honorifice et decenter conductum fuit, et sub hoc lapide marmoreo hic humatum, cujus animæ propitietur Deus. Pro cujus quidem Agnetis prosperitate dum vixerit, & pro cujus anima, cum ab hac luce migraverit, speciales ordinantur memoriæ, et orationes per Gardianum et Capellanos Collegii predicti juxta compositionem et Statuta inde ordinata perpetuis futuris temporibus devote fiendæ.

Here lyeth George Clifton, Esqʳᵉ, who was Sonne & heyre apparant of Sʳ Gervas Clifton, of Clifton, Knt. & Dame Winifride his wife, who marryed Winifride yᵉ daughter of Sʳ Anthonie Thorold & Dame Anne his wife, one of yᵉ daughters & heyres of Sʳ John Constable, of Kynalton, Knt. which George had issue by his said wife, Gervas Clifton, & dyed att Clifton the first day of August, Anno Dñi 1587, & was of yᵉ age of 20 yeares & 7 moneths.

[p. 33]

Neare lyes a faire & auncient Monument of Free-stone, raysed about a yearde from yᵉ ground, on yᵉ top of which lyes one armed cap-a-pee, & his wife by his side. Noe inscription, only two or three fayre Eschocheons on yᵉ side of yᵉ Monument, wherein are impaled *Clifton* with a Fretty coate in which a Canton per pale & a ship in it, quarterly with a Saltier, Erm. which is *Nevile* (of Rolleston).

Ex Australi parte ejusdem Ecclesiæ, A brave & stately Monument :
Here lye yᵉ Bodies of Gervas Clifton of Clifton in yᵉ County of Nottingham, Knt. & of Dame Marie his first wife, daughter of Sʳ John
Nevile, of Cheete in ye County of Yorke, Knt. & of Dame Winifride
his second wife, yᵉ daughter & heire of William Thwaytes of Owlton in
yᵉ County of Suffolke, Esqʳᵉ, which Dame Marie deceased yᵉ 10ᵗʰ day
of Aprill, Anno Dñi 1564, & yᵉ said Gervas deceased yᵉ 20ᵗʰ day of
Januarie, Anno Dñi 1587. And yᵉ said Dame Winifride deceased—.

This Inscription is about yᵉ verge of yᵉ Monument, on yᵉ top of it
lyes himself in compleate Armour between his two wives, all in perfect
features & full proportion. On yᵉ right side by their Mother are yᵉ
portraytures, armes & names of five children, viz., Elizabeth, Frances,
Robert, Gervas & Anthony. Under Elizabeth empaled, B. a Bende
betweene 6 Escallops, Arg. with S. semy of Cinquefoiles, a Lyon
rampant, Arg. She was yᵉ first wife of Peter Freschevile of Staveley,
Esqʳᵉ ; yᵉ other foure dyed unmarried. These were yᵉ children he had
by Nevile. On yᵉ left side by his Mother, George Clifton ; under him
empaled *Clifton & Thorold.* At yᵉ end of yᵉ Monument, 1. Empaled,
Clifton with Arg. on a Saltier G. a Crescent, Gold, *Nevile.* 2. *Clifton*,
impaled with Quarterlie, Arg. a Crosse, Sa. Frettie of yᵉ first, *Thwaites*,
& Sa. a Lyon ramp. crowned, Or.

In the Windowes South :

B. a Bend between 6 Escallops, Arg. . . .	*Freschevile*
Arg. a Chevron betw. 3 Eagletts displayed G. . .	*Franceys*
S. Semy of Cinquefoiles, a Lyon ramp. Arg. . . .	*Clifton*
B. a Lyon rampant, Or.	[*Braytoft*]
Arg. a Lyon ramp. double queue, S. . . .	*Cressy*
Arg. a Fesse between 3 Escallops, G.	*Dorthorp*
G. 6 mascles voided, 3, 2, 1, d' Or. . . .	*St. Andrew*

The Crest :—In a Coronett G. a Peacockes bodie, Paly of 4, Arg. &
Sa. winges displayed —in divers places.

In Ecclesia de Wilne juxta Sawley in com. Derbie.

Hic jacent Hugo Willughbie de Risley, Armig. et Isabella uxor ejus
filia Gervasii Clyfton, Militis, qui Hugo obiit 12⁰ die Septembris, Anno
Dñi 1491 ; Et predicta Isabella obiit 3⁰ die Maii, Anno Dñi 1462.
There for *Willughby* is Erm. 3 Barres, which impales with *Clifton* of
Clifton in Notts.

Here under this Tombe lyeth Hen. Willoughbee, Esq , the which
hath nr̃allie his life departed yᵉ 3ᵈ day of September, Anno Dñi 1514.
There Willughbie beares yᵉ right Arms of *Willughby*, & quarterlie with
Clifton. The Crest—a Peacockes head.

[p. 34].

Record' de Termino Trin : A° 30 Hen. VI, rot. 26. 18 Julii (1452).

Rex &c. Cum nos 18 die Julii A° Regni nostri 29° (1451) com-
miserimus Gervasio Clifton, Armig., et Johanni Scot, Armig., custodiam
duarum partium Manerii de Skirbecke, Wikes, et Frampton cum suis
pert. in com. Lincoln—Habendam a festo Paschæ tunc ultime preteritæ
ad finem 12 annorum &c. Reddendo cxxij^l per ann.

Carta penes Comitem de Clare.

Sachent toutes gents que sont en present et que sont avenir que jeo
Gervays de Clifton, Chr. ay donee, grantee, et par ceste ma presente
chartre confermee a mon bien ame amy Richard de Bevercotes un
Heaume, cest-a-savoir, un Tufte de Plume, la moite, cest-a-dire
paramont de plume noir, et lautre moite, cest-a-dire, par aval de plume
blaunc—A avoir et tenir le dite heaume oue toutes ses apurtenaunts a
l' avant dit Richard, et a ses heires franchement, bien, et in pees a
touts jours. Et jeo l' avant dit Gervays et mes heires l' avant dit heaume
oue ses apurtenaunts a l' avant dit Richard et a ses heires countre
touts gents garantirons a touts jours. En temoigniance de quele chose
a cest ma presente Chartre ay mys mon seal. Cestes gents temoignes,
Monsr. Johan Seigneur de Gray de Codenore, Monsr. Johan de
Loudham, Monsr. Johan Dannesley, Hugh Dannesley, Richard de
Biron, et altres. Doñ a Clifton, Lundy proscheyn apres la Feste
Seint Ambrose l' an du regne nostre Seigneur le Roi Richard secund
apres le Conquest Dengleterre tierce (1380).

Clausi de A° 5 Edw. IV, m. 6 (1465-6).

Gervasius Clifton, Miles, et Matilda uxor ejus, nuper uxor Roberti
de Willughby, concessimus Antonio Wydevile, dño de Scales et de
Newcelles, Maneria de Candelesby, Halem, Lamley, Saawdon, Boston,
Plesley, Gippesmere, Goureton, Drainfeld, Baseford, Quinton, Rasin,
Lacton, Belcheford ac Tuxford, cum redditu de Deincourt ibidem in
com. Linc. Nott. Derb. et Warw. Necnon in Tumby, excepto magno
bosco vocato Tumby Woods, alias Tumby Chase in dicto com. Linc.
quæ nuper fuerunt Radulphi Dñi Crumwell, una cum advocacione
Ecclesiarum, Capellarum, et Cantariarum eisdem pertinentium.

Escaetria de A° 17 Edw. II, No. 36 (1323).

Inquisicio capta apud Clifton in com. Nott. coram Escaetore Dñi
Regis, 11° die Augusti A° regni R. Edwardi filii R. Edwardi 17°, post
mortem Gervasii de Clifton. Juratores dicunt quod predictus Gervasius

nulla tenuit terras &c., die quo obiit de Dño [p. 35] Rege in capite ut de Corona &c. Sed dicunt quod tenuit maneria de Clifton et Willeford cum pert; in predicto com. Nott. de Thoma de Ver et Agnete uxore ejus per servitium militare &c. Item Juratores dicunt, quod predictus Gervasius de Clifton tenuit apud Brouton quoddam Manerium de Dño Rege in capite, ut de honore de Tutburie, racione forisfacturæ Thomæ nuper Comitis Lancastriæ per servitium feodi Militis unius &c. Dicunt etiam quod Robertus de Clifton filius Gervasii filii et heredis predicti Gervasii est ejus heres propinquior, et est ætatis viginti et quinque annorum et amplius.

Escaetria de Aº 1 Edw. III, No. 33 (1327).

Inquisicio capta coram Gulielmo Truswell, Escaetore Dñi Regis citra Trentam, virtute Brevis &c., apud Clifton in com. Nott. die Lunæ proximo post festum S. Nicholai, Aº regni R. Edwardi III, post conquestum 1º &c., post mortem Roberti de Clifton. Juratores dicunt quod predictus Robertus non tenuit &c. Et quod Gervasius filius predicti Roberti de Clifton est ætatis xiv annorum, et maritatus fuit per predictum Robertum patrem suum Margaretæ filiæ Roberti de Pirpount.

This Gervas marryed afterwards Isabell Harbard, als. Finch, yᵉ widdow of William Scott of Scotts-Hall in Kent, of whom this Epitaph in yᵉ Chancell of Braborne Church in Kent. On yᵉ Monument yᵉ Coate of *Finch*, first joyned with *Scotts*, & after in another Scutcheon with *Clifton*.

Hac necis in cella prudens jacet hic Isabella*
  Quæ nulli nocuit sed Domino placuit.
Sponsa fuit fata venerabilis et peramata
  Clifton Gervasii Militis egregii,
Ante fuit dicta Wilhelmi Scotti relicta
  Harbard vocata, vel Finche certe scies
Dicitur hic alias . . . mille quater centum
  Petit L cum septem . . . Monumentum.
Novembris Daca bis hiis numerando dabis.

Another.

Gervasium Clifton istam genuisse Johannam
  Stã lege cui John Digge sociatus erat.

* By this woman he had two daughters, Joane marryed to John Diggs, & Isabell marryed to John Germingham. Hee was one of yᵉ first Mayors of Canterbury, none but persons of a good quality for a long tyme used to be chosen Mayors thereof, but yᵉ best of Kent.

Escaetria de A° 22 Edw. III, p. 2, No. 59 (1348).

Inquisitio capta &c., coram Johanne de Vaus, Escaetore &c., A° 22° Edw. III. Juratores dicunt quod non est ad dampnum nec prejudicium Dñi Regis aut aliorum si Dñus Rex concedat Gervasio [p. 36] Clifton, Chr. quod ipse Gervasius undecim messuagia, quinque virgatas et unam bovatam terræ et tres solidatas redditus cum pert. in Staunton in yᵉ Wold et Clifton juxta Nottingh. et advocacionem Ecclesiæ ejusdem villæ de Staunton dare possit et assignare tribus Capellanis Divina pro salubri statu ipsius Gervasii et Isabellæ uxoris ejus in Ecclesia S. Mariæ de Clifton juxta Nottingham singulis diebus celebraturis. In cujus rei testimonium &c.

Escaetria de A° 32° Hen. VI (1452).

Inquisitio capta apud Nott. die Jovis proximo post festum S. Michaelis Archangeli A° regni Henrici VI, post conquestum 32°, coram Johanne Saynton, Escaetore &c., post mortem Gervasii Clifton, Militis. Juratores dicunt quod predictus Gervasius &c., et quod predictus Gervasius obiit 8° die Decembris, A° 32 Hen. VI. Robertus Clifton, Armig., est filius et heres ejusdem Gervasii propinquior, et ætatis triginta annorum et amplius.

Escaetria de A° 18 Edw. IV, No. 25 (1478).

Inquisitio capta in com. Nott. 7° die Junii, A° 18° regni Edw. IV, post mortem Roberti de Clifton, Militis. Juratores dicunt quod predictus Robertus tenuit Maneria de Clifton juxta Nottingham et Willeford una cum advocacionibus Eccles. eorundem Maneriorum, quæ tenentur de Johanne le Scrope, Milite, ut de Manerio suo de Langer in predicto com. Nott. per servitium unius denarii per ann. pro omnibus servitiis. Et quod predictus Robertus seisitus de Manerio de Hoddesake cum soca ejusdem manerii, vizᵗ., Hoddesake-holme, Wodehous, Oule-cotes, Harmeston, Flixthorpe, Stirop, Letwell, et Gildingwells, cum suis pert. per quoddam scriptum suum sigillo ipsius Roberti Clifton ad arma signatum, dedit et concessit cuidam Magistro Roberto Clifton, Archidiacono de Est-riding in com. Ebor., Clerico, filio suo et aliis, Habendum et tenendum dictum Manerium cum pert. suis eisdem Magistro Roberto &c. Quorum unus superstes est adhuc, et se tenet intus in Manerio predicto cum pert. per jus accrescendi. Predictum Manerium de Hoddesake cum soca ejusdem tenetur de Rege ut de honore de Tykhull, parcella Ducatus Lancastriæ per servitium trium feodorum Militum. Et quod predictus Robertus Clifton, Miles, obiit 9° die Aprilis ultimo preterito. Et quod Gervasius Clifton, Armig., est filius et heres ejusdem Roberti propinquior, et est ætatis XL annorum et amplius.

Escaetria de A° 7 Hen. VII (1491).

Inquisitio capta apud Blythe in com. Nott. 30º die Octobris, A° 7º Hen. VII, coram Thoma Hunt, Escaetore Regis in com. predictis, virtute Brevis Dñi Regis, post mortem Gervasii Clifton, Militis. Juratores dicunt quod Gervasius Clifton, Miles, in dicto Brevi nomi- [p. 37] natus, nulla tenuit &c. Sed dicunt quod dictus Gervasius diu ante obitum suum fuit seisitus in dominico suo, ut de feodo, de Maneriis de Clifton juxta Nottingham, Willeford, Broughton Sulney, una cum advocacionibus Eccles. de Wilford. Clifton et Broughton in com. predicto cum pert. Ac de Manerio de Hoddesake cum soca ejus dem manerii, Viz^t., Hoddesake-holme, Oulecotes, Harmeston, Flix- thorp, Sterup, Letwell et Gilden Wells cum pert. in com. predicto. Et sic inde seisitus &c. Virtute quorum doni et concessionis iidem Gervasius et Agnes uxor ejus fuerunt seisiti in predicto Manerio &c. Et quod predictum Manerium de Hoddesake cum soca ejusdem manerii, cum pert. valet per annum in omnibus exitibus ultra reprisas XL libras. Et quod predictus Gervasius Clifton obiit 12º die Maii ultimo preterito. Et quod Robertus Clifton, Clericus, est filius et heres propinquior dicti Gervasii Clifton in dicto Brevi nominati, et est ætatis triginta annorum et amplius.

Note.—That Agnes was his second wife & not ye mother of this Robert. Shee overlyved her husband. Robert Clifton, Clerke, pre- sented himselfe to his spiritual livings, & gave his temporall estate to his brother Gervas, after knighted. Robert dyed unmaried.

Escaetria de A° 9 Hen. VIII (1517).

Inquisitio capta apud Notingham in com : Nott. ultimo die Novem- bris A° 9º regni R. Henrici VIII, coram Escaetore dicti comitatus virtute Brevis, post mortem Roberti Clifton, Armig. per sacramentum &c. Qui dicunt quod dictus Robertus Clifton die quo obiit fuit seisitus in dominico suo, ut de feodo, de Maneriis de Clifton juxta Nott. et Wilford cum advocacionibus Eccles. de Clifton et Wilford, et patronatu advocacionis Collegii et Cantariæ de Clifton predicto, ac mille acris terræ, quinquaginta acris prati, quadraginta acris pasturæ, viginti libratis redditibus cum pert : in Clifton et Wilford in com : predicto. Et sic inde seisitus per literas suas patentes juratoribus in evidenciis extensas sub sigillo dicti Roberti concessit Hugoni Clifton fratri predicti Roberti unam annuitatem sive annualem redditum v^l per ann. exeuntem de dicto Manerio de Wilford ad terminum vitæ dicti Hugonis, qui quidem Hugo Clifton adhuc superstes est, et in plena vita existit &c. Insuper Juratores dicunt quod dictus Robertus fuit seisitus de Manerio de Hoddesake cum soca &c. Et Gervasius Clifton, Miles, pater Gervasii Clifton, Militis, et avus predicti Roberti, concessit annuitatem &c. In- super Juratores dicunt quod dictus Robertus Clifton seisitus fuit de

Manerio de Stanton super le Wolde &c. et de centum acris terræ, quadraginta acris pasturæ, viginti acris bosci cum pert. in Kings Carleton in
Lynricke in com : pred : et de [**p. 38.**] messuagiis et terris in Misterton,
Bonney, et Willughby super le Wolde in com : pred : Lound, Shafles-
worth, Bawtry, Blyth, Newthorp, et de Manerio de Broughton in com :
pred.   Et quod dictus Robertus Clifton obiit 3° die Septembris ultimo
preterito ; Et dicunt quod Gervasius Clifton . . . est filius et heres
dicti Roberti propinquior, et est ætatis unius anni 26° die Martii ultimo
preterito.

Escaetria de A° 30 R. Elizabethe, p. 1, N°. 22 (1588).

Inquisitio capta apud Nottingham in com : Nott. 16° die Aprilis A°
regni Reginæ Elizabethæ 30°, virtute commissionis, post mortem
Gervasii Clifton, Militis, nuper de Clifton in com : pred : defuncti, per
sacramentum &c.   Qui dicunt quod predictus Gervasius in vita sua
fuit seisitus in dominico suo, ut de feodo talliato sibi et heredibus de
corpore suo legitime procreatis, de et in Manerio de Clifton cum pert :
ac de viginti messuagiis, decem cottagiis, sex toftis, triginta gardinis,
viginti pomariis, uno molendino ventritico, nonagentis acris terræ, et
triginta acris prati, quingentis acris pasturæ, viginti acris bosci, quad-
ringentis acris jampnorum* et brueræ,† libera piscaria in aqua de
Trent, et decem libratis redditibus cum pert : in Clifton pred : in
Glatton et Gedling in com : pred : et de advoc : Ecclesiæ de Clifton
predictæ.   Idemque Gervasius sic inde seisitus existens quendam
Finem levavit in curia nuper Regis Philippi et Mariæ apud Westmon.
in Octabis Purificacionis Beatæ Mariæ Annis regnorum dicti nuper
Regis et Reginæ 3° et 4°, coram &c.—Justiciariis.   Et postea a die
Paschæ in quindecim dies Annis eorumdem nuper Regis et Reginæ
ibidem, inter Galfridum Taylard. Armig. et Franciscum Nevill, gen.
querentes, et predictum Gervasium Clifton, Mil. deforcientem, de
Manerio, tenementis et advocacione pred : cum pert : (inter alia)
Ibidem recitatur Finis predictus verbatim de terris predictis et de
duobus messuagiis, duobus toftis, viginti acris terræ, quindecim acris
prati, viginti acris pasturæ cum pert : in Eastwayte et Newthorpe in
com : Derbie, Ad usum predicti Gervasii et heredum masculorum de
corpore ipsius Gervasii.   Et si contingat quod idem Gervasius obierit
sine herede masculo de corpore suo legitime procreato, tunc post
decessum ipsius Gervasii predicta &c. remanerent [**p. 38.**] Richardo
Clifton et Janæ uxori ejus, et heredibus masculis de corporibus suis
inter eos legitime procreatis, Et si contingat quod iidem Ricardus et
Jana obierint sine herede masculo &c. tunc post decessum ipsorum
Ricardi et Janæ predicta integre remanerent heredibus masculis de
corpore ipsius Richardi legitime procreatis.   Et si nullus heres

---

* *Jampnum*, Furze, gorse.   † *Bruera*, Heath, heather.

masculus de corpore ipsius Richardi fuerit legitime procreatus, tunc predicta &c. remanerent integre Johanni Clifton generoso, filio et heredi apparenti Gulielmi Clifton, de London, armigeri, et heredibus masculis de corpore ipsius Johannis legitime procreatis. Et si contingat quod idem Johannes obierit sine herede masculo de corpore suo legitime procreato, tunc post decessum ipsius Johannis, predicta &c. integre remanerent Gulielmo Clifton, generoso, fratri predicti Johannis et heredibus masculis de corpore ipsius Gulielmi legitime procreatis. Et si contingat quod idem Gulielmus obierit sine herede masculo de corpore suo legitime procreato, predicta &c. integre remanerent rectis heredibus predicti Gervasii, prout per unam copiam ejusdem Finis juratoribus predictis super captionem hujus Inquisicionis in evidenciis ostensam plene liquet. Virtute cujusquidem Finis idem Gervasius fuit de predictis &c. seisitus in dominico suo, ut de feodo talliato, Vizt. sibi et heredibus masculis de corpore suo legitime procreatis, remanere inde, ut profertur, existente. Et ulterius dicunt quod predictus Gervasius Clifton in vita sua fuit seisitus in dominico suo, ut de feodo, de et in Maneriis de Hodsake et Carleton in Lyndricke cum pert : in com : predicto, ac de et in XL messuagiis, X cottagiis, XXX toftis, III molendinis aquaticis, uno molendino Fullonico, X columbariis, XL gardinis, XL pomariis, MCC acris terræ, CCC acris prati, MD acris pasturæ, CCC acris bosci, MM acris jampnorum et brueræ, ac XL solidatis redditibus cum pert : in Hodsake predicta, Hodsake-holme, Flixthorp, Wodehouse, Oldcotes, Carleton in Lyndricke, Wodehouse Leyes, Kilset-Holmes & Wigthorp in dicto com : Nott. necnon de advocacione Hospitalis S. Johannis Evangelistæ de Blyth in dicto com : Nott. ; ut de feodo et jure. Et quod Gervasius sic inde de premissis seisitus quendam finem levavit in curia Dñæ Reginæ nunc apud Westmon : in Octabis S. Michaelis, Aº regni dictæ Reginæ nunc 7º, inter Robertum Cressie et Richardum Handley, querentes, et predictum Gervasium et Winifridam tunc uxorem ejus deforcientes ; Cujus Finis tenor sequitur in hac inquisicione ad usum ipsius Gervasii et Winifridæ et heredum ipsius Gervasii. Et ulterius Juratores dicunt quod predictus Gervasius sic inde (ut profertur) seisitus existens, ac etiam in vita [p. 40.] sua seisitus existens in dominico suo, ut de feodo talliato sibi et heredibus suis de corpore suo legitime procreatis, de et in Maneriis de Wilford et Broughton cum pert : in dicto com : Nott., ac de et in diversis terris, tenementis, et hereditamentis in Wilford et Broughton predictis, ac in Willughbie et Bunney in com : predicto, ac etiam seisitus existens in dominico suo, ut de feodo, de et in uno messuagio, uno cottagio, duobus gardinis, duobus pomariis, viginti acris terræ, octo acris prati, et viginti acris pasturæ, cum pert : in Broughton predicto nuper perquisitis per predictum Gervasium de quodam Ricardo Byard quendam Finem levavit apud Westmon : in Octabis S. Hillarii, Aº 24º regni Reginæ nunc, inter Henricum Perpoynt, Armig. Franciscum Beaumont, Armig. Johannem Markham, Armig. et Philippum Thirwhit, Armig. querentes, et Gervasium Clifton, Mil.

deforcientem, de Manerio de Wilford cum pert: ac de XXXVIII
messuagiis, XVII cottagiis, XXXVIII toftis, IV molendinis aquaticis,
uno molendino ventritico, duobus columbariis, XL gardinis, MCC acris
terræ, CCLX acris prati, CCCCXC acris pasturæ, XL acris jampnorum
et brueræ, et septem solidatis redditibus cum pert: in Wilford, Broughton Sulney, alias Over Broughton, Willughbie juxta le Waldam,
Bunney, Hodsake, Woodhouse, Fleetesthorpe et Owcotes, ac de libera
piscaria in aqua de Trent, necnon de advocacionibus Eccliar. de Wilford et Broughton, quæ &c. predictus Gervasius recognovit esse jus
ipsius Henrici &c. Et ulterius predicti Juratores dicunt quod dictus
Finis ultime mentionatus fuit ad opus et usus sequentes, Vizt. de et in
Manerio de Wilford, ac de et in omnibus terris predicti Gervasii in
Wilford, Broughton, Willughbie et Bonney, exceptis omnibus illis
clausuris et pasturis in Broughton predicto, vocatis Willughby Closes,
et omnibus aliis terris dicti Gervasii in Broughton tempore levacionis
Finis predicti in tenura Wilelmi Reyner et Hugonis Bradshawe, Ad
usum Georgii Clifton, Armig. tunc filii et heredis apparentis predicti
Gervasii et Winifredæ uxoris suæ pro termino vitarum suarum, et eorum
diutius viventis, et post eorum decessum ad usum primogeniti filii
predicti Georgii Clifton de corpore predictæ Winifredæ uxoris suæ
legitime procreati, et heredum masculorum de corpore predicti primogeniti filii legitime procreandorum ; Et pro defectu talis exitus ad usum
predicti Gervasii Clifton heredum et assignatorum suorum imperpetuum. Similiter ibidem de aliis [p. 41.] terris in Hodsake, Woodhouse,
Oldcotes, et Flixthorpe, prout per Indenturam tripartitam datam 20°
die Januarii, A° Reginæ nunc 24°, inter pred: Gervasium ex prima
parte, et predictos Henricum Pirpount, Franciscum Beaumont,
Johannem Markham, et Philippum Tirwhit, ex tertia parte, confectam
patet. Constat preterea in hac inquisicione de diversis aliis terris ad
diversos usus particulariter limitatos concessis &c.

Prefatus Georgius Clifton obiit 5° die Augusti ultimo preterito apud
Clifton, et predicta Winifreda uxor ejus eum supervixit, et adhuc
superstes est. Et quod Gervasius Clifton 20° die Januarii ultimo
preterito apud Clifton pred: obiit, et quod Gervasius Clifton est
consanguineus et heres propinquior ipsius Gervasii Clifton defuncti,
Vizt. filius et heres predicti Georgii Clifton defuncti filii et heredis
apparentis, dum vixit, predicti Gervasii defuncti. Et quod predictus
Gervasius Clifton consanguineus fuit ætatis quatuor mensium et
viginti unius dierum.

[p. 42.]
Richard Duke of Yorke & Regent of France, 18 Hen. VI, made
Gervas Clifton Captaine of Ponthoise neare Paris, whom yᵉ French
King beseiged with all his forces hee could make & tooke yᵉ towne by
assault & yᵉ captaine & slew 400. But before he could effect it he
lost 3000 men & more, when as the whole Garrison of yᵉ English there
were but one thousand. *Holinshed*, p. 1265.

The 14th of Edward IV, ye Monday after ye battell of Tewkesburie, Edmund Duke of Somersett, John Lonstrother, Priour of St. Johns, Sr. Gervas Clifton, Sr. Thomas Tresham, & twelve other Knights & Gentlemen were beheaded in ye Markett Place of Tewkesburie. *Holinshed*, p. 1460.

Saturday ye 6^d of June, A° 2 Eliz., 1560, the Lord Grey, Lord Lieutenant in Scotland, Mr. Secretarie Cecill, & Mr. Ralph Sadler, betwixt three & four of the Clocke in ye afternoon, gave order that there should be noe peece shott nor show of hostilitie made till seaven of ye Clocke ye same night, & herewith sent Sr. Gervas Clifton unto all ye Souldiers that warded ye trenches & bulwarkes on ye west side of Leith, to commande them to observe ye like order, & Sir John Nevill was sent with ye like commande to ye souldiers that lay in Somersetts Mount. On ye morrowe, being Sunday ye 7th of June, Sr. Francis Leake & Sr. Gervas Clifton accompanyed with two French gentlemen were sent to ye Toune of Leith to signify to Mons. Doysell, ye Bpp. of Amiens, La Brosse, Martignes & other of ye French Lords & Captains, that they were come thither by commandement from ye commissioners to cause ye peace already concluded to be proclaymed. which accordingly was done. Immediately after proclamation ended Sir Francis Leake & Sir Gervas Clifton were brought to Monsr. Doysell's lodgings, where was prepared for them a banquet of 30 or 40 dishes. *Holinshed*, p. 1813.

Ex Cambden's Huntingdon, p. 369.

Parum hinc Leighton abest ubi splendida ædificia Gervasius Clifton, Eques auratus, inchoavit.

[pp. 43, 44 blank.]

Lincolne.

IN PALATIO EPĪ LINCOLN'.

Over yᵉ doore att yᵉ entrance into yᵉ Hall in yᵉ Stone worke—A Cross sarcely, which as it is painted in many places in yᵉ Hall is Arg. a Cross sarcelé, Sab.

In introitu ad Capellam, in Fenestra :—

Istam, Virgo, novellam do tibi, meque Capellam,
Alnwick, tu pia, natum fac mihi propitiatum.

In yᵉ Chappell in every window memorialls of yᵉ saide Alnewick, as

O Benedicte satis Flos et Rosa Virginitatis
Luminis ad regnum duc Alnwick, Virgo, Wilelmum.

O Pater ! O Proles ! O Consolatio ! Flamen
Quem refovere soles, Alnwick, ostende solamen.

Triplex persona, sed simplex in deitate
Wilelmum dona celis Alnwick, precor a te.

O Lux æterna, qua fulget turma superna,
Post vitæ cursum rapias Alnwick tibi sursum.

Principis almifici Genitrix, O digna patrona,
Alnwick Pontifici, precor, assistas prece prona.

Principis . . . . celi dulcedine plena,
. . . . . . Alnwick succurre Wilelmo.

In a large & high Bow window in the Great Hall—The pictures of many of yᵉ Kinges of England, but much mangled & defaced ; yᵉ Inscriptions for yᵉ most part gone, yet here & there something to be read, Vizᵗ.,

Willm̄us Bastard regnavit annis 21.

And of William Rufus, noe great freinde to yᵉ Clergy, this spitefull Distich :

Grata sagitta fuit Willelmum quæ perimebat,
Dira morte perit, qui dira frequenter agebat.

[p. 46.]

 Henrici Regis discretio summa patrabat
 Neglectæ legis . . . . . dum reparabat.
with other such like fragments.

Insignia in Fenestris.

Or, 3 Lyons passants, gardants, B. . . . . *Denmarke*

These ⎧ A lyon rampant G. . . . . . . ⎫
3 per ⎨ Jerusalem . . . . ⎬ *Ermeny*
pale ⎩ B. 3 Barres Arg. over all a lyon ramp. G. . ⎭

Quarterly ⎰ France semy, a Bend compony Arg. & G. . ⎱ *Naverne*
   ⎱ G. an escarbuncle, nowed & flowered d' Or. . ⎰

Gules, a Lyon rampant, double queue, Arg. . . . . *Boheme*

B. a Crucifix, d' Or . . . . *Prester John*

Arg. 5 Escocheons in crosse B., in each of which as many
  Plates, all in saltoyre . . . . . *Portingall*

Argent, 5 Pallets, G. . . . . *Arragon*

Quarterly ⎧ Jerusalem . . . . ⎫
   ⎨ Argent, 3 barwayes B., over all a Lyon rampant ⎬ *Cyprus*
   ⎩   G. crowned d' Or. ⎭

Quarterly ⎰ Jerusalem . . . . . . ⎱ *Naples*
   ⎱ France semy, a labell of 3 . . . . ⎰

G. a Lyon rampant Or, holding a Battle Ax, Sable . . *Norway*

B. a Cross patonce between 5 Martlets d' Or . . . *St. Edward*

B. 3 Crownes d' Or, 2 & 1 . . . . . . *St. Edmund*

G. a Crosse crossed d' Or

. . a Crosse Argent.

B. 3 Crownes d' Or . . . . *St. Edmund*

Argent, a Lyon rampant G.

G. a Lyon rampant d' Or.

 Depict' super murum—His Maties Atchievements.

 The Armes of Dr. Williams, Bp. of Lincoln, empaled betweene those
of yᵉ Bishopricke & of yᵉ Abbey of Westminster.

[p. 47.]

ECCLESIA SC̃I SWITHINI.

In Fenestra Aquilonari.

Empaled ⎰ Argent, 2 Barres B.
   ⎱ G. a Crescent surmounted of an estoyle d' Or. . [*Touke*]

Quarterly, France and England.

Quarterly ⎰ Sa. a Crosse engrayled d' Or . (*Ufford*) ⎱ [*Willoughby*]
   ⎱ G. a Crosse sarcely, Argent . . (*Beke*) ⎰

Empaled ⎰ G. a Crescent surmounted of an estoyle d'Or. . [*Touke*]
   ⎱ Argent, 2 barres B.

 Under this last is yᵉ picture of a man with this name inscribed—
Ricardus Touke.

54   LINCOLNE.

In Fenestra Australi :—Checky d'Or & B. a Cheife, Erm.

In Fenestra Orientali Cancelli :—

Argent, 3 Pallets between 4 Mulletts in Bend Sa., a mullett difference   .   .   .   .   *Thymelby*

Argent, on a Bend between 2 Dolphins nayant Sa., 3 Eagletts displayed of yᵉ first   .   .   .   .   .   .   *Younger*

Stephanus Thymelby, Recordator | Civitatis Lincolñ'.

In Insula Boreali :—

Hic jacent Martinus Mason | bis Pretor Civitatis Lincolñ, | et Maria uxor eius. Obiit ille | 17° Augusti, illa ult. Julii, 1590.

Willūs Skolfeld, bis Maior, 3° | electus obiit 22 Sept., 1587.

Margeria uxor Hugonis Willugh | by, olim Vice-comitis Lincolñie obiit | 13 Januar' 1518.

Johes Middlebroke, servus St. | Thymelby, Arm. Recordatoris | Civitatis, obiit 23° Decembris | A° 1587.

[p. 48.]

ECCLESIA SC̃I BOTOLPHI.

This Church is of very auncient building, being framed in yᵉ fashion of a Crosse, yᵉ Steeple standing in yᵉ middle of yᵉ Church, in wᶜʰ there is onely this Coate of Armes in yᵉ window :

G. on a Bend B. 3 Lyons passants gardants, d'Or, betweene 9 Billets, Arg. 3, 2 & 1 on cheife, & 3 on base.

ECCLESIA SC̃I MARCI.

In Fenestra Orientali Cancelli :—

Empaled { Quarterly, d'Or et G. a bordure Sa. bezanty, on yᵉ first Quarter a flowre de Lize, Sa. } *Rochford* Argent, 3 Flowres de Lize betweene 9 Crosses botony fitchy Sa. a bordure G. } *Hillary*

Quarterly, d'Or & G. a Bordure Sa., bezanty   .   .   .   *Rochford*

In capella Boreali :—Thomas Knight, Mercator | Lincolñ, Obiit 24° Junii, 1423. | Alicia uxor.

Alexander filius Thome | Knight, obiit 19° Decembris, 1458.

Argent, a Chevron & 2 Estoyles in cheife, Sa.

Argent, on a Bend Sa., 3 Escallops.

[p. 49.]

ECCLESIA SC̃I BENEDICTI.

In Fenestra Orientali :—

G. on a Bend B. 3 lyons passants gardants d'Or betweene 9 Billets, Arg.

G. on a Fesse B. 3 lyons pass. gard. Or, betweene 8 Billets, Arg.

Quarterly, France semy, with England.

In Fenestra Australi :—

Arg. a Chevron G. between 3 torteaux . . . . *Sherard*

In Fenestris Cancelli et Ecclïæ :—

Arg. a Chevron betweene 2 Escallops on cheife, & a Cross, botony fitchy upon a Fernier in bast G. *quinquies.*

In Fenestra Australi :—

Argent, a Chevron betweene 2 Crescents, & a Crosse botony fitchy Sa. . . . . [*Gegge*]

Eadem Insignia ad murum affixa; necnon super ostium Ecclïæ sculpt'. &c.

In a North Chancell a Monument of Sapcote, on wch is his Coate of Armes, Vizt : On a Chevron 3 Escallops between 3 Dovecotes, *Sapcote*

His crest—a Goates head couped, collered & crowned.

Johannes de Wickforth unus Benefactoȓ huius Ecclesiæ.

A Monument on ye South wall of ye Chancell (in a plate of brass) of Alice Clarke, wife of Richard Clarke of Wollarton, the parents of Richard Clarke, then Recorder of Lincoln, Año 1513 : about it written—

. . . Virgo Mater tuam compassionem . . .

. . . animam meam ad æternam | Trinitatem. . . .

Thomas Hodgson Maior existens | obiit 11° die Septembris, a° 1587.

Augustinus Gabitus Alderman | nus obiit 20° die Maii, a° 1590.

[p. 50.]

ECCLESIA SC̃Æ MARIÆ IN WIKFORD.

In Fenestra Cancelli :—

Quarterly, Arg. & Sa. on a Bend G. 3 flours de lize, Or.

In Fenestra Australi Ecclesiæ :—

Thomas de Wellington . . . .

. . . uxor Gilerdi de Harple | me dedit.

John Williamson, a benefactor to the next window there.

In Fenestra Boreali Navis :—

Argent, 2 bars nebuly Sa. on cheife a Lyon passant gardant d'Or . . . . [*Merc. Stap*]

Gules, a fret of 6 peices Arg. . . . . . *Hodleston*

Orate p. aĩa Radĩ Hodelston | dudum Maioris Civitatis Linc̃. | ac Mercatoris Stapulæ Calesiæ, | et Agnetis, Isabellæ, et Catharinæ | consortum suarum, qui hanc | Fenestram fieri fecerunt.

In Campanili :—

On a flatt stone ye portraytures traced of John Hodgson & Jane his wyfe, he holding her by ye hande & (having been buryed some space before her) upon her being layd with him was engraven a Scroll from his mouth—Welcome.

On a gravestone, | Hic jacet Gregorius Ion Armig^r. | quondam unus
Justiciariorum | ad pacem et quorum in Civitate | Lincolñ. qui obiit
7° die . . . .

Depicta in Cancello :—
Sa. a Chevron engrayled between 3 Falcons Arg. . . . *Ion*
Argent (on) a Cross engrayled between 4 Doves Sa. 5 Bezants . *Welcome*

[p. 51.]

ECCLESIA SCI MICHAELIS IN MONTE.

In Fenestra Australi Cancelli :—
The picture of a Chevalier upon whose Surcoat are these Arms—
Argent, 3 lyons passants G.

In Muro Boreali :—
    Virgo Dei genitrix, Rogero sis mihi tutrix.
    Virgo poli-thronis animam tu trans. . .
Petrus Acland publicus | Notarius obiit duodecimo | die Novembris, A° 1590.

[p. 52].

ECCLESIA SCI MARTINI.

In Fenestra Boreali Capellæ :—
G. a crescent surmounted of an estoyle in pale, d'Or. . . [*Touke.*]
Ermyn, a Gryphon segreant G. . . . . . *Grantham.*
Argent on a chevron between 2 crescents, & a cross botony
    fitchy Sable, a mullet of ye first. . . . . *Gegge.*
Empaled { G. a crescent surmounted of an estoyle d'Or.
       { Arg. 2 barrs B.

In Australi Fenestra Cancelli :—
Arg. a fesse between 2 bars gemeaux G. . . . *Badlesmere.*
Ermyn, a crosse engrayled G. . . . . . *Norwood.*

In Fenestra Navis :—
B. a fesse between 3 buckes heads cabossed d'Or.
Empaled { Arg. a bar Sa. . . . . . . [*Bussy.*]
       { Arg. a bend, & annulet on cheife, Sa . [*Pagnell.*]
    Tumulus lapideus super solum : | Hic jacet Fremmanus* | Grantham
Mercator et bis | Maior Civitatis Lincoln', qui | obiit 26° die Julii, A°
dñi 1455, et | Elena uxor ejus quæ obiit . . .

Upon a Tombe of Freestone these ensueing Escocheons :—
Empaled { Ermyn, a Gryphon segreant G. . . .. *Grantham*
       { G. a Crescent surmounted of an Estoyle d'Or. . [*Touke*]

---

* *Fremmanus* is evidently a mistake for *Semannus* ; Seman Grantham was Mayor
of Lincoln in 1429 and 1450.—*Ed.*

Empaled { Grantham.
            { Argent 2 Bars B.

Empaled { Grantham.
            { Arg. on a Chevron between 2 Crescents & a
                     Crosse botony fitchy Sa. a Mullet d'Or.   . *Gegge*

Empaled { Grantham.
            { Arg. a Fesse Sa. between 3 Magpies, Proper. . *St. Poll*

Empaled { Quarterly, *Grantham* with y⁰ 4 former Empalements.
            { Or, on a Chevron between 3 Annulets G. as
                    many crescents of the first. .   .   . *Sutton*

Empaled { *Grantham* &c, quarterly.
            { G. 3 Bees volant Arg. a border engrayled d'Or. [*Girlington*]

Empaled { *Grantham.*
            { G. 3 Mullets Argent. .   .   .   .   . *Hansard*

Empaled {
     Quarterly { Grantham.
                    Arg. 2 Barrs B.
                    G. a crescent surmounted of an estoyle d'Or
                    Gegge.   [*Touke*]
                    Seynt Poll.
     Quarterly { B. a Cheife indented d'Or   .   . [*Dunham*]
                    Arg. a Cinquefoil pierced between 3 } [*Bowet*]
                      Rayne deares heads Sa. }
                    G. Bezanty, a Canton Ermyn .   . [*Zouch*]
                    Sa. 5 Lozenges voyded in pale d'Or.

Empaled { Grantham, and all these 8 quartered.
            { Sa. a Fesse d'Or between 3 Asses passants Arg. *Ayscough*

A little below this is a stately Monument of alabaster raysed up from a Pedestall graduated from the Basis; above which is a broade Bordure, & therein sixe children in lively proportion cut out in the stone, & soe (rising up higher) it is made up to a perfect quadrature in the Area above (which is a very large flat) upon which lyeth a chevalier in complete armour parcell guilt, his wife on his right hande, their Statuas (for proportion, visage, complexion) effigiated so as it gives a perfect representation of themselves as they were being alive, their handes elevated. As for the front of itt above it hath att either ende two Antickes with torches helde downward. The other devices (though very lively cut) yet they are but of homely conceite, Viz^t. two Pick-axes crossed on the one side, two spades on the other, then a Booke, under which is a Spade & two Torches putt out; likewise a Crosse, & upon the top of that a Death's Head betweene an Houre glasse & a Booke. Over them (which covers the whole surface of the Monument) is a fayre & large Canopye supported att either ende from the Base of the Area with two goodly columns of Touch*, in the

---

* *Touch*, that is Touchstone, a hard black slaty stone, so-called from its being used to test the purity of gold or silver, the quality of the metal being judged from the colour of the streak which it leaves on the stone.—*Ed.*

Concave whereof are rowes of Roses fretted with golde.   In the front
above their Statuas is the Table of Inscription of Touch, whereon in
golden letters written—Here lyeth Dame Fraunces | Grantham. one of
yᵉ daughters | of yᵉ [p. 54.] Right honᵇˡᵉ | Sʳ John Puckering, Kt. some
| tymes Lord Keeper of yᵉ great | Seale of England, & late wife | of
Sʳ Thomas Grantham | in the County of Lincolne, Kt. | by whom he
had issue foure | Sonnes, vizᵗ. Vincent, Thomas, | Robert & Fraunces,
& two | Daughters Elisabeth & Jane. | Shee departed this life | att
London 26ᵒ Jan. Aᵒ 1618.

On yᵉ one side of the Monument stande his Armes empaled wᵗʰ
hers, Vizᵗ :—

Ermyn, a Griphon segreant G. his fore-legs d'Or   .   .   *Grantham*
Sable, a Bend fusilly cottised, Arg.   .   .   .   .   *Puckering*

In the middle is *Grantham* quartered wᵗʰ some other coates before
described. On the other side the Atcheivements of *Grantham* empaled
with her Atcheivements, Vizᵗ :—

Quarterly
{
   Sa. a Bend fusilly cottised Arg.   .   .   .   *Puckering*
   Argent, a Mullet of 5 poyntes G.
   Ermyn, on a Fesse G. 3 annulets d'Or.
   Argent, 3 Pallets B.
   Argent, 2 Bars Sa. yᵉ first engrayled.
}

The next Quadrature above is adorned at either side with two
Pyramids of Touch.   In the middst in a fayre Sheilde are depicted his
armes with the usuall bearings, as are before described.   And (as a
Coronis upon yᵉ top of all) standeth upon a base the Picture of Charity,
as a naked woman having two children hanging on her breasts, two
more in her armes, & others clinging about her ; Shee shewing to cast
an eye of pitty upon them all.

Sʳ Thomas Grantham lyeth there buryed neare unto her Monument.

[p. 55.]

On yᵉ East side of yᵉ same Chancell,—A Monument of Free-stone
raysed up to a meane height, on which is written—

Charissimæ atq. honestissimæ | Uxori suæ, Janæ
Filiæ Thomæ | Tayleri, quæ obiit 11ᵒ die Martii |
Aᵒ Dñi 1591 ex puerperio Thomæ | filii sui, hic juxta
Matrem | suam sepulti, Georgius Anton | hujus
Civitatis Recordator in | veri atq. inviolati conjugalis
A | moris testimonium hoc poni | voluit.
Fidem post Funera servo.

A Gravestone—El. Filia Thomæ Taylor, uxor | Willĩ Aiscogh de
Stallinburgh | Filii et hæredis Edrĩ Aiscough | de Kelsey, obiit 6ᵒ die
Novembris, | Añᵒ Dñi 1590.

[p. 56.]

ECCLĪA. SCĪ. PETRI IN EASTGATE.

Fenestra Occidentalis ad Boream :—

Party per pale G. & Vert, an Eagle displayed Argent.

The same Coate in severall places empaling the Armes of the city of Lincoln. | Orate pro Joħe Eyleston.

In Fenestra Boreali supra :—

Quarterly Sa. et Or.

G. on 2 Chevrons Argent 6 Flours de Lise.

Arg. on a Chevron betweene 3 Martlets, Sa. a Flower de Lize d'Or.

Orate pro aīa Joħis Eyleston | et Joħis filii ejus.

In Feñ. Orientali :—

Joħes Verdon. Or, a fret G. . . . . . . *Verdon*

G. a Bend Ermyn ; a labell of 3 poyntes. . . . . [*Rie*]

In Fenestra Australi :—

G. 5 Fusills, a labell of 5 poyntes.

Or, a playne Crosse Sa. a file with 5 lambeaux G. . . [*Vescy*]

In Choro Boreali—Tumulus lapideus :—

Petrus Efford publicus Notarius et | Archidiaconatus Registrarius, obiit | 10° die Januarii, A° dñi 1511.

Super Sedulam :—

Arg. a Chevron between 3 Martletts, Sa.

Hic jacet Elizabetha quondam uxor | Walteri Tailboys . . . quæ obiit | 19° die Maii A° dñi 1477, cujus &c.

Super hunc lapidem :—

Empaled { A Saltier, on a Cheife 3 Escalops. . . *Tailboys*
         { A Chevron between 3 Cinquefoyles.

Depicta super laqueare :—

Sa. a Crosse sarcely betweene 4 Fusills Arg.

Argent a Crosse molyn Sa.

Empaled { Party p. pale G. & V. an eagle displayed Arg.
         { Arg. a Chevron betw. 3 Martletts Sa.

Argent, a Saltier G. on a Cheife of the second 3 Escalops of
the first. . . . . *Tailboys*

[p. 57.]

G. a Chevron between 3 Roses Argent.

Empaled { Quarterly { Arg 3 six-foyles G. . . . [*Darcy*]
         {   { Sanguine, a Lyon rampant Arg. . *Wymbish*
         { Quarterly Arg. & Sa. over all a Bend G. . [*Everingham*]

Quarterly { Argent, 3 Fusills in fesse G. . . . *Montacute*
          { Or, an Eagle displayed Vert. . . *Monthermer*

B. a Saltier between 4 Floures de Lize, Or. . . . [*St. Hugh*]

G. a Chevron Verry, between 3 Flowers de Lize, Or.

G. a Crescent betweene 6 Crosses botony Or.

[p. 58.]

ECCLESIA CATHEDRALIS.

In Fenestra Orientali orbiculari :—
Checky, Or & G. a cheife Ermyn. . . . . . *Tateshale*
Quarterly Arg. & G. in yᵉ 2 & 3 a Fret Or, over all a Bend Sa. . *Spenser*
G. a Crosse sarcely Ermyne. . . [*Ant. Beke, Bp. of Durham*]
G. a Fesse between 6 Martlets Or. . . *Beauchamp of Holt*
Checky, Or & B. . . . . *Warren*
G. 3 Lyons pass. gard. Or, a File with 3 Lambeaux B. [*E. of Lancaster*]
Party per pale, Or & Vert, a Lyon ramp. G. . . . . *Bigod*
England, with a Labell of 5 poyntes, B. Besanty.
Or, a Lyon rampant, Purpure. . . . . . . *Lacy*
Or, 3 Chevrons G. . . . . *Clare*
B. a Bend Arg. cotised betw. 6 Lyons ramp. Or. . . *Bohun*
Quarterly G. & Or, in the 1st Quarter a Mullet of 6 points Arg. . *Vere*
Quarterly Or & G. over all a Bend Vert.
G. a Fesse betweene 6 Crosses botony, Or. . . . *Beauchamp*
Argent, a Crosse patonce, B.

In Capella Cantelupi, ex Fenestra :—
G. a Fesse checky Arg. & B. between 3 Leopards' faces jesant
Flowres de Lize, Or. . . . . . . *Cantelupe*

Nicholaus Cantelupe Fundator Collegii | et duodecim Presbyter-
orum.
Quarterly { B. a Fesse dauncette betw. 6 Escalops, Arg.
{ G. on a Bend 3 . . Heads betw. 6 . .
Party per pale, G. & Vert, an Eagle displayed Arg. . . *Eyleston*
Empaled { Arg. a Cheife G. over all a Bend engrayled B.
{ upon yᵉ Cheife an annulet of the first. . *Leeke*
{ Quarterly, Or & G. a border Sa. Besanty. . *Rochford*
Argent, a Chief G. over all a Bend, B. . . . . *Crumwell*
Barry of 6 peices, Arg. & B. in cheife 3 Lozenges G. . *Flemming*

Super Tumulum :—
Quarterly { G. 3 Lyons pass. gard. Or, a Border Arg. . [*Holland*]
{ Bendy, of 10 peices, G. & Arg.
{ Sanguine, a Lyon ramp. Arg. . . . [*Wimbish*]
{ Arg. 3 Six-foiles pierced G, ... [*Darcy*]

The Sex-foyles & yᵉ Lyon per se hinc inde.
Cantilupe & Zouch sculp. super ædes Collegii.

B. 2 Chevrons Or, betw. 3 Roses Arg. . . . . . *Roscel*
Joħes Roscel Eꝑus Lincolñ, prius | Roffensis. fundator Capellæ
ibidem et sedis de | Buckden, Angliæ Cancellarius, | obiit Anno
Milleno C quater atque viceno, | Bis septem junctis.*

---

* Sanderson gives a much longer Epitaph for Bishop Roscel or Russel, consist-
ing of twelve Latin Hexameters, of which the two last are :—

[p. 59.]

Verus celuy Je suis.

Arg. a Chevron betw. 3 Crosses botony fitchy Sa. . . [*Russel*]

Ermyn, a Chevron party Or & Sa. . . . . [*Cosyn*]

Barry of 6, Arg. & B. in cheife 3 Lozenges G. on y^e . . *Fleming*
    2nd Bar a Mitre Arg. ; on ye 3rd a Mullet Sa. . . *Epus*

Ricũs Fleming Epus Lincolñ | ibidem sepultus Capellam construxit | ad ostium boreale ultra Chorum.

Barry of 6, Ermyn & G. 3 Crescents Sa. . . . . *Waterton*

In Fenestra juxta Ostium Boreale:—

Orate pro bono status Thomæ . . . | Utriusque Juris Doctoris, qui hanc Fenestram | fieri fecit.

Barry of 6, Arg & B. in cheife 3 Lozenges G. . . *Flemming*

Arg. a Cheife G. over all a Bend, B. . . . . *Crumwell*

B. a Chevron betw. 3 Wolfes-heades erased Or. . *Chedworth*

Joñes Chedworth Epus Lincolniensis | obiit die Sĉi Clementis A° Dñi 1471.*

Thomas Dymoke de Friskeney | obiit primo die Februarii, A° Dñi 1547, | A° Regis Henrici octavi 13°.

Willũs Dymoke, filius et hæres Thomæ | Dymoke de Friskeney, obiit 16° Aprilis, | A° Dñi 1549 : Elizabetha uxor ejus, filia | Joñis Harrington de Exton, Militis.

Robtus Dymoke, filius unicus Wilti | Dymoke de Friskeney, obiit 13° die Septembr. | A° Dñi 1593 : Anna soror eius et hæres, re | licta Caroli Bolle, et Bartholomæi Armyn, Armigeroñ.†

Quarterly ⎰ Sa. 2 Lyons pass. Arg. crowned Or ; a crescent . *Dymoke*
         ⎟ B. a Saltier betw. 4 Crosses formy Or. . . *Friskeney*
         ⎟ Arg. a Chevron betw. 3 Bulls pass. Sa . *Tourney*
         ⎱ The 4th as the 1st.

Roḡus Dalyson Sacræ Theologiæ professor Præcentor | et Canonicus Resident' Eccliæ beatæ Mariæ Lincolñ, | obiit 24° die Julii, A° Dñi 1566.

" Anno milleno, C quater, quaterque viceno,
    Bis septem junctis, vitalia lumina claudo."
He built the palace at Buckden and this chapel in which he was buried ; he died at Nettleham, 30 Jan., 1494. The first coat of arms is that assumed by the bishop, the second that of his family. " Verus celuy je suis " appears to have been the motto adopted by him, the second and third syllables forming his name 'Rus-cel.' It was engraved with his arms on two silver basins belonging to the Cathedral. (*Dugd. Mon.* VIII, 1280.)—*Ed.*

* Sanderson gives Bishop Chadworth's Arms as "three Goats' heads erased." and has preserved his Epitaph of twenty Latin Hexameters.—*Ed.*

† Sanderson gives the Epitaph of Mrs. Anne Armyn, the sister and heir of Robert Dymoke ; she died, as it says, 18 Aug., 1616, s.p., leaving her first cousin, Thomas Cracroft, of Fulletby, her heir.—*Ed.*

[p. 60.]

Wiltus Dalyson, unus Justiciar. de Banco | Regis, filius Wilti Dalyson de Laghton, | obiit A⁰ primo Elizabethæ, A⁰ Dñi 1558 : | Elizabetha uxor ejus, filia Robti Dighton de Sturton | parva : Filii eorumdem Wiltus, Robtus, Roḡus, | et Thomas : Filiæ, Elizabetha, Jocosa, Barbara, | Maria, Jana.

Super alium hoc Epitaphium :—

> Quis jacet hic? Puer est Johannes. Unde propago?
> E Dalysonorum gente decennis erat.
> Tam puer extinctus? Mortis scelus illud et error.
> Cur? Quia tam sapuit, credidit esse senem.
> Quis pater illius? Thomas. Quæ mater? Et Anna,
> Unde? Litelburio stemmate clara. Sat est.

In variis Fenestris :—

Empaled — Quarterly
- Arg. a Chevron betw. 3 Crosses botony within a Bordure Sa. besanty. . . *Fitzwilliam*
- Arg. 2 Barrs engrayled Sa. . *Staynes*
- Sa. a Frett Argent. . . . . *Harington*

Thomas Fitz-William de Malberthorp | Arm. obiit A⁰ Dñi 1474. Margareta | Harington uxor ejus obiit Año Dñi 1463. | Quorum Filii, Ricardus, Willũs, Johannes, | Thomas : Filiæ, Elizabetha, Johanna, Aleanora, | Jocosa, Margareta, Beatrix.

Maria filia Georgii Fitz-William | de Malberthorp, Armig. obiit 27⁰ die Novembris, | A⁰ Dñi 1607 ; nupta prius Riĉo Hiltoft : | 2ᵈᵒ Antonio Nevile : 3ᵗⁱᵒ Francisco | Bullingham.

Or, on a Chevron G. 3 Martlets Arg. betw. as many Flowers de Lize, Vert. . . . . *Hiltoft*

G. a Saltier, Ermyn. . . . . *Nevile*

B. an Eagle displayed Arg. on a Cheife, Or, 3 Crosscrossletts, G. . . . . . . *Bullingham*

Each of these three Coates empaling the ensueing quarterings.

[p. 61.]

Quarterly
- Lozengy, Arg. & G. . . . . *Fitz William*
- Arg. a Chevron betw. 3 Crosses botony, within a Border, Sa. besanty. . . . *Malberthorp*
- Arg. 2 Barres engrayled Sa. . . . *Staynes*
- B. a Lyon ramp. Arg. . . . . . *Montalt*

Vert, on a Chevron betw. 3 Hindes trippants, Or, as many Estoyles G. . . . . *Robinson*

Johes Robinson Precentor Ecclesiæ.

Sa. 3 Musyons,* Erm. . . . . *Walker*

Georgius Walker, Medicinæ Doctor.

---

* *Musyon*, a Wild Cat, the emblem of Burgundy. Readers of Sir Walter Scott will remember his use of the term in *Quentin Durward.—Ed.*

Empaled { B. on a Chevron Or, 3 Roses G. a Canton Erm. . *Randes*
{ B. a Saltier Arg. . . . . . . *Yorke*

Randes his Crest—on a Torce Or & G. a Sword Arg. pointe in cheife, pomel hilt & Neuf Or, supported by two Lyons paws, Gules.*

Icy gist Dame Katherine Duchesse de | Lancastre, Jadys feme de le tres-noble et tres | gracious Prince John Duk de Lancastre | Fitz a tres-noble Roy Edward le tierce, le | (*sic*) quelle Katherine morust le X Jour du | May, l'an de grace 1403, des queux almes | Dieu ayet Mercy et pitie. Amen.

Empaled { Quarterly, *France*, semy of Flowers de Lize, } *Duke of*
{ & *England*, a file of 3 pointes Ermine. } *Lancaster*
{ G. 3 Catherine Wheeles, Or. . . . . *Roet*

Juxta hanc tumulatur Filia Johanna, et super tumulum hæc :—
G. a Saltier Argent . . . . *Nevile*
Quarterly, England & France semy, a Border gobony, Arg. & B. *Beaufort*

    Filia Lancastris Ducis Inclita, sponsa Johanna
      Westmorland primi subjacet hic Comitis :
    Desine, Scriba, suas virtutes promere, nulla
      Vox valeat merita vix reboare sua.†

[p. 62.]
Argent, on a Chevron G. a Falcon volant of yᵉ 1ˢᵗ, betw. 3 Ogresses ; on a Cheife Or, a Rose of the 2ⁿᵈ betw. 2 Leopards' faces B. . . . . . *Longland Epus*

Longa terra mensuram eius Deus dedit, *Job II.*

Joħes Longland Eꝑus Lincolniensis tempore Hen. 8ᵛⁱ, Capellam construxit ad Austrum : Obiit 7° die Maii, A° Dñi 1547 apud Manerium suum de Wooburne in Comi- -tatu Buckingh. sepultus apud Eaton juxta Windsore.

    J. Shepey canus jacet his sub marmore planus,
    Lincoln' Decanus, dum vixit corpore sanus,
    Gratus et humanus ; cui Crux est Samaritanus.
    O mortalis homo ! Memorare novissima, plora,
    Esto memor, timor atq. tremor sit mortis in hora,
    Talis eris, qualis ego sum : pro me (precor) ora.

Lucia uxor Wilħi Wray de Ashby in Com. | Linc. Militis, Filia Edri. Mountagne de Bough | ton in Coɱ. Northampt. Militis, Obiit primo | die Martii A° Dñi 1599.

---

* Sanderson gives at length the Latin Epitaph of Thomas Randes, Commissary and Official of the Archdeaconries of Lincoln and Stow. He died 17 Feb., 1608, and his wife Mary, daughter of Thomas Yorke, esq., 23 Feb., 1596.—*Ed.*

† Sanderson supplies four more lines of her epitaph, which tell us that she died on the Feast of St. Brice, 13 Nov., 1440.—*Ed.*

Gulielmi **Wraii*** preclari Nobilis uxor,
Fæminei sexus splendor, virtutis imago,
Illustris jacet hic ; quænam sua Lucia dedit
Lucia, quæ luxit terris, nunc lucet Olympo ;
Libera mente canens divinos cælitus hymnos
Quæ modo, dum vixit, captiva mente sonabat,
Ac velut exilio ad patriam revocata triumphat.

(This wretched Epitaph, I beleive, was made by her sonne, yᵉ owle
& changeling Sʳ John Wray ; however yᵉ Lady was a good woman.)

Empaled
{
Quarterly
{
B. on a Cheife d'Or, 3 Martletts, G. . *Wray*
Arg. on a Chevron Sa. 3 Cinquefoyles
pierced of yᵉ 1ˢᵗ, between as many
Falcon's heads, erased, B. . *Jackson*
}
Arg. 3 Fusills in fesse G. a border Sa. . *Mountagne*
}

Christopherus Massingberd Archidiacon' Stow, Obiit 8° die Martii,
A° Dñi 1553.

B. in cheife a Sanglier Arg. in bast 3 Quaterfoyles, Or. . *Massingberd*

Henricus Sapcote, bis Maior Lincolñ, | Clericus generalis Decañ. et
Capituli, | Consistarii Episcopalis Registrarius Prin | cipalis, (ac etiam)
Archidiacoñ Lincolñ et Stow, | Obiit 27° die Julii, 1552. Jana uxor
ejus | decessit 24° die Maii Año Dñi 1546.

[p. 63.]

Wilłus Sapcote, Canonicus et Præ | bendarius, et Rector Eccłiæ de
Waddington, | Obiit 9° die Septembr. A° Dñi 1565.

Margareta Fynes Vidua Obiit 26° | die Octobr. A° Dñi 1486 ; Tum-
ulus ex australi parte Chori.

Super Lectrinam æream in Choro :—
Ad laudem Dei et honorem gloriosæ | Virginis Mariæ hanc Lectri-
nam contulit | bonæ memoriæ Margareta Fynes,—cujus | aïæ propit-
ietur Deus. Amen.

Sʳ Thomas Wright, sometyme Sacrist of ye Collegiate Church of
Lincolne, Maister of Cantelupe Colledge & Chauntery, parson of
Wykenby, died yᵉ 23ʳᵈ of January, 1516.

Robtus Mounson unus Justiciarioⁱ de Communi Banco obiit 24° die
Septembr. A° Dñi 1583. Elizabetha uxor ejus, filia et hæres Joħis
Dyon, Armig.

Quem tegat hoc marmor, si forte requiris, Amice,
Lunam cum Phæbo jungito, nomen habes.
Luce patrum clarus, proprio sed lumine major,
De gemina merito nomina luce capit.

---

* Marginal Note by G. Holles :—"Vir quidem plane simplex et honestus, alias
vero nulla virtute aut claritate præditus."

Largus, doctus, amans, aluit, coluit, recreavit,
Musas, Jus, Vinctos, sumptibus, arte, domo.
Tempora læta Deus post tempora nubila misit,
Læta dedit læte, nubila ferre pie.
Et tulit et vicit, super et sua lumina vectus
Fulget apud Superas, Stella beata, Faces.

Empaled
{
  Or, 2 Chevrons G. . . . . . *Munson*
  Quarterly
{
    Or, a Saltier B. on a Cheife G. 3
    Saltiers humets of yᵉ 1ˢᵗ . . *Dyon*
    Barry of 6, Arg. & G. a Canton, Erm.
}
}

[*Marshall*]

Hic jacet Magister Thomas de Corbrig quondam Canonicus istius
Ecclïæ. Cujus aïæ propitietur Deus. Amen.

On a Cross fitchy — 3 Escalops. . . . . . . *Corbrig*

[p. 64.]

Hic sunt sepulta Viscera Alianoræ | quondam Reginæ Angliæ,
consortis | Regis Edwardi filii Regis Henrici. | Cujus aïæ propitietur
Deus. Amen. Pater Noster.

(Tumulus Marmoreus cum statua ærea desuper in Capella Sõæ
Mariæ versus Orientalem Fenestram.)

Philippus Tylney, Armig. Canonicus et Residentiarius
Cathedralis Ecclïæ Bẽæ Mariæ Lincolñ, Filius
Frederici, Filii Philippi Tylney, Militis :—Uxor
ejus Isabella, filia Edmundi Thorp de Ashwelthorp
in Com. Norfolciæ, Militis, et Dñæ, Johannæ de Scales
consortis suæ, amitæ Thomæ Dñi de Scales. Obiit
penult' die Octobr. Año Dñi 1453.*

Sir William Tyrwhit of Kettleby, Knight, died 1522 :—

Marryed (Anne) the daughter of Sʳ Robert Constable, of Flamburgh, Kt.

Empaled
{
  G. 3 Lapwings, Or. . . . . . *Tyrwhit*
  Qnarterly, G. & Verry, over all a Bend, Or. . *Constable*
}

Wiłłus Atwater, Sacræ Theologiæ Doctor, et Regum
Henr. 7ᵐⁱ et 8ᵛⁱ Sacelli prius Decanus, mox eoŕdem
a conciliis, postea huius precelebris Ecclesiæ Ep̃us
præsedit annos 6, menses 3 : Obiit Año ætatis
suæ 81°, consecracionis 7° a Xp̃o nato 1520, Febr. 4ᵗᵒ.

Barry wavee of 6, Or & G. on a Chevron G. a Rose & 2
Pauncies slipped. . . . . . . *Atwater*

---

* Sanderson adds an inscription of 16 lines of English verse, describing the life
& lineage of " Sir Philip Tilney—In youth esquier, & so wedded to his wyf."—*Ed.*

Wiłtus Smith quondam Coventr. et Lichfeldensis, deinde Lincolniensis Ep̄us, obiit 2º die Januarii, Año Dñi 1513.*

Arg. a Chevron betw. 3 Roses G. . . . . . . [*Smith*]
G. a Saltier Erm. betw. 4 Flowers de Lize, Or. . . [*St. Hugh*]

Dnūs Joħes de Multon, Miles:—
Sa. 2 Barres, in cheife 2 Annulets Arg. . . . . *Multon*

[p. 65.]

Ricardus Bevercotes quondam Receptor generalis Ecclesiæ, obiit 5º
die Junii, Año Dñi 1546.
Arg. a Cross patonce B. a labell of 3 pointes G. . . *Bevercotes*

Orate pro aïa Mʳⁱ Thome Burgh, nuper | Canonici Ecclesiæ Colle-
giat' Derbiæ, | ac Rectoris Ecclesiaꝛ de Fulbecke et | Market Overton,
Obiit 12º die Martii 1527.
Arg. on a Saltier Sa. 5 Cygnets of yᵉ first. . . . . *Burgh*

Edmundus Yerburgh, Armig̃. duxit | Margaretam Filiam Vincentii
Grantham, | Armig̃. Obiit 28º die Febr. Año Dñi 1590.†

Empaled { Party per pale . . . a Chevron betw. 3
Chaplets, all counter-charged. . . *Yerburgh*
Ermine, a Griphon segreant G. . . *Grantham*

Vincentius Tothoth, in Sacris Canonibus | Baccalaureus, Rector
Ecclĩe de Burton | juxta Bitchfeld, et Vicar : de Stallingburgh | et
Gousil, obiit primo die Martii, Año | Dñi 1529.

Tumulus Marmoreus—Joħes Mackworth, Decretoꝛ Doctor, | Can-
cellarius illustrissimi principis | Henrici filii Regis Henrici 4ᵗⁱ, Decanus |
Ecclĩæ B̃eæ Mariæ Lincolñ.
Party per pale indented, Sa. & Erm. a Chevron G. fretty Or. *Mackworth*

In Fenestra—*Mackworth.*
G. a fesse betw. 2 Barres gemels Arg. . . . [*Badlesmere*]

Thomas de Aston, Archidiacoñ Stow, Canonicus Ecclĩæ Cathedralis
Lincoln, obiit 7º die Julii, Aº 1401.
Arg. a Mullet Sa. a border engrayled. . . . . . *Aston*
Quarterly { Arg. a Crosse humet betw. 4 botony, Or. . *Jerusalem*
B. semy of Flowers de Lize, a Lyon ramp. Or. *Beaumont*

In Fenestra ex opposito horologii :—
Or, a plaine Crosse Sa. a labell of 5 pointes G. . . . [*Vescy*]

[p. 66.]

In muro Capellæ Australis—Tumulus lapideus Georgii Tailboys,
Milit', et Elizabethæ uxoris cum Insigniis sequentibus—

---

* Here too Sanderson gives the epitaph more fully, and adds six lines of Latin
verse.—*Ed.*

† Sanderson gives this epitaph also more fully, adding that Edmund Yerburgh
and Margaret Grantham "habuerunt inter eos exitus Carolum, Franciscum, et
Fidem," and giving other quarterings for *Yerburgḣ.—Ed.*

Empaled { Arg. a Saltier, on a Cheife G. 3 Escallops of ye 1st. *Tailboys*
{ Arg. on a Pale Sa. a demi Lucy hauriant Or. . *Gascoigne*

Hic jacet Magister W. . . | Tailboys, quondam Canonicus istius |
Ecclesiæ, filius venerabilis viri Georgii Tailboys | Militis, et Dñæ
Elizabethæ uxoris eius : Obiit | . . . Año Dñi MCCCCC. . .

Hic jacet Joannes Gynewell, Ep̄us | Lincoln, qui obiit 5° die
Augusti, A° Dñi | 1362, et suæ consecracõis 15mo, | Cuius aïa in
perpetua pace requiescat.

Ex parte Australi Cancelli :—
Hic jacet Dñus Johannes Tram, | Sacrista istius Ecclesiæ, Canoniĉ.
Staff. | et Rector de South Hikham, et Capellanus | Cantariæ Kath-
arinæ Ducissæ Lancastr', | qui obiit 6° die Martii Año Dñi 1494.

> Thomas de Saperton gist ycy
> Dieu luy grant sa mercy
> Jadys servant Esquier
> A Sire Johan de Welborne tresourer
> Que del mound fichee son departer
> Del moys de June le jour primer
> L'an de Crist, si vous plest,
> Mille tres-cent septante et sept.
> Ditz par sa charity
> Pater noster et Ave.

Thomas Marshall Capῐus Cantar̄ Dñi Bartholomei Burghwash
Militis, Obiit 5° die Maii, Año Dñi 1539. [p. 67.] Capella ipsius
Bartholomei juxta tumulum et Capellam Flemming Episcopi.

Tumulus lapideus in Ambulatorio ære totaliter coopertus : Hugo
de Edlington, Senior, Civis et Mercator Lincolñ, obiit die Sabbati
Vigil' Sc̃i Jacobi, Año Dñi 1333.

In Capella Australi : Effigies et Insignia Thomæ Burgh Militis
Sangeorgeani Ordinis, cum limbo semilunari.

IN PALATIO EPISCOPI.

Arg. a Crosse molin, Sa. . . . . . . *Buckingham**

Joħes Buckingham Ep̄us (ut dicitur) sæpissime in Fenestrarum
limbis et ostiis ligneis cum dicto : *Delectare in Domino.* Ab Urbano
5° Papa provisus A° 1362, trans. Coventr. et Lichf.

Party per chevron embattelled G. & Arg. 3 Roses counter-
changed . . . . *White*

---

* *Arg. a cross moline, Sa.* were not the Arms of Bishop Buckingham, but of
Bishop Alnwick, who built a Chapel and several rooms in the Palace, and whose
motto, *Delectare in Domino,* was inscribed on the great Cross, silver-gilt, given to the
Cathedral by him. Bishop Buckingham's proposed translation to Coventry and
Lichfield, which he would not accept, was in 1398.—*Ed.*

Joħes White Epus Linc. temp. Reïnæ Mariæ.
B. 3 Mylers Or.

Insignia Regis Henrici 8^{vi} et Katherine Howard uxoris suæ bis in
Palatio, semel in Capella, Viz^t :—

Empaled {
    France & England . . . . *Hen. VIII*
    B. 3 Flowers de Liz. in pale Or. betw. 2 } *Katharine*
        Flasques Erm. each charged with a Rose } *Howard*
    G. quartering *Brotherton, Howard,* &c. }

Super murum sculpt' juxta Veteres Vicar' Arma Coronæ ex dextra :—
A Cross botony ex sinistra.
A Fesse betw. 6 Crosse crosselets.

Ex orientali parte Vicariorum :—
Insignia Epi Buckingham, et Juxta *Breton,* ejus offiċ.

In nave Ecclesiæ :—
Hic jacet Henricus Fotherby Arm. qui obiit . . .*

[p. 68 blank.]

Kingerby.

[p. 69]

In Fenestra Aquilonari :—
Argent, on a Fesse G. 3 Flowers de Lize, Or . . . *Disney*

Effigies bellatoris prædicta arma gestantis in eadem fenestra.

Sub hac fenestra tumulus lapideus super qnem duo bellatores tibiis
in crucem conversis, quorum unus gestat super pectus tres Leopardos.

On the side of this Monument these Escocheons :—
1. A Chevron between 3 Birdes.
2. Three Leopards passants . . . . [*Amundeville*]
3. Three Leopards passants with a Labell of three . [*Amundeville*]
4. A Manch.
5. Barruly of 14 peices, 3 Chappelets . . . [*Greystoke*]

In Fenestra Orientali Effigies duorum bellatorum hæc arma gestantium, Viz^t :—
Argent, on a Fesse G. 3 Flowers-de-Lize, Or . . . *Disney*

In altera Fenestra :—3 Leopards.

In Fenestra Occidentali :—
Argent, on a Fesse G. 3 Flowers-de-Lize, Or . . . *Disney*

---

* Sanderson completes this epitaph—" Qui obiit sexto die mensis Februarii,
Anno Dom. MCCCCLXX."—*Ed.*

In the Quire :—On a flatt gravestone the halfe portrayture of a man, his hands elevated, on his right arm hangs this escocheon, A Chevron betw. 3 birdes ; on his left hand this—On a bend 3 Mullets of 5 poyntes peirced. Above him 2 Escocheons :—

1. Two Lyons passant.
2. Barry of 12, 3 Chappelets . . . . [*Greystoke*]
    Patronus, Thomas Puckering, Miles.
    Vicarius . . . . Whitwicke.

𝕶irkby.

[p. 70.]

In a North window of yᵉ Church a man holding a Cup ; On eache hande of him divers kneeling ; under him this motto :—Gilda de Ouresbi me fecit.

In a South window :—

Argent, 2 Lyons passant Gules.

In the Quire :—A fayre Tomb raysed above yᵉ ground, where lyes John Wildebore & his wife at his feete. The Tombe is of a great length. He lyes in compleate armes gilt ; Upon his surcoat *three Boares passants, Ermine.* In divers places of the Monument three Boares & an Escarbuncle. Under his head lyes his helmet & his crest, A Boare sejant Erm. The Inscription thus :—His jacet Johannes Wildebor, qui | obiit tertio Nonar' Octobris, Año Dñi | Millesimo trecentesimo Nonagesimo | octavo. Cujus anime &c.

Above his wives head two Escocheons :—

Three Boares passants Ermyne . . . . . *Wildebore*
A Chevron betw. 3 Bulls passants . . . . . *Tourney*

The Inscription thus :—Hic jacet Dña Margareta quon | dam uxor Joħis Wildebore, cujus | animæ &c.

Other monuments in yᵉ Quire much defaced when the Quire was taken downe.

In Fenestra Australi in Cancello :—

G. an Eagle displayed Arg. membered & bequed, Or ; on a
    Bend Azure 3 Escallops Or. . . . . [*Suthill*]
Azure, a Hinde tripping Golde.

Long Ouresby.

[p. 71.]

In yᵉ East window of yᵉ Church yᵉ portrayture of a man in compleate armour ; Upon his Surcoate –

Gules, 3 Mullets, Argent. . . . . . . *Hansard*

Behinde him two Sonnes.

In the next glasse his wife & 4 daughters in blew, all kneeling ; underneath this written :—Orate pro animabus Roberti | Hansardi de Ouresby, Aliciæ | uxoris eius, eoͬ filioͬ et filiæ | qui me fecit fieri.

In the North window of yᵉ Chancell these quartered :—

1. B. a Chevron Arg. betw. 3 Mullets Or. . . . [*Hilyard*]
2. Barry of 4, Arg. & B. on 3 Torteaux G. as many Mullets, Arg.
3. Blew, 2 Barres G. a Flower de Lize, Or.
4. As the First.

Percy & *Lucy* quartered.

G. a Lyon ramp. Arg. . . . . . . *Mowbray*

In a South window of the Chancell :—Johannes de Glentham Vicarius me fecit. A white Rose neare by the Vicar.

Patronus Thomas Munson, Miles et Baronettus.
Vicarius . . . West.

Stow Beae Mariae.

[p. 72.]

This Church is built Minster-like, & was first founded by Leofricus & his Countesse Godiva, who likewise here founded an Abbey which was after transferred to Eignesham.

In a West window of the Church :—

Quartered { Gules, a Saltoyre, Or.
{ Arg. on a Chevron Sa. 3 Leopards-faces of yᵉ 1ˢᵗ.

On a Gravestone yᵉ portrayture of a woman, hir handes elevated, a huke on her head : this engraven in old characters :—

All ye men that ben in life
Pray for me (that) was Fucke wife.

On a monument in the Chancell this Inscription :—Neare unto this place lyeth buried the | bodyes of Mʳ Thomas Holdbech, yᵗ some-tymes | dwelt in Stowe Parke, with Anne his wife, | daughter of

Anthony Yaxley, of Yaxley & | Mellis, Esq. wch said Anthony* deceased y^e | 9th day of September Año Dñi 1581 ; & | the said Thomas deceased ye first day of | Aprill Año Dñi 1591 ; & they left ishue | onely one Sonne named Edward.

Empaled { Quarterly { Vert, 5 Escallops in saltoyre Arg. . *Holebech* / Arg. on a Cheife B. 3 Lyons-heads / rasy, of ye first. / Ermine, a Cheveron Sa. betw. 3 Mullets, voyded G. *Yaxley*

Holbech's Crest, a Pelican's head within a Coronet, Arg.

In the North window of the Chancell :—

Empaled { The Armes of the Bishoppricke of Lincolne. / Arg. on a Chevron G. betw. 3 Torteaux an Eagle / displayed Or . . . 3 Hurtes. . [*Longland*]

Cotes Magna.

[p. 73.]

In the Quire :—

Empaled { B. a Fesse dauncy Erm. betw. 6 Crosse-crosse- / lets, Arg. . . . . . *Barnardeston* / Vert, a Saltoyre engrayled Arg. . . . *Hawley*

Barnardeston's Crest—a Hynde regardant.

On a Gravestone :—Orate pro aīabus Thomæ de Barnar | deston Militis, filii Thomæ Barnardeston | defuncti, dum vixit, de Mikel-Coates in | Com̃. Linc̃. et Elizabethæ uxoris | prædicti Thomæ, nuper filiæ Georgii | Newport (dum vixit) de Pellam in Com. Herford, Armiğ.

On the Stone in Brass an embleme of the Resurrection with this inscribed, Vizt :—In the worship of the Resurrection of our Lord & the Blessed Sepulcher, & for the Soule of Sr Thomas Barnardeston, Knight, & Dame Elizabeth his wife, & of your Charity, say a Pater Noster, Ave & Creed, & ye shall have an hundred dayes of pardon to your meed—Which Sr Thomas deceased the 29th of June Año Dñi 1503. On whose soule Jhesus have mercy. On the stone 8 sonnes & 7 daughters.

His word—Jhesu fili Dei miserere mei.

Hers—Fiat voluntas sua.

* *Sic*, but evidently a mistake for Anne, see [p. 191.]—*Ed.*

On the same Monument empaled :—

A Fesse daunsy Erm. betw. 6 Crosse-crossletts . *Barnardeston*

A Fesse betw. 3 Crescents . . . . . *Newport*

On a high Monument—*Bernardston* p. pale with :—

Sa. a Bend betw. 2 cotises flowry Or . . . . *Bromflet*

Bernardston per pale with :—

Or a Fesse daunsy Sable . . . , . . *Vavasor*

On a Gravestone :—Hic jacet Dña Johanna Barnardston de Magna Cotes . . . Aº Dñi 1453.

On another :—Hic jacet Isabella quondam Uxor Roḡi de Barnardston Arm̃. cujus aīe &c. Her portrayture in brasse.

On another :—Thomas South Rector obiit 1593.

[p. 74.]

Hic jacet Johannes de Bar | nardston, Rector istius Ecclesiæ | qui obiit in festo Sci Martini Anno | Dñi 1406. Cujus aīe &c.

 Patronus . . . .

 Rector, Abraham Smith.

Ḧelyng.

In yᵉ great window of yᵉ Quire :—

Or, a Cross engr. G. in yᵉ dexter quarter a Cornish Chongh,

 Proper . . . . *Mussenden*

On a Tombe of free-stone :—Hic jacet Franciscus Missenden Arm̃,| qui obiit sexto die Martii Año regni | Reginæ Elizabē undecimo 1569.

On the side of the monument *Mussenden* paleth—

Sa. a Fesse Or, betw. 3 Asses passants Arg. hoofs, maynes &

 tayles as yᵉ second . . , . . . *Ayscough*

James yᵉ sonne of Frances Mussenden lyeth by him under a Marble.

Hic jacet Thomas Mussenden, Miles, | qui obiit decimo die Septembris Año | Dñi 1550.

In severall places of yᵉ Tomb, Per pale, *Mussenden*, with *Saint Pol & Goodricke.*

Hic jacet Thomas Mussenden | Arm̃ⁱᵍ qui obiit 3º die | Februarii Año Regis et Reginæ | Philippi et Mariæ quinto.

On yᵉ Stone :—*Mussenden*, per pale with

Sa. a Fesse betw. 3 Papillions Arg. . . . . *Girlington*

In a table *Mussenden* Per pale with
Sa. a playne Crosse Or, betw. 4 Flowers de Lize, Arg. . *Morison*

These in the Windows :—
Argent, a plaine Crosse B.
Argent, a Chief B.

𝕴𝖗𝖇𝖞.

[p. 75.]

On a Gravestone :—Of your Charity pray for the Soule of John
Godricke, Preist. late Parson of this Church, on whose Soule Jhesu
have mercy.—Viventes in carne, orate pro defunctis quia moriemini.

In the East window :—

Quarterly { G. a Castle Or . *Castile* } Per pale with
{ Arg. a Lyon ramp. Sa. . *Leon* }
France & *England*, a file with 3 lambeaux, Erm. . . *Lancaster*
Quarterly, *France* & *England*.
France & *England*, a labell of 3, Argent.

In a South window :—
Argent, 3 red Roses.
Arg. fretty, a Cheife Sa. on yᵉ sinister point a Rose, Arg. . *Rydford*
Gules, 3 Buckles of a belt, Or. . . . . . . [*Malet*]

In the next window :—
Arg. fretty a cheife Sable . . . . . . *Rydford*
Arg. an Inescocheon Sa. an Orle of red Roses.
Rydford, with a Mullet pierced, Arg.

In the next window :—
Argent, fretty ; a Cheife Sa. . . . . . *Rydford*
Per pale { Arg. fretty, a Cheife Sa. . . . . *Rydford*
{ G. 3 Buckles Or . . . . . . *Malet*
Arg. fretty, a Cheife Sa. a Mullet of 5, pierced Arg. . *Rydford*

In a North window :—
Arg. an Inescocheon Sa. voyded of yᵉ feilde ; an Orle of red Roses.
Per pale { Arg. Fretty, on a Cheife Sa. a white Rose . *Rydford*
{ Arg. an Inescocheon Sa. an Orle of red Roses.
Arg. Fretty, a Cheife Sa. on yᵉ dexter poynt a Buckle Or *Rydford*

In the Church :—
On a Torce Arg. & Sa. an Arme & hande holding a Holly-bush—yᵉ
Crest of Densell Holles.

This Motto over yᵉ Armes—Esperance aid to hardy.

Almost in every window of yᵉ Church & the Chancell yᵉ Armes of
Hollys, sometymes alone, sometymes quartered with other Coates, &
sometymes empaled with Sheffeild.
Sa. a Bend betw. 2 Talbots passants Arg.
Arg. a Chevron betw. 3 Garbes, G. . . . . [*Sheffield*]

[p. 76.] In yᵉ Chancell of this Church lyes buried under a playne stone without any inscription the bodye of Denzel Hollys, Esq., eldest son of Sʳ William Hollys, of Haughton in the County Nottingham, Knight, who by his wife Elianor daughter to Edward Lord Sheffeild (slayne by yᵉ Northfolke Rebells in Kett's rebellion) had issue John Hollys, the fiıst of that name Earle of Clare, William who dyed a youth, Sʳ George Hollys, Knight, & Thomas Holles who was Leiutenant-Collonell to the Lord Veres regiment in yᵉ Netherlands, Frances wife of Sir Francis Coke, of Trusley in Com̃. Derb., Jane wife of Thomas Saunderson of Lincolnes Inne, Esqʳ., & others wᶜʰ dyed unmarryed.

Sʳ George Holles & Thomas Holles Leiutenant-Colonell (boeth famous souldiers in yᵉ Netherlandes warres, & borne here) were the principall honnours of this place.

Sʳ George Holles lyes buried in the Abbey of Westminster close by Sʳ Francis Vere. His Statua in full proportion & compleate armour, standing upon a fayre area of white Marble, a commanding staffe in his right hande, his left arme bearing his sheilde, whereon depicted these Coates quarterly :—

Ermine, 2 Piles in poynte Sa. . . . . . . *Holles*
Arg. a Lyon ramp. Gules . . . . *Estley*
Sa. a Crescent surmounted of a Mullet, Arg. . . . *Densell*
Arg. 3 Chevernells Sa. . . . This is put for *Trenewith*

His difference—a Mullet. His left eye (which he lost in yᵉ Seige of Ostend) put out. The Inscription this :—

Georgio Holles Eq. Anglo-Brit:' clariss: Penatibus oriundo, Rebus Militar.' sic a pueritia dedito, ut castrorum alumnus nasci videretur, qui postquam cuncta quæ decerent nobilem, stipendio in Belgio fecerat, Ordinum ductor suæ gentis supremus (vulgo Sergeant Major Generalis) Declaratus est. Augustæque Trinobantum pacifice excessurus, Hic propter Franciscum Verum Imperatorem suum et Consanguineum, Cui tamen periculis quam sanguine conjunctior, ambitu honestissimo componi voluit.

Johannes Frater Comes de Clare Fratri merentissimo mœrentissimus Posuit. Vixit A.L.M. III. D. IIII.
Ob. XIIII Cal. Juni, A.D. MDCXXVI.

Patronus, Comes de Clare.
Rector, Radulfus West. Vide plura p. 86.

[p. 77.]

Stalingburgh.

In the upper ende of the North Isle :—
A fayre Tombe of Marble under which lye buryed Sir William Aiscogh & Dame Margery Hiliard his wife. Upon the Tombe there is

the portrayture of himselfe in compleat armoure. Upon his surcoat his Armes, Viz^t :—

Sa. a Fesse d'Or entre troys Asses passants d'Argent, maynes,
tayles, & hoofes as ye Second. . . . . *Ayscogh*

His wife by him hir garments adorned with these coates quarterly, Viz^t :—

B. a Chevron Arg. betw. 3 Mullets of 5 pointes, Or. . *Hylyard*
On a Bend 3 Escalops betw. 6 Cups covered.

This Epitaph :—

> Ossa sub hoc gelido Willhelmi Militis Ayscugh
> Marmore, non parvo munere, pressa jacent,
> Cui conjuncta jacet sua Margeria pudica,
> Filia Roberti Militis hæc Hylyard.

Maritus—Scā Trinitas, unicus Deus, miserere nobis.
Uxor—Libera nos famulos tuos, O beata Trinitas.

In a fayre Tombe of white Marble :—A Chevalier in compleat armour, his wife by him in full stature reclining upon a cushion : Upon a tableture of Touch this Inscription in golde letters :—

Memoriæ Meritiss: cl: D. Edwardi Ayscogh de Kelsey in Com. Linc. Equitis aurati, ex antiqua Hansardorum Familia oriundi, et uxoris ejus optimis meritis Estheris, Thomæ Grantham, Armig. Filiæ. Obiit ille Martis die nono, Año Dñi 1612.

Anagr̄. { Edouardus Aiscolghe.
{ Gaudes Io clarus Deo.

At ye heade & feete of this Tombe upon a tableture these coates depicted Quarterly, Viz^t.—

1. Sab. a Fesse, Or, betw. 3 Asses passant, Arg. &c. . *Ayscogh*
2. Or, a Bend B. . . . . *Cathorp*
3. Gules, 3 Mulletts Argent. . . . . . *Hansard*
4. Chevrony of 6 peices Arg. & Gules.
5. Arg. a Saltier G. on a Cheife of ye 2nd 3 Escalops of y^e
 1st ; a Trefoyle difference. . . . . *Taylboys*
6. B. a Crosse chequy Arg. & Gules. . . . *Cokefeild*
7. G. 2 Chevrons & Border Or. . . . . *[Charnel]*
8. Sa. a Chevron betw. 3 Pillars Or. . . *[Bullingbroke]*
9. Ermyne, 2 Chevrons Gules. . . . . *[Seymore ?]*
[p. 78.]
10. Arg. an Inescocheon & Orle of Cinquefoyles Sa. . *[Hedworth]*
11. Arg. 3 red Roses ; a file with 3 lambeaux Sa. . . *[Darcy]*
12. Barry nebuly of 6 peices Or & Sa. . . . . *Blunt*
13. Arg. 2 Wolves passants Sa. a Border Or, charged with
 Saltoyres Gules. . . . . . . *Ayala*
14. Or, a Castle B. . . . . *Sanchia*
15. Verry, Arg. & B. . . . . . . *Beauchamp*
16. Vert, a Saltoyre engrayled Or. . . . . *Franke*

17.   Arg. 5 Fusills in fesse G.   .   .   .   .   .   [*Hutton*]
18.   Party per pale Arg. & G. 3 Bends counterchanged.   .   *Dallington*

Upon yᵉ toppe of this Monument arched over, a halfe Statua, in yᵉ right hande a leading staffe, his head reclining upon his left, on the top of all upon a Torce his Crest, vizᵗ. an Asse passant ; under which— Franciscus Aiscough, Eques auratus, pater infrapositi Dñi Edwardi.— Below :

> Profuit hic patriæ Franciscus, strenuus, almus,
> Bello, Marte suo, Pace, suo ingenio.

Upon the side of Sʳ Edward Ayscoghs Monument above mentioned on a Pedestall eight sonnes & as many daughters, & these ensueing Escocheons expressing the matches of his children.

1.   *Aiscogh* empaled with—
     Or, a Greyhound cursant Sa. betw. 3 Leopards-faces, B.
           a Border engrayled Gules.   .   .   .   .   *Henneage*
2.   *Aiscogh* with—
     B. a Chevron betw. 6 Escalops Arg.   .   .   .   .   *Hatcher*
3.   *Aiscogh* with—
     Sa. a Fesse Chequy, Arg. & B. betw. 3 Horse-heads,
           erased.   .   .   .   .   [*Higham*]
4.   Arg. on a Bend Sa. 3 Owles of yᵉ First.   .   .   .   *Savile*
     Empaled with *Aiscogh*.
5.   *Hatcher* empaled with *Aiscogh*.
6.   Arg. 3 Bugles* passants Sa.   .   .   .   .   .   *Metcalfe*
     Empaled with *Aiscough*.
7.   *Savile* empaled with *Aiscogh*.
8.   Arg. on a Chevron B. 3 Crescents Or, between 3
     Trefoyles, slipped, Vert.   .   .   .   .   .   [*Williamson*]
     Empaled with *Aiscogh*.

[p. 79.]

Under a flatt marble lyes the body of William Ayscogh, Esq. sonne & heire of Sʳ Edward, who dyed 4 Feb. 1610.   He marryed Katherine daughter of William Henneage, of Haynton, Esq. by whom he had three Sonnes, two Williams deceased, and Sʳ Edward now living, & Katherine wife of Thomas Hatcher, Esq.

Upon yᵉ Stone their Coates empaled in brasse, vizᵗ.—
A Fesse between 3 Asses passants.   .   .   .   .   .   *Aiscogh*
A Greyhound cursant betw. 3 Leopards-faces B a Border
     engrayled.   .   .   .   .   *Henneage*

In the uppermost Window of yᵉ Quire :—
Gules, 3 Lyons pass. gard. barways in pale, Or.   .   .   .   *England*
Arg. 3 Roses within a Border engrayled G.   .   .   .   .   *Darcy*
G. a Chevron betw. 10 Crosse-crosseletts flowry, Or.   .   .   *Kyme*

---

* *Bugle*, i.e. a young Bull, Latin *Buculus*, or Calf, for Metcalf.—*Ed.*

In another :—

G. a Lyon rampant Argent. . . . . . *Mowbray*

In another :—

Quarterly, *Aiscogh*, & Or, a Bend, B. empaled with . . *Cathorp*

1. Arg. a Saltoyre G. on a Cheife of the 2nd 3 Escalops of
   ye 1st ; a trefoyle difference. . . . . . *Taylboys*
2. B. a Crosse chequy, Arg. & Gules. . . . . *Cokefeld*
3. G. 2 Chevrons within a Border Or. . . . . [*Charnel*]
4. As the First ; these last 4 quarterly.

Aiscogh empaling :—

B. a Chevron Arg. betweene 3 Mullets, Or. . . . *Hilliard*

Quarterly *Aiscogh, Cathorpe, & Taylboys* empaling Paly of 6,
   Arg. & B. . . . . [*Strelley*]

Aiscogh empaling :—

Or, 3 Piles in point Sa. a Canton Erm. . . . [*Wrottesley*]

Aiscogh empaling :—

B. a Fesse betweene 3 Floures de Lize Or, quartered with Vert, an
   Eagle displayed with 2 Heads Or.

Taylboys empaling these two following quartered :—

1. Quarterly Erm. & Chequy Or & Gules . . [*Gibthorpe*]
2. Arg. 2 Barrs G. a Border Sa. . . . . [*Thorpe*]
3. As ye Second.
4. As ye First.

Taylboys empaling :—

Quarterly { B. a plaine Crosse, chequy Arg. & G. . [*Cokefield*]
          { Vert, an Eagle displayed with 2 Heads Or.

Quarterly, *Aiscogh, Cathorp, & Taylboys* empaling

Quarterly { B. a Crosse chequy Arg. & G. . . [*Cokefield*]
          { G. 2 Chevrons within a Border Or . . [*Charnel*]

[p. 80.] The Crosse chequy, *Taylboys, Cathorpe & Aiscogh* quarterly,
empaling Quarterly, 1. Gules 2 Chevrons within a Border Or. 2. The
Eagle. 3. Gules a Fesse betw. 3 Flowers de Lize, Or.

Lastly in this Church these 6 Coates quarterly :—

1. G. a Fesse betweene 3 Flowers de Lize Or.
2. Vert, an Eagle displayed wth 2 Heads Or.
3. Vert, a Saltoyre engrayled Arg. . . . . *Hawley*
4. Erm. on a Canton Arg. a Saltoyre engrayled Sa.
5. G. a Crosse botony Arg. an Escalop Arg. on ye dexter quarter.
6. Gules 3 Mullets Arg. . . . . . . *Hansard*

All these empaled with

Quarterly { Gules, 3 Lapwings Or . . . . *Tyrwhit*
          { Gules, a Cheife indented Or . . . . *Grouall*

[p. 81.]

Barton upon Humber.

IN ST. MARYES CHURCH.

In yᵉ East Window of the Quire :—

1.

Quarterly { Arg. a Crosse patée betw. 4 Crosses humet Or *Jerusalem*
{ B. Semy of Flowers de Lize a Lyon ramp. Or *Beaumont*
Underwritten—Rex Hierosolomiæ cum Bello-Monte locatur.

2.

Quarterly { *Beaumont.*
{ B. 3 Garbes Or   .   .   .   .   .   [*Buchan*]
Underwritten—Bellus Mons etiam cum Bogwan consociatur.

3.

Quarterly { *Beaumont.*
{ *England*, on a Labell 9 Flowers de Lize, Or   [*Lancaster*]
Underwritten—Bellus-Mons iterum Longo-Castro relegatur.

4 defaced.

Underwritten—Bellus-Mons   .   .   .   .   Oxoniæ   .   .   .

On a Marble Gravestone in the Quire the portrayture of a man cutt in Brasse, about his head in a plate of Brasse this is ingraven, vizᵗ :—Credo qᵈ Redemptor meus vivit, et in novissima die resurrecturus sum, & in carne mea videbo Salvatorem meum.

About yᵉ Stone this :—Hic jacet Simon Seaman quondam Civis Vinitarius ac Aldermannus Londoñ, qui obiit xjº die Mensis Augusti Año Dñi MºCCCCºXXXºIIIº, cuius aïe et oïum fidelium defunctoꝛ propitietur Deus.   Amen.   This Escocheon :—
Barry wavy (of 6 Arg. & B.) a Crescent (Or)   .   .   .   *Seaman*

On another Gravestone :—Hic jacet Riĉus Haubord quondam Capellanus Parochïis istius loci, qui obiit primo die mensis Aprilis, Año Dñi 1471 ; cuius aïe &c.

[p. 82.] On the North wall of the Quire :—An elegant Monument of white marble raysed from the ground to a great height, on the top whereof stands an Angell holding a Trumpett ; below which a round Pillar of Touch, about which is wreathed in golden letters this :—Columna resurgendi Fides.   Underneath on a fayre Quadrature of Touch this in golden letters :—

Jucundissimæ Memoriæ piæ prudentis Matronæ, Janæ uxoris Johannis Shipsea, Rectoris Ecclesiæ de Saxby, quæ obiit in puerperio Maii 19º 1626, Ætatis suæ 22º.   Fuit natu generosa, fide docta, virgo casta, conjux fidelissima, laus sexus, viri gloria, modo Cælicola.   Underneath this Distich :—

Such Walls doe build God's house, true living stones,
Ingraven, as wee, by God, God's holy ones.

Upon yᵉ Woodworke in yᵉ Church these Coates depicted :—

1. B. a Griffon segreant Or, membred & bequed G.   *Rex Bohemiæ*
2. Quarterly { Gules, a Castle, Or . . . } *Rex Hispaniæ*
             { Arg. a Lyon ramp. P. . . . }
3. Quarterly { B. 3 Flowers de Lize, Or. . . } *Rex Angliæ*
             { G. 3 Leopards pass. gard. Or. . }
4. Or, an Eagle displayed wᵗʰ 2 heads, Sa. . . *Imp. Alemanniæ*
5. B. 3 Flowers de Lize, Or. . . . . . *Rex Franciæ*
6. G. a Lyon ramp. Or, armed & langued B.
7. Per pale Or & Arg. a Crosse patee betw. 4 Crosses
   humets, counter-changed. . . . . *Rex Hierosolymæ*

In another row below, these Coates :—

1. Paly of 6, Or & G. . . . . . . *Rex Navcrniæ*
2. B. a Lyon ramp. Or, queue fourche nowy G. . *Rex Arragoniæ*
3. Or, a Lyon ramp. within a double tressure counterflory G. *Rex Scotiæ*
4. Or, semy of Torteaux, 3 Leopards pass. gard. B. . *Rex Cypriæ*
5. G. a Crosse patoncee nowed set on degrees Arg. . *Rex Hungariæ*
6. Arg. 3 longe Boates in pale barwayes Or, at every ende a
   Serpents-head, G. . . . . . *Rex Portugalliæ*
7. G. a Horse saliant Arg. bridled & saddled Vert, yᵉ bosses
   & stirrups Or. . . . . . . *Rex Poloniæ*

[p. 83.]

On the other side of yᵉ Woodworke these in two Rowes :—

Quarterly { B. a Fesse betw. 3 Leopards-faces, Or. . *De la Pole*
          { Arg. on a Bend G. 3 payrant Winges conjoynd Arg.
                                                    Wingfield
Quarterly { Or, a Lyon ramp. B. . . . . . . *Percy*
          { G. 3 Lucies haurient Arg. . . . . *Lucy*
G. a Saltoyre Arg. . . . . *Nevile*
B. semy of Flowers de Lize, a Lyon ramp. Or. . . *Beaumont*
Chequy, Or & B. a Fesse G. . . . . . *Clifford*
Quarterly { Sa. a Crosse engrayled Or. . . . *Ufford*
          { G. a Crosse sarcely Sa. (*sic.*) . . . . *Bec*
G. 3 Water-bougets, Or. . . . . . . [*Ros*]
Or, a Bend Sa.
Quarterly Arg. & G. fretty Or, a Bend Sa. . . [*Le Despencer*]

In yᵉ lower Row :—

Quarterly { Arg. 3 Chapletts, G. . . . . . *Lascells*
          { Barry of 4, Arg. & B.
G. a Chevron Erm. betw. 3 Crosses pomels Arg.
Sa. a Bend flowry Or. . . . . . . *Bromflet*
G. a Crosse patonce Or. . . . . . . *Latymer*
B. 3 Crescents Or. . . . . *Rither*

B. Fretty of 8 peices Arg.   .   .   .   .   . *[Etchingham]*
Arg. on a Bend cotised, Sa. 3 Mulletts of yᵉ 1ˢᵗ.   .   . *Rowth*
G. 3 Mulletts Arg.   .   .   .   . *Hansard*
Or, 3 Barways B. on yᵉ middle bar an Annulet Or.   .   .   . *Aske*
In a Window—G. a Lyon ramp. Verrey.   .   . *Everingham*

Over Mʳ Everinghams seate :—
. . . a Trefoyle slipped Vert.
Quarterly, Arg. & Sa. a Bend G.
Arg. a plaine Crosse Sa. a Mullett G. in yᵉ sinister quarter.
Arg. a Bend wavy B.

These three following empaled togeather :—
1. G. a Lyon rampant Verry.   .   .   .   . *[Everingham]*
2. Arg. a plaine Crosse, Sa. a Martlett G. in yᵉ dexter quarter.
3. Arg. a Bend wavy Gules.

[p. 84.]

ST. PETER'S CHURCH.

Quarterly { Sa. a Crosse engrayled Or.   .   .   .   . *Ufford*
          { G. a Crosse sarcely Arg.   .   .   .   . *Bek*

Quarterly { G. on a Saltoyre Arg. a red Rose.   .   .   . *Nevile*
          { G. on a Fesse betw. 6 Crosse-crosseletts Or, a
          {   Crescent, Sa.   .   .   .   . *Beauchamp*

In yᵉ same Window below :—

Empaled { Barry of 10 peices, party p. pale Or & B.   . *Bernetby*
        { Arg. on a Bend cotised Sa. 3 Annulets of yᵉ 1ˢᵗ . *Dawney*

In yᵉ same Window the portrayture of one in compleate Armour, & his wife by him, boeth of them kneeling : Under written this :—

Orate pro anima   .   .   . Barnabe
Et Margarete consortis suæ, qui hanc
Fenestram fieri fecit.

In yᵉ next pane :—

Empaled { Arg. 3 Escalops G.
        { Barry of 10 peices, party p. pale B. & Or.   . *[Barnetby]*

Empaled { Arg. semy of Crosse-crosseletts 3 Cinquefoyles
        {   pierced G.   .   .   .   . *Saltmarsh*
        { Arg. on a Bend cotised Sa. 3 Annulets of yᵉ 1ˢᵗ. . *Dawney*

In another pane of the window a strange but very fayre, large & orient Escocheon.   It seemes to be these two Coates empaled, vizᵗ :—
Barry of 10 peices parted p. pale counter charged B. & Or, & Barry of 10 peices parted p. pale counter-changed Or & B.

Beneath this window lies the following Monument :—
[p. 85.] Upon a Marble the Portrayture of a Man in compleate Armour, cutt in brasse, with this Inscription :—Hic jacet Robertus Barnetby de Barton, Armiğ. qui obiit 21⁰ die mensis Septembris A⁰

Dñi 1440. In eleaven severall places about yᵉ Stone are written these words, Mercy and Grace. I fynde in an old manuscript belonging once to the Abbey of Thornton neare this place, these words, vizᵗ. Aᵒ Dñi 1241, Solut' Magistro Joħi Barnetby pictori pro Tabula et Tabernaculo magni Altaris depingend' 15ˡⁱ &c. And it is not unlikely (if we consider yᵉ strange mixture of Colours in yᵉ afore expressed Coate) that the Auncestor was a Paynter.

In yᵉ Quire :—
B. a Crosse patonce betw. 4 Martletts, Or, regard. one another
                                                    S. Edward
G. 3 Lyons pass. guard. Or . . . . . . *England*
Barry of 6, Or & B. a Bend G. . . . . . . *Gant*
B. semy of Flowers de Lize, a Lyon ramp. Or, over all a
   Bendlet compony Arg. & B. . . . . *Beaumont*

In yᵉ Closett windows in yᵉ North Isle :—
Beaumont (as above) in every pane.
Effigies Bellatoris et Feminæ, uterque gestans scutum predictum.

In yᵉ same Window this Escocheon :—
Arg. a Crosse botony G. resting on a segment of a Circle G. betw. 4
   Inescocheons Az. semée de liz, Or, a Lyon ramp. of the last
   debruised by a Bend comp. Arg. & G.

[p. 86.]

Irby juxta Grimesby.*

On a gravestone :—Hic jacet Johannes Malet . . . obiit . . . et Elianora uxor sua . . .

On another :—Hic jacet Johannes Malet . . . qui obiit . . . et Agnes uxor ejus . . .

In yᵉ East window of the Church :—Three Friars with shaven crowns, the first in greene, the second in blew, the third in Russett. Underwritten— Orate pro benefactoribus hujus operis.

Patronus, Comes de Clare.
Rector, Radulfus West.

Skartho.

Argent, 6 Crosses botony fitchy Sa. 3, 2, 1.
Argent, a plain Cross Gules.

---

* *Irby*, see *antea* p. 75.—*Ed.*

Clee.

On a pillar over the Fount :—Hæc Ecclesia dedicata est in honore Sc̃æ Trinitatis et Sc̃æ Mariæ V. IIIñ. Martii a Dño Hugone Lincolniensi Ep̄o Anno ab incarnatione Dñi M°C°XC°II° Tempore Ricardi Regis.

[p. 87.]

South Ormesby.

In the Windowes :—

Empaled { B. 3 Barres Or , ... *Constable*
{ G. semy of Crosses fleury, a Cinquefoyle Or *Humfreville*

Arg. 3 Barres G. in cheife a Greyhound cursant Sa. . *Skipwith*

B. 3 Cinquefoyles, Or . . . . *Bardolfe*

B. a Lyon rampant Ermine . . . . . . *Fitz-Simon*

Quarterly Ermine, & Chequy Or & G. . . . . *Gibthorp*

Empaled { *Skipwith.*
{ Quarterly, Sa. a Crosse engrayled Or, & G. a
{   Crosse sarcely Arg. . . . *Willughby*

Empaled { *Skipwith.*
{ Or, on a Chevron G. betw. 3 Flowres de Lize,
{   Vert, 3 Martletts d'Argent . . . *Hiltoft*

Empaled { B. semy de Lize, a Lyon ramp. Or . . *Beaumont*
{ B. 3 Cinquefoyles Or . . . . *Bardolfe*

On a gravestone :—Orate pro animabus Wilhelmi Skipwith Militis, et Agnetis uxis eius, qui quidem Wiłłus obiit Año Dñi 1485.

Patronus—Willughby Skipwith Arm.
Rector—Raphael Throckmorton.

Ketsby in Parochia de Ormesby.

Dñus Manerii, Wiłłus Skipwith, Arm.   Non ibi Ecclesia.

Wivelsby, Hole, Jtterby, Thrinscoo.

Villulæ in Parochia de Clee, ubi non Ecclesiæ.

[p. 88.]

Burgh in the Marsh.

In a Window in the North Isle :—

Erm. on a Cheife dented G. 3 Crosses Thau, Arg. . *Thurland*

Erm. on a Fesse G. a Mullet, Arg. . . . . *Quadring*

Quarterly { Arg. a Fesse Gules.
{ B. a Chevron betw. 3 Lozenges, Arg.

Empaled { Arg. a Fesse Gules.
{ Erm. on a Fesse daunsy G. 2 Leopards-heads, Arg.

In another Window—Orate pro animabus Joħis Halding et Matildæ ux̄is eius.

On a gravestone :—Hic jacet Gilbertus Knaresburgh Armig. qui obiit 17° die Mensis Januarii Año Dñi 1442.   Cuius animæ propicietur Deus.

Another :—

Quis jacet hic? Leonardus Palmerus generosus.
Quæ conjux dilecta fuit? Catherina.   Quis hæres?
Christopherus (cui nupta Anna est).   Quis filius alter?
Robertus.   Gnatæ quot erant? Tres, Elizabetha,
Ac Maria ac Helena.   An superant? Superant.   Ubi mens est
Defuncti rogitas? Dubio procul astra petivit.

Obiit — die Martii Año Dñi 1610, Ætatis suæ 70.
On a Fesse 3 Escallops.

[p. 89.]

Partney.

In the Windows :—

Empaled { Quarterly, *Castile* & *Leon.*
{ Quarterly, *France* semy & *England.*

Empaled { Quart- { Sa. a Crosse engrayled Or.(*Ufford*) }   [*Willoughby*]
{ erly { G. a Crosse molin Arg.   . (*Beke*) }
{ G. 3 Leopards-faces jessant de Lize Or.   .   *Cantelupe*

Thomas Havyn & Mary his wife.
On yᵉ wood-worke of yᵉ Font – Margery Hert.
On yᵉ Crosse—Orate pro animabus Thomæ Athaven et Mariæ uxoris, quorum aīabus propitietur Deus.   Amen.

Hundleby.

Quarterly { Sa. a plaine Cross engragled Or.   .   .   .   *Ufford*
{ G. a Crosse molin Argent.   .   .   .   .   .   *Beke*

Sawsthorp.

In a window :—The face of a woman like a Votisse ; Underneath hir name, Amabilla Charnells.

[p. 90.]

Rathby.

In a window:—Argent, on a plaine Crosse B. a Mound ensigned with a Crowne Or.

In another:—G. a Crosse molin Arg.   .   .   .   .   *Beke*
G. 2 Keyes in Saltoyre, yᵉ sinister surmounted of yᵉ dexter Arg.

In another:—Sa. a plaine Cross engrayled Or.   .   .   *Ufford*

In many places of the windows (not upon escocheons) are Crosses molin Arg. & Eagles displayed with 2 heads Or.

In the Chancell window:—The pictures of a man & his wife boeth attired in blew, kneeling, their handes elevated & expanded. Their Word—Sc̃a Maria, Ora pro nobis.

In yᵉ next pane the pictures of a man & a youth behinde him. The youthe girde with a red belt, yᵉ man having a hood of red hanging downe his backe, boeth their handes expanded. Their Word—Sc̃e Johannes, Ora pro nobis. Alonge the bottome of yᵉ whole window this inscription:—Orate pro animabus Roberti Staynes et Johannæ uxoris eius, et Walteri Freeman, Rectoris Ecclīe istius.

Taylboys was anciently Lord of this Mannour, who had a Chappell here (called Taylboys Chappell) now ruyned.

[p. 91.]

Spilsby.

In the Windows:—

Empaled { Quarterly {	Sa. plaine Crosse engrayled Or.	} *[Willughby]*	
	G. a Crosse sarcely Arg. .		
Gules, a Crosse patonce Or.			*Latimer*
Quarterly { Sa. a plaine Crosse Or.			*Ufford*
G. a Crosse sarcely Arg.			*Beke*
Empaled { Quarterly, *Ufford & Beke.*			
G. 3 Lioncells passants Arg. . . .			*Strange*

In two other panes *Beke*, yᵉ Quarterings defaced.

In another Window:—

Quarterly { Sa. a plaine Crosse engrayled Or. . .		*Ufford*
G. a Crosse sarcely Arg.		*Beke*
Gules, a Crosse patonce Or.		*Latimer*

In another:—

Quarterly { Gules, a Lyon ramp. Or. . . .		*Fitz-allen*
Checquy, Or & B.		*Warren*

Quarterly, *Ufford & Beke.*

Gules, a Crosse patonce Or. . . . . . *Latimer*

Empaled   { Quarterly, *Ufford & Beke.*
 { G. a Crosse patonce, Or. . . . . *Latimer*

In yᵉ North Isle :—A stately Monument raysed with three pillars to the top—Sixe severall Tables of Inscription on it in golden letters : in the first five the Scripture usually read at burialls, beginning Homo natus est &c. In the sixth this:—The Wiseman & yᵉ foole, | The Emperour & yᵉ slave, | The riche, yᵉ poore, yᵉ weake, yᵉ stronge, | Death coucheth like in grave.

Empaled   { Or, fretty of — peices, B. . . . *Willughby*
 { G. a Crosse sarcely, Arg. . . . . . *Beke*

Empaled   { Quarterly, *Willughby & Beke.* . . *Willughby*
 { G. Crusilly, 3 round Buckles Or. . . *Roseline*

Empaled   { The 3 former quarterly. . . . *Willughby*
 { Sa. a plaine Crosse engrayled Or. . . *Ufford*

Empaled   { All 4 quarters. . . . . . *Willughby*
 { G Besantee, a Canton Erm . *Zouche of Haringworth*

Empaled   { All quartered. . . . *Willughby*
 { G 2 Lyons pass Arg . . . . *Strange*

[p. 92.]

The West side of the same Monument Before yᵉ Front of it is raysed a fayre Tombe of Freestone adorned with these Escocheons :—

Empaled   {

Quarterly { Or, Fretty B. . . . . *Willughby*
 G. a Crosse sarcely Arg. . . . *Beke*
 G. Crusilly, 3 round Buckles Or . *Roseline*
 Sa. a plaine Crosse engr. Or . . *Ufford*

Quarterly { G. a Lyon ramp. Or . . . *Fitz-allen*
 Sa. a Frett, Or . . . *Maltravers*

Empaled   {

Quarterly { Or, Fretty B. . . . . [*Willughby*]
 G. a Crosse sarcely Arg. . . . | *Beke*
 Sa. a Crosse engrayled Or . . [*Ufford*]
 G. a Lyon ramp. Or . . . [*Fitz-allen*]
 Sa. a Frett Or . . . . [*Maltravers*]

Quarterly { Or, a Lyon ramp. double queue Sa. . *Welles*
 G. a Fesse daunsy betw. 6 Cross-cross-
      letts Or . . . . *Engayne*
 Barry of 6, Erm. & G. 3 Crescents Sa. *Waterton*

Empaled   {

Quarterly { *Willoughby, Beke, Roselyne, Ufford, Fitz-alane*
      & *Maltravers* quarterly, with a Crescent
      difference, *Welles, Engayne & Waterton.*

Quarterly { G. 2 Bends Or, betw. 3 . . Sa.
 Arg. a Chevron betw. 3 Buckles.

Empaled   { Quarterly, *Willughby* &c.
 { B. a Castle with a Scaling Ladder on yᵉ top, Or.

Empaled { Quarterly {
Barry of 10 peices, Arg. & G. a Lyon
    ramp., crowned Or . . *Brandon*
B. a Crosse sarcely, Or . . . *Bruyn*
Lozengy, Erm. & Gules . . *Rokeley*
}
Quarterly, *Willughby* &c.

Empaled { Quarterly {
Or, 3 Battering Rammes in pale, barways B. *Bertie*
A Castle triple-towered.
}
Quarterly, *Willughby* &c.

Empaled {
Quarterly, *Bertie, Willughby,* &c.
Quarterly {
Quarterly G. & Or, a Mullet in ye dexter
    quarter, Arg. . . . *Vere*
Vert, a Lyon ramp. Arg. vulned sur
    l'epale . . . . . *Bulbecke*
Barry wavy of 6, Arg. & B. . . *Samford*
Arg. a Fesse betw. 2 Bars gemells G. *Badlesmere*
Arg. a Saltoyre, Sa. betw. 12 Cherrys G.
    slipped Vert. . . . *Sergeaulx*
Arg. 3 Chevrons Sa. . . . *Archdeacon*
}
}

[p. 93.]

Empaled {
Quarterly {
Barry of 6, Arg. & B. 3 Torteaux in
    chiefe . . . *Grey of Ruthin*
Or, a Maunche G. . *Hastings, E. of Pembroke*
Barruly, Arg. & B. an Orle of Martletts G.
    Valence, E. of Pembroke
}
Quarterly, *Willughby,* &c.
}

The inscription :—Sepulchrum Dñi Ricardi Berty et Dñæ Catharinæ Ducissæ Suffolciæ, Baronissæ de Willughby et Eresby, Conjugum. Ista obiit decimo nono Septembris 1580 : Ille obiit nono Aprilis 1582.

The outward surface of the Monument bearing a very faire & large quadrature, ye frontispeice whereof is all fretty work garnished with Roses, disposed into two partitions being very fayre & large concaves almost from ye Top, y^e-arch-work raysed from two pillars in the middle, & at either ende adorned with 3 statuas. | The first an Hermite in his proper weede & habitt, holding his staffe in his right hande, his beades hanging downe ; over his head in an escocheon *Willughby & Beke* quartered. | The second Statua (which is in ye Middle) a Sarracen naked crowned, advancing ye Atcheivement of *Ufford & Beke* quartered.| The third a Wildman, his head girt with an oaken wreath, advancing the sheild of *Berty*, & the Castle triple-towered quartered. Under the feete of every Statua is a Death's head. | Upon a squared verge above the Hermite is a Bat displayed : Over the Sarracen something defaced : Over the Wildman a Saracen's head with a crowne of Gold, set on a Torce Or & Sable. On the top all over every Statua an Antique, ye offsprings of Tyme ; Under their feete Deaths heads.

The uppermost Monument in ye partition of ye 2 Quires :—

On yᵉ North side :—
A Bend betweene 6 Martletts.
6 Lozenges voyded, 3, 2, 1.
A Lyon rampant double queue . . . . . *Welles*
Billety, a Fesse daunsy . . . . . . *D'Eyncourt*
Semy of Crosse-crosselettes a Cinquefoyle. . . . *Umfreville*

[**p. 94.**]

In yᵉ North Chancell :—A fayre Monument of white Marble, upon yᵉ Area whereof lyes reclining a lady vayled, as in childebed, at her feete an infant in a cradle covered with a mantle of greene ; att either ende of the Monument two squared Peristillions of marble supporting two fayre pillars of Touch with yᵉ chapiters on yᵉ top curiously fretted with gold, ensigned with 2 escocheons, yᵉ first of them defaced, yᵉ other beares

Arg. on a Chevron engrayled B. betw. 3 Martletts Sable, 3
   Crescents Or. . . . . . . *Watson*

The second Quadrature raysed upon yᵉ first Arch-wise ; on yᵉ top whereof is this Atcheivement, vizᵗ, Quarterly, *Berty, Willoughby, Beke, Ufford, Fitz-alane* & *Maltravers, Welles* & *Engayne.* The Crest, a Batt displayed, mantled G. doubled Arg. In yᵉ concave of this Quadrature a Cheifetaine in his compleate armour guilt & embroidered, holding in his right hande a Batune ; below at his feete his Gantlett at his right hande, his helmet at his left. Himselfe in his full proportion & perfect feature as stepping forward in his commande. Within the hollowed concave of yᵉ first Quadrature 2 tables of Inscription in Touch, whereon in golden letters is written, in yᵉ first this :—

This presents unto you the worthy memory of the right-honᵇˡᵉ Sʳ Peregrine Berty. Knight, Lord Willoughby of Willoughby, Beake & Eresby, deservedly employed by Queene Elizabeth as generall of hir forces in the Low Countreys & in France, as Embassadour into Denmarke, & Lastly as Governour of Barwicke, where he dyed in the 47ᵗʰ yeare of his age, Aᵒ 1600, Leaving ishue by his wife yᵉ Lady Mary Vere, daughter to John Earle of Oxford 5 sonnes & daughters, Vizᵗ Robt. Lord Willoughby, Generall of yᵉ English forces in Denmarke, Peregrine, Henry, Vere, & Roger, & this vertuous Lady Catharine, wife to Sʳ Lewis Watson, of Rockingham, where she dyed in childebed yᵉ 15ᵗʰ of February, 1610, desiring to be here buried wᵗʰ her Father, for whom at her request, & for herselfe in his owne affection, the sayd Sʳ Lewis hath erected this Monument as a marke of boeth their virtues to all posterity, Aᵒ Dñi 1612.

Upon the frontispeice neare the Verge of the first quadrature is impaled *Watson* & *Berty.* Upon the front above the Basis of the Monument two compartments of Touch in which this Epitaph.

    Ut pereundo parit prolem, proh ! mortua Phœnix,
     Sponsa, peris, prolem sic pariendo tuam.

Sponsa, vale, *katharôs** vivens, **Catharina valeto** ;
Vixisti ut *katharos,** sic Catharina peris.
Quid dixi? Catharina peris? Non, alta Tonantis
Tecta petens rutili vivis amata polo.

On a gravestone—the pourtrayture of a lady, hir handes conjoined &
elevated ; about yᵉ stone these 8 escocheons :—

1. *Mortimer.*
2. *Bohun,* Erle of Hereford.
3. Quarterly, *Ufford & Beke* . . . . . *Willughby*
4. Bezantee wᵗʰ a Quarter Ermine . . . . *Zouch*
5. 3 Water Bougets . . . . . . *Ros*
6. Semy of Flowres de Lize, a Lyon rampant . . *Beaumont*
7. A Lyon with a double queue . . . . . *Welles*

Empaled { *Ufford & Beke* . . . . . *Willughby*
         { *Zouch* of Haringworth . . . . . *Zouch*

Written in a brasse plate about it :—Hic jacet Margeria quæ fuit
uxor Wilłi de Willoughby, Dñi de Eresby, quæ obiit A° Dñi 1391.

The uppermost Monument in yᵉ partition of the 2 Quires on the
North side :—

A Bend between 6 Martlets.
6 Mascels voyded, 3, 2, 1.
A Lyon rampant queue furchee . . . . . *Welles*
Billety, a Fesse daunsy . . . . . . *Deyncourt*
Semy of Crosses fleury, a Cinquefoyle . . . . *Umfreville*

[p. 96.]
In yᵉ Quire :—A Fayre Monument of Freestone wrought artificially,
on which lyes a fayre Statua of marble of a Cavalier in compleat
armour, his helmet encircled with a chaplet of Roses, under his Feet a
lyon.   The Statua lyes upon a fayre wrought stone of Alabaster (being
as yᵉ cover & closer of yᵉ Monument) curiously embroydered wᵗʰ divers
well polisht Images, each of them under arched workes, embatteled
above & wrought out of yᵉ stone.   At yᵉ head ende of yᵉ man an
angell guardian, body & winges azure, clasping in his handes an
escocheon, whereon a Crosse sarcely—*Beke.*

On the front these escocheons, Vizᵗ :—
A Crosse engrayled—*Ufford.*   Besanty—*Zouch.*

Empaled { a Cross sarcely . . . . . . *Beke*
         { a Cross engrayled . . . . . *Ufford*

6 Escalops, 3, 2, 1—*Scales.*   Upon a Fesse 3 Roundles—[*Hunting-
feld.*]   At the feete, Fretty of 8 peices—*Willughby.*

Lower in yᵉ Quire :—A very fayre Monument of Alabaster wrought
& embattled on yᵉ foreside. on the which lyeth on the nearer side a
Lady, on hir left hande hir husband, boeth in their full proportions :
Hee in compleate armour, his handes erected, a lyon under his feete,

---

* These two words are in Greek type in the original.—*Ed.*

under his head a Sarracens head crowned sett upon an helmett, close to which is a sheild wherein *Ufford* & *Beke* quarterly. Hirs is a rare peice of workmanship. Upon hir head a cawle of Fretty worke with double roses, a fillet of embroidery of Diamondes & Pearles turned up from hir brow the whole breadth of hir forehead, hir necke all bare, hir gowne according to y⁰ due proportion of hir body, sitting close above & so by degrees falling & closing to the slender of hir midle, downe along before a fayre border of buttons with stringes hanging downe on either side thereof, tasseled below, & above on either side entwined & fastened to two table Diamondes, a border of Goldsmithes (worke) of Akornes branched going acrosse over hir breast, & soe alonge downe [p. 97.] towards hir middle, & then turned rounde to hir trayne behinde ; hir sleeves close with a border along from y⁰ elbow, seamed with Pearles, hir cuffes covering hir handes to the knuckles, ringes upon hir fingers. Hir head couched upon a Pillow, which lyes upon a Boulster tasseled at either ende, supported by two Antiques couchant with longe beardes, & cowles about their neckes, & sitting bare-footed. Under hir feete 3 little Beagles wᵗʰ collars of rounde Beades.

On the side of it divers escocheons, the colours worne, onely yet there is to be seene on one 6 Mascles. on another coate Besantee, as it seemes, then 6 Mascles againe on y⁰ side to y⁰ Quire. At their feete there is empaled a Saltier, with Crosse Patonce. No Inscription.

On an old flat Marble much defaced :—At the head & at the lower ende of this gravestone are empaled :—On a Fesse 3 Roundles, & a Crosse sarcely. On one of the sides the Fesse with Roundles empaled with a Lyon rampant. On another side the Crosse sarcely empaled with a Coate not discernable : then y⁰ Crosse sarcely alone.

A very auncient Monument standing in the middle of the Quire :— On which lyes y⁰ pourtrayture of a Chevalier crosse-legged, in compleate armour, his handes elevated, upon his left arme his sheild, in which a Crosse sarcely, his sword hanging in his belt buckled upon his belly, y⁰ belt and scabbard garnished in divers places with crosses sarcely ; under his feete a lyon. On his right hande lyes his wife, hir handes elevated, about hir head a border of Roses, under hir feete a Talbot ; on hir right an Escocheon in which a Fesse & Border. On the side of y⁰ Monument [p. 98.] where the woman lyes, are divers Escocheons ; one seemes to be a Griffon, with Semy of Crosse-crosseletts fitched. Another seemes to be 3 Roundles on a Fesse ; y⁰ rest defaced. On his side a Crosse sarcely : at the head a Crosse engrayled. Some other escocheons about it. At the endes 4 old great & high Pillars set with the statuas of men & women : Much defaced & ruyned.

On another gravestone :—In a plate of brasse rounde about a large stone of marble, this Inscription, vizᵗ :—

DN DNM* qui fuerat apud Eresby nunc tumulatur
Vermibus esca datur hic, sed veniam modo sperat
Mors caro cara cinis, Christi nono ruit anno
Cæli quem scamno duc Christe precum medicinis
Anno . . . .
. . . . bene respice nomen
Ejus cognomen satis invenies ibi nudum.

[p. 99.]

Swallow.

In yᵉ East window of yᵉ Quire :—
Or, a Chevron G. a Cheife Verry   .   .   .   . [*St. Quintin*]
Arg. a Chevron betw. 3 Marygolds Gules.

On a gravestone :—Hic jacet Walterus Peddington quondam Rector
istius Ecclesiæ qui obiit Año Dñi 1432.

Briggesley.

No entry.

[p. 100.]

Castor.

The North Isle hath a Quire built by the Family of Houndon, as a
Hounde on the top set as a Finiall doeth show.   Within it lyeth (as yᵉ
Tradition goes) Sʳ John of Houndon : his effigies of stone in the full
proportion & compleat armour ; his handes closed & erected : at his
head two Angells supporting his pillow att either ende.

A little below without yᵉ partition lyeth under an arch in the wall
another of yᵉ same family (as yᵉ Townesmen say) much more ancient,
crosse-legged, his helmet & gorget of Male curiously wrought, as likewise upon his armes & legges, his sword hanging in a belt, upon which
lyeth a broad target, his surcoate large plaighted, a small fillet of gold
distinguisheth his helmet by the browes & about yᵉ head from yᵉ rest
of yᵉ same worke, & mayle below ; a Hounde under his feete.

Almost over against this on a high built Monument of stone in full
proportion (as the Tradition goes) lieth the wife of the afore-named
Sʳ John of Houndon, hir handes closed & erected.   This Quire
belongeth to William Trowsdale, of Houndon, Esq. to which family
yᵉ inheritance of Houndon descended.

---

* *Sic*, no doubt the name was illegible when Holles copied it.—*Ed.*

Houndon bore for his armes:—G. 3 Chevron wayes, Arg. in the dexter quarter a Talbot's head couped Arg.—*Houndon.*

In yᵉ South Quire belonging to Sʳ Rafe Maddison:—A Quadrature of white Marble sett in yᵉ wall raysed Archwayes from 2 columnes, within which in a Tabliture of Touch in golden letters this inscription:—Hic jacet Edwardus Maddison Miles, filius Christopheri, et nepos Gulielmi de Unthank in Com. Dunelmensi, qui duxit in uxorem Annam filiam [**p. 101.**] Witti Roper de Eltham in Coṁ. Cant. Arṁ. De eadem genuit Edwardum, Christopherum, Johannem, Aliciam, et centesimo Anno ætatis suæ obiit 14° die Februarii, Anno Salutis 1553. Over this is the effigies of himselfe, armed, with gilt spurres, his handes erect, kneeling at a deske on which is a booke ; Above all his Atchievement of Armes, Vizᵗ:—

Quarterly
{
Arg. a Chevron betw. 3 Martlets Sa.   *Maddison*
. . . 10 Closets.*
Arg. 2 Barres G. in chief 3 Torteaux .   . [*Aungevin*]
Barry of 6, Or & Vert.
}

His Crest, an Arm extended, in his hande a Battle-axe.

His Motto—Væh Timido.

[**p. 102.**]

Cokerington.

In yᵉ Church at yᵉ upper ende of yᵉ South Isle :—

A monument whereon a statua of marble, in its coate armour, his heade reclining upon his right hande, his sworde lying by his side ; this coat on yᵉ wall in white marble, Vizt :—

B. a bend Or, a mullet difference . . . . . *Scrope*

The crest a plume of feathers issueing out of a coronet, G. his motto—Arma Virumque cano. The escocheon supported with two Cornish Choughs. Underneath this inscription :—The thrice noble Sʳ

---

* G. Holles's draughtsman has here evidently mis-read the text, and has mixed together the imperfectly emblazoned bearings of two distinct quarterings, figuring the chevron of the former as charged with the bars, or closets, as Holles calls them, of the latter. Happily in this case Sir Edward Maddison's monument with its escutcheon may still be seen at Caistor. It shows us that while the first quartering is *Arg. a Chevron between 3 Martlets, Sa.* being the arms of *Merlay* of Unthank which the Maddison family, having married the heiress, adopted for a time, instead of their paternal coat, *Arg. 2 Battle-axes. Sa.* ; the second represents a quartering brought in by *Merlay*, and would be more fully described as *Barry of 10 argent & gules within a bordure azure charged with 8 martlets or*, being the armes of *Merlay* of Morpeth.

Yet another mistake is that the mason has put William, instead of John, Roper in the inscription, Anne the wife of Sir Edward Maddison, having been in fact daughter of John Roper of Eltham, and sister of William Roper, the husband of Margaret More —*Ed.*

Adrian Scroope, Knight, deceased December ye 10th 1623.   His Epitaph—

> Toombes are but dumbe Lay-bookes, they only keepe
> Their names alive, who in their woombes doe sleepe ;
> But who would pen the Virtue of this Knight
> A Story (not an Epitaph) must write.

Upon a pedestall raysed from ye side of ye tombe ye portraytures of 7 sonnes, wth this written, Similis in prole resurgo :—Two daughters kneeling & 2 lying in a cradle wth this—Pares et impares.

In ye South window . . . Joñis Howton et Agnetis uxoris . . . et Edmundi Howton—

In ye North window . . . Howton et Aliciæ uxoris Dñi Wiłłi Howton.

In another—Dñi Nicholai Howton 1519.

In ye glasse their pictures & their wives & some children, 2 of ye men having blacke tippets about their neckes, sett with white crosses.

Thomas Hopkinson—Robertus Raynold—Joñes Wren, in a North window.

Quarterly *France* & *England*.

[p. 103.]

Old   Hanworth.*

B. a Crosse botony Or.

Spridlington.

On ye North side of ye Quire a man in compleate armoure, a shirt of Mayle, his sheild on his left arme, his sword hanging in a chayne about his necke, & buckled about his belly, wth a girdle embossed with brasse bosses, Spurres on his heeles.   Tradition calls him Sr John Stokes.

Toft.

On ye Fount Stone :—

1. A Chevron.
2. Quarterly.

---

* *Sic*, but intended for Cold Hanworth.—*Ed.*

3. A Bend betw. 3 Crescents, a cheife Ermine . . *Fulnetby*
4. 3 Crescents, a cheife Ermine . . . . . *Fulnetby*
5. A cinquefoyle pierced —.
6. A playne Crosse —.
7. 2 barres —.

On a gravestone :—Here lyeth the body of William Yates & Anne his wife, departed this life Novembr 2° 1619.

[p. 104.]

Lowth.

In Fenestris :—

Or, a lyon rampant double queue Sa. . . . . *Welles*

Quarterly { Sa. 3 conyes heads rased Arg. . . . *Conisholme*
Arg. on 2 barres Sa. 6 Bezantes, a border engrayled Or.

Arg. on a fesse betw. 6 Martlets Sa. 3, 2, 1, a crescent of ye first.
Barry of 6, Arg. & G. on cheife a Greyhounde cursant Sa. collared Or . . . . [*Skipwith*]
G. a playne Cross, Argent.

On yᵉ next pane a Chevalier in compleat armour, his surcoat G., on which a playne crosse Arg. over all his breast.
Arg. 2 chevrons Sa. betw. 3 Ogresses.
(Arg.) A lyon passant & billets in border, G.

Quarterly { Sa. a Crosse engrailed, Or } *bis*. . . *Willughby*
G. a Crosse sarcely, Arg. }

Sa. 2 barres Nebuly Arg.
B. 2 barres Verry.
Arg. a Goate trippant, chayned & attired Or.
Sa. a saltier Arg.
Sa. an escalop betw. 3 crosses botony fitchy Arg.

In Campanili—

Empaled { Quarterly { Arg. a chevron betw. 3 crosses botony } *Mable-*
Sa. a border Sa. bezanty . . } *thorpe*
Arg. 2 barres engrayled Sa. . . *Staynes*
Sa. Fretty of 8 peices, Arg. . . [*Harrington*]

Thomas Fitz-William de Malberthorpe Armiger.

On a gravestone :—Orate pro anima Venerabilis Viri Dñi Thomæ Sedbery quondam Vicarii istius Eccliæ, qui obiit 18° die Septembris, 1504.

On another in a plate of Brasse :—Pray for ye Soule of Simon Lincolne, sometyme Marchant of the Staple, who dyed 25° Aprilis 1505.

On ye stone :—Nebuly a lyon passant in cheife.

[p. 105.]

On another :—

     . . . Ordine pleno
Quadringenteno quarto pariter atque deno
Fulgens ut Stella sua conjux hic Isabella
Sub petra duraque jacebat dum paritura
Spiritus amborum . . .

On a flat marble in a leafe of Brasse:—Anna Laughton wife of Thomas | Broxholme Esqr Marryed after | to William Gilby, gentleman, who died | the 28^h of March 1600, Ætat. 55.

Empaled { A Fesse wavy betw. 3 estoyles . . . *Gilby* / On a Fesse a mullet betw. 3 crosse-crosseletts fitched . . . . . . } *Laughton*

On ye North Wall :—Roger Stut dyed Maii 1° 1604.

In ye Quire, on ye Wall, in white marble :—

Fida Comes, custos que thori fidissima casti,
   Cui vir solus amor, solaque cura domus.
An tua ferali deplorem carmine fata ?
   Qua sine triste mihi vivere, dulce mori :
An cælo invideam, quod te rapuitque tenetque,
   Delicias animæ, dimidiumque meæ ?
Sancta sed eternæ vetat hec sententia mentis,
   Ordine quo certo stat sua cuique dies.
Signa, locus, Tabulæ, justi Monumenta doloris
   In te animi, Conjux, sunt Monumenta mei.
     Ad viatorem.
A sacro huic Cineri flores da, serta, Viator,
   Hic crocus, hic violæ, hic spica Cilissa cadat.
Illa sui nuper, dum vixit, gloria sexus,
   Magdala flos jacet hoc flore tegenda loco,
Carolus Yarbroughius cum lacrimis posuit—
     Obiit Maii 19° 1606, Ætat. 37.

[p. 106.]

In a lozenge wrought in stone, this Inscription :—

Frances Bradley daughter of John | Fairfax Esq. together wth hir husband | John Bradley, Sonne of Thomas Brad | ley Marchant of the Staple, & hir | two Sonnes Tho. Bradley, & John Doc | tour of Phisicke ; she died 15° Apri | lis 1608.

On the top of ye lozenge :—

Empaled { Or, a chevron G. betw. 3 crosses patee fitchee Sa. *Bradley* / Arg. 3 barres gemeus G. over all a lyon rampant Sa. . . . . . . } *Fairfax*

At ye right corner :—

Empaled { Bradley.
Party p. chevron Arg. & G. on a cheife of the 2nd
3 leopards' faces ; a crescent in bast, Or . *Chapman*

At the left corner :—

Empaled { Bradley.
Sa. on a fesse Arg. a lyon passant of ye 1st betw.
3 dolphins nayant of ye 2nd.

At ye bottom of ye lozenge :—

Quarterly {
Or, a chevron G. betw. 3 crosses formy fitchy Sa. *Bradley*
Arg. a chevron betw. 3 Gryphons heads, erazed G. *Tilney*
Barry of 6 peices G. & Arg. on a canton . . .
    a crosse flowry d'or.
Or, a bend sinister B.
Arg. a chevron betw. 3 martletts Sa.
Arg. a Fesse betw. 2 lyons passants guardants Sa.

[p. 107.] In a square peice of blacke Touche in ye wall :—

Here lyeth Richard Bound D^r of Phi | sicke, ye sonne of Robert Bound D^r & | Phisitian to ye late Duke of Norfolke. | He departed this life at ye age of 46, | & left behinde him his elder Brothers | Alexander & Nicholas, D^{rs} in Divi | nity, August 8°, 1603.

Or, on a Bend, B. 3 Floures de Lize erect, Or   . . *Bound*

On the South wall in ye Quire this inscription in Touch :—

Here lyes buryed the corpes of Ed | ward Heron, Esq., Servant to Queene | Elizabeth, sonne of Thomas Heron, | Brother to Sr Nicholas Heron K^{nt} | of the House of Edgecombe by Croyden | in the County of Surrey, who had to | wife Olive Bretton daughter to Tho | mas Bretton of Flemingham in ye Coun | ty of Norfolke Esq. who after ye death | of Thomas Heron was marryed to S^r | George Henneage of Haynton, Knight, | he died August 29, 1596.

G. a chevron betweene 3 Herons Arg. .   .   . *Heron*
Quarterly per Fesse endented Or & G. on ye dexter quarter a
  Mullet Sa. .   .   .   .   .   . *Bretton*
Or, a Greyhound cursant betw. 3 Leopards' faces B. a border
  engrayled G. .   .   .   .   . *Henneage*

[p. 108.]

Tuxford, Notts.

In orientali fenestra Cancelli :—

Orate pro anima Thomæ Gunthorpe, | Prioris de Novo Loco in Shirwod, qui | Cancellam istam ædificavit A° Dñi | M°CCCC°LXX XX°V°.

In prima fenestra Australi Cancelli :—

G. 3 Lyons passant gardant Or ; on a cheife B. yᵉ Virgin with
   Christ in her armes sitting in a Castle Or . *Newstead Abbey*
  Subscriptio :—Arme Monasterii de Novo Loco in Shirwod.

In fenestra 2ᵈᵃ :—

Quarterly { B. 3 flowers de lize Or . . . . [*France*]
    { G. 3 Lyons passant guardant Or . . [*England*]

  Subscriptio :—Arme Regis Angliæ Fundatoris de Novo Loco in
Shirwode.

In 3ᵗⁱᵃ Fenestra :—

G. a bend gobony B. & Arg., charged with 3 suns in their
   glory betw 2 Lyons-heads erased Arg., a border
   gobony, B & Arg . . . . *Gunthorpe*

  Subscriptio :—Arme Thomæ Gunthorpe Prioris de Novo Loco in
Shirewode.

In 4ᵗᵃ Fenestra :—

Sa. a bend betw. 6 crosses botony Arg. . . . *Lungvillers*

  Subscriptio :—Arme Joħis Lungvillers quondam patronus istius
ecclesiæ.

In Fenestra in Navi Eccliæ :—

All 4 in { Quarterly Arg. & Sa. a bend fusilly Or . *Cheyney*
pale, in yᵉ { G. a fesse dauncy between 6 crosse crosslets Or *Engayne*
same { Chequy, G. & Arg. . . . . *Vaux*
Escocheon { 4, defaced.

[p. 109] Subscriptio :—Orate pro anima Joħis Cheyney, Militis, qui
istam fenestram fieri fecit
    Juxta effigies Joħis Cheyney Militis.

In Fenestra opposita :—

Crumwell { Quarterly { G. a crosse sarcely Arg . .} *Willughby*
     { Sa. a crosse engrayled Or . .}
   { Arg. a cheife G. over all a Bend B. . . *Crumwell*

Neare to this Escocheon in the same window the picture of a Lady,
hir goune adorned with the ensignements of *Beke, Ufford* & *Crumwell*;
over hir head this inscription—Orate pro anima Dñæ Matildæ uxoris
Dñi Robti Willughby quæ illam fenestram fieri fecit.

In proxima fenestra :—

Orate pro animabus Johannis Stanhop et Catharinæ uxoris.

In yᵉ same window, he & his wife kneeling, over hir gowne :—

B. a crosse sarcely Or . . . . . [*Molyneux*]

On a flat gravestone in yᵉ North Isle :—

Obitus Ricardi Stanhop filii et hæredis Ricardi Stanhop de Rampton
Militis, qui obiit 2° die Mensis Martii, A° regni Regis Henrici vj
decimo, Cuius animæ propitietur Deus. Amen.

At the head of the stone on ye right hande, in an escocheon :—
A bende betw. 6 cross-crossletts, wch is Lungvillers coate, put for Stanhope.

In ye uppermost window of ye North Isle :—
The picture of a man in a red roabe wth longe yellow hayre, underwritten Eduardus Stanhope.

[p. 110.] Under an arch in ye same wall the effigies of a woman, in alabaster which, tradition sayes, is one of the Stanhopes.

Neare this is an old defaced Monument of Alabaster, whereon there remaynes the one halfe of a man in compleat armour, having on his breast the coat of Lungvillers, Vizt.—
A Bend betw. 6 cross-crosselets.

A monument* of Sr John White & his wife upon which are empaled—

Empaled { G. a Chevron Verry betw. 3 Lyons ramp. Or . *White*
Arg. a lyon rampant within a bordure engrayled Or (*sic*) . . . . . . *Harper*

[p. 111.]

Haughton neare Tuxford.

This mannour gives the title of Baron to the present Erles of Clare. †
It is seated on ye verge of ye Forest of Shirewood, & therefore more triumphes in pleasantnesse than richnesse of soyle ; & yet the best part of it is not unfertile. It is very well watered, ye River Idle running quite through it (as a lesser brooke doeth in another part) encompassing the house rounde about in its passage. The house itselfe is old building, little uniformity in it, as being built at severall tymes. The oldest part of it is ye Tower at ye entrance (as it should appeare by some escocheons cut in stone on ye sides of it North & South) built by some of the Family of Lungvillers or of Stanhope (for that family likewise for a tyme bore Lungvillers Armes for their owne paternal coate). The escocheons on ye South are these underneath—
A bend dexter between 6 cross-crosselets (three times).

* Thoroton (*Notts*. III, 225) gives not only the Arms, but the Inscription on this Monument, viz. "Hic jacet Johannes White, miles, filius et hæres Thomæ White, Armig. (servi quondam Philippi et Mariæ Regis et Reginæ Angliæ) et Agnetis Cecill, sororis Willielmi Cecill Baronis de Burghleigh, summi Angliæ Thesaurarii : qui quidem Johannes obiit in festum nativitatis Domini Anno 1625. Dorothea uxor charissima predicti Johannis White, filia Johannis Harpur de Swarkeston in Com. Derb. militis, in piam posteritatis memoriam et spem certam futuræ resurrectionis monumentum hoc posuit. Obiit . . die . . Anno." It was never filled up.—*Ed*.

† This account of Haughton by Gervase Holles, whom he describes as "one of his Majesties Masters of Requests, a great lover of antiquities," is quoted by Thoroton in 1677 (*Notts*. III, 359-61).

A bend sinister D°.

The bend sinister empaling the bend dexter

[p. 112.] These 3 on y° North side :—1. a bend dexter betw. 6 cross-crosselets ; 2. a bend sinister D° ; 3. a cross moline.

It appeares that y° Hall was built by y° last Sʳ William Holles, as appeares by this ensueing which is carved in stone on either side the entrance doore, & expresses y° yeare of the Lord his name & rebus.

On either side a holly branch with berries bearing a shield.

| W : H. A° Kⁱ 1545. | —This on the right hande. This on the left hande— | W : H. A° Dⁱ 1545. |

[p. 113]

On a flat gravestone in the Chapell :—

Jesu merci. Lady helpe. A bend betw: 6 cross-crosselets, empaling a cross within a bordure. | Orate pro aĩa Johannæ Stanhope uxoris Henrici Stanhope, Arm. Cuius aĩe &c.

North side of this gravestone lyes buried y° body of Sʳ William Hollys Knight qui obiit 18° die Jan. A° Dñi 1590 ; & Anne his first wife, daughter & co-heire of John Densell of Densel in y° county of Cornewall, Serjeant at law ; and Jane his seconde wife, daughter of Sir Richard Grosvenour, Knight, wᶜʰ Jane dyed without issue.

On y° outside of y° Chappell close by y° North wall lies y° pourtrayture of a Lady elegantly carved in Freestone, hir head supported by an angell, at hir feete . . . . No Inscriptions.

In y° Porch two other pourtraytures without Inscriptions ; they doe seeme by their habitts to have bin chaplaynes.

In Fenestris Capellæ :—

Empaled	Quarterly	Ermine 2 piles in point Sa. . .	Holles
		Arg. on a chevron betw. 3 crosse-crosselets Sa. 5 crescents of y° 1ˢᵗ .	Scopham
	Quarterly	Sa. a crescent surmounted of a mullet, Arg.	Densel
		Arg. a chevron G. betw. 3 Moore's heads, Proper . . .	Wenlocke

Quarterly {
Ermine, 2 piles in point Sa. . . . . *Holles*

Arg. on a chevron betw. 3 cross-crosselets Sa. 5
crescents of yᵉ 1ˢᵗ . . . . *Scopham*

Quarterly Or & G. on a bend Sa. 3 crosses formy
Arg. . . . . . . *Hanham*

Sa. a Crescent surmounted of a mullet in pale
Arg. . . . . *Densell*
}

[p. 114.] In fenestris Mansionis hujus Manerii hæc quæ sequuntur quam sæpissime.

1. *Holles* & *Scopham* Quarterly (with Crescent difference).
2. *Holles* & *Scopham* Quarterly, empaling *Densell* & *Wenlocke*.
3. Quarterly : 1. *Holles*. 2. a lion rampant (*Eastley*). 3. *Scopham*.
   4. *Hanham*.

[p. 115.]

Claxby.

In australi fenestra in Navi Eccłiæ :—
B. a Mullett of 6 pointes, Arg. peirced Sa. a border engrayled G.

In murum Australem Chori :—
A fayre monument of Freestone, on yᵉ top whereof as a finiall a large escocheon, whereon :—

Empaled {
Quarterly {
G. a merlin, Arg. . . . *Witherwike*

B. a mullet of 5 pointes Arg. pierced
Sa. a border engr. G.

Arg. a saltier betw. 4 Mullets G.

Arg. a saltier engr. Sa.

Arg. a Moore's heade couped, Ppr.

G. a bend fusilly, & on a cheife 3
mullets Arg.
}

Quarterly {
Lozengy, Arg. & G. . . *Fitz William*

Arg. a chevron betw. 3 crosse-crosselets, a border Sa. Besantee . *Mablethorpe*

Arg. 2 barres engrayled Sa. . . *Staynes*

Arg. a Lyon rampant, B.
}
}

On yᵉ right hande a Bird (Merlin) for Witherwicke's Crest, on yᵉ left, In a crowne a plume of feathers Argent, Fitzwilliam's Crest. Below one kneeling against a deske, his wife and daughter kneeling over against him. Beneath them in a large Area this inscription, Here lieth John Witherwicke, Esq. | Lord of this Towne, who deceas'd the | 25ᵗʰ day of December, Anno Dñi 1595. | He had to his first wife Katherine | Litlebury, & by hir no ishue living. After | he marryed Elizabeth Fitz-william | daughter of Wm. Fitz-william of Ma | blethorpe Esq., & by hir had ishue Ju | dith his sole daughter & heyre now li | ving Anno Dñi 1605.

On a flat gravestone underneath in a plate of Brasse Fitzwilliam's Coate & Crest, & this Inscription :—

Gulielmus Fitz-William, Arm̃. Anno ætatis suæ supra LXXX arma militiæ hujus deposuit.

[p. 116.] Uuderneath this Epitaph :—

> Weepe, poore men, weepe, heere our Mortality
> Laid a Maister in Hospitality.
> How he was religious, pious, constant,
> Twenty seaven Quietus est's demonstrant.
> From worldly troubles he never founde true rest,
> Untill from God he had Quietus est.

At the bottom of the Epitaph thus :—Anno Dñi 1634, mense Julii die 13° Vivit in æternum.

Another gravestone in Brasse :—

Empaled { Or, 2 chevrons G. . . . . . *Munson*
{ Lozengy, Arg. & G. . . . . *Fitz-william*

Here lyeth the body of Mary Monson wife of John Monson of Northorpe in the county of Lincolne, Esq. & daughter of William Fitz-William of Claxby in the said county Esq. who departed this life the 29th day of August, Anno Dñi 1638.

Upon a plaine Stone in yᵉ Quire :—
Hic jacet Dña Matilda de Witherwicke, cujus animæ &c.

Under an Arch there hath been an olde monument wholly defaced.

On a gravestone neare by :—
Hic jacet Joħes Witherwicke, cujus animæ propitietur Deus.

[p. 117.]

Laceby.

In australi fenestra Chori :—
Arg. 2 barres G. in cheife a Greyhounde cursant Sa. collared Or. *Skipwith*

In orientali fenestra Chori :—
G. a crosse engrayled, Argent.

Thetford.

In Fenestris :—Thomas Woodthorpe, 1495.
Arg. 3 palletts betw. 4 Mullets in bend Sa. . . . *Thimelby*
G. a cinquefoyle pierced betw. 3 crosse-crosselets d'Or. . *Umfravile*

In Baptisterium :—

Thimelby & *Umfravile* empaled.

Empaled { Chequy Or & G. a cheife Ermine . . *Tateshall*
{ B. fretty Arg. (y⁰ cheife part defaced).

[p. 118.]

Gunby.

In choro :—

On a fayre flatt marble the pourtrayture in brasse of a Judge in his Roabes, a girdle about his waste, & a knife like a Fawcheon hanging in it. On either side of him an escocheon in Brasse—that on yᵉ right hande defaced ; on yᵉ left hands this, Viz^t :—

Empaled { 3 Palletts on a cheife, a lyon passant guardant . *Lodyngton*
{ A cinquefoyle betw. 8 crosseletts flowry, 3, 2, 2, 1. *Umfravile*

Under his feete a lyon couchant guardant ; beneath this :—

Loudington William sancto tumulo requiescens,
Justus erat, quoniam (sit) celesti dape pascens.

Hic jacet Willielmus de Lodyngton | quondam juris Justiciarius | illustriss : Dñi nr̃i Regis Henrici | quinti de communi Banco, qui | obiit nono die mensis Januarii | A° Dñi 1419. Cujus aĩe &c.

In Ecclesia :—

On a fayre blew stone the pourtrayture in brasse of Sʳ Thomas Massingbeard in his armour compleate, & his wife ; on yᵉ Stone these armes :—

1. 3 Quaterfoyles a Seinglier passant in cheife, une croix sur le pall (l'epaule) . . . . . *Massingbeard*
2. Ermine a fesse . . . . *Bernake*
3. 3 Helmets within a bordure engrayled . . . *Halliday*
4. On a crosse humet 5 escalops between 4 lyons rampant.

About the tombe this inscription :—Sʳ Thomas Massingbeard, Knight & Dame Johan his wife specially desireth all reasonable creatures to give laud & prayes of yʳ charity unto our . . . Kinge & Queene.

[p. 119.] In australi Fenestra Ecclesiæ :—

G. a lyon rampant guardant Or, *bis*.

Empaled { *Massingbeard*.
{ *Fitz William*.

Patronus Thomas Massingbeard, Arm. Rector . . .

Humberston.

In hac Ecclesia jacent Herbertus Lacon, Gen. quondam proprietarius Abbatiæ de Humberston, & Dorothea, filia sua secunda, uxor Freschevilli Holles, Armig̃. cui duos peperit filios Willielmum et Darceum, qui uterque puerulus obiit.

Riby.

In a North window :—
Chequy, Arg. & G. a bend Sa.   .   .   .   .   .   *Bekering*

This coate stands agaynst the knees of a man kneeling, a booke before him, his gorget of male, that & all his armour white, a helmet on his heade ; over his head written :—

. . . Dei miserere mei :

below thus :—   . . . Thomæ . . . ekeri . .

In y⁰ Chancell South :—Arg. a playne crosse G.

North window :—The picture of S. George with y⁰ red Crosse on his sheild.

In a West window :—Thomæ Mosson . . fieri fecit.

There yet remaynes of this name in the Towne, who all bury under this window.

[p. 120.]

Witham juxta Boston.*

In Fenestris :—
Barry of 6 peices Or & B. a bend G.   .   .   .   .   .   *Gant*
Johes Gisburn de Bredlinton.
Arg. 3 lyoncells passants, over all a bend B.
G. 3 escallops d'Or.
G. 2 barres, & 3 estoyles in cheife Or.
G. a fesse between 3 escallops Ermine.
Or, a crosse engrayled Sa. over all a bendlet compony, Arg. & G.
Empaled { Checquy Or & G. a cheife Ermine   .   .   *Tateshall*
{ Arg. a Bend engrayled Gules .   .   .   .   *Culpeper*

[p. 121.]

Mansfield in Shirewood.

In Fenestris Chori :
Quarterly { 1. Arg. a lyon ramp. Sa. a border of cinquefoyles,
G.   .   .   .   .   .   .   *Pierpoint*
2. Arg. 6 Annulets, 2,2,2.   .   .   .   *Manvers*
3. B. 3 Hedge-hogs, Or   .   .   .   .   *Heriz*

This escocheon is supported with two beasts like Fummards Sa. :— the Crest a beast like a Fummard or Pole-cat, Arg.

---

* *Sic*, but perhaps Witham on the Hill, juxta Bourne, where Gilbert de Gant held lands.—*Ed.*

A little below in the same pane one in compleat armour, white, parcell guilt, his head bare, his lockes yellow, before him a booke open, lying as it were on a carpett embroydered with cinquefoyles, kneeling upon a like carpett, his handes closed & elevated. Underneath written :—Orate pro anima . . . Pierpount.

In the next pane a woman in red kneeling, hir handes closed & elevated. In the next a man with a shaven crowne kneeling, a Booke open before him.

Blackewall uno Magistrorum.

Per pale { Sa. a stag couchant Arg.
{ Arg. an eagle displayed Sa.

Johannes Deane.

In occidentali Fenestra Chori :—

Quarterly { B. 3 Floures de Lize, Ermine . . . . . *Burgh*
{ Or, 3 Pallets Sa. . . . . . . *Athole*
{ Or, a lyon rampant B. . . . . . *Percy*

Another defaced escocheon remayning onely thus :—3 bends, 2 barrs nebuly, 2 barrs, a cross fleury, 2 coates defaced ; empaling Per pale— 1. defaced ; 2. 3 barrs nebuly.

[p. 122.] In Orientali Fenestra :—

Empaled { Sa. a stag couchant Arg.
{ Arg. an eagle displayed Sa.

Empaled { Arg. a Foxe head erased Sa.
{ G. 2 chevrons Arg.

B. a barre Arg. betw. 3 lyoncells rampants Or.

In Australi Fenestra :—

England.

B. billety, a fesse dansy d'Or . . . . . *D'Eyncourt*

Arg. 2 barrs & a canton G. a border engrayled Or.

G. 3 lyons passants gardants in pale barways Or ; over all a bendlet B.

B. semy of crosse-crosseletts ; 3 sex-foyles Arg. . . *Darcy*

Vairè Or & Gules . . . . *Ferrers*

Arg. 3 crosses botony fitchy Sa. on a cheife 3 mullets Or, pierced.

In muro australi effigies bellatoris ex familia Trusbuttorum, ut ab incolis dicitur.

A brasse plate on a gravestone :— Here lyeth the Corps of John Chambers & Alys his wife, who lived togeather in the feare of God 33 yeares, & had Issue togeather 7 sonnes & 7 daughters, & when they had thus well run their race, John departed this life godlily, & Alys forsaking this worlde did cleave unto Christ, who receaved hir unto his mercy the first day of April 1564. God Grant them a joyfull resurrection in Christ Jesus their Savyour. Amen.

On ye left hande under ye North ende of ye Altar lieth Dorothy, ye first wife of Gervase Holles of Great Grimesby in y^t county of Lincolne, Esq., togeather with her little Infant, of whom she dyed in childbirth ; boeth under a square Freestone without Inscription.

[**p. 123.**]   Upon y^r wall next hir grave hanges a square Table lozenge-wayes, whereon their armes & this inscription :—

The blazon of y^t armes in ye greater escocheon* :—

1. Ermine 2 piles in pointe Sa.   .   .   .   .   *Holles*
2. Arg. on a chevron betw. 3 crosse-crosselets Sa. 3 crescents of the first   .   .   .   .   .   .   *Scopham*
3. Quarterly Or & G. on a bend Sa., 3 crosses formy fitchy of the first   .   .   .   .   .   .   *Hanham*
4. Sa. a crescent surmounted of a mullet in pale Arg.   .   *Densel*
5. Arg. a chevron G. betw. 3 Moores heads couped Or   .   *Wenlocke*
[**p. 124.**]   6.   Gules a chevron between 3 Rose-trees, trunked & eradicated Or   .   .   .   .   *Skewys*
7. B. a plaine crosse betw. 4 leopards-faces Or   .   *Kyngston*
8. Ermine between a cheife & chevron Sa. a leopard's face Or   .   .   .   .   *Pourdon*

These coates quartered are empaled with :—

1. Barry of 8 peices Ermine & Gules   .   .   .   *Kircketon*
2. Sa. a pheon Arg. a crescent Or, difference   .   .   *Nichol*
3. Arg. a chevron G. a Labell of 3 Sa.   .   .   .   *Prideaux*
4. As the first.

The escocheon on the right hande :—

Empaled { *Holles, Scopham, Hanham, & Densel.*
{ B. a Bend betw. 6 escalops Argent   .   .   *Frescheville*

The escocheon on the left hande :—

Holles, Scopham, Hanham, Densel.
B. a crosse betw. 4 leopards faces Or   .   .   .   .   *Kingston*

The crest on a Torce Arg. & Sa. a Blackamore'e head. Proper, half-faced, a jewell in his eare, about his head a wreath Arg. & Bl. a crescent Or, for difference.

The motto :—Nec pudore rubens, Nec timore pallens.

---

* In the escutcheon as figured these eight coats are several times repeated so as to form 20 quarterings, arranged thus :—
1. Holles, 2. Scopham, 3. Hanham, 4. Kingston, 5. Pourdon :—
6. Densel, 7. Wenlocke, 8. Skewys, 9. Pourdon, 10. Kingston :—
11. Kingston, 12. Pourdon, 13. Holles, 14. Scopham, 15. Hanham :—
16. Pourdon, 17. Kingston, 18. Densel, 19. Wenlocke, 20. Skewys.—*Ed.*

[p. 125.]

Gresby, Caburne, Withcol, East Halton, Bradley.

(No entries.)

[p. 126.]

Limbergh Magna.

Patronus :—Willus Pelham, mil. Vicarius . . .

Normanby.

(No Entry.)

Toft.

On the Font these escocheons :—1. a chevron ; 2. Quarterly ; 3. a Bend betweene 3 crescents, a cheife Ermine ; 4. Three crescents a cheife Ermine ; 5. a Cinquefoile peirced ; 6. a plaine Crosse ; 7. two Barres.

A gravestone of William Yates & Anne his wife, who dyed 2 November 1619.

Hanworth.

B. a crosse botony d'Or.

Hacthorne.

Limbergh parva.

[p. 127.]

Uzleby, Lissington.

East Ravendale, West Ravendale.

(No Entries.)

Walmesgare.

This church was new-built in yᵉ yeare . . . by Lyonell Skipwith, grandchilde of Sʳ William Skipwith of Ormesby, & son of John Skipwith & Elianor his wife, daughter of John Kingston of Great Grimesby, Esq. It is a very handsome little Pile, & vaulted underneath ; In which vault lyes buryed yᵉ said Lyonell Skipwith.

[p. 128.]

North Kelsay.

East window of yᵉ Chancell :—
Arg. a chevron B. betweene 3 red roses– *bis.*

South window of yᵉ Chancell :—
G. a crosse Sarcely, Arg. . . . . *Beke*

North window of yᵉ Chancell :—
Arg. a chevron Sa. betweene 8 Martletts, d'Or, five above &
three below . . . . *Hardreshill*

(These Martlets are yellow, but I conceave they should be Gules, & then it is Hardreshill's coate who (aunciently & for a long tyme) was Lord of this mannour).

In prima Australi fenestra ecctiæ :—
Arg. a crosse sarcely G.
Arg. a chevron B. a file with 3 Lambeaux G.

In secunda Fenestra Australi :—three bendlets.
Arg. a chevron Sa. betw. 8 Martlets in orle, d'Or . *Hardreshill*

In tertia Fenestra Australi :—
Arg. 3 bars Sa. . . . . *[Bussy]*

In Fenestra boreali :—. . . Thomæ Bard, . . .

Under this Window, a little on yᵉ right hande, a hollow Arch under the wall, on yᵉ Flore of which a Square freestone wᵗʰ yᵉ picture of a man, & this Inscription :—

Hic jacet Jones Wyga qui fecit | istam Insulam, et qui obiit die | Aplorum Simonis et Judæ Aᵒ Dñi | 1372. Cujus aïe ppitietur Deus. | Amen. Att yᵉ head a crosse fleury.

[p. 129.]

Alesby.

In Fenestris Cancelli :—
Arg. 3 Hawkes' lures Sa. *ter.*
Arg. 3 Hawkes' lures Sa. a crescent Sa. in the middle of yᵉ
escocheon ; *bis.*

In Australi Fenestra Eccliæ :—
Party p. fesse Arg. & G. a Lyon ramp. so parted, Sa. & as the first ; *ter*.
The same with a Cinquefoile Arg. on the Lyons breast.

In Fenestra boreali . . . Martini quondam . .

In Fenestra Orientali :—
Sa. a bend counter-embattled Arg. empaling
Arg. two chevrons Sa. a chief defaced.

On a gravestone :—
. . Joħes Martin quondam Rector | istius Eccliæ, qui obiit |
. . . Novembris . . .

[p. 130.]

Broughton cum Manneby
& Kaylesthorpe.

On a gravestone in the Middle Isle :—
Hic jacet Dominus Joħes Goldsmith | quondam pñus hujus . . .
qui obiit | Anno Dñi 1477. cujus aīe p̄pitietur | Deus. Amen.

On a gravestone in yᵉ Quire :—
Hic jacet Dñus Thomas Vaus | quondam Rector istius Eccliæ de |
Broghton, cujus aīe &c.

On another :—Hic jacet Margareta filia Roberti | de Halton.

On a blew stone in a plate of Brasse :—
Here lyeth the body of Katherine | Anderson onely daughter of
Steven | Anderson of Broughton in yᵉ County | of Lincolne, Esq. &
of Katherine | his wife, daughter to Sʳ Edwyn | Sandys, of Ammersley
in yᵉ County | of Worcester, Knight, who died the | twenty fifth of
September Anno | Dñi 1640.

Under an Arch in yᵉ North wall of yᵉ Quire :—
A fayre. & auncient Monument of Freestone, on the Frontispeice of
which are three Escocheons, That in the middle beares Fretty, a
chiefe ; That on the right beares two Lyons passants ; On the left
hande, the Fretty coate with the chiefe is empaled with the two Lyons.
At the two extreames of the Frontispeice a Lyon rampant, but not
upon an Escocheon.

[p. 131.] On the top lieth a chevalier in compleat armoure with his
wife on his left hande, boeth in full stature & proportion. His surcoate
Fretty with a cheife, his Gorget of mayle, a Collar of SS about either
of their neckes, his right hande reaching over his body, & holding hir
by yᵉ right hande ; in his left hande he holdes his right hande Gantlet ;
under his head a high Helmet (on which a Ramme for his crest), &

under his feete a Lyon holding in his mouth a longe Scrowle, but noe Inscription; onely on his lefte legge (which certainly is but lately done) these wordes engraven, vizt—Here lyeth Sr Henry Retfurth (lego Rydford).

At the foote of this on ye grounde lyeth a fayre blew Marble, on which in Brasse the effigies of a man & his wife accurately done ; he is in compleat armoure, his Gorget mayle, his handes closed at his breast (as likewise hirs), either of them holding a heart betweene their handes ; a Lyon under his feete, a Talbot at hirs.   There have bin 4 Escocheons in brasse at the head, & an Inscription rounde about, but all torne away.   Not unlikely some Monument of the Rydfords, who had fayre possessions in these parts.

In Fenestra Australi :—

P. pale { Arg. Fretty Sa. a cheife Sa.   .   .   .   .   *Rydford*
        { G. 2 Lyons passants Arg.   .   .   .   .   .   *Strange*

In alia Fenestra :—

Arg. Fretty Sa. a cheife defaced   .   .   .   .   .   *Rydford*
A cheife G. the coate defaced.

[p. 132.]

West Rasen.

In boreali Fenestra Eccłiæ :—

A Bishop in his Pontificalibus, holding in his left hande a hammer, a horse leg with his hoofe, & nayles in the shoe lying over above his right knee, & above that over his right hand neare his breast a heart (as it seemes) enflamed, streaming out droppes of blood.   On ye top of ye window :—

G. a cinquefoyle peirced Arg.   .   .   .   .   .   *Powger*

Below this (raysed up close to the wall) is a fayre Monument of Alabaster, upon ye flatt of which (being a very fayre & large Stone) are traced 3 pictures of ye husband, wife, & their sonne, with these following Inscriptions, Viz^t :—

Hic jacet Johannes Suthell, | Dñus de West-Rason, qui obiit | 4to die Maii, A^o Dñi 1445.

Hic jacet Johanna Powcher, | Dña de West-Rason, quæ obiit | 19° die Julii, A^o Dñi 1451, quoƨ | aĩabus propitietur Deus.

Hic jacet Henricus filius | Joħis Suthell . . . cujus . . .

Under ye husband's feete in an Escocheon an Eagle display'd : at hir feete a Cinquefoyle cutt in ye Stone.

On ye head of ye Monument these 3 Escocheons :—

(I. Three*.   II. a bend between in cheife six ermine spots, in base 3 crescents in bend.   III. a cinquefoile.)

---

* It is difficult to say what the objects here figured are intended to represent ; they resemble a stem or handle from the top of which five sails or wings project fan-wise.—*Ed.*

On ye side of ye Monument these other 3 Escocheons next
ensueing :—

[p. 133.]   I. a bend ; II. a chevron engrailed between three martlets ;
III. Ermine, on a canton an Eagle displayed.

In orientali Fenestra Cancelli :—
Sa. a Cinquefoyle Arg. peirced G.
G. a Lyon rampant d'Or.
Arg. on a cheife Sa. 2 Mulletts d'Or peirced.

(— a fesse dancettée between ten billets, 4 in cheife & 3, 2, 1 in
base —.   On a bend six fleurs de lis).

In Fenestra Australi Cancelli :—
Or, a Lyon rampant B.   .   .   .   .   *Percy*

In Orientali Fenestra Insulæ Borealis :—
England.
Or, a plaine crosse Sa.   .   .   .   .   .   .   [*Vescy*]
G. 5 Fusils in fesse d'Or.

Below these on ye middle parte of ye window a Chevalier in compleat
armour, his Gorget & Helmet of golde, his Helmet rounde curiously
wrought on ye top, Argent. His wife by him, she having a Huke on
hir head, ye labels hanging downe on either side, they boeth kneeling,
he on ye left side of a sheilde, she on ye righte, they boeth advancing
ye same on high.   The Coate is :—
G. a Cinquefoyle Arg. peirced   .   .   .   .   .   *Powcher*

Underneath in old characters these broken fragments .   .   .   .   .
OMO .   .   .   .   CAISE .   .   .   & the next pane   .   .   .   P
.   .   MAVD SA .   .   .   M .   .   .

[p. 134.]   In alia Fenestra Insulæ Borealis :—
This Atcheivement, vizt Gules a Cinquefoyle Argent, pierced. Upon
ye Helmet a Chapeau G. having two pendents behinde, on which
standes above a Cinquefoyle Argent, peirced, & another below ; y^e
endes with buttons & tassells ; the Crest, an Escallop Argent. The
Coate is hung up.

In proxima Fenestraa :—
England.
G. 5 Fusills in fesse d'Or.
(— on a bend — 4 crosses moline —).

In ye same window the pictures of a man & a woman in a very large
proportion. For their fashion differing from others in this kinde, She
on ye right hande, he on ye left. She in a gowne of Red, hir hayre
twined about hir browes, as in ye fashion of a wreath, having a garland
above hir head, & under hir head a pillow curiously wrought with gold,
hir right hand close to hir breast lifted up, in hir left hande she holdeth
a booke.   The man standeth in the other pane, lapped about with a
mantle of Red, barefoote & bare-leg'd, laying his right hande upon his

left breast, his head uncovered, & just over him this Coat :—
Or, a playn Crosse Sa.

Over hir head a Coate which seemeth to be farre auncienter then yᵉ
other Coates of yᵉ Cinquefoyle Argent in Gules.   It is blazoned thus :—
Arg. a Cinquefoyle pierced G. within an Orle of Besantes.

Below them in olde characters :—PRIEZ PVR ESTEVEN | SIBRI
PVR   SA   MERE | MARGARET—& these following fragments
. . .   AVSI REDEV . .   DE . . EVS . . ENA . .
IT . . MERCI.

[p. 135.]   In another window :—
The picture of yᵉ murdring of Sᵗ Thomas Bekett.   Foure Souldiers
armed with their swordes bent against him, the foremost of them
having upon his sheild a Crosse formy Sa.   The Archbishop is pictured
twice ; once in his Pontificalibus with his Crosse advanced, holding in
his left hande a chalice.   Then again, lower, as despoyled of all his
Episcopal attyre, bowing downe, & offering his necke to yᵉ smiters.

In orientali Fenestra Insulæ Australis :—
Quarterly, *France* (semy) & *England*, a File with 3 Lambeaux,
Argent.

The same, quartered with Barry of 6, Or & G.
Quarterly, *France* (semy) & *England*, a File with 3 Lambeaux,
      Ermine   .   .   .   .   .   .   [*Lancaster*]
Chequy, Arg. & G.   .   .   .   . [*Vaux*]
Arg. on a Bend, B. Crosses formy d'Or.

(— two bars wavy — on a chief — 3 martlets —).

(— a saltire — in fess point a roundle charged with a cinquefoil —).

Below on yᵉ window are foure pictures.   Upon the first pane a
woman wᵗʰ a Huke* on hir head, like a Tippet, hir handes elevated.

The 2ᵈ is a Chevalier in compleat armour, his Dagger pendent
before, his handes closed & elevated, a paire of Beades hanging
betweene his fingers, under him this Fragment . . SHIER . .

The next a Chevalier having his *Baltheum Militare honoris* more
curiously wrought lozenge-wayes, his Armour close to his hippes guilt,
& adorned more than the other, his handes closed, & elevated. his
Beades hanging down. [p. 136.]   Under him in certain broken
Fragments . . ETESTAIE . .   ET PVR . .

At yᵉ other ende (as at yᵉ first) a woman kneelinge having about hir
necke a Gorget, or close Rayle comming low downe almost to cover hir
shoulders ; over hir head a Huke* comming downe on either side hir
face, & lined with Furre.   Under hir this Fragment . . a . . .
gafen me . . .

---

* *Huke*—a kind of Cape with a hood, made of cloth or stuff pleated, the upper
part gathered and sewed together with a tassel on the top. *Oxford English Dict.*

Over hir head at either ende the Cinquefoyle Argent in a field G. . . . . *Powger*

In Australi Fenestra :—

G. a Cinquefoyle Argent peirced . . . . . . *Powger*
(— a bend compony —).

Above this Escocheon is a man kneeling, his handes elevated, having about him a gowne or mantle of Azure, his necke all bare, on his head a round close Capp, his hayre turned up, & curled above his forehead, & hanging downe something behinde; above his head these Fragments in Saxon characters:—PVR . . . ER NEMO. And below on either side of him . . TECA . . R . . CV . . A . . FEME MAVDE ECES . . ESTER . . TE . . FEN . . RI . . RVNT.

In alia Fenestra Australi :—

England.

Or, a Lyon rampant, Purpure . . . . *Lacy*
Or, 3 Chevron-wayes G. . . . . *Clare*

In ye North Isle this Atcheivm^t of Armes paynted on the wall :—

1. Quarterly, G. & Verry a Bend Or . . . . *Constable*
2. G. a Pale fusilly Or.
3. Or, a cheife B. . . . . [*De Lizures*]
4. Chequy Or & G. on a cheife of ye 1st a Lyon passant Sa.

[p. 137.] [*Cumberworth*]

5. Arg. 2 Bars engrayled Sa. . . . . . . *Staynes*
6. Arg. a Chevron betwene 3 Martletts, Sa.
7. G. an Eagle displayed, Arg. . . . . . . *Sothill*
8. Arg. a Bend Sa. . . . . *Paynell*
9. G. a Cinquefoyle Arg. peirced . . . . . . *Powcher*
10. G. a Lyon rampant Verry . . . . . *Everingham*
11. Or, on a plaine Crosse Sa. 5 Flowers de Lize, Or.
12. The last as ye First . . . . *Constable*

Below in a Scroll this Motto :—Sois ferme. The Crest a Ship in harbour Sa. These letters R.A.S. in severall panes of a Window neare by.

Market Rasen.

Quarterly, G. 3 Lyoncells passants gardants Or.
B. 3 Floures de Lize, Or ; over all a File with 3 Lambeaux Arg.
Princeps Walliæ

[p. 138.]

Newton (by Toft).

In australi Fenestra chori :—

G. a Crosse botony d'Or . . . . [*Paynell*]

Welton.

In boreali Fenestra Eccłiæ :—
Arg. 2 Bars gemeus Sa. a Border engrayled G.

Below in Saxon letters—DE APPLYN, just over which is a man kneeling gowned.

In another Window these Fragments :—
. . . FRAT . . NIT . . FIERI FECIT.

In alia Fenestra :—
Arg. 3 Fusills in fesse Sa. each charged with a Plate.

In the same Window these Fragments :—
. . . VB . . . DE . . . TRE . . . EDEL . .

On a gravestone :—Hic jacet Riĉus Stokes quon | dam Rector Eccłiæ hujus qui | obiit Año Dñi 1403, &c.

Upon a Table hung upon a wall in yͤ Chancell :—
[p. 139.] Memoriæ Henrici Tayler | viri digni in artibˢ Maḡri, | quondam Socii Cl. Collegii Sĉi | Joħis Baptistæ Cant' hic se | pulti, amoris ergo dictatum per | familiarem suum G. W. Obiit | 19° die Junii 1619.

> Mi Taylere vale, quem Mors male sustulit ultra
> Expectatum Mors, sed non dominabitur ultra.
> Qualis enim fueras, fueris post fata superstes,
> Vir juvenis, doctus, facundus, sale facetus,
> Ingeniosus, amans, adamatus, dignus in omni,
> Celebs, modestus ; quid et hæc morientur in unum ?
> Mors tua damna tuis, nec in ullo profuit ulli,
> Terra tui terram teneat, meliora supersunt.

Netleham.

In australi Fenestra Ecclesiæ :—
B. on a Chevron engrayled Or, 2 red Roses slipped between
   3 Doves' heads erased Arg. holding in their bills
   Olive-branches Proper   .   .   .   .   *Holbech*
This coate ensigned yͤ top wᵗʰ a Miter d'Or.

Neare by is a large Monument of Freestone, on the which the said Armes are engraven on the head, & on the side, where is also one of the heads single with the Flower in it. It is yͤ Monument of Bishop Holbech.

In the Wall neare thereunto :—UX. S. C. | Dorotheæ Nethercootes ejusque | animulæ candidiss. quæ ad celos | evolavit [p. 140.] 29 Junii 1603, ob | pietatem, castitatem, modes | tiam, multasque suavitates, ac gratas gratias ; | Tres, quos tulit liberos optima spe ac specie, | Martham, Mariam, Thomam. | Denique ob familiam probe | curatam ac sobolem, Gualterus | Nethercootes Conjunx moes | tissimus, æterni desiderii et | amoris ergo posuit.

On yᵉ Basis of two Pillars at yᵉ endes—Vitæ—Morti.
In the middest :—In utrumque paratus.

These Armes empaled :—

Empaled { Ermine, a Bend engrayled G. a Cheife B. . *Nethercootes*
{ B. on a Chevron Or, 3 Roses G. a Canton Erm. . *Randes*

Someretby.*

In boreali Fenestra Chori :—
Arg. 3 Chaplets with Roses, Gules . . . . *Lascels*
G. 3 Mascles Arg.
G. 4 Fusills in fesse Arg. a Border engrayled, Or . . *Nevile*

[p. 141.]

Severby.

In boreali Fenestra :—
The picture of a man & his wife in very Orient Colours ; she in a garment of Blew buttoned downe before, a Gorget of white about hir necke, a Tippet comming downe either side hir head, having about hir temples a Chaplet, hir handes elevated, having gloves on them, which are buttoned above.

He in a red Gaberdine, his Gorget blew, yᵉ foreparts of his garment white, yᵉ hayre of his head shed in yᵉ middest, & hanging downe on either side.

Priez pur Geffray de Thoresby
et pur Johanne sa feme.

Arg. 3 Martlets Sa.
Sa. a Chevron betweene 3 Estoyles of 6 pointes, Arg. on yᵉ
chevron a Crosse botony fitchy . . . *Thoresby*

A most curious lively peice of yᵉ Virgin Mary as mourning ; hir armes a-crosse, with hir head bowing downe & countenance dejected ; hir inner garment before red, & hir sleeves of the same colour, having about hir a blew mantle curiously Imbordred.

In alia Fenestra :—
Sᵃ Juliana having in hir handes yᵉ legges of a Kite, or yᵉ like, yᵉ rest of yᵉ body of him being hid by hir garment, which is of yellow colour curiously fimbriated.

---

* Somerby near Brigg.—*Ed.*

In yᵉ other pane Sᵗ Peter holding a Church in his right hande, in yᵉ other 2 Keyes, his inner garment yellow embrodered, yᵉ outward red & curiously wrought.

In alia Fenestra :—
. . . DE MOMBY . . .

In this window is yᵉ story depicted of yᵉ killing of Thomas Becket. The pictures of 4 armed men with swordes, he kneeling & holding up his handes, having a Garland about his head ; above an Angell having a † mounted above his forehead.

[p. 142.]   In another pane a Pilgrime having on his head a close blew Bonnet, upon which an Escallop, his hayre yellow, longe lockes, & beard spread, with a short coate to the elbowes something close, having depicted upon in severall places flames of fire, holding in his right hande a Pilgrim's Staffe ; he hath upon him 2 coates or garments, yᵉ outward one shorter then yᵉ inmost, bare-foote, having by his side a bagge or scrip. on which is an Escallop above, & another below ; holding in his left hande a booke clasped.

In yᵉ middle pane yᵉ picture of a woman, whose inner garment is yellow, having about hir a white mantle (closed before with a button), curiously fimbriated ; hir right hande extended ; hir left within hir garment ; hir hayre yellow.

In Australi Fenestra :—
On the top a roundle of Orient purpure.

Kirkeby.

Arg. a lyon passant in cheife & a Delfe* in bast d'Or.
G. an Eagle displayed Arg. over all a Bend B. charged with
      3 crosseletts d'Or.

[p. 143.]

Lindwood.

In Australi Fenestra :—
Quarterly, *Jerusalem & Beaumont*.

Quarterly { B. 3 garbes d'Or   .   . *Comin, Comes Boughan*
{ B. semy of Flowers de Lize, a lyon ramp. d'Or. *Beaumont*

In pale { *Beaumont.*
{ *England.*

In pale { *Beaumont.*
{ Quarterly G. & Or, on the 1ˢᵗ quarter a Mullet, Arg.   *Vere*

---

* *Delf*—a square heraldic bearing, supposed to represent a square-cut sod of turf.—*Ed.*

In pale { *Beaumont.*
{ G. a lyon rampant Verry . . . *Everingham*
B. semy of Flowers de Lize, a lyon rampant d'Or . *Beaumont*

In orientali Fenestra Insulæ Australis :—

Paly of 6 peices Or & G. on a cheife of ye 2nd 3 escallops of
ye 1st . . . . . . *Bayus, de Baiocis*

Paly of 6 peices Arg. & G. on a cheife of ye 2nd 3 escallops
of ye 1st . . . . *Bayus*

Paly of 6 peices Arg. & Sa. on a cheife of ye 2nd 3 escallops
of ye 1st . . . . . . *Bayus*

G. a Fesse between 3 Escallops d'Or . . . *Chamberlaine*

In ye same window the memorials of divers Kings & Saints :—Viz^t.
Scūs Joħes Baptista—S. Paulus—S. Edwardus - S. Edmundus—S.
Vincentius - S. Antonius Ep̄us—S. Nicholaus Ep̄us—S. Cordelius—
S. Ciprianus—Gaspar R. Coloniæ. All these have their pictures, as
likewise divers of ye Apostles ; & these fragments in Saxon characters,
Viz^t. . . . EBAYVS . . MHO . . RE . . . & in
the same characters, Viz^t. MEMORIAE BEATAE MARIE ET
OMNIVM SANCTORVM, & EGO SVM A & O.

In Nave Eccłiæ :—Two fayre Marble stones ; on the one is plated
in Brasse a man, & his wife by him ; on the [p. 144.] other a man
single.* On ye first stone below the two pictures these barbarous verses
are engraven, Viz^t :—

> Qui contemplaris lapidem modicum, rogo, siste
> Et precibus caris dic salvi sint tibi Christe
> Spiritus in requie Lynwood sine labe Johannis
> Ejus et Aliciæ consortis pluribus annis.
> Anno milleno, C quater, nono quoque deno
> Mense Virum Jani Mors hiče tulit Johanni
> X quater atque tribus annis hi corde jocundi
> Convixere, quibus nati fuerant oriundi
> Septem, qui pedibus tot gaudent pulvere tundi.
> Vermibus ecce cibus : Sic transit gloria mundi.

Below their feete the Portraytures of seaven children in Brasse, with
this verse :—

> Hos septem natos fac, alme Deus, tibi gratos.

On the stone this Coate :—

A chevron betweene 3 Holly leaves . . . . *Lyndwood*

---

* These two fine Brasses which still exist commemorate respectively John and
Alice Lynwood, the father and mother, and John Lynwood the brother, of the
celebrated Canonist, William Lynwood, Bishop of St. David's, 1442. The elder
John died Jan. 1419, the younger on St. Praxedes' day, 21 July, 1421. The bearing
it their coat of arms should evidently have been described not as Holly, but as Lin-
den leaves in allusion to their name.—*Ed.*

On the other stone neare it :—

Hunc lapidem cernens Linwood memorare Johannis,
Quem Mors præveniens mundo Domini tulit annis
M.C. quater, X. bis uno Julii quoque mense. A° 1421.
Festo Praxedis mortis quæ corruit ense,
Sicque patris tumulo nati tumulus sociatur,
Quo velut in speculo mortis tibi mentio datur.
Ergo qui transis, magno, medio, puer an sis,
Mundas funde preces, nobis sic sit Veniæ spes.

In Fenestra Aquilonari :—

. . . BOUTINGHAM ET JOHANNE . . .

In altera Fenestra :—

. . . Ricus . . Capus . . fecit ista . . .

In Fenestra Orientali :—

One kneeling on a mantle of Redd, his handes closed, & erected, two gold ringes on two of his fingers.   His word this ensueing, Viz^t.— [p. 145] Me tibi sancta pia totum commendo Maria.

Over against him att ye other side of the window below one kneeling in redd, his handes closed, & erected. Over his shoulder hanges a belt studded with silver & embrodered, whereat hanges a short sword (or rather) dagger ; His word—Mater Dei Miserere Mei.

This inscription in the window :—

Orate pro animabus . . . de | Wyche et Margaretæ uxoris | suæ qui me fieri fe . .

In Cimiterio :—On a tombe neare ye Steeple ende, there is engraven in a fayre sculpture this—Hic jacet Dñus . . | . . quondam Rector | qui obiit A° Dñi M°CCC°LXXXX° | VI° : Cujus ãie propitietur Deus, Amen.

Ingraven below on ye north side of the Monument :— A chevron between 6 escallops, which stands reversed.

[p. 146.]

Whickenby.

In australi Fenestra :—

Or, a lyon rampant B.	*Percy*
G. a sexfoyle peirced betw. 12 crosses botony d'Or . .	*Umfraville*
B. semy of flowres de Lize, a lyon rampant, Or, a bend compony Arg. & G.	*Beaumont*
B. a bend betw. 6 Martletts Arg.	*Lutterell*
Paly Arg. & G. on a cheife of ye 2nd, 3 Escallops of ye 1st .	*Bayus*
G. a fesse betw. 3 Escallops d'Or	*Chamberlayne*

Over this coate is placed ye picture of St. Michaell (it seems his

tutelary Angell), peircing a Dragon in the mouth with a speare, having on a robe of Redd, adorned with escallops d'Or.
G. on a fesse betw. 3 escallops d'Or a mullet Sa. peirced *Chamberlaine*
G. crusuly fitchy, a lyon rampant Arg. . . . *De la Ware*

In Fenestra Orientali :—
The picture of S. Laurence tormented on a gridiron; Underwritten ICI LE PASSION St LAVRENCE. Under it in Saxon letters also RADVLFVS ME FECIT.

Depict' super Murum—Arg. a cheveron betw. 3 lapwings G.
G. a cheveron betw. 3 snaffles d'Or.

[p. 147.]

Burton juxta Lincolne.

In orientali Fenestra Chori :—
Or, on a cheveron G. 3 crescents of ye first betweene so many annulets of the second. *Bis.* . . . . *Sutton*

On a plaine gravestone in the Quire :—Hic jacet Robtus Sutton Armiger | maritus Dñæ Margaretæ filiæ Tho | mæ Sutton Militis Dñi Dudley, nu | per relictæ Joħis Gray Militis, Dñi | Powys, qui obiit 25° die Mensis No | vembris Año Dñi 1545. Cujus aïe | propitietur Deus.

On ye Monument two Escocheons :—

Quarterly
{
1. On a Chevron 3 crescents betw. 3 annulets . *Sutton*
2. A chevron betw. 3 garbes . . . *Sheffeld*
3. 3 boares heades couped.
4. Fretty.
}

Per pale
{
Sutton.

Quarterly
{
A lyon ramp. double queue . . *Dudley*
2 lyons passants . . . . *Somery*
A lyon rampant . . . [*Charleton*]
A saltier engrayled . . . [*Tiptoft*]
}
}

[p. 148.]

Barnetby.

In Fenestra Cancelli :—
England, on a file with 3 lambeaux B. 9 Flowres de Lize Or.
[*E. of Lancaster*]

In altera Fenestra :—In a square panel.
B. a crosse formed of pearls, or white beades.

In Australi Fenestra :—
The portrayture of some monster or monstrous man, being in shape & apparell like a man, but having ye head of a Kite. Before kneeles a

man, as suppliant, & offering something to him (as if it were mony or
something that fills the handes), & reaching out his handes to receave
the same. By him stands a Cabinet filled with some things that
seeme squared & large. Neare (& as it were looking over the man
offering), standes one looking up, & pointing with his finger to yᵉ head
of yᵉ monster, as though he seemed to give him notice, what a one he
was, & that he should mynde his head :—What this Hieroglyphicke
may mean Quære ?

In Fenestra Aquilonari :—
A bend fleury & counter fleury . . . . . . *Kelke*

In a North window in divers parts of it this word :—COVENANE,
& over it a bird upon a scroll, in which is—GAVNG . . PARTER.

[p. 149.]

Kirketon in Lindesey.

This toune was the auncient inheritance of the Duke of Cornewall,
of which Duchy the Freeholders holde their lande.

In orientali Fenestra Cancelli :—
B. a mace (or scepter) in Pale d'Or.

In Fenestra Insulæ Orientalis Eccliæ :—
Robertus Hardenby, & Agneta uxor ejus.

Neere this window lyeth a Chevalier in compleat armour & full proportion, crosse-legg'd, his sheild a very large one, his handes elevated.

In alia Fenestra :—
Barry of 6 peices Arg. & G. 3 crescents Sa. . . [*Waterton*]

There was sometimes of the name of Brocklesby Gentlemen
inhabiting & having land here.

[p. 150.]

Beakeby.

In Cancello :—
A large Tombe of white alabaster, upon the flatt whereof about a
yard high lyeth in full proportion a Chevalier in compleat armour. with
his wife on his left side, their handes elevated. Under his feet an ape
guardant, his heade girt wᵗʰ an oaken wreathe. On yᵉ area above is a
carpett diapred & rolled up att yᵉ head & feete, on which they lye.
Under hir heade a pillow, at hir feete a lyon. On the sides alonge in
a border betw. 2 verges graduated yᵉ 128 Psalme in metre, beginning
at yᵉ head ende & so alonge. disposed in foure paragraphs, each con-
tayning foure verses to yᵉ ende. Above yᵉ pedestall below is another

bordure in which are 21 children, Sonnes & Daughters in their statuas, of which there be foure infants in their swathing clothes : & under them (in another bordure) ye severall escocheons of their differenced armes.

On ye Wall side adjoyning is raysed another Quadrate supported by two columnes of ye same within the squared of which in a Table of inscription in blacke letters is :—Hic jacet Robertus Tirwhit | de Ketleby, Miles, qui obiit | 13° die Novembris Año Dñi | 1581. Ac etiam Elizabetha | uxor ejus quæ obiit — — | die —. Below, — Vigilate et orate, quia nescitis diem et horam. The sides of it hollowed, adorned with carved worke, ye edges whereof are garnished with golde. On ye toppe is a death's head in the midle. At one ende Fame with hir trumpett ; under which are written—Fame soundeth on high. On the other Time winged, with a fore locke, holding in one hande [p. 151.] a Sickle, in ye other an Houre-glass ; Under which is written —Time trueth doeth try. On ye toppe in a Quadrate finiall their arms, Viz^t :—

Empaled	Quarterly	G. 3 lapwings d'Or	. . .	*Tyrwhit*
		G. a cheife endented d'Or	. .	*Grovale*
	Quarterly	G. a lyon ramp. Arg. on a border Vert, 8 escallops Arg. . .		*Oxenbridge*
		B. a frett Arg.	. . .	*Itchingham*

Upon ye helmet on a Torce Or & G. a Lapwing's head erased, all supported with two Salvages with clubs in their hands, mantled G. doubled Or. His motto in a scroll below, Viz^t.—Temps esproua verite. His sword & helmet hange up.

In superiori parte Cancelli :—A very fayre Monument of white marble ; on the flatt whereof above is one kneeling in compleat armour on a wrought cushion before a deske. On ye other side his wife in a gowne of scarlet, the sleeves turned up Ermine. The 2nd Quadrature is raysed up arch-wise, the Frontispeice of which is adorned, is support- ed with two fayre columns of Carnation marble, the coronides whereof are curiously diversifyed with billetty worke fretted with golde. These upholde the whole surface of ye worke, above which hath first an half canopy imbellished with roses on ye concave. Above which is another quadrature adorned at either ende with two pyramides of blew marble. This partition is of very curious workemanship with a costly aurificium round about it, within which are cornucopias, & powdered also with other severall fruites. Above (as a Finiall) is an escocheon incircled in a Ring set about wth Roses, npon which is depicted ye armes of Tyrwhit empaled with Mannours Erle of Rutland wth all ye quarterings apperteyning to either family.

Upon ye table of Inscription (being of Touch) in golden letters is written :—
[p. 152.] Here lyeth the right Honble the Lady Briget daughter of John Earle of Rutland, Lord Rosse, Baron of Helmesley, Trusbut &

Belvoire, wife of Robert Tyrwhit of Ketleby, Esq. sometimes of y^e
Privy Chamber to Q. Elizabeth, & in speciall grace & favour. Of
nature milde, of spirit noble, of speech affable, of countenance amiable,
nothing proud of hir place, & fortunes, & using hir grace rather to
benefitt others than hirselfe. Who having bin long visited wth sickenesse ye 10th day of July, 1604, finished this mortall life, leaving
behinde hir 4 children, William, Robert, Rutland, & Bridget. In
memory of whom, as also of himselfe, whensoever it shall please God
to call him from this Vale of Misery, her deare husband Mr Robert
Tyrwhit att his costs erected this Monument.

Below this comely Epitaph :—

> Heus, hospes ! Qui negligenter præteris
> (Sortis memor fortasse non satis tuæ)
> Sta ; donec hic quæ dormiat, cognoveris,
> Brigitta, claris clarior parentibus,
> Virtute, castitate, moribus probis
> Bonisque, quæ vere beant clarissimam,
> Formam cui suæ parem dederat Venus.
> Terra sub ista nescio quid pulveris
> Habet vetusti, et obsoleti, et putridi.
> Heu ! fata sævis sæviora Tigribus !
> Non sic decebat, obsecro vos, ut prius
> Quam se videret vivere, et lustrum satis
> Quintam peregisset, nigrantem regiam
> Proserpinæ subiret intractabilis,
> Illa, illa longis digna sæclis vivere.
> Et nunc maritus, heu, misellus in toro
> Vacuo gemens, lugensque, et incusans Deos
> Frustra suam desiderat Turturem.

[p. 153.] In the midst of the Chancell is a Tombe of marble without
inscription, which is saide to be the monument of Robert Tirwhit a
Judge in the dayes of King Henry the 4th.

Upon a flatt stone there is a plate of brasse :—Here lieth Elizabeth |
Skipwith, wife of William | Skipwith, sonne & heyre | to Sr John
Skipwith of Ormes | by, daughter to Sr William | Tirwhit of Ketleby.

In Orientail Fenestra Cancelli :—
B. 3 (? water-bougets) Arg. on a chief G. 3 bezants.*

Tirwhit's Crest :—a Salvage man d'Or, holding in his hand a club
Vert.

---

* These arms are tricked, not blazoned, in the manuscript.—*Ed.*

[**p.** 154.]

Waddington, Praebenda de Lincoln.*

In Fenestra Orientali Cancelli :—
Arg. 3 barrs Sa. . . . . *Bussy*
Quarterly { Arg. 5 Fusills in fesse G. . . . . . *Hebden*
{ G. a Bend Ermine . . . . *Rie*

In Fenestra Orientali Insulæ Australis :—
Orate pro bono statu Francisci | Mering et Annæ consortis suæ | qui istam fenestram . . .

Quarterly {

Arg. on a chevron Sa. 3 escallops Or ; a mullet } *Mering*
    of 6 points Sa. pierced of the 1st . . }

G. a Saltier Ermine . . . *Nevile of Rolleston*

Arg. on a Bend Sa. 3 mullets of 6 points of the
    1st betw. 6 Lyons passants gardants of the 2nd.

Arg. a chevron betw. 3 escallops G.

Neare hande a Monument of marble, but no Inscription ; tradition speakes it one of the Meringes. Note, the Mannour house is yet called Mering-Hall.

In Fenestra Australi Eccłiæ :—
Arg. 3 bells Sa. clappers B. a canton of ye 2nd.

On a gravestone :—Hic jacet Alexander Southwicke, | insignis hujus Eccłiæ pastor, qui | obiit Martii 16° Año 1606.

Tumulus marmoreus ære fixus :—Hic jacet Wiłłus Plumtre | Rector de Hogarton in Coɱ. | Nott.' qui obiit sexto die | Octoƀ. Año Dñi 1545.

Ex ære fixo ad murum borealem Cancelli :—

[**p.** 155.] Corpus Johannis sub humo concluditur Herdi,†
    Illius at famam claudere terra nequit.
Doctor in arte fuit Medica, qua profuit Anglis,
    Atque Tui verbi, Christe, minister erat.
Historias quatuor descripsit carmine Regum,
    Anglica gens quorum sub ditione fuit.

---

* Waddington never was a Prebendal Church ; the mistake probably arose from the fact that John Herd the rector, whose epitaph Holles gives, held the prebend of Lafford with the rectory.—*Ed.*

† John Herd, M.D., was instituted to the rectory of Waddington, 13 Sept. 1565, on the presentation of Thomas Tailor, of Lincoln, gent. He had been installed as Prebendary of Lafford, *al.* Sleford, in Lincoln Cathedral 19 Oct. 1557, and as Prebendary of York Cathedral, 14 April, 1559. He wrote in Latin verse, as mentioned in his epitaph, an " Historia Anglicana heroico carmine conscripta," dedicated to Sir Wm. Cecil, and containing the reigns of Edw. IV & V, Rich. III & Hen. VII. It has not been printed, but forms *Cotton MS. Julius.* C. II. 136. He died early in 1588.—*Ed.*

Edwardi quarti, et quinti, ternique Ricardi,
Septimi et Henrici bellica gesta refert.
Hic etiam scripsit Catechismum carmine stricto,
Quo pueros docuit dogmata sacra Dei.
Hæc faciunt Herdi laudem Monumenta perennem
Quam nunquam poterit tollere tempus edax.

[p. 156.]

Saxby.

In Fenestra Orientali :—

Paly of 6, Arg. & B. on a Bend Sa. 3 annulets d'Or　　.　　*Sanderson*
Sa. a fesse betw. 3 lambes passants Arg.　.　　.　　.　　.　*Lampton*

Sanderson with a baronet's inescocheon.

Empaled {　*Sanderson.*
Sa. a· cheveron engr. betw. 6 crosselets botony
fitchy d'Or, charged wth 3 flowers de Lize, B. *Smith*

In Fenestra Australi :—

G. a chevron betw. 3 axes' heads Arg. a cheife wavy, Arg. & B.

Sanderson with a Talbot Sa. on the Helmet.

Paly of 6 Arg. & B. on a Bend Sa. 3 Annulets d'Or　　.　*Sanderson*
Ermine, a griphon segreant G.　　.　　.　　.　　.　*Grantham*

Empaled { *Sanderson.* { *Sanderson.* { *Sanderson.*
{ *Lampton.* { *Sandon.* { *Hiltoft.*

In Cancello :—A monument of ashler stone reared up against the
North wall to a convenient height, on either side having 2 little
Pyramides of blewish marble.　Above ye first Quadrature in ye table of
inscription (coloured blacke) in golden letters is written:—Robert
Saunderson of Fillingham Esq. the youngest sonne of Nicholas
Saunderson of Reresby, & Agnes his wife, married Katherine, the
youngest daughter of Vincent Grantham of St. Katherines by Lincolne, Esq., by whom he had Issue, 3 Sonnes, Viz^t—Nicholas, Robert,
& Thomas, & 3 daughters, Anne, Faith, & Katherine, living all at his
death.　He feared the Lord, & trusted in him, & he prospered in his
wayes.　He built for his habitation 2 howses att Fillingham, where he
lived very worshipfully being in Commission of ye peace, & kept good
hospitality untill ye 63rd yeare of his age when [p. 157.] being visited
with sickenesse he prepared himselfe by faith & repentance for y^e
heavenly Jerusalem ; & having purchased this Lordship, he willed his
body to be buried in this place, & commended his Spirit into ye handes
of his Redeemer. & soe leaving a house of Clay for a Mansion of
glory, he died at Fillingham Novembr. 2°, 1582.

Katharine his wife was after married to William Rookeby of Skiers in the county of Yorke, Esq. Aug. 30, 1585, with whom she lived 30 yeares with much contentment & joy in ye Lord, & in ye 74th yeare of her age changing a living death into everlasting life, she died there Martii X°, 1615.

On a compartment above are depicted his armes upon a sheilde, Viz^t.—

Empaled {
  Paly of 6, Arg. & B. on a bend Sa. 3 annulets } *Sanderson*
  d'Or, a crescent difference   .   .
  Ermine a Griffin sergreaunt G.   .   .   .   *Grantham*
}

His motto—Jeo suœve velaut a plaire.*

His crest—A wolves head Proper, devouring of a childe, his legges & buttocks appearing out of ye wolves' Jawes.

Hæc ad murum posita in Australi termino Eccliæ :—

Attende tibi
Quia Mors hodie mihi, cras tibi,
Si non es pro te modo Sollicitus,
Quis erit pro te in futuro?
Tria sunt vere, quæ me faciunt flere ;
Primum quidem durum, quia scio me moriturum.
Secundum vero plango, quia moriar, et nescio quando,
Tertium autem flebo, quia nescio ubi manebo.

Memento mori—Memorare novissima.

[p. 158.]   Bonis bene, malis male.

Ubi vultus, ubi speci   )   Unde superbi   )
Ubi genæ, ubi aur | Quid est homo nisi li |
Ubi nares, ubi luc | De limo homo pri |
Ubi lingua, ubi dent | Mortem vitare nequi |
Ubi venæ, ubi fauc | es.   Si nos terra si | mus.
Ubi cutes, ubi pell | Ad terram terra redi |
Ubi venter, ubi ren | Terra quid est nisi fi |
Ubi manus, ubi ped | Si nihil est nisi fu |
Ubi corpus, ubi vir | Ergo nihil su |
Consumpserunt omnia verm   )   Ideo studea |
    Cunctorum fin   )   Ut parati si   )
    Mors, et verm   } is.
    Fovea, cin   )

Memento mori—Memorare novissima.

A hande holding a crowne in a chayne with these verses underneath :—

Nubibus en duplici vinctum diadema catena
Quod procul a nostro sustinet orbe manus.
Non alia te lege Deus, Jacobe, legavit
Quem regere Imperio fecit et esse Virum.

---

* *i.e.*—Je suis veillant à plaire.—*Ed.*

[p. 159.]

Bagenderby.

In Fenestra Aquilonari Ecctiæ :—

B. 3 Cinquefoyles d'Or . . . . *Bardolfe*
Quarterly { Arg. a cheife G. over all a Bend B. . . . *Crumwell*
Quarterly { Chequy d'Or & G. a cheife Ermine . . *Tateshall*
Sa. 2 lyons passants Arg. crowned d'Or . . . . . *Dimoke*
Arg. a chevron betw. 3 crosses botony G. . . . . *Copledike*
Lozengy Ermine & G. . . . . *Rokely*

In Australi Fenestra :—

Quarterly, *France & England.*
G. 3 water-bougets, Arg. . . . . *Rosse*
Arg. a saltier G. on a cheife G. 3 escallops Arg. . . . *Taylboys*
Quarterly d'Or & G. a border Sa. besanty . . . . *Rochford*
B. 3 whips ye hafts d'Or, strings Arg. . . . . . } *Abbatia*
G. 3 board knives, hafts d'Or, blades Arg. . . . . } *de Crowland*

In alia Fenestra Aquilonari :—

Argent, 3 red roses.

Below ye picture of St. Thomas Becket receaving woundes from 3 knights there pictured, thrusting their swordes into him. On ye other side ye decollation of some legendary Saint. Under, att ye root of the window is writted this, Viz^t :—PRIEZ PVR ROB . . . TIE ORMSBY ET PVR PHILLIP SVN FRERE.

In Fenestra Campanilis :—

G. a crosse fleury d'Or.
Quarterly { Arg. a chevron betw. 3 crosse-crosseletts Sa. a border Sa. besantee . . . . *Mablethorpe*
Quarterly { Arg. 2 barrs engrayled Sa. . . . . . . *Staynes*
G. a crosse botony d'Or.

This last coate, boeth here & in all places where I fynde it, is in a very large & fayre escocheon, larger & fayrer than of most coates of armes I meete with.

Lapis marmoreus in Cancello :—

Thomas Enderby & Agnes sa femme | giseunt ycy
p. Dieux de lour Almes | p sa grace eyt mercy.

[p. 160.] Ex ænea fimbria super lapidem marmoreum sicut et prior ; Orate pro anima Albini de | Enderby qui fecit fieri is | tam ecctiam cum campanili, | qui obiit in Vigilia Sc̃i Mat | thiæ Ap̃li, Añno Dñi 1407.

Tumuleus lapideus :—Here lyeth John Gedney, Esq. | & Isabell his wife daughter | of Edward Grantham of Dun | ham : John died Año 1533 ; | Isabell died 1536.

Upon a quadrature of freestone carved, raysed upon ye north wall of ye chancell a man in armour, kneeling before a deske, his 2 sonnes behinde him ; His wife wth 2 daughters on ye other side, kneeling also, their handes elevated : below written :—Here lyeth Andrew Gedney, | Esq. & Dorothy his wife. They | had Ishue, Richard, John, Mary, | & Katherine. Dorothy died 7° | Junii 1591, & Andrew died ——.

On ye top at either ende a chapiter, in ye middest an Houre glasse, under wch in blacke letters :—

Omne quod exoritur, e terra fit, et moritur.

Armes on ye top :—

Empaled { Quarterly { Arg. 2 barbells in Saltier B. . . *Gedney*
Arg. a fesse B. betw. 2 barrulets Sa. . *Enderby*
Barry of 8 Arg. & G. in cheife a Greyhound Sa. . *Skipwith*

1. A Hart couchant regardant.
2. The wheele of a Clocke.
3. A crowne.
4. One playing on a citterne.
5. 2 spears in saltier, in bast a Phæon.
6. A Virgin, having Christ (taken from the crosse), in hir lap.
7. A crosse compassed about with a crowne of thornes.
8. An empty escocheon.

[p. 161.]

Bullingbroke.

The castle of Bullingbroke was built by William de Romara, Earle of Lincolne, & ennobled by the birth of King Henry the 4th, who from thence tooke his sirname. Heretofore it was a famous structure, but now gone much to ruine & decay. The Towne standes in a bottome, & ye castell in ye lowest part of it, compassed about with a large moat fed by springs. It is most accessible on ye South West part, ye rest being encompassed by ye Hills. As for ye frame of the building it lyeth in a square, the area within the walls conteyning about an acre & a halfe, ye building is very uniforme. It hath 4 stronge Forts or Ramparts, wherein are many roomes & Lodgings, the passage from one to another lying upon ye walles, which are embattled about. There be likewise 2 watch Towers all covered with lead. If all ye rooms in it were repayred & furnished (as it seemes in former tymes they have bin), it were capable to receyve a very great Prince with all his trayne. The entrance into it is very stately over a fayre drawbridge : The gate house is a very uniforme & strong building. Next within ye Porter's Lodge is a payre of low stayres which goe downe into a dungeon, in wh. some reliques are yet to be seene of a Prison house. Other 2 Prisons more are on either side. The building itselfe is of a sandy stone, hewen of a great square out of ye rockes thereby, which though it abide the weather longe, yet (in process of tyme) it will moulder, especially if wett gett within it, which hath bin yᵉ decay of many places of yᵉ wall, where yᵉ roofe is uncovered. There be certain roomes within yᵗ castle (built by Queene Elizabeth of freestone), amongst which is a fayre great chamber with other lodgings.

In a roome in one of yᵉ Towers of yᵉ castle they usually kept their auditt once by yᵉ yeare for yᵉ whole Dutchy of Lancaster, having ever bin yᵉ prime seate thereof, where all yᵉ recordes for yᵉ whole county are kept.

[p. 162] The constable of the castle is Sir William Mounson, Lord Castlemayne, who receaveth a revenue out of yᵉ Dutchy lands of 500ˡⁱ pʳ annum, in part of payment of 1000ˡⁱ yearly given by the King to the Countesse of Nottingham his Lady. One thing is not to be passed by, affirmed as a certaine truth by many of yᵉ inhabitants of yᵗ towne upon their owne knowledge, which is, that yᵗ castle is haunted by a certaine spirit in yᵉ likenesse of a Hare ; which att the meeting of yᵉ Auditors doth usually runne betweene their legs, & sometymes overthrows them, & so passes away. They have pursued it doune into yᵉ Castle yard, & seene it take in att a grate into a low cellar, & have followed it thither with a light, where notwithstanding that they did most narrowly observe it (& that there was noe other passage out, but by the doore or windowe, yᵉ roome being all close framed of stones within, not having the least chinke or crevice,) yet they could never fynde it. And att other tymes it hath bin seene to run in at Iron-grates below into other of yᵉ Grotto's (as their be many of them) & they have watched the place, & sent for Houndes, & put in after it ; but after a while they have come crying out

[p. 163.] In Fenestra Orientali Cancelli :—

G. 3 lyons passants gardants d'Or ; a labell of 3, each charged
    with 3 flowres de lize of yᵉ second   .   .   *Comes Lancastr.*

Empaled { *Castile* & *Leon*, Quarterly.
    France & *England*, Quarterly ; a labell of 3, Arg.
      each charged with 2 (Flours) de Lize, Sa.

Or, a lyon rampant Purpure   .   .   .   .   . *Lacy*
B 3 garbes d'Or   .   .   .   .   *Meschines, Com. Cestr.*

Quarterly { Sa. a cross engrailed d'Or   .   . *Ufford* } *Willughby*
         G. a cross moline Arg. .   .   .   . *Beke* }

Arg. a fesse betw , 3 Bugles* trippant Sa.   .   .   .   [*Metcalfe*]

In Fenestra Orientali ad dextram Navis :—

B. 6 lyoncells rampant d'Or, 3, 2, 1.   .   .   .   . *Longespee*
Lancaster.
France & *England*, Quarterly.
Lacy.

---

* The text has Bugles, i.e. Calves, see p. 76, but dogs, Beagles, are here figured.—*Ed.*

G. 3 lyons passant, Arg. a labell of 3, d'Or, each charged
with a lyon ramp. Purpure . . . [*Ebulo le Strange*]

In prima Fenestra Australi :—

B. 3 garbes d'Or . . . . *Meschines*
Chequy d'Or & B. a bend G. . . . . . *Clifford*
Quarterly Arg. & G. yᵉ 2ⁿᵈ & 3ᵈ charged with a fret d'Or ;
over all a bend Sable . . . . . *Spenser*

Fæmina gestans in veste sex leones aureos erectos, *Longespee*
una cum leone purpureo conjunctos . . . *Lacy*

In secunda Fenestra Australi :—

G. a fesse Verry betweene 3 Leopards heads jesant Flowres
de Lize d'Or . . . . *Cantilupe*
G. a cross molyn Arg. . . . . . . *Beke*
B. a fesse dauncee betw. 10 billets d'Or . . . *Deyncourt*

In Campanili :—

Quarterly, *France* & *England.*
Quarterly, Or & G. a border Sa. bezanty . . . *Rochford*
Or, a chevron betw. 10 crosses botony Sa. . . . *Slight*

Orate pro bono statu . . . Ducis Aureliæ
Ad hoc campanile . . . Aᵒ r. r. Heñ.

Quarterly {
Arg. a chevron betw. 3 Martlets Sa. . . [*Argum*]
Chequy Or & G. on a cheife Arg. a lyon passant
Sa. . . . . . . [*Comberworth*]

[p. 164.]

South Elkington.

In Campanili :—

G. a cinquefoyle peirced between 8 crosse-crosselets d'Or . *Umfreville*

North Elkington.

In Fenestra Orientali Cancelli :—

Arg. a bend between 6 Martletts, G.*
Arg. a bend G.

In Fenestra Insulæ Aquilonaris :—

Or, a Fesse betw. 3 Mullets of 6 pointes Sa. a bendlet, Arg.
. . . 3 Swans . . . betw. 6 crosse-crosseletts, fitchy.

---

* This coat is coloured—Az. a bend between 6 martlets, Arg., which are the
arms of Luttrell.—*Ed.*

[p. 165.]

Hagworthingham.

In Fenestra Insulæ Australis :—
Party per fesse G. & Arg. a pale counter-changed ; 3 falcons
    of yᵘ second.
Sa. a bend betw. 2 cotises fleury   .   .   .   .   [*Kelke*]
Quartered with Arg. 3 escallops, G.

In Cancello :—
Hic jacet . . . Radilston quondam | Rector istius ecclesiæ.

Hæc depicta in Ecclesia :—

Empaled { Arg. 3 lyons passants gardants G.   .   .   *Littlebury*
{ G. 3 crescents d'Or, a canton Erm.   .   .   *Dalison*

Empaled { Erm. a bend G. betw. 2 bendlets d'Or.
{ *Litlebury*.

Empaled { Sa. a crosse engrayled d'Or.   .   .   .   *Ufford*
{ Erm. a bend G. betw. 2 bendlets d'Or.

The crest a Saracen's head proper upon a crowne flowry d'Or,
mantled G. doubled Ermine.

Empaled { *Litlebury*.
{ . . . 3 crosse-crosseletts.

Empaled { *Litlebury*.
{ Ermine 2 bars G.   .   .   .   .   [*Kirketon*]

Empaled { *Litlebury*.
{ G. a fesse betw. 3 water-bougets Arg.   .   .   [*Meres*]

On a gravestone of blew marble in yᵉ body of yᵉ Church is pour-
trayed in Brasse one in compleate armour, bearing upon yᵘ manches of
his coate of armes on either side, 2 crescents to be discerned. Betweene
his feete a right hande couped. The rest is all defaced.

[p. 166.]

Welton juxta Ludam.

In Fenestra Aquilonari Ecclesiæ :—
Barry of 6 G. & Arg. a bend engrayled Sa.

In Fenestra Orientali :—
B. 2 bars nebuly Arg.

In Cancello :—on a peice of brasse fixed on yᵉ wall these armes, &
this inscription, Vizᵗ :—

Empaled { Or, a saltier G. surmounted of another of yᵉ first ;
{   on a cheife G. 3 saltiers engrayled d'Or   .   *Dyon*
{ . . . 3 bars . . a canton Erm. crescent difference.

Hic jacet corpus Johannis Dyon | Armigeri.

His gravestone of blew marble, on which in a border of Brasse :—
Here lyeth the body of John | Dyon, Esq. who departed this | lyfe
yᵉ 24ᵗ day of May Anno | 1575.

> Earth treades on earth, & mould upon moulde ;
> . . . . shineth as golde,
> Yet Earth must be Earth sooner then he would.

Upon a Freestone in yᵉ middle of yᵉ Quire :—
Hic jacet Thomas Asgarby Rector | Eccłiæ de Welton juxta Ludam
| qui obiit . . . die . . . Año dñi | MᵒCCCCᵒXXᵒ cujus
animæ &c.

Under an arch in yᵉ wall in yᵉ North Isle of yᵉ Church :—
Hic jacet Isabella uxor Joħis | Gee quæ obiit in festo . . | Año
dñi 1386, cujus aïæ &c.

[p. 167.]

Harrington.

In Fenestra Orientali :—

Empaled { — a lyon rampant —.
         { Argent, a fesse B.

In Fenestra Aquilonari :--

Empaled { Arg. a chevron betw. 3 crosses botony G.   .   *Copledike*
         { Lozengy, Ermine & G.   .   .   .   .   *Rokely*

Neare by a fayre Monument of marble, yᵉ plates of brasse on yᵉ side
of yᵉ wall defaced.

Under an arch upon yᵉ South wall lyes the portrayt of a cheifetaine
of huge proportion, all in compleat armes.   Hee lyeth crosse-legged,
his sheild a vast one covering his left side, his surcoate of armes loose,
a lyon under his feete.

Upon a fayre blew Marble in yᵉ middle of yᵉ Quire cut in brasse :—
Orate pro anima Joħis Copuldyk | Armigeri, qui obiit 15ᵒ die Martii |
Aᵒ Dñi 1480, ac pro anima Margare | tæ nuper uẍis ejus quæ obiit .
. . die | . . . Aᵒ Dñi . . . quorum ani | mabus ppitietur
Deus.   Amen.

The arms of this Monument defaced ; onely there appears
         on a cheife endented 3 crosses Tau.   .   .   *Thurland*

At yᵉ lower ende of yᵉ Quire in Brasse set in yᵉ wall :—
Here lyeth Sʳ John Copledike, Kt. late | of Harington, deceased :
he died the | twelfth of December 1557 ; & Elizabeth | Litlebury his
wife, who died the 12ᵗʰ of | May 1552.

Their pictures (his in compleat Armour) & their armes above, all in
brasse.

Empaled {
   Arg. a chevron betw. 3 crosses botony G.   .   *Copledike*

   Quarterly {
     Arg. 2 lyons passants gardant G. . *Littlebury*
     Barry of 6, Ermine & G.   .   .   *Kirkelon*
     Arg. a bend betw. 6 crosse-crosselets
        botony fitchy B. . . [*Woodthorp*]
     G. 3 crescents d'Or; a canton Ermyne *Dalyson*
     — 3 lockes in true love.

On yᵉ other side by hir Littleburyes coat alone.

[**p. 168.**] A litle above a fayre Monument of blew marble built up to a convenient height upon yᵉ wall, arched, yᵉ topp flowry, in proportion square, supported from yᵉ flatt stone by two pillars, within yᵉ hollow on a plane 2 portraytures of yᵉ Man & his wife cut in Brasse ; under wᶜʰ this Inscription :—Here lyeth John Copledike Esq. | sonne & heire of John Copledike | Kt. late of Harington, deceased, | who died 4ᵗᵒ Aprilis 1585, & Anne | Etton his wife who died 10° Julii | Año 1582.

Over this his Armes, Quarterings & Crest, Vizᵗ. a . . . head ishuing out of a crowne : Then *Copledike* alone.

On yᵉ other side by hir :—Sa. on a bend d'Or 3 Hazle leaves Vert betweene 2 lyons passants gardants of yᵉ second.

About this Tombe theis several escocheons :—

Quarterly {
  Arg. a chevron betw. 3 crosses botony G.   .   *Copledike*
  . . on a saltier engrayled 5 mascles   .   . [*Leake ?*]

Quarterly {
  Copledike.
  . . a bend . . a cheife . . .   .   . *Harrington*

Quarterly {
  Copledike.
  Lozengy, Erm. & G.   .   .   .   .   . *Rokeley*

Empaled {
  Copledike.
  . . on a fesse 3 roundes . . .   . [*Huntingfield*]

Empaled {
  Copledike.
  Quarterly G. & Verrey, a Bend d'Or.   .   . *Constable*

Empaled {
  Copledike.
  . . a chevron betw. 3 Griffons' heads erased . [*Tilney*]

Empaled {
  Copledike.
  Erm. on a cheife endented G. 3 crosses Tau Or *Thurland*

Empaled {
  Copledike.
  Or, on a cheveron G. betw. 3 annulets of the 2ⁿᵈ
       as many crescents of yᵉ first   .   . *Sutton*

Empaled {
  Copledike.
  . . on a bend . . 3 mulletts.

Empaled {
  Copledike.
  Arg. 3 lyons passants gardants G.   .   . *Littlebury*

On yᵉ other side over against this another reasonable fayre Monument, raysed upon yᵉ wall, of white marble, from 2 columns arched ; within the concave whereof are two little portraytures of yᵉ man & his wife kneeling, himselfe in compleat armour parcell guilt, Shee on yᵉ other side [p. 169.] in black ; their handes elevated. A little Sonne behinde him, & a daughter behinde hir : two little Pyramides of Carnation Marble (raysed from yᵉ flatt Tombe stone) empaling them. Under them this Epitaph :—Here lyeth yᵉ body of Francis Copledike | Esq. brother & next heyre of John Cople | dicke, Esq. wᶜʰ John Copledicke was son | & heyre of John Copuldicke of Haring | ton in the county of Lincolne, wᶜʰ foresaid | Francis died yᵉ 24ᵗʰ of December 1599, | which foresᵈ Francis married Elizabeth | one of yᵉ daughters of Lyonel Reresby of | Thryborgh in the county of Yorke, Esq. & | had with hir one son & a daughter which | died in their infancy. Upon a quadrate Finiall his Atchievement, in which are depicted theis 6 coates quartered ; Vizᵗ.—

Quarterly
{
Arg. a chevron betw. 3 crosses botony G. . *Copledike*
B. a saltier betw. 4 crosses botony d'Or . . *Friskeney*
Or, on a fesse G. 3 plates . . . *Huntingfield*
Lozengy, Ermine & G. . . . . . *Rokeley*
Or, a cheife G. over all a bend B. . . . *Harington*
Or, on a saltier engr. Sa. 5 mascles of yᵉ 1ˢᵗ. . [*Leake ?*]
}

The same Escocheon is depainted also a little lower over him, & on the womans side also with hirs empaled, Vizᵗ :—

Quarterly
{
G. on a bend Arg. 3 crosses botony, Sa. . . *Reresby*
B. billetty ; a Fesse dauncetty d'Or . . *Deincourt*
Arg. upon a Fesse betw. 2 bars gemews G. 3 floures de lize d'Or . . . *Normanvile*
Arg. 3 barwayes G. on a canton of yᵉ 2ⁿᵈ 3 fusills of yᵉ first . . . . . . [*Bosvile*]
G. 3 buckes trippant Arg. . . . . [*Swift*]
Bendy of 8 peices G. & Arg.
}

Upon the Fount :—*Copledike* alone, & the same wᵗʰ some of the former coates empaled, Vizᵗ : wᵗʰ the Griphons' heads erased ; with the roundells on Fesse ; with yᵉ Saltier ; wᵗʰ yᵉ lozengy coate. In yᵉ square of it, wᶜʰ joyneth upon the wall is to be seen a caterfoyle peirced betw. 3 crosses botony. The stooles in yᵉ Church have yᵉ coate of Copledike carved upon yᵉ heades of them.

[p. 170.]

Keleby.

In Fenestra Aquilonari Eccᵗiæ : —
Arg. a chevron between 3 crosses botony fitchy Sa. . [*Russel*]
Sa. a mullet of 6 pointes Arg.

In alia Fenestra :—
Arg. a mullet of 6 pointes Sa.
Arg. a fesse between a Bend in base, & in chief a leopard's head between 2 cinquefoyles sable.

Below (in 3 severall panes) a Man & his wife & daughter (as it seemes) kneeling, their handes erected ; he in a loose surcoate, yellow hayre, his sword hanging poynt downewards in a Belt about his belly. Underneath thus :—

Orate pro aïabus Roberti | Cosson, et Margarete ux̃is ejus | qui hanc fenestram fieri fe | cerunt.

In yᵉ quire a low monument of freestone covered wᵗʰ a flatt Marble, on which in Brasse a man in armes, by whose side his wife ; att their feete 3 sonnes, Edward, Francis, & Thomas, & 4 daughters, Vizᵗ : Dorcas, Elizabeth, Mary, & Joane   Upon a plate of Brasse below this inscription :—Here under this stone lyeth buryed | in yᵉ mercy of God yᵉ body of Edward | Ayscough, Esq., sonne of Sʳ Wm. Ayscogh | Kt., wᶜʰ Edward died 6° Aprilis, A° Dñi | 1558, & Margaret his wife.

Upon˙yᵉ tombe this Escocheon.
(G.) 2 barrs humets (Arg.) betw. 3 lyons passants (Or).

In Orientali Fenestra :—
In severall panes—A man with a woman on either side of him, all kneeling. Under one is written in Saxon letters, ELENE QVE FVIT VXOR LAVRENCI ; Under the other AGNES COSSON ; [p. 171] under him ROBERTVS FILIVS LAVRENCI. Above their heades this—ORATE PRO . . . ROBERT FIL. LAVRENCI QVI HOC OPVS FIERI FECIT.

In yᵉ north quire—A Monument in the wall of white alabaster, within yᵉ orbicular hollow of it a woman vayled, hir handes erected, over hir head this escocheon :—
Arg. 2 bars G. in chiefe a mullett S. pierced, a crescent
    difference, Or   .   .   .   .   *South*
Arg. a plaine crosse G. voyded of yᵉ feild, charged with 5
    crosses botony fitchy of the second, between 4 cinque-
    foyles Sa. peirced.

Below under hir picture—Franciscus South, Eques auratus | suæ Matris manibus verendis | hoc Monumentum posuit.

    Alicia en hic Southa cubat ter longa Vicenis.

[p. 172.]

Belesby.

In insula australi Eccłiæ :—Hic jacet Wiłłus de Belesby | Miles, Senior, cujus aïæ ꝑpicietʳ | Deus. Amen.

Upon this monument (which is a very fayre one of blew marble) is cutt one single coate, which is a saltier.

In orientali Fenestra ejusdem Insulæ :—
Sa. a saltier d'Or   .   .   .   .   *Belesby*

B. a bend between 6 martletts, Arg. . . . . *Lutterell*
G. 3 Pick-axes Arg. . . . . *Pigot*
Joħes Browne obiit 1461.

On a white freestone in yᵉ Quire :—Hic jacet Mʳ Nicholaus Davison |
quondam Rector, qui obiit 18° | die Novembris A° Dñi 1418, | cujus
aïe &c.

Hic jacet Dñus Willelmus | Inthinston, quondam Rector | Eccłie de
Belesby, qui obiit | 8° Calend Maii, A° Dñi 1318, | cujus aïe &c.

[p. 173.]

Thorganby.

Arg. 3 chevronels brased in bast, on a cheife Sa. 3 mullets of
yᵉ first peirced ; a crescent difference . . . *Danby*.

Orate pro aïabus Ricardi Danby de | Thorganby, et Margaretæ uxis |
ejus, qui fecerunt hunc lapi | dem, A° Dñi 1452, Quorum | aïabus
ppitietʳ Deus. Amen.

On a flatt stone in yᵉ Church :—Hic jacet Thomas Wylde | nuper
Rector de Thorganby, | qui obiit 4° die Octobris, A° | Dñi 1472.
Cujus aïe &c.

Kevermond.

On yᵉ north side of yᵉ Church, neare the wall, upon a fayre & broade
white freestone (having yᵉ proportions of a man & his wife very
exquisitely cutt, & shadowed in lines) is written :—Hic jacet Joħes de
Keuermond | qui obiit . . . · The other halfe on yᵉ womans side—
Hic jacet Katherina quondam | uxor Joħis Keuermond, que obiit |
Cał. Julii, Año Dñi 1399.

[p. 174.]

Binbrooke Scae Mariae.

In Cancello :—
Vert, a saltier engrayled Arg. . . . . . *Hawley*
In alia Fenestra :—Walter Curtas.

Binbrooke Sci Gabrielis.

In Fenestra orientali :—
G. 5 Fusils in fesse d'Or . . . . . . *Newmarch*
Or, 5 Fusils in fesse G. a bend B.

On a Gravestone in yᵉ Chancell :—
    Spiritus Henrici de Stenaldburne pace fruatur,
    Ipse Vicarius hic, primitus eique datur.

In yᵉ Church :—Hic jacet Dñus Joħes Win | quondam Vicarius Eccłiæ Sēi | Gabrielis, qui obiit in die Sēi | Georgii Año Dñi 1401.

Randby.

In Nave Eccłiæ :—Orate pro aïa Dñi Radulphi | Crumwell, qui incepit hoc | opus Año Dñi 1450.

[p. 175.]

Beningworth.

In Nave Eccłiæ :—WILLIAM IRBE [? GOSLE].

In Insula Boreali :—Hic jacet Elizabetha quondam | uxor Joħis Iwardby, filia Joħis | Hennege de Hainton, Armigeri, | cujus anime &c.

In Fenestra :—Orate pro bono statu Joħis Coek.

In Fenestra Orientali :—Orate pro aïabus Roberti Jonson | et Agnetis . . . aïabus | omnium benefactorum.

In Fenestra Australi :—
G. a plaine crosse Arg.
Vert, a saltier engrailed Arg.   .   .   .   .   .   *Hawley*
Vert, 3 [? horse-pickers], Arg.*

In Fenestra Boreali :—Orate pro bono statu Henrici | Hansard, et aïa Joħæ consortis | suæ defunctæ.

G. 3 mullets Arg.   .   .   .   .   *Haunssard*
G. 3 lapwings d'Or   .   .   .   .   *Tirwhit*
. . . per bast endented . . . a ring dove.

[p. 176.]

Kirkeby-super-Bane.

In yᵉ windowes of yᵉ Parsonage House :—
Quarterly, *France & England*   .   .   .   .   *Rex Angliæ*
Quarterly, *Ufford & Beke*   .   .   .   .   .   *Willughby*
Quarterly, *Percy & Lucy*   .   .   .   .   .   *Northumberland*
Arg. a lyon rampant G.
Party p. pale Arg. & Sa. a crosse sarcely counter-changed.
Purpure, a crosse flowry betw. 4 lyons ramp. Arg.
G. a bend Arg.

---

* These arms are only tricked   The charges are probably horse-pickers, and if so, the arms are those borne by the family of Metringham — *Ed.*

Empaled { . . . 2 bars nebuly Arg.
 { G. 3 lapwings d'Or . . . . . *Tyrwhit*
Empaled { Arg. a saltier, on a cheife G. 3 escallops Arg. *Taylboys*
 { Arg. on a pale Sa. a Lucys head couped d'Or *Gascoyne*
Sa. 2 lyons passants Arg. crowned Or . . . . *Dymoke*

P. pale { Or, a crosse parted Arg. & G.
 { G. a chevron betw. 5 cinquefoyles in cheife & 6 in
 { orbicular forme in bast d'Or.

Quarterly { B. 3 flowers de Lize Arg. . . . . [*Burgh*]
 { Or, a lyon rampant B. . . . . . [*Percy*]
 { Paly of 6 peices Sa. & Or . . . . [*Athole*]

In Cancello Eccɫiæ :—

Lambard Ricardus jacet hac petra tumulatus,
Istius Ecclesiæ quondam Rector fuit ille ;
Quique hunc cancellum noviter fecit fabricari.
En Missale dedit, necnon sua qui bona plura.
In quarto die deno Januar' petit astra,
Anno milleno, C quater LI minus inde.
Æternam requiem cui semper det Deus. Amen.

On another flatt stone next yᵉ former :—

Bulliar Willielmus jacet hic tumulatus,
Istius Ecclesiæ Rector quondam fuit ille,
Ac Crucifixorium noviter fecit fabricari,
Qui Gradile dedit, crucem que cætera plura,
Qui demum obiit XI die Mense Decembris,
Anno milleno quincentum Decimo vere.

In Fenestra Eccɫiæ :—Wiɫɫus Bulliar.

[p. 177.]

Thimbleby.

On a gravestone :—Hic jacet Gulielmus Braken | burgh, et Emmota
uxor ejus, qui | quidem Gulielmus obiit 6° die | Januarii Año Dñi
1476, quorum | aīabus ppitietur Deus. Amen. The pictures of them-
selves upon yᵉ stone, & of 10 children—all in brasse.

Baumbergh.

In Fenestra :—
Arg. a plain cross G.
G. a fesse betw. 6 crosselets botony fitchy Arg. charged with
 as many Mullets Or, peirced G.
Sa. a Bend betw. 6 Mullets Or, peirced G. . . . *Briton*

In yᵉ Church on a flatt marble stone in Saxon characters :—ICI :
GIST : MARGARE | TA : DE : LACI : QE : FV : | LA : FEME :
GWILLE | AME : DE : MOVSTE.

[p. 178.]

Burgh super Bane.

In Fenestra Orientali :—
Vert a saltier engrayled Arg.   .   .   .   .   *Hawley*

Empaled { Vert a saltier engrayled Arg.   . . .   *Hawley*
Arg. semy of crosses botony, a lyon ramp. queue
fursh nowed G. crowned Or .   .   .   *Rowse*

In yᵉ Quire under a flatt free-stone :—Hic jacet Agnes quondam
uxor | Thomæ Blount primo-filia et he | res Johannis Hawley, Dñi de |
Burgh, quæ obiit 14° die Octo | bris A° Dñi 1462, cujus aïe | propit-
ietur Deus.

There is a defaced Monument of blew Marble affixed in yᵉ wall.

Hemingby.

Hic jacet Dñus Johes Midd, | quondam Rector Eccliæ de He |
mingby, qui obiit . . . | Januarii, Año Dñi 1397, cujus | aïe &c.

In Fenestra :—Orate pro Johe de Northby, | et Catherina .   .   .

[p. 179.]

Cuningsby.

In Fenestra Orientali Cancelli :—

Quarlerly { Verry, a fesse G. fretty d'Or   .   .   .   *Marmyon*
Sa. 2 lyons passants Arg. crowned d'Or . . *Dymoke*

Empaled { G. a frett of 8 peices d'Or.
B. 3 garbes d'Or.

G. a lyon rampant d'Or   .   .   .   .   .   *[Fitzalan]*
Sa. a sword in pale Arg.   .   .   .   .   .   *[Kilpec]*
Sa. 2 lyons passants Arg. crowned d'Or   .   .   .   *Dimoke*
Arg. 3 flowers-de-lize betw. 6 crosse crosseletts fitchy Sa. a
border G.   .   .   .   .   .   .   *Hillary*
Arg. a playne crosse G.
G. a playne crosse Arg.

Tumulus lapideus :—Hic jacet Anna filia Thomæ | Dymoke Militis
Dñi . . | et Margaretæ consortis suæ, quæ | obiit A° Dñi 1462, &c.

Verry, a fesse G. fretty d'Or . . . . . *Marmyon*
Or a lyon rampant double queue Sa. . . . . *Welles*

In muro boreali ære sculptum :—Orate pro aïa M^{ri} Joħis de Croxby quondam | Rectoris istius Eccłiæ, qui dedit annualem | redditum XX^s annuatim imppetuum, et | in secunda Feria primæ hebdomadæ Quad | ragesimæ habitantibus in Conningsby scđm | formam Evidentiæ suæ distribuendorum.

This Charity hath ceased for many yeares, ye Evidence having been sacrilegiously stolne out of that Monument within ye wall, as by ye loosening of ye plate of Brasse may appeare.

In Fenestra Occidentali Capellæ Orientalis :—Orate pro aïabus . . Hatcliffe | . . . uxoris suæ . . fenestram.

Sa. 3 welles Arg. *Bis.* . . . . *Wellis*
Empaled { Sa. 3 welles Arg. . . . . . . *Wellis*
{ B. 2 bars d'Or, over all a lyon ramp. G. . *Hatcliffe*
Sa. a sword in pale Arg. . . . . . . [*Kilpec*]
Arg. a fesse daunce betw. 3 Talbotts-heades erased Sa. . [*Spayne*]
Arg. a fesse betw. 3 cootes Sable . . . . . [*Coote*]
[p. 180.] B. 2 bars d'Or, over all a lyon ramp. G. . *Hattecliffe*

Orate pro bono statu H. Wellis | notarii publici . . . | Hatcliffe uxoris suæ, et sequelis eorum . . . hanc | fenestram fieri fecerunt Año | Dñi 1460.

In superioribus Fenestris Borealibus :—
G. a cinquefoyle peirced betw. 8 crosse-crosselets d'Or . *Umfravile*
Quarterly { Sa. a crosse engrayled d'Or . . *Ufford* } *Willughby*
{ G. a crosse sarcely Arg. . . . *Beke* }
G. 3 water-bougetts Arg. . . . . *Ros*
Or, a lyon rampant double-queue Sable. *Bis.* . . . *Welles*
Arg. a crosse patonce G.
Arg. a cheife G. over all a bend engrayled B. . . . [*Leek*]
Chequy Or & G. a cheif Ermyne . . . . *Tateshale*
Ermyne, a fesse G. . . . . *Bernake*
Arg. a cheife G. over all a bend B. . . . . *Crumwell*
Sa. 2 lyons passants Arg. crowned d'Or . . . *Dymoke*
Or, on a fesse G. 3 plates . . . . . . *Huntingfeild*
Quarterly Or & G. a border Sa. bezanty . . . . *Rochford*
G. a cross molyn, Arg. . . . . *Beke*
Quarterly Or & G. a border Sa. bezanty ; on ye 2nd quarter a
Garbe, Arg . . . . *Rochford*
Quarterly &c. an Annulet on ye 2nd quarter . . . *Rochford*
B. crusilly, a lyon rampant Arg.— *Bis.*
Arg. 3 shell-snayles Sa.
Dymoke — Crumwell — Holland.
Quarterly, *France* & *England*—a labell of 3, Arg.
Quarterly, *France* & *England*—a labell of 3, Erm.

In Fenestra Orientali :—Orate pro aïabus fratrum, et | sororum Gildæ Bëæ Mariæ de | Cuningsby, qui istam fenestram | fieri fecerunt.

This is a fayre window adorned with the genealogy of yᵉ Kinges of Israell & Judah, David lying along through yᵉ whole bottome, from whose roote branch out yᵉ severall stems. In one part of it below yᵉ picture of King Edward yᵉ first crowned &c.

Edwardus Primus regnavit annos   .   .   .
Orate pro Matilda de Padholme, | et Alicia   .   .   .

[p. 181.]   On a gravestone :—Hic jacet Dñus Thomas Butler | quon-dam capellanus Gildæ Bëæ | Mariæ Cunningsby, qui obiit 10 | die Mensis Decembris Año Dñi | 1510, Cujus aïe &c.

Another :—Pray for the Soule of John Smith of | Cunsby, some-time M'chant of yᵉ Staple | of Calis, which died in yᵉ yeare of Oʳ Lᵈ | God 1470, & Jonet his wife, wᶜʰ died | yᵉ 24ʰ day of November in yᵉ yeare | of our Lord God 1461.
And all Good people yᵗ this Scripture reade, or see,
For their soules say a Paternoster, Ave Maria, & a Creed for charity.

On another yᵉ Portraytures of a man & his two wives on either side of him in Brasse, with this inscription, Vizᵗ :—Pray for yᵉ Soules of Richard Whete | croft of Coningsby, M'chant of yᵉ Sta | ple at Calice, & sometimes Lieu | tenant of yᵉ same. & Jane & Margaret | his wives, wᶜʰ Richard deceased yᵉ | 23 day of November Aᵒ Dñi 1524.

In yᵉ parlour of yᵉ Parsonage house :—

Arg. a crosse engrayled G. betw. 4 water-bougets Sa. .	*Bourchier*
Quarterly { G. billetty d'Or, a fesse Arg.	*Lovayne*
Quarterly, *Crumwell & Tateshale*.	
B. a manche d'Or	[*Conyers*]
Empaled { Sa. 3 Lyons passants gardants Arg.	
Sa. 2 Lyons passants Arg. crowned d'Or .	*Dymoke*
Empaled *Dymoke & Marmyon*.	
[p. 182.] Verry, a fesse G.	*Marmyon*
Or, a Lyon rampant, double queue Sable . . .	*Welles*
Empaled { A coate defaced.	
Welles.	
Empaled { Verry, a fesse G.	*Marmyon*
B. a manche d'Or	[*Conyers*]

All these escocheons are in two windowes, in wᶜʰ two windows are also these Verses :—

Alme Deus cæli Croxby tu parce Johanni,
Hanc ædem fieri benefecit sponte Jo. Croxby,
Anno milleno quater C LX quoque terno.

In yᵉ other windowes :—

Barry of 6, Erm. & G. 3 Crescents Sa. . . .	*Waterton*
Quarterly, *Ufford & Beke*	*Willughby*

Verry, a fesse G. . . . . *Marmyon*
Ermine, 5 fusills in fesse G. . . . . . *Hebden*
Arg. a crosse sarcely Sa.
Empaled { Quarterly, *Crumwell* & *Tateshale* . . *Crumwell*
{ B. a fesse between 6 Billets d'Or . . . *Deyncourt*
Empaled *Dymoke* & *Welles*.
Sa. an arming Sword Pile in poynte Arg. . . . [*Kilpec*]
Empaled { Arg. 3 Bulls passants.
{ G. on a chevron Arg. 3 Pomeis.
Empaled { Arg. a fesse dauncè betw. 3 Talbots heads,
{ erased Sa. . . . . . [*Spayne*]
{ Arg. a fesse between 3 Cootes Sa. . . . [*Coote*]

[p. 183.]

Croxby.

In Fenestra superiori Insulæ Borealis :—
Sa. a chevron between 3 Mullets Arg. *bis*.
Arg. a chevron, Sa. between 2 [? nails*] in chief, a garbe in bast.
1. Thoresby. 2. . . . .

Stainton in le Hole.

— a chevron between a Mullet in chief, 2 in bast ; in chief 2
[? nails*], in bast a garbe.†

[p. 184.]

Tateshale.

A gravestone in yᵉ upper ende of yᵉ Chancell :—Hic jacet nobilis
Baro Raðus | Crumwell, Dñus de Crumwell | quondam Thesaurarius
Angliæ, | et fundator hujus Collegii, cum | inclita Consorte sua Mar-
gareta | filia et una hæredum Dñi | Dayncourt ; qui quidem Radus |
obiit 4° die Mensis Januarii | Año Dñi 1455 : Et predicta | Margareta
obiit 15° die Mensis; | Septembris, Año Dñi 1454, | quoꝝ. aïabus
ppitietur Deus.

Upon yᵉ tombe these 2 escocheons cutt in Brasse :—
1. *Crumwell* & *Tateshale* quartered.
2. *Deyncourt*.

---

* The charges are like nails, points downwards, with square heads and a
protuberance about one-third of the way down.—*Ed.*
† This coat is a combination of the two preceding ones, one of the mullets of
the first being inserted between the two nails of the second, and the two others
added on either side of the garbe in base. These coats are tricked only, and not
blazoned.—*Ed.*

On another Tombe, or Gravestone next to this, is y⁰ portrayture of a
Lady cutt in Brasse, with this following inscription :—
Hic jacet nobilis Dña Matilda | uxor Roꞗti Dñi de Willughby |
Militis, et consanguinea et hæres | illustris Dñi Raꝺi nuper Dñi |
Crumwell fundatoris hujus | Collegii, et specialis benefactrix | ejusdem
Collegii, quæ obiit 30° | die Augusti Año Dñi 1497. | Cujus aɪæ
ꝑpitietur Deus.*

Escocheons on the tombe at the upper corners :—

Quarterly { 1 & 4. A bend between 6 crosses-crossletts. . *Lungvilliers*
for *Stanhope*
2. *Crumwell.* 3. *Tateshall.*

Empaled { Quarterly *Ufford & Beke. Willughby.*
Stanhope.

[p. 185.]   On y⁰ lower corners these two :—

Empaled { Quarterly *(defaced).*
Quarterly, 1 & 4. *Stanhope.*
2 & 3. *Crumwell & Tateshall,* quarterly.

Empaled { . . . a lyon rampant . . . . [*Clyfton*]
Stanhope.

On y⁰ other side North y⁰ portrayture of a Lady cut in Brasse upon
a Monument with these foure ensueing Escocheons, one at every
corner :—

Quarterly { 1. Defaced.
2. *France & England* quarterly, a label of 3 points.
3. . . . a fesse—
4. *Crumwell & Tateshall,* quarterly.

Empaled { . . . a bend engrayled . . . [*Ratcliff*]
Crumwell & Tateshall, quarterly.

Quarterly, *Stanhope & Tateshall.*
Quarterly, *Stanhope* with *Crumwell & Tateshall* quarterly.

The inscription :—Orate pro aɪa Dñæ Johannæ | Crumwell, quæ
obiit decimo die | Martii Año Dñi 1490. Cujus | aɪæ ꝑpitietur Deus.†

---

* Matilda Lady Willoughby was a daughter of Sir Richard Stanhope by
Matilda sister of Ralph Lord Crumwell, and was one of her uncle's heirs. She
married, 1st Robert, Lord Willoughby of Eresby, who died 1454 ; 2nd Sir Thomas
Nevill, son of Richard, Earl of Salisbury, who was killed on the Yorkist side at
Wakefield in 1460 ; 3rd Sir Gervase Clifton, who was beheaded as a Lancastrian
after the battle of Tewkesbury in 1471. Thus the escutcheons on her tomb represent,
first, her own arms, *Stanhope*, quartering *Crumwell* and *Tateshale* ; then their empalement with *Willoughby*, her first husband ; then an empalement defaced, which must
be for *Nevill*, her second husband ; then as empaled with a lion rampant, for *Clifton*,
her third husband.—*Ed.*

† Joan Lady Crumwell, sister of Lady Willoughby, married 1st Sir Humphrey
Bourchier, created Baron Crumwell in her right, who quartered the royal arms in
right of his grandmother, Anne daughter and eventually sole heir of Thomas Plan-
tagenet, Duke of Gloucester. He was killed at the battle of Barnet in 1471, and she
married secondly Sir Robert Ratcliff, whose arms were Arg. a bend engr. Sa.—*Ed.*

Next under another fayre Monument of blew marble (as the former) the picture of one also inlayd in Brasse, adorned rounde about wth a border of curious workemanship in Brasse, wth the pictures & names of some Saxon Kinges as Edmund, Edward, Etheldred, Ethelbert : there is noe [**p.** 186.] Inscription, onely this ensueing Escocheon upon either side of him—. . on a chevron between 3 bugle horns . . two roses slipped . .

In ye body of ye Chancell under a blew marble inlayd in Brasse :—
Vir Virtute virens Gulielmus vulgo vocatus
More micuit mire intus bene morigeratus,
Hujus Collegii de Tattershale secundus
Prudens Præpositus, et egenis semper habundus.
Hic Eboracensis fuit Ecclesiæ Cathedralis
Canonicus, Rector et de Ledenham specialis,
Sacræ Scripturæ Baccalaurius arte probatus,
Jam sub tellure fit vermibus esca paratus.
Octobris dena mensis cum luce novena
Mense prima moritur, cujus corpus sepelitur,
Mil. Dñi. C. quater. L. sexto continuatur,
Spiritus in celis ejus sine fine locatur.*

On ye North side under a marble :—Orate pro aïa M^ri Joħis Gigur | baccalaurei Theologiæ, custodis | hujus Collegii, ac etiam . .; | Collegii Marton in Oxonia, qui | obiit 12° die . . .

On ye woodworke in ye lower ende of ye Quire curiously carved in Capitall letters this :—Ad honorem et gloriam Dei Opt. | Max. et decorem domus ejus | hoc opus factum est Anno Dñi | 1424.

[**p.** 187.] Betweene ye Chancell & ye Church under ye arched Roofe : —Hic jacet Hugo . . . quondam | servus Dñi Raði de Crumwell Mi | litis Dñi de Tatshall, qui obiit ul | timo die Septembris A° 1415.

In Fenestris :—The History of ye Passion depainted.

In another :—Hells Torments, where are divers Creatures bound togeather in a chayne ; amongst whom one with a Crowne, another with a Mytre on his head, ye Divell tormenting them ; & under is written :—Sic affliguntur pænis, qui prava sequuntur.

The History of Hermogenes y^t raysed up Devills, & of Guthlake (ye Saint of ye Fens) & of Catherina, who cast them into ye Sea, y^t Hermogenes & Philetus raysed.

The History of Cosdre with his decollation.

In Fenestris ex latere Australi :—
Arg. a cheife G. surtout a Bend B. . . . . *Crumwell*

---

* William More, or Moor, whose name is here played on, was presented to the Wardenship on the resignation of Thomas Ripholme in 1443, and died on the 9th or 19th October, 1456. In the last line but two of his epitaph " Mense prima moritur " appears to be a mis-reading for " Mente pia moritur."—*Ed.*

Quarterly, *Crumwell*, with Chequy d'Or & G. a cheife Ermyne *Tateshall*

G. a lyon rampant d'Or . . . . . . *Fitz-Alane*

Arg. 3 Cinquefoyles; & a Canton, G. . . . . *Driby*

Bendy of 10 peices, Arg. & G. . . . . . *[Cailli]*

Ermyne, a fesse G. . . . . . . *Bernake*

B. a fesse daunce between 10 Billets d'Or . . . *Deyncourt*

G. 10 Annulets d'Or . . . . . . *[Old Crumwell]*

Chequy d'Or & G. a Bend Ermyne . . . . *Clifton*

Quarterly, *Crumwell & Tateshale.*

Empaled { Arg. a cheife G. surtout a Bend B. . . *Crumwell*
{ Arg. a chevron B. a File with 3 Lambeaux d'Or.

Barry of 6, Arg. & B. a Bend G. . . . *Grey of Rotherfield*

Verry, a fesse G. . . . . . . *Marmyun*

Arg. a cheife G. surtout a Bend B. a labell of 3 Erm. *Crumwell*

Lozengy, Arg. & G. . . . . . . *Fitz-William*

Ex latere Boreali :—

Empaled { Chequy d'Or & G. a Bendlet B.
{ Lozengy, Arg. & G. . . . . *Fitz-William*

B. a Crosse patonce Arg.

Party p. pale G. & Sa. a Lyon ramp. Arg. crowned d'Or *[Bellers]*

Arg. 3 water-pots covered G. a Border Sa. bezanty . *Monboucher*

Empaled { Arg. a cheife G. over all a Bend B. . . *Crumwell*
{ Party p. pale G. & Sa. a Lyon ramp. Arg. crowned
        d'Or . . . . , . *[Bellers]*

Arg. a chevron betw. 3 Pots covered G. a Border Sa. bezanty.

[p. 188.]   Arg. a cheife G. surtout a Bend B. a labell of 3 d'Or.

Barry of 6, Arg. & G. a Bend engrayled d'Or . . . *Grey*

Crumwell, with a Labell of 3 Ermyne.

In Fenestris utrinque super portas Australem et Borealem :—

Orate pro aĩa Radulphi nuper | Dñi Crumwell et Tateshale, | Thes-
aurarii Angliæ, et fundatoris | hujus Collegii.

The Roode loft 1524.

G. a Saltier Arg. a File with 3 lambeaux B. . . . *Nevile*

Lozengy, Sa. & Erm. on a cheife Sa. 3 Lillies Arg. . *Wainflet*

Epus Winton, cujus Insignia sculptata super utramque porticum in
Saxo.

Thomas Howard, geñ, et Beatrix consors ejus vitriaverunt Fenestram
borealem in honore Scæ Catherinæ ; cujus passio ibidm̃.

Empaled { Arg. a chevron chequy d'Or & G. betw. 3 Flesh-hookes Sa.
{ B. a fesse between 3 Storkes Arg.

Arg. a chevron betw. 3 Catherine wheeles d'Or.

Deyncourt super portam Collegii.

Super Crucem in foro Villæ *Crumwell & Tateshale* paling *Deyncourt*, &
per se *ter*.

Gravestones in yᵉ Church.

Hic jacet Thomas Gibbon artium | Liberalium Mgr. Rector nuper de | Wiberton, Socius et precentor hujus | Collegii, qui obiit 16° die mensis Ja | nuarii A° Dñi 1506, Cujus &c.

Another.

Orate pro aīa Dñi Henr̃. Porter
Capti, quondam Socii Collegii de
Tatshall, ac precentor' ejusdem
Eccłiæ, qui obiit 12° die Martii
Año Dñi 1519.

Another.

[p. 189.]

Hic jacet Edwardus Okey
Nuper unus sex Clericorum hujus
Collegii. qui obiit 29° die Januarii
Año Dñi 1519. Cujus &c.

In Insula Australi.

Hic jacet Rĭcus English artium
liberalium Mgʳ Socius ac precentor hujus
Collegii, et Vicarius Eccłiæ de Burwell
qui obiit 29° die Martii A° Dñi 1522.

Another.

Orate pro aīa Mʳⁱ Robti Sudbury, sa-
-cræ Theologiæ Baccalaureus nuper
Rector . . . . ac quondam
precentor et socius hujus Collegii, qui
obiit 19° Decembris, Año 1482.

Under yᵉ arched Worke of yᵉ Partition between yᵉ Chancell & yᵉ body of yᵉ Church, thus :—

Orate pro aīa Robti de Whalley
. . . . hujus Collegii qui
hoc opus fieri fecit A° Dñi 1528.
Cujus aīe ppitietur Deus. Amen.

Within a Chappell on yᵉ North side of a fayre flatt Marble, on wʰ this Epitaph :—

Have mercy on yᵉ Soule (good Lord) we thee pray
Of Edward Hevyn layd here in Sepulture.
Wᶜʰ to thine honour this Chappell did array
With ceiling, deske, perclose, & pourtrayture,
And paviment of Marble longe to endure,
Servant of late to the excellent Princesse,
Mother to King Henry, of Richmund Countesse.

The Armes on ye Gravestone are :—

Empaled {
A chevron betw. 3 Boares heades couped, having
    so many Pomeis in their mouths ; on y^e
    chevron a crescent . . . . *Hevyn*
A chevron betw. 3 Bulls heades.
}

[p. 190.]

Cauenby.

In the Hall of Edward Tourney of Cauenby, Esq. these auncient &
very fayre Escocheons in ye windowes :—

G. 3 Lyons passants guardants d'Or . . . . *England*
England, on a labell B. 9 Flowers-de-Lize Or . [*E. of Lancaster*]
Quarterly, *Castile & Leon.*
Chequy, d'Or & B. . . . . *Warenne*
B. a bend Arg. cotised betw. 6 Lyoncells ramp. d'Or . . *Bohun*
Or, a lyon rampant purpure . . . . *Lacy*
Or, a lyon rampant B. . . . . *Percy*
Party p. pale d'Or & Vert, a lyon ramp. G. . . *Comes Pembrochiæ*
B. billetty, a Fesse dauncetty d'Or . . . . *Deyncourt*

In another window :—
G. 3 Bulls passants in pale barways d'Or.

In ye parlour :—

Empaled {
Arg. a chevron betw. 3 Bulls passants Sa. . *Tourney*
Or, on a chevron betw. 3 annulets G. as many
    crescents of ye first . . . . *Sutton*
}

Tourneys crest over ye empalement, which is a Crosse formy Arg.

[p. 191.]

Memorabilia in Eccl'iis com. Lincoln.

Stow Beae Mariae.

Obiit Thomas Holbeche 15° Aprilis, Año 1591.   Anna uxor 1581.
In muro Australi Cancelli lapideus Tumulus.

Empaled {
Quarterly {
5 Escallops in Saltier . . . *Holbech*
on a cheife 3 lyons-heades erased.
}
Ermine, a chevron betw. 3 mullets peirced . . *Yaxley*
}

In Fenestra boreali :—
Arg. on a chevron G. a falcon volant, Arg. betw. 3 ogresses :
    on a cheife Arg. a rose G. & 2 leopards-faces B.
Joħes Longland Eр̄us Linc. temp. Hen. 8.
Empales ye armes of ye Bishopricke of Lincolne.

[p. 192.]

Cotes juxta Stow.

In Fenestra Orientali Cancelli :—
G. on 3 fusills in fesse Arg. as many roses G.
G. 3 mullets, & a martlet Arg. in bast . . . . *Hansard*
Empaled { G. a crosse Tau betw. 3 mullets Arg. . . *Hansard*
{ V. a chevron betw. 3 mullets Or . . . *Pudsey*

In Fenestra boreali Navis :—
Quarterly { G. 3 mullets, Arg. . . . . . *Hansard*
{ G. 3 lapwings Or ; a martlet, Arg. . . . *Tirwhit*
Vert 3 bowes bent G. liè Or ; in bast an escallop Arg.
Hansard with an annulet empales *Pudsey*.

In Fenestra australi Navis :—
G. 3 mullets, in bast a Martlet Arg. . . . . , *Hansard*
Arg. a Flowre de Lize Sa. . . . . . *Fishburne*

Tumulus alabastr. in Choro :—
Hic quondam in orbe vivens Hansard Henricus humatur,
Armiger, arma gerens, honor sic cito superatur.
Uxores binas habens, Joanna Aliciaque vocantur,
Sub lapideque latens, horum et corpora in pace locantur.
Cum hoc Epitaphio insignia *Hansard* et *Pudsey* ut supra.

Juxta Cancellum tumulus lapideus :—
Hic simul humati jacent generosi prostrati
Hansard Henricus, uxor Joanna, Ricardus
Filius, et hæres eorum, cui detur Nardus.
Cælicus Rex Jĥus quibus sit modo ppitius. Amen.

3 Lapwings [*Tirwhit*]. 3 Mullets [*Hansard*].
3 Seingliers trippant with a Mullet.

Wiłłus Fuljam Armiger | Obiit 1487 X° Novembris.

Sa. a bend between 6 escallops Or . . . . *Fouljamb*

[p. 193.] Juxta murum borealem Cancelli :—
Antonius Butler Armig. obiit 5to die Septembris, 1570.
Empaled { Arg. on a chevron B. 3 cups covered d'Or betw. }
{   as many demy-lyons passant gardant G. } *Butler*
{   crowned Or . . . . . . }
{ Or, on a cheife Sa. 3 martlets of ye 1st . *Wogan*

In muro Australi :—
Gulielmus 2^{dus} filius ejusdem An | tonii Obiit 28° die Aprilis A°
1590 : Duxit | Elizabetham filiam Georgii Yorke ; Priscilla | unica
eorum proles obiit infans.
Empaled { *Butler*.
{ Arg. a saltier B. . . . . . . *Yorke*

Carolus Butler primogenitus filius | ipsius Antonii obiit 17° die
Aprilis A° 1602 : | Dowglassia uxor ejus 3ᵗⁱᵃ filia Marmaduci | Tyrwhit
de Skotter, Armiḡ.

Empaled { *Butler.*
{ G. 3 lapwings d'Or, a mullet difference   *Tyrwhit of Scotter*

[p. 194.]

Leagh.

In Fenestra Orientali Cancelli :—Rogerus de Spalding Rector hujus
| Eccīiæ has Fenestras fieri fecit.

Mᵈ quod Rectoria de Gait-Burton et Leagh quondam fuere possessiones Prioratus de Spalding.

Statua lapidea viri, tibiis in crucem transversis, in scuto gestantis :—
A Bend within a border counter-compony, *Trehampton*, ut opinor.

In Fenestra Orientali Insulæ Borealis :—
G. 3 lyons passants gardants Or, a labell of 3 Files.
Chequy Or & B.   .   .   .   .   *Warren*
B. crusilly, a lyon rampant Or   .   .   .   .   .   *Brewes*
Arg. a Bend G. a border counter-compony Or & B.   .   *Trehamton*
Arg. a Bend G.   .   .   .   .   ut opinor

Effigies Viri et Feminæ gestantium super pectora le Bend & Border
counter-compony, et in manibus Ecclesiam—*Trehamton.*

In Fenestra Boreali Navis :—
G. a lyon rampant double queue Or   .   .   .   [*Burghershe*]
Arg. a bend G. a border counter-compony Or & B.   .   *Trehamton*
B. crusilly, a lyon rampant Or   .   .   .   .   .   *Brewes*

In Fenestra Occidentali :—
Arg. on a Bend B. 3 cinquefoyles Or, pierced G.

Gait Burton.

No Entries.

[p. 195.]

Glentworth.

Tumulus Christopheri Wray | Militis Capitalis Justitiarii Angliæ |
qui obiit 7° die Maii Año Dñi 1592, | Año 34° Elizabethæ Reginæ.

Epitaphium :—
    Quisquis es, O hospes, manes reverere sepultos,
    Qui jacet hic nostri gloria Juris erat ;

Christopherus Wraius, re Justus, nomine Verus,
  Quique pia micuit cognitione, fide.
En, fuit! en, non est! Rapidum rotat omnia Fatum.
  Heu, moritur nobis ; ipse sibi superest.
Terram terra petit, cinem cinis, ætheraque æther ;
  Spiritus ætherei possidet astra poli.

Empaled
 Quarterly
 { B. on a cheife Or, 3 Martlets G. . *Wray*
 Arg. on a chevron Sa. 3 cinquefoyles
   peirced of ye 1st betw. as many
   falcons heads erased B. . . *Jackson*
 Quarterly
 Arg. a chevron betw. 3 Papillions Sa. a
   crescent difference . . *Girlington*
 G. a chevron betw. 3 sufflues,* Or.
 G. on a bend Arg. 3 leopards-faces B.
 Sa. a fesse Ermine betw. 3 Goates
   heads erased Arg.

Wray's Crest—an Estrich Or.
Girlington's—a demy Griffon sergreant Sa.

[p. 196.]

Willerton.

In Fenestra Orientali Cancelli :—
Arg. on a Bend cotised Sa. 3 annulets of ye first . . *Dawney*
G. a crosse Or . . . . *Crevecœure*
Sa. 3 Roses Arg. on a cheife party p. pale B. & G. a Flowre
  de lize, & a Lyon pass. gard. Or.
Dawneys Armes again, with his word, Vizt.—Dread Shame.

Tumulus in muro Boreali :—
Nicholaus Sutton obiit 6to die | Decembris Año Dñi 1602, ætatis |
suæ 88°.

Empaled
 { Or, on a chevron between 3 annulets G. 3
   crescents of ye first . . . . *Sutton*
 Arg. a saltier engrailed Sa.

Empaled
 { *Sutton.*
 Arg. a fesse betw. 3 Falcons-heads erased Sa.

Quarterly
 { *Sutton*, with a Crescent difference.
 Or, a lyon rampant, double queue, Vert.
 G. 3 boares heads couped Or.
 Arg. a saltier engrayled Sa.

Juxta, Tumulus super solum :—
Hic jacet Nicholaus Sutton, Ar | miger, qui obiit 6to die Martii |
Año Dñi 1556.
Sutton's Creast—On a Torce Or & G. a Boares head d'Or, coupee.

---

* *Sufflues*—tricked as Spades.—*Ed.*

Scotter.

[p. 197.]

In Cancello ad austrum tumulus marmoreus ære inscriptus :—
Hic jacet Wiłłus Tyrwhit, Miles, | qui obiit 19° die Martii, Año Dñi
| 1541.

G. 3 lapwings Or   .   .   .   .   *Tyrwhit*

Juxta Cancellum in muro :—
Marmaducus Tyrwhit 4^{tus} filius | Wiłłi Tyrwhit, Militis, obiit 21° |
die Januarii Año 1599, Ætatis | suæ 66° ; Uxor ejus fuit Helena | filia
Leonelli Reresby.

Empaled { G. 3 lapwings, Or, with a Mullet difference   .   *Tyrwhit*
{ G. on a Bend Arg. 3 crosses botony Sa.   .   *Reresby*

In muro Boreali Cancelli :—
Donate cineri Bonner corpus Nicholai.
Rector præsentis fuit Ecclesiæque Magister
Artibus, O genitrix sedibus . . . atque Minister,
Ergo tuum Natum rogito sibi propitiatum.
. . . Obiit . . . . Julii, 1511.

[p. 198.]

Bliton.

In Fenestra Orientali Cancelli :—
Lozengy Or & G. a labell of 5 pointes B.
Arg. a lyon rampant G crowned Or, a border Sa bezanty.

                                                 [*E. of Cornwall*]

In Fenestra Boreali Cancelli :—

Empaled { Quarterly { Barry of 6 Erm. & G. 3 Crescents Sa. . *Waterton*
{ G. a mullet Arg.
{ Arg. on a Fesse dauncee Sa. 3 Bezants   *Burgh*
{ Sa. fretty Or   .   .   .   .   [*Belleau*]
{ Sa. 3 Mattocks, Arg.   .   .   .   .   [*Pigot*]

In Fenestra Orientali Navis :—On a bend 3 cinquefoyles. Effigies
viri et fæminæ gestantium super pectora eadem insignia.

In duabus Fenestris Borealibus :—Priez for y^c Gild of Corpus Xti
quilk y^is window garte mak.

In Fenestra Occidentali juxta ostium :—
Party p. pale counter-changed Arg. & B. a chevron G.

Springthorpe cum Sturgathe.

Empaled { Arg. on a Bend Sa. 3 leopards-faces of ye first ; in cheife a
{   Flowre de lize Sa.
{ B. a lyon rampant Or.

[p. 199.]

Coringham magna. Somerby.

Coringham parva. Pauthorpe.

Aby. Dunstall.

Præbenda Eccłiæ Lincolniæ concessa a Rege Henrico primo. Cancellum super Statuam.

Empaled { . . on a Bend, 3 escallops.
{ A saltier.

Tumulus Marmoreus muro boreali, cum effigie desuper.

Hic jacet Magister Wiłłus de | Lagare quondam Archidiaconus | Lincolniæ, et Prebendarius hujus | Eccłiæ.*

In Fenestra Orientali :—

Arg. a saltier G.—*bis.*

Arg. on a saltier G.—a crescent.

Empaled { Barry of 6, Erm. & G., 3 crescents Sa.   .   *Waterton*
{ G. a mullet Arg. &c.

In Fenestra Orientali Insulæ Borealis :—

Barry of 6 peices, Erm. & G. 3 crescents, Sa.   .   .   *Waterton*

In Fenestra boreali :—

Empaled { Quarterly { *Waterton.*
{ { G. a mullet peirced Arg.
{ { Sa. Fretty Or.   .   .   .   .   *[Belleau]*
{ { Arg. on a Fesse dauncee Sa bezantes   .   *Burgh*
{ Arg. on a saltier engr. Sa. 9 annulets Or   .   .   *Leake*

In Fenestra Australi Insulæ Orientalis :—

Quarterly { 1 & 8, Party p. pale Arg. & Vert 3 Crescents G.   *Topcliffe*
{ Barry of 6, Erm. & G. 3 Crescents Sa.   .   *Waterton*
{ Sa. a Tower Arg.   .   .   .   .   .   *[Towers]*
{ Arg. a chevron, on yᵉ dexter point a Cinquefoyle Sa.
{ Sa. Fretty Or   .   .   .   .   .   *[Belleau]*
{ G. an annulet Arg.
{ Arg. on a Fesse dauncee Sa. 3 bezantes   .   *Burgh*

* William de la Gare held the Prebend of Corringham from 1276 till his death : he became Archdeacon of Lincoln in 1280, and died in December, 1290. His tomb still remains in Corringham Church.—*Ed.*

Carleton.

[p. 200.]

Tumuli super humum ex ære, marmore et lapide fixo :—

Hic jacet Joħes Munson Miles, qui | obiit 26° die Maii, Año Dñi 1542, et Do | rothea uxor ejus &c.

Empaled { Or, 2 chevrons G. in cheife a crescent . . *Munson*
{ G. a fesse betw. 3 water-bougets Erm. . . . *Meres*

Hic jacent Wiħus Munson, Armig. | qui obiit 15° die Octobris, Año 1558, et | Elizabetha uxor ejus, filia Roberti | Tirwhit Militis, quæ obiit 8ᵛᵒ die Octo | bris, Año Dñi 1546 &c.

Empaled { Or, 2 chevrons, & 2 crescents in cheife G. . *Munson*
{ G. 3 Lapwings Or. . . . . . *Tyrwhit*

Hic jacet Joħes Munson, filius et | hæres apparens Wiħi Munson, Arm. | qui obiit 17° die Novembris, Año | Dñi 1552.

Empaled { *Munson.*
{ Or, a plaine Crosse Vert . . . . *Hussy*

Joħes Munson, Miles, obiit 20° | die Decembris, Año Dñi 1593.

His Banner & Sheild ; his armes without a difference, his Crest yᵉ Moone griping the Sun, Or, his colours Or & G.

His motto—Prest pur mon pais.

Munson & Meres sculpt. super lignum in Ingressu Cancelli.

In Fenestra Orientali Cancelli :—

Arg. a Bend Sa. . . . . *Paynell*

In Fenestra Australi Cancelli :—

Or, 2 chevrons G. . . . . . . *Munson*
G. a fesse betw. 3 Water-bougets, Erm. . . . *Meres*
Empaled { Or, 2 chevrons, G. . . . . *Munson*
{ G. 3 lapwings, Or. . . . . . *Tyrwhit*
Quarterly, G. & Verry, a Bend, Or . . . *Constable*

In Fenestra Australi Navis Superiori :—

Arg. a chevron G. betw. 3 Water-bougets, Sa. . . . *Hill*
Empaled { *Hill*, with a mullet on yᵉ chevron.
{ Arg. a chevron B. a label of 3 points G.

Fenestra inferior juxta ostium :—

Quarterly { B. a crosse molin, Arg.
{ Lozengy, Erm. & G. . . . . *Rokeley*

[p. 201.]

Ganesburgh.

Tumulus marmoreus cum effigiebus alabastrinis Thomæ Burgh, Militis aureæ Periscelidis, et uxoris ejus.*

In Fenestra Insulæ Australis :—

Empaled { Quarterly { B. 3 flowres de lize Erm. a labell with 3 files, Arg. . . . . *Burgh*
Or. a lyon rampant B . . . . *Percy*
Or, 3 Pallets, Sa. . *Comyn, Comes Atholiæ*
G. on a chevron Or, 3 estoyles Sa. *Cobham of Sterborough*

Burgh & his quarterings within yᵉ Garter.

Empaled { B. 3 Flowres de lize, Erm. . . . . *Burgh*
Quarterly { G. 3 water-bougets, Arg. . . . *Ros*
G. a fesse betw. 2 bars gemells Arg. a crescent B. & wheel within Arg. [*Badlesmere*]

Empaled { B. a cheife, & 3 chevronels braced in bast Or. *Fitz Hugh*
B. 3 Flowres de lize Erm. . . . . *Burgh*

An Arme coupee Arg. lie Or, Vulgo Manfere.† } Burgh's crest
A Falcon volant Erm. collared wᵗʰ a crowne Or. } & supporters.

G. 3 Grey-houndes cursant Arg.
Arg. a saltier Sa.
Arg. a manch, Sa. . . . . *Hastings*
Chequy Arg. & Sa. a Bend G.
Arg. a lyon rampant G. crowned Or ; a border engrayled Sa. bezantee . . . . . [*Earl of Cornwall*]

In muro Australi Insulæ Australis :—

Tumulus Agnetis filiæ Christopheri Draper Militis, Aldermañ. Londoñ, et unius her. ejus, primæ Conjugis Wiłłi Hickeman (postea Militis,) quæ obiit 22° Feb., 1599. Elizabeth filia senior, Wiłłi Willughby, heř. apparentis Caroli Dñi Willughby de Parham, uxor secunda.

---

* Sir Thomas Burgh, knt. was created K.G. and Baron Burgh of Gainsborough in 1487 : he was the son of Thomas Burgh, esq. by Elizabeth, daughter and coheiress of Sir Henry Percy, knt. styled d'Athol, his mother having been daughter and heiress of David de Strabolgi (not Comyn), Earl of Athol. He married Margaret, daughter of Thomas Lord Ros, and is represented by the 2ⁿᵈ coat of arms, empaling *Ros* and *Badlesmere* quarterly, as well as by the coat within the Garter. He died in 1496 : and the 1ˢᵗ coat, empaling *Cobham*, is that of his son and successor, Sir Edward Burgh, knt. who became a lunatic and was never summoned to Parliament. He married Anne, daughter of Sir Thomas Cobham, and niece and heiress of Reginald, Lord Cobham, of Sterborough, co. Surrey. The other coats record alliances of the Burgh family, Margaret a daughter of Thomas Lord Burgh, having married Sir George Tailbois, knt. who died in 1538, and another, Elizabeth, having married 1ˢᵗ, Richard, 6ᵗʰ Baron Fitzhugh, who died in 1487 ; and 2ⁿᵈ, Sir Henry Willoughby, of Wollaton, knt. who died in 1528.—*Ed.*

† *Manfere, i.e. Fr.* Main ferrée, an iron-clad hand, mailed fist, or gauntlet.—*Ed.*

Empaled {
Party p. pale endented Arg. & B.   . .   *Hickman*

Quarterly {
  Arg. on a Fesse G. a mullet of ye first &
    2 cuppes Or, betw. 3 annulets of ye 2nd *Draper*
  Erm. on a cheife B. 3 lyons ramp. Or.
  Erm. a Fesse chequy Arg. & Sa.

Fenestra Orientalis in Ludo litterario :—

Empaled { Arg. a Saltier, on a cheife G. 3 escallops, Arg. . *Taylbois*
B. 3 Flowres de Lize, Ermine   . . . . *Burgh*

Empaled { Quarterly, *Fitz-Hugh* & *Marmyon.*
Burgh.

Empaled { Or, on 2 bars G. 3 water-bougets Arg.
                    [*Willoughby of Wollaton*]
B. 3 Flowres de Lize, Erm.   . . .   *Burgh*

Dñus Georgius Tailbois me fieri fecit.
Dña Elizab. Fitz-Hugh me fieri fecit.

Wiberton.

[p. 202.]   Tumulus marmoreus :—
Ici gyst Adam de Franton Ky | trespassa en l'an 1325 le 28 Jour |
de December, prietz pur sa alme. | Ici gyst Sybill sa feme. . . . |
trespassa   MCCC . . .

In Fenestra Boreali :—
Sa. a crescent Or betw. 2 roses in cheife & a mullet in bast
  Arg. . . . . [*Witham*]
In scuto funebri :—
Lozengy Arg. & G. wth a mullet . . . . *Fitz William*

Frampton.

In Fenestris Austral. Cancelli :—
Or, on a fesse G. 3 plates . . . . *Huntingfeild*
G. a crosse sarcely, Arg. . . . . . . *Beke*
Or, on a fesse G. 3 plates . . . . *Huntingfeild*
Arg. 3 lyons passants gardants G. . . . . *Littlebury*

In Fenestra Boreali :—
G. 3 Bars Ermine . . . . . . *Kirketon*

In Fenestra ad dextram Campanilis :—
G. a crosse engrayled Or . . . . . *Ufford*
Arg. a chevron betw. 3 crosses botony G. . . . *Copuldike*
G. 3 Bars, Ermine . . . . . *Kirketon*
The window bordered wth G. a Bend, Erm. . . . *Ry*
Ad sinistram : —
Or, on a fesse G. 3 Plates—*bis* . . . . *Huntingfeild*
Arg. a chevron betw. 3 crosses botony G. . . *Copuldike*

[p. 203.]

Boston.

Villa de Boston incorporata fuit in Burgum 14° die Maii año 37 Hen. VIII (1546).

In Fenestra Australi Cancelli :—

Barry of 6, Arg. & B. in cheife 3 lozenges G. a Mitre on ye second Bar, *Ricus Flemming Ep'us Lincoln, quondam Rector istius Eccl'iæ.*

Sa. a crosse engrayled, Or		*Ufford*
Quarterly { G. 3 water-bougets, Arg.		*Ros*
Arg. a Fesse betw. 2 Bars gemells G. .		*Badlesmere*
Quarterly { Sa. a crosse engrayled, Or, *Ufford* . }		*Willughby*
G. a crosse sarcely, Arg. *Beke* . }		
Quarterly { Arg. a cheife B. over all a Bend G. . .		*Crumwell*
Chequy, Or & G. a chief Ermine . . .		*Tateshale*

In Fenestra boreali Cancelli :—

Or, a lyon rampant double queue Sa.	*Welles*
Empaled { *Welles* with a labell of 3, Arg.	*Welles*
Quarterly, *Ufford* & *Beke*	*Willughby*

In Fenestra occidentali ex dextra Campanilis :—

Sa. a crescent Or, betw. 2 roses in cheife & a mullet in bast, Arg. . . . . [*Witham*]

Arg. a Fesse, & a mullet in cheife Sa.—*bis.* . . . [*Dale*]

In Fenestris Campanilis :—

Sa. a chevron between 3 bells, Arg. . . . . [*Bell*]

Plures Fenestræ Campanis circumductæ :—

Sa. a crescent, Or, between 2 roses in cheife & a mullet in bast, Arg. . . . . [*Witham*]

Quarterly, *Ufford* & *Beke—Willughby.* The crest a Saracen's head.

G. 3 water-bougets, Arg.	*Ros*
Quarterly { Arg. a cheife G. over all a Bend B. .	*Crumwell*
Chequy, Or & G. a cheife Ermine . .	*Tateshale*
Arg. a chevron betw. 3 rams-heads erased G. . .	[*Cheryton*]

Tumulus marmoreus ære fixus :—

Hic jacet Wiłłus Smithe quondam Vicarius istius Eccłiæ, in decretis Baccalaureus, et Præbendarius Præbendæ de Hather, Prebend. in Cathedrale Ecctia Linĉ. qui obiit 13° die Aprilis, Año Dñi 1505. Cujus &c.

Tumuli marmorei in Terra :—

Hic jacet Dñus Wiłłus Bonde Bac | calaureus Theologiæ, quondam Rec | tor Eccłiæ de Stekeney, qui obiit | 15° die Decembris Anno Dñi 1485. | Cujus animæ &c.

[p. 204.] Hic jacet Dñus Wiłłus Newton, | Rector medietatis Eccłiæ de Leverton, | qui obiit 16° die Novembris, 1545.

In Choro majori versus Austrum : –
Ricus Bolle de Haugh filius Rici et Mariannæ uxoris suæ, filiæ Johis Fitz-William de Malberthorp, bis Vice-comes comitatus Lincolniæ, sæpe Provinciam gerens in Scotia et Anglia, obiit 6° die Februarii Año Dñi 1591. Jana filia Wiłłi Skipwith, Militis, prima uxor, per quam Carolus, Maria nupta Antonio Tourney de Cauenby, Anna Leonardo Cracroft, Gertruda Leonardo Kirkeman de Keale, et Ursula Johi Kirkeman desponsatæ ; Anna, 2da uxor, per quam nullus exitus : Margareta 3^{tia} conjux, per quam Ricus, Johes, et Johanna.

Robertus Towneley, Contrarotulator Portûs, et Aldermannus Boston obiit 8° die Martii, Año 1585. Johanna uxor ejus relicta Rici Skepper de East Kirkeby sepulta jacet apud East Kirkeby.

Quarterly {
Arg. a fesse, in cheife 3 mullets, Sa. a crescent difference . . . . . . *Townley*
Sa. 3 goates saliant, Arg. . . . . *Gateford*
}

Johes Nutting obiit in Crastino | Nativitatis Bëæ Mariæ 1380. Litera | Dñicalis G. Agnes uxor ejus obiit 26° | die Novembris, Año 1420.

To ye mortall coarse, y^t lyeth here under stone,
Was of Roger Shavelocke ye wife clepyd Jone.
Of London he was Citizen, on Pilgrimage he went
To our Lady of Walsingham, with full good intent,
And so header* to y^{eir} countrey, disporting in y^{eir} life.
But cruell death, y^t spareth none, he took away ye wife
In ye yeare of our L^d 1488, ye day of Ascension,
All good Christian pepull pray for hir of y^r devotion.

Johes Leeke Mercator de Boston | obiit ultimo die Februarii Año Dñi | 1527. Alicia et Johanna uxores ejus . . .

[p. 205.] Hic jacet prostratus Ricus Frere tumulatus,
Gildam dilexit quam munere sæpe provexit.
Anno milleno C obit quater et duodeno
Bis Julii senoque die migravit amæno.
Uxor et Alicia sepelitur, juncta Johanna.
Spreverunt vitia, gustant cæli modo manna.
Audit quique pie Missam cum voce Mariæ
Alte cantatam per Gildæ vota locatam.
Papa dies donat centum veniæque coronat
Nonus ei vere Bonifacius, hunc reverere.

Johes Dale Mercator Stapulæ (Fenestrarum Reparator) obiit 16° die Februarii Año Dñi 1482.
. . . a Fesse & a crescent in cheife . . . . . *Dale*

---

* Header, *i.e.* Hither.—*Ed.*

Riᶜus Brigges, Aldermannus Boston, erexit quatuor . . . 23⁰
die Martii 1584.

In choro Sᶜorum Petri et Pauli ad Boream :—
    Ut referunt Metra Mercator olim vocitatus,
    Pescod sub petra Walterus hic est tumulatus,
    Qui quinto Julii discessit ab orbe Kalendas
    MC ter octo cui nonageno mage prendas.
    Multa Petri Gildæ bona contulit ex pietate.
    Vestis et versus Pisis interstinctæ.

Requiescens in Dño Henricus Butler obiit 11⁰ die Augusti A⁰ 1601.
Ætatis suæ 30⁰.
Arg. on a chevron B. 3 cups covered Or, betw. as many demy-
    lions pass. gard. G. an annulet difference   . . *Butler*

To his Crest—on a Torce Or & B. a Horse-head erased quarterly
Arg. & Sa.

Fenestra cum limbo Clavium et Gladiorum a litera P pendentium,
Vizᵗ :—

Alanus filius Robᵗi Lamkin, quondam Canonicus professus Monasterii bēæ Mariæ de Barlinges, obiit undecimo die Maii Año Dñi
1498.

In Navi Ecclesiæ :—
Thomas Gull obiit 7⁰ die Decembris Año Dñi 1420.

Thomas Robertson Mercator Villæ Calisiæ obiit . . . die Mensis
. . . et Elizabetha uxor ejus quæ obiit 25⁰ die Aprilis Año Dñi
1495, et Maria uxor altera quæ obiit 2⁰ die Julii Año Dñi 1520.

[p. 206.] Joħes Robinson Arm. Mercator Stapulæ villæ Callisiæ,
Anna, Elizab; Elizabetha et Alianora uxores ejus. Fundavit duos
Capellanos in Gilda bēæ Mariæ Virginis in Ecctia Parochiał Sᶜi
Botulphi de Boston imppetuum celebraturos p aīabus &c. Obiit circa
annum ætatis suæ 72, primo die Mensis Martii, Año Dñi 1525.
(B) a fesse dauncee betw. 3 falcons (Or)

Athelardus Kate Mercator Stapulæ Aldermannus Gildæ Corporis
Christi obiit in Vigilia Sᶜi Matthiæ Año Dñi 1501. Uxores ejus Anna
ac Dña Elena.

Hic jacet Willūs Reade de Boston gen. qui obiit Año 1400.
Quarterly $\Big\{$ a fesse betw. 3 griphons heads erased
          . . . 2 chevrons wᵗʰ an annulet.

Robᵗus Trygge, Mercator de Boston, et Alicia uxor ejus ; Obiit ille
25⁰ die Augusti Año 1436.

    Ecce sub hoc lapide Thomas Flete sistit humatus
    Vi mortis rapidæ, generosus semper vocitatus,
    Hic quisquis steteris ipsum precibus memoreris,

Sponsam defunctam simul Aliciam sibi junctam.
MC quater quadringeno quoque deno.   (1450.)
Martia quarta dies exstat ei requies.

Schola ibidem fundata Año 9° Elizab. Wiłło Ganocke Maiore ;
Gualtero Woodroffe primo Ludi-Magistro, Año Dñi 1567.

In Fenestris :—

Empaled { G. 2 lyons passants Or, a border Arg.
         { Or, a chevron G. . . . . . .   *Stafford*
Arg. a fesse & 3 Martlets in cheife Sa.
Or, on a chevron G. 3 martlets Arg. betw. 3 Flowres de Lize,
     Vert . . . .   [*Eltoft*]

[p. 207.]

ﬁﬁﬅ﬏﬉﬏ﬅﬅ﬏ Fishtoft.

Cancellum :—
Or, on a fesse G. 3 Plates—*ter* . . . .   *Huntingfeild*
G. a crosse patonce Or ; a border Sa. charged with crosses
     botony, Arg.
G. 3 crownes, Or.
Empaled { Quarterly, *Ufford & Beke* . . . .   *Willughby*
         { Sa. a bend betw. 6 crosses botony, Arg. . *Lungvillers*
Quarterly, *Crumwell & Tateshall*.
Sa. a crosse engrayled . . . .   [*Ufford*]
B. a bend, Or ; a labell of 3 poyntes Arg. . . . .   *Scrope*
Or, on a fesse G. 3 plates . . . . .   *Huntingfeild*
Quarterly, *Ufford & Beke* . . . . . .   *Willughby*

Hic jacet Dñus Joħes Wessington | quondam Rector Ecclîæ de Fish-
toft, qui | obiit 30° die Martii, A° Dñi 1416, &c.

In Fenestra Insulæ Borealis, vulgo Robertsons :—
Quarterly, *Ufford & Beke* . . . . . .   *Willughby*
Quarterly, *France & England*.
Empaled { Quarterly, *Ufford & Beke* . . .   *Willughby*
         { Sa. a Bend betw. 6 crosses botony, Arg. . *Lungvillers*

Super murum depicta :—
         (Vert, on a chevron Arg. 3 cinquefoyles pierced G.
         | betw. as many Harts trippant of yᵉ 2ⁿᵈ
Empaled <   *Francis Robertson of Risinprise*
         | Arg. on a cheife G. 2 annulets braced of yᵉ first,
         (over all a Bend engrayled, B. . .   [*Leeke*]

Super sedilia 5 :—
A chevron betw. 2 annulets braced. }
3 crosses botony, in cheife a lyon passant } *ter*
Ermine, on a Bende a mullet, in cheife 2 annulets braced—*bis*
                                             [*Barnake*]

In Fenestra Campanilis :—
Orate pro aïabus Galfridi Paynell et Annæ uxoris ejus.

Empaled { G. 2 chevrons, Arg. . . . . . *Paynell*
{ G. a fesse betw. 3 water-bougets, Erm. . . *Meres*
Party p. pale, B. & G. a Pellicane, Arg.

In Fenestra Insulæ Australis :—

Empaled { G. 2 chevrons, Arg. wth a martlet . . . *Paynel*
{ Arg. a cheife G. over all a Bend engrayled B. with
an annulet . . . . . . *Leeke*

Paynel's Crest—A Drake's head rased B.

Tumulus juxta ingressum Cancelli :—
Orate pro aïabus Galfridi Paynel, Armig. et Annæ uxoris ejus : obiit
ille . . . die Mensis . . . A° Dñi . . . Illa 14° die
Aprilis, Año Dñi 1521.

[p. 208.] On ye last monument :—
G. 2 chevrons Arg. . . . . *Paynell*
G. a Fesse betw. 3 water-bougets, Erm. . . . . *Meres*

Tumulus marmoreus ære celatus.
Tumulus Margeriæ uxoris Riĉi Goodinge.

3 combes (*Tunstall*) 3 speare-heades (*Goodinge* or *Goodwin*).
Riĉus Goodinge in laudem uxoris hos lugubres versus posuit . . .

Leverton.

In Fenestra orientali Cancelli :—
G. 3 garbes Arg. a border Sa. bezantee. Subscribed Dñus Joħes
Clement, Miles.

Utrinque in cancello :—
Pur l'amour de Jhesu Christ
Priez pur luy que moy faire fist.
Orate pro aïa Joħis Clement et Matildæ uxoris ejus.

Butterwicke.

In Campanili :—
G. 3 water-bougets, Arg. . . . . *Ros*
Arg. on a cheife G. an annulet of ye first, over all a Bende
engrayled B. . . . . *Leek*
. . . Prioris de Freston.

ffreston.

In Fenestra Cancelli :—

Empaled { *Copledike* & *Rokeley* quartered.
On a chevron between 3 annulets, 3 crescents . *Sutton*

Empaled { *Vavasor*, Sa. a fesse dauncy Or.
Sutton.

In Fenestra boreali :—

Arg. on a cheife G. 2 annulets braced Arg. over all a Bende engrayled B. . . . . *Leeke*

Arg. a cheife G. over all a Bend engrayled B. charged with a martlet, Or. . . . . *Robertson*

Effigies Viri gestantis super pectus :—

Arg. on a cheife G. an annulet ; over all a Bend engr. B. . *Leeke*

Effigies Fæminæ gestantis super tunicam :—

Quarterly, Or & G. a border Sa. bezanty . . . *Rochford*

Arg. on a Fesse between 3 escallops Sa. 3 crosses botony fitchy of y⁰ first.

Sanguine, a crosse patonce Or ; a border B. semy of crosses botony Arg.

In Fenestra Campanilis :—

B. 3 pillars flaming fire, Arg.

Sa. a chevron between 3 garbes Arg.

Arg. a chevron between 3 crosses botony G. . . *Copledike*

Empaled { *Copledike*.
Lozengy, Erm. & G. . . . . . *Rokeley*

Quarterly { G. 3 water-bougets, Arg. . . . . . *Ros*
Arg. a Fesse betw. 2 bars gemels G. . *Badlesmere*

Quarterly, Or & G. a border Sa. bezanty . . . *Rochford*
Leeke & *Rochford*.

Arg. 3 Hurtes betw. 7 crosses botony fitchy G. . *Ricus Dawse*
Sed sunt arma Clement uxoris ejus, ut dicitur.*

In Insula boreali effigies æneæ Viri et Fæminæ cum hoc epitaphio:—

Ecce necis speculum, celeri venit aspera gressu
Mors quoscunque rapit falce rapace sua.
Hic jacet in tumulo Symon cognomine Clarcus,
Providus æternas alliminavit opes.
Charus erat cunctis ; multos ditavit amicos ;
Pauperibus miseris maxima dona dedit.
Terra tenet corpus, Superis animumque relinquo,
Ast sua nobiscum munera multa manent.
Funde Deo laudes, Frestonia, celiferenti,
Qui tibi tale dedit (teque parente) bonum.

---

* *Clement* however elsewhere bears Gules, 3 garbes, Arg. within a border, Sa. bezanty. Richard Dawse appears to have been one of the principal landowners in Frieston at the end of the 16th century, being assessed at £8 to the subsidy of 1591. —*Ed.*

Sique diem quæris, annum, seu tempora Mortis,
 Quæ sequitur liquido linea scripta docet.
Prædictus Symon Clarke | obiit 10° die Febr. Año 1607. Maria |
nuper uxor ejus obiit 5° die Aprilis | proximo sequente Año Dñi 1608.

[p. 210.]

Bennington.

In Fenestris Austraĭ Cancelli :—
B. a chevron, Ermine.
Sa. a fesse betw. 2 Leopards' faces & a Flowre-de-lize, Arg.
Arg. a chevron betw. 3 garbes, Sa. . . . . *Darby*
 Orate pro aĭa Mᴿⁱ Robti Knolle, | Rectoris Eccłiæ de Bennington,
qui istam | fenestram fecit fieri, Año Dñi 1410.
Sa. gutty, 3 morters Arg.
Sa. a fesse betw. 2 Leopards' faces & a Flowre-de-lize, Arg.
Arg. a fesse dauncy betw. 3 Cockatrices heads rased, Sa. *Tamworth*
The Fesse, Leopards-faces, & Floure-de-lize—*Ter.*
. . . 3 Catharine-Wheeles, & a border engrayled.
The Fesse, Leopards-faces, &c.
Or, a Griphon passant.
 Fenestra Australis juxta ostium :—
Arg. on a chevron Sa. 3 Mullets peirced of yᵉ first betw. as many
 Lyons-heads rased G.—*Bis.*
 Ad loca stellata duc nos, Katherina beata.
G. 3 water-bougets, Arg. . . . . *Ros*
Empaled { . . . a chevron, Erm. betw. 3 cinquefoyles, Arg.
    { Arg. a chevron betw. 3 garbes, Sa. . . . *Darby*
Effigies Wiłłi Wainflet Eᵽi Winton.
Lozengy, Sa. & Erm. on a cheife Sa. 3 lilies, Arg. . *Wainflet*
G. 3 crosses botony fitchy, Arg. a Border, B.
Arg. a Saltier, B. . . . . [*Yorke?*]
B. crusilly, a lyon rampant, Or. . . . . . [*Brewes*]
B. 3 cinquefoyles pierced, Or. . . . . *Bardolfe*
Empaled { *Ufford* & *Beke*, Quarterly . . *Willughby*
    { Sa. a bend betw. 6 crosses botony, Arg. *Lungvilliers*
    { B. a saltier engrayled betw. 4 crosses botony, Or *Friskeney*
Quarterly{ Arg. on a cheife G. an annulet, Or ; over all a
    {   Bend engrayled, B. . . . *Leeke*
Insignia Riči Friskney, Arm̃. qui obiit Año Dñi 1583.
His Crest—3 Ostrich Feathers Or betw. 2 . . . G.
Super Sedulam juxta Cancellum :—
Empaled { Arg. a chevron betw. 3 garbes, Sa. . . *Darby*
    { G. 3 garbes Arg. a border, Sa. bezanty . [*Clement*]
Item in Fenestra Orientali ad austrum.

[p. 211.]

Leeke.

Appropriatio Collegii Cantilupi in Civit. Lincolñ.

In cancello in muro Australi :—
Tumulus lapideus cum effigie Militis tibiis in crucem transversis—
Leak, ut dicitur.

Altera effigies alabastrina in medio Cancelli :—Thamworth, ut dicitur,
. . . | Rector Eccłiæ de Leek, et Fundator is | tius Chori, qui obiit
Año Dñi 1332 | . . die . . . Mensis, Cujus &c.*

Depicta super murum :—

Quarterly {
  Arg. a fesse dauncy betw. 3 cockatrices heads,
      erased, Sa. . . . . . *Thamworth*
  G. 3 garbes Arg. a border Sa. bezanty . . *Clement*
}
                                  ut opinor.

Eadem Insignia sæpius super Sedulam ex sinistra Cancelli, cum
pluribus fascibus Lıliorum :—Circumscript' Me plest bene.

Ex opposito sedula *Leek*, et supra depict' :—
Arg. a cheife G. over all a Bend engr. B. . . *Leake of Leake*

In Fenestra Australi Navis :—

Empaled {
  Quarterly, *France* & *England*.
  Naples.
}

In Campanili :—
Arg. a saltier, on a cheife G. 3 escallops of yᵉ first . *Taylboys*

Quarterly {
  Arg. a cheife G. over all a Bend B. . . *Crumwell*
  Chequy, Or & G. a cheife Erm. . *Tateshale*
}

Benefactores ad construccionem ejusdem

[p. 212.]

Wrangle.

Eccłia de Wrangle appropriata Abbïæ de Waltham.

In Fenestra Orient. Insulæ borealis :—
Arg. a crosse engr. betw. 4 crosses botony fitchy, G.
Sa. a crosse betw. 2 Floures de lize & as many Annulets Quart'ly, Arg.

Borealis Prima Insulæ :—
Orate pro aîa Joħis Harald et Aliciæ uxoris ejus, qui hanc fenestram
fieri fecerunt.

Borealis Secunda :—

Quarterly {
  Ufford
  Beke
} . . . . *Willughby*†

---

* The name of this Rector of Leake, which deserves to be recorded, was Walter
de Spaldyng who was instituted in 1307, and died before Oct., 1332, when his successor was instituted.—*Ed.*

† Note yᵗ yᵉ Lᵈ Willughby (for a good while after yᵉ match with Uffords heire)
bore *Ufford* & *Beke*, Quarterly, for yᵉ paternall coate of armes.

Quarterly, Erm. & Chequy Or & G.   .   .   .   *Gipthorp*
Fenestra Navis borealis prima :—
Quarterly, *France & England*, a border gobony Arg. & B.
Beaufort Dux Somerset
England, a border B. semy of Floures de Lize, Or.
Holland, Dux Exoniæ
Quarterly { G. a fesse betw. 6 crosses botony Or   .   *Beauchamp*
{ Chequy, Or & B. a chevron Erm.   (*Old E. of Warwick*)

Orate pro aïabus Joħis Haliday quondam Vicarii de Wrangle, Alani Haliday, et Agnetis uxoris . . . Haliday Clerici, qui hanc fenestram fieri fecerunt.

Fenestra infima . . . Reade . . . Wiħi frïs . . .
Super cooperculum Baptisterii sculpt.

Orate specialiter pro aïa Wiħi Keuing quondam Vicarii istius Eccħiæ cujus aïæ &c.

Fenestra Occidentalis ex dextra Campanilis :—
Quarterly { G. 3 water-bougets, Arg.   .   .   .   .   *Ros*
{ Arg. a Fess betw. 2 barrs gemells G.   .   *Badlesmere*

In Fenestra superiori boreali Navis :—
Quarterly { Arg. a cheife G. over all a Bend B.   .   *Crumwell*
{ Chequy, Or & G. a cheife Erm.   .   .   *Tateshale*

In Insula Australi :—
G. on a Bend Arg. 3 Shovelers, Sa.   .   .   .   .   *Read*

Joħes Reade, Miles, filius Wiħi Reade.
Depicta super murum I.R. cum signo Mercatoris.

In Cancello, Fenestra Orientalis :—
Thomas de Weyversty Abbas de Waltham me fieri fecit.

[p. 213.]   Super trabem transversam in Cancello :—
Orate pro bono statu Ricardi Rede Mercatoris, et pro aïabus Joħis Rede, et Margaretæ parentum ipsius Riči, qui hoc opus fecit Año Dñi 1528.

Tumulus marmoreus cum ære et Versibus :—
Here lyeth John Reede, sometyme Marchant of yᵉ Staple, & Margaret his wife. He dyed the 24ᵗʰ day of October 1503; She yᵉ 27ᵗʰ of March 1503.

[p. 214.]

Wainflet.

Eccħia ommium Sanctorum.
In choro Australi :—
Statua alabastrina viri cujus pulvillus ab Eꝑo et Monacho sustentatus ; et inferius ad caput bini Angeli gestantes Insignia aurea periscelide cincta, quorum dextrum :—

Lozengy, Sa. & Erm. on a cheife Sa. 3 lilies, Arg. . . *Wainflet*
Alterius colores fugerunt

Novissima memorare.—Credo videre bona Dñi in terra viventium.—
Bursa, Pugiunculus, et globuli Oratorii ad cingulum. Tumulus ligno
inclusus. Ut dicitur, Pater est Willi Wainflet Episcopi Wintoñ.*

In Fenestra Australi Cancelli :—
Orate pro aïa Willielmi Hewarbe Prioris de Kyma, et Joħis Bardnay.

In Schola Villæ per Eρ̄um fundata Arma prædicta semel in Fenestra
Orient. cum effigie sua, et 'Vulnera quinque Dei sint medicina mei'
bis in Fenestra Occidentali In quolibet rhombulo Lilium inspersum.

[p. 215.]

Friskney (Rectoria).

Tumulus lapideus juxta ostium :—
Effigies Viri tibiis in crucem transversis, gestantis in scuto :—
A saltier betw. 4 crosses formy, *Friskeney*, ut dicitur.

In cancello :—
Orate pro aïa Joħis Michel, Juñ, qui fieri fecit substantiam hujus
Cancelli.

Depicta super tabulas Cancelli :—
    Istum Cancellum si quis Clerus ingrediatur,
    Aut legat, aut cantet, aut ipse foras gradiatur.
    Sed si quis Laicus intret sub culmine cultûs,
    Offerat, et redeat, cum Sanctis ordine fiat,
    Non intus maneat albis quin sit co-opertus.

In Orientali Fenestra Insulæ Australis :—
Orate pro aïa Joħis Michel qui istam fenestram fieri fecit.
In Fenestra Australi :—
G. 2 Lyons passants, Or . . . . . . *Pedwardyn*
G. a crosse patonce, Or . . . . *Latimer*
Quarterly { Arg. a chevron betw. 3 crosses botony G. . *Copuldyke*
          { Lozengy Ermine & G. . . . . . *Rokeley*

Fenestræ Australes inferiores Navis :—
Arg. 3 conies' heads erased, Sa. . . . . *Conisholme*
Arg. on 2 bars Sa. 6 bezants ; a border engr. Or.
Or, on a Fesse Vert, 3 garbes Or.

---

* This was the tomb of Richard Patten, father of the great bishop, William of
Wainfleet, representing his recumbent effigy with purse, poniard and prayer-beads
(Bursa, Pugiunculus, et Globuli Oratorii) at his girdle. It was wantonly broken up
at the destruction of All Saints Church in 1718, but has since been re-erected in the
chapel of Magdalen College, Oxford, William of Wainfleet's foundation. The figures
however of his two sons, William the bishop and John a monk, which supported his
pillow, have unfortunately been lost.—*Ed.*

G. 2 lyons passants Or, a border Arg.

G. crusilly botony fitchy, a Lyon ramp. Or . . [*La Warre*]

Quarterly, *Crumwell* & *Tateshale.*

Sanguine, a crosse patonce Or, a border B crusilly botony, Arg.

B. a crosse patonce betw. 4 Lyons ramp. Arg.

Empaled { *Ufford* & *Beke* . . . . . *Willughby*
{ G. bezanty ; a canton, Ermine . . . . *Zouch*

G. a crosse patonce, Arg.

Empaled { Quarterly, *Ufford* & *Beke* . . . . *Willughby*
{ G. 2 lyons passants, Arg. . *Strange of Knocking*

In Campanili :—

G. a crosse patonce, Arg.

Quarterly { Or, a lyon rampant B. . . . . . *Percy*
{ G. 3 lucyes hauriants, Arg. . . . . *Lucy*

Quarterly, *Ufford* & *Beke bis* . . . . *Willughby*

G. bezanty ; a canton Ermine . . . . . *Zouch*

[p. 216.] Arg. a fesse dance betw. 3 cockatrices heads rased Sa.

Tamworth

B. a saltier betw. 4 crosses formy Or . . . . *Friskeney*

Arg. on a Bend B. a bezant.

In Fenestra Orientali Insulæ borealis :—

G. a cinquefoyle peirced within an orle of crosses botony, Or. *Umfravile*

Quarterly { Or, a lyon rampant, B. . . . . . *Percy*
{ G. 3 luces hauriants, Arg. . . . . . *Lucy*

G. 3 luces hauriants, Arg. . . . . . . *Lucy*

Arg. 3 bars G. . . . . *Multon*

G. a crosse patonce, Arg.

Orate pro aïabus Henrici Comitis Northumbriæ et Matildæ uxis ejus.

In Fenestris boreal. Insulæ borealis :—

Lozengy, Or & G. . . . . *Creoun*

G. 2 lyons passants, Or . . . . . . *Pedwardyn*

Or, on 3 crescents as many plates . . . . *Longchamp*

Arg. 3 cinquefoyles peirced, G. . . . . . [*Darcy*]

G. a crosse sarcely, party ꝑ pale, Erm. & Or.

Orate pro aïabus Walteri Pedwardyn et . . . uxoris ejus, qui has fenestras fieri fecit in honore bēæ Mariæ.

Fenestræ boreales superiores Navis :—

G. 2 lyons passants, Or . . . . . . *Pedwardyn*

Arg. 3 chaplets, G. *Bis* . . . . . . *Lascells*

Fenestræ boreales inferiores Navis :—

Arg. 3 chaplets, G. . . . . *Lascells*

Tumulus ex marmore et ære :—

Piers Jonson et Agnes sa feme gysont icy,
Deus de lour Almes ꝑ sa grace eyt mercy.

[p. 217.]

ḫaulton ḫolgate.

In Choro Australi :—

Party p pale, B. & G. a Lyon ramp. Arg.—*bis*   .   .   *Haulton*

Quarterly { Party p pale, B. & G a Lyon ramp. Arg.   .   *Halton*
{ Arg. 2 chevrons G. a label of 3 pointes, Or.

Sub muro Statua lapidea bellatoris, tibiis in crucem transversis, gestantis in scuto :—Leonem &c.—Sir Henry Halton, ut dicitur.

In Fenestra occidentali ad dextram Campanilis :—

. . . . Stayndrop et Agnetis . . . .

Empaled { . . . . .
{ *Ufford* & *Beke*   .   .   .   .   *Willughby*

Quarterly { Party p pale, B. & G. a lyon ramp. Arg.   .   *Halton*
{ Arg. 2 chevrons G. a label of 3 pointes, Or.

Empaled { Arg. 2 bars G.
{ G. 3 water-bougets, Arg.   .   .   .   .   *Ros*

Quarterly, *Ufford* & *Beke*   .   .   .   .   *Willughby*

Quarterly { Party p pale B. & G. a lyon ramp. Arg.   .   *Halton*
{ Arg. 2 chevrons G. a label of 3 pointes, Or.

Tumulus marmoreus triangulus :—

Sire Walter Bek gist ici,
De Ky alme deu s'eit merci.

Orate pro pulsatoribus Campanarum qui fecerunt Fenestram.

Kele, West.

In hac Ecclia sepulti jacent Willus Holles et Darcy Holles, pueruli filii Frescheville Holles, Arm̄. ex Dorothea 2da uxore sua, filia Herberti Lacon.

In Fenestra boreali :—

B. a lyon's head erased betw. 5 crosse crosseletss, Arg.   .   *Tothby*

[p. 218.]

Maram.

In Fenestra australi Cancelli :—

Empaled { Arg. a crosse Sa.
{ Arg. on a crosse G. a bezant.

Empaled { Arg. a crosse Sa.
{ Quarterly Arg. & G. on ye 1 & 4 quarter a Popinjay, Vert,
{   membred & beked G.

In Fenestra occidentali ex sinistra Campanilis :—
Orate pro aīa Joñis Tott, Agnetis et Helenæ uxorum ejus, et specialiter pro Andrea Tott Artium Baccalaureo, qui istam fenestram lapidari, necnon vitreari fecit.

Super Fulchrum ex parte australi : —
Quarterly, *Ufford & Beke* . . . . . . *Willughby*
. . . 3 crosses portate . . . 2 chevrons betw. 3 roses . . .
. . . a crosse . . . a lyon passant . .
Domus mea domus Orationis vocabitur—1591.

Stickford.

In Cancello :—
O cæli Janitor, Markby . . . Priori
De Stickford aperi . . . portam meliori.
Armiger æthereus . . .
Dñus Willus de Markby . . .

In Fenestra orient : —Roɓtus Tomson et uxor ejus me fecerunt.
In Fenestra australi :—Dñus Willus Markby me fecit.
Quarterly, *France & England* ⎱ utrinque super porticum lapide
Quarterly, *Ufford & Beke* ⎰ sculptum.

[p. 219.]

Sibsey.

Ex sinistra Cancelli :—
Arg. a cheife G. over all a Bend engrayled B. on the cheife
an annulet Arg. . . . . *Leek*
Super laqueare juxta Cancellum depicta :—
Est Homo nascendo, Vitulus mortem patiendo,
Est Leo fremendo, Volucris sua regna petendo.

Stikney.

Fenestra Cancelli Orientalis :—
Quarterly, *France* Semy & *England* . . . *Ricus 2ᵈᵘˢ Rex*
Or, an Eagle displayed, Sa. . . . . *Anna Regina sua*
G. a crosse botony, Or.
Quarterly, G. a lyon ramp. Or, & Chequy, Or & B. a border
engrayld, Arg.
B. 3 garbes, Or.
B. 3 crownes Or.

Fenestra borealis :—
Or, 3 chevrons, G. . . . .   *Clare*

In Campanili :—

Empaled { Arg. a fesse dauncy betw. 3 Talbots' heads, erased Sa. . . . . . . *[Spayne]*
{ Arg. a fesse betw. 3 Cootes, Sa. . . . . *[Coote]*

Arg. a fesse betw. 3 Cootes, Sa. . . . . . *[Coote]*

Empaled { B. a saltier betw. 4 crosses patee, Or.
{ Sa. a bend betw. 6 annulets, Or.

Pray for yᵉ Soules of . . . Totyll . . . to the building of this Steeple.

Fenestra occidentalis juxta Campanile ad dextram :—
Arg. a fesse betw. 3 Cootes Sa. . . . . . *[Coote]*

Empaled { The Fesse & Talbots' heads . . . *[Spayne]*
{ Sa. a Bend betw. 6 annulets, Or.

Empaled { The Fesse & Talbots' heads . . . *[Spayne]*
{ G. a fesse dauncy betw. 10 billets, Arg.

Ad sinistram :—
A coote with a scrowle in hir mouth—Disce semper vivere.
A talbot's head with a scrowle—Learn to live ever.   Hoc sæpius.

In Fenestra australi Navis :—
G. 3 spades, middle point in cheife, Arg.

Empaled { B. a fesse betw. . . . Or.
{ Ermine . . .

[p. 220.]

Kirketon in Holland.

G. a chevron Or, betw. 3 combes, Arg.
G. 3 bars Arg.
Arg. a chevron betw. 3 eaglets, a border engr. Sa.
G. a lyon ramp. . . . an annulet.
B. a crosse patonce Arg.
B. a fesse betw. 10 billets, Or . . . . . *Deincourt*
Arg. 3 bars Sa. a bend G. . . . . . . *Buschy*
G. a crosse sarcely Arg. a bend B. . . *Rob'tus Benale, Miles*
Sa. a chevron Arg. betw. 3 crosses engr. Erm. . *Valentine Champneys*
Arg. a chevron betw. 3 griffons' heads erased G. . . *Tilney*
Arg 3 hurtes betw. 7 crosses botony fitchy G

Empaled { G. a fesse betw. 3 water-bougets, Erm. *Rogerus Meres, Miles*
{ The Hurtes & Crosses fitchy.

Johes Meres Miles, et ejus nominis complures in diversis fenestris.

Empaled { G. a fesse betw. 3 water-bougets, Erm. . . *Meres*
{ G. 3 roses Arg. . . . . . *Cleymond*

Empaled { *Meres.*
{ Arg. a bend betw. 6 Martlets, Sa. . . *Tempest*

Quarterly { Arg. a fesse dauncè betw. 6 billets, G. . *De la Laund*
{ *Meres. Tempest.*
{ Arg. a crosse betw. 4 Falcons' heads erased, G.

Quarterly, Vert & G. over all a lyon rampant.

In Litleburies Isle :—

Fenestra Australis vitreata per Henricum Asty Militem et Aliciam uxorem ejus.

Ibidem insignia—*Meres, Cleymond,* & Billety a crosse botony fitchy.

Empaled { G. a fesse betw. 3 water-bougets, Erm, . . *Meres*
{ Or, 2 pallets G. a canton Erm.

Empaled { Or, 2 pallets G. a canton Erm.
{ Or,* a fesse betw. 3 water-bougets, Erm. . *Meres*

Orate pro aïa Alani Burton qui istum fontem fieri fecit,
Gilda Scissorum—Gilda Textricum—
Fraternitas Scæ Helenæ.
Kirkston, Merketstede, & Meres.
Skeldich, (Willington,) Eudike & Kirketon Holme.

[**p.** 221.]

Algerkirke.

Ex utraque parte Fenestrarum Superiorum :—
Orate pro bono statu Nicholai | Robertson de Algerkirke, Mercatoris | Stapulæ Villæ Calisiæ, et Isabellæ Consortis | suæ, qui fieri fecerunt istas Fenestras | suis sumptibus, tam in lapidatione quam | in vitreatione, Año Dñi 1492. | Obiit Nicholaus 26° die Martii 1498. Altera uxor Alicia sepulta in Ecclesia Sči Botulphi | in Boston 12° die Sepetmbris Año 1458.

Tumulus marmoreus ære circumscriptus : —
Scis Jhesu Christe, quod non jacet hic lapis iste,
Corpus ut ornetur, sed spiritus ut memoretur.
Quisquis eris, qui transieris, sta, perlege, plora.
Sum quod eris, fueramque quod es, pro me, precor, ora.

Ex utraque parte Fenestrarum :—
Arg. a cheife G. over all a Bend, engrayld B. a martlet, Or. *Robertson*
Arg. 3 maces Sa. . . . . *Pulvertoft*

In Choro boreali : —
Orate pro aïa Tho. Robertson quondam | Mercatoris Stapulæ Villæ Calisiæ, qui obiit 27° | die Maii Año Dñi 1531, Et Elizabethæ uxoris | ejus quæ obiit 25° die Aprilis Año 1495, | et Mariæ uxoris suæ quæ obiit 2° die Julii Año Dñi | 1520.

---

* *Sic,* but should be Gules.—*Ed.*

Here lyeth John Saunders Citizen & | Draper of London Merchant
of the Staple | of Calice, who died the 10th of September 1507.
Statua cujusdam Religiosi in cæmeterio.
Campanile in medio Eccłiæ cum pyramide plumbo cooperta.

[p. 222.]
Sutherton.

In Fenestra Orientali Insulæ Australis :—
G. 3 escocheons Or.
B. 3 escocheons Or.
    Cecilia de Campo me fecit.

In Fenestra Boreali :—
B. semy of Flowres de Lize, a lyon rampant Arg.
Or, 2 bars G. in cheife 3 torteaux   .   .   .   .   .   [*Wake*]
    In Fenestra Occidentali : – Hugo de Cranemere.
B. 3 knives, Arg. }
B. 3 scourges Or. } [*Abbatia de Croyland.*]
G. 3 lyons pass. guard. in pale barways   .   .   .   *England*
Quarterly, *Castile & Leon.*

In Fenestra Australi juxta Ostium :—
Chequy, Or & B. a border G. charged with lyons pass. guard.
    Or, a quarter Erm.   .   .   .   *Dreux Comes Richmundiæ*

In magna Fenestra Occidentali :—
    Orate pro aïa Joħis de Campo.

Or, on a fesse G. 3 water-bougets Arg.   .   .   .   .   *Boug*
B. 3 wheate-ears Or, slipped Vert   .   .   .   .   .   *Grandorge*
    Depicta in tabulis utrinque super Statuas,
    Egidius pater Hüfri obiit 1602.

Spalding.

In Fenestra Boreali superiori :—
Orate pro aïa Wiłłi Hariot Militis, | Mercatoris Stapulæ Calisiæ, et |
Pannarii Civitatis London.

Super sedile :—
A fesse engrayl'd betw. 3 lyons rampant.

[p. 223.]
Wigtoft.

In Australi Fenestra :—
Or, 3 bendlets B. a label of 4 pointes G.
    Priez pur l' alme Richard de Castirtone—Eɓi Sarum.*

---

* There was no Bishop of Sarum of this name. Richard de Casterton was one
of twelve knights returned out of Holland in 1324, and was probably attached to the
service of one of the bishops.—*Ed.*

In Fenestra Orientali Navis :—

G. a bend Ermyn . . . . *Ry*
Arg. 3 lyons pass. guard. G. . . . . . . *Litlebury*
G. 3 bars Ermyn . . . . *Kirketon*

Fenestra borealis :—
Arg. a chevron betw. 3 crosses botony G. . . . *Copuldike*
Quarterly G. & Or, in the 1st quarter a crosse sarcely Arg.

Fenestra borealis superior :—
Empaled { Arg. a bend betw. 6 Martlets Sa. an annulet . *Tempest*
{ Arg. on a bend Sa. 3 lyons passants, Or . *Hawtry*

Fenestra Australis superior :—
Arg. a cheife G. over all a bend engrayld B. . . . *Leyke*

Orate pro aĩa Nicholai Robertson Mer | catoris Stapulæ Calisiæ, et
Isabellæ uxoris suæ.

𝔚𝔢𝔰𝔱𝔬𝔫.

Arg. a chevron engr. betw. 3 ravens, Sa.
            Thomas Halmere de Weston.

Effigies Viri gestantis in scuto, et in vestitu :—The chevron & ravens.
Effigies Viri gestantis in scuto, vizᵗ :—Arg. 2 barrs G.
            Lambertus de Westone.

Tumulus marmoreus in Choro boreali :—
Hic jacet Lambertus, et Matilda uxor ejus.   Orate pro eis.

In Fenestra Orientali :—
Orate pro aĩabus Lamberti de Weston, et Matildæ ux̃is ejus.

[p. 224.]

𝔖𝔴𝔦𝔫𝔰𝔥𝔢𝔳𝔢𝔡.

Fenestræ Australes :—
G. crusilly botony fitchy a lyon ramp. Arg. . . *La Warre*
      { *La Warre.*
      { B. 3 leopards' faces jessants floures de Lize, Or *Cantelupe*
Empaled { G. a bend, & 2 bendlets above, Or . . *Grelle*
      { Lozengy, G. & Verry . . . . . . *Tregose*
Orate pro bono statu Thomæ Dñi de la Warre.

La Warre & *Grelle* carved upon 2 seates in yᵉ Chancell, ad
dextram.*

---

* Roger, Lord de la Warre, summoned to Parliament, 27 Edw. I-4 Edw. III,
married Clarice, daughter and co-heir of John de Tregoz, a great Herefordshire
Baron. His son John married Joan, daughter of Robert, and sister and heir of
Thomas, Lord Grelle, by whom he obtained Swineshead and Sixhill.—*Ed.*

Empaled { Arg. a chevron B.   .   .   .   .   .   *Locton*
           { G. 3 bendlets Verry.

In Insula Boreali :—
Barry Bendy Or & G.   .   .   .   .   .   .   *Holland*
Or, a chevron betw. 3 annulets G. as many crescents of the first   *Sutton*

Effigies Viri et Fæminæ super vestes gestantium arma, ipse Holland ; illa Sutton.

In Fenestra Boreali :—
Empaled { G. on a fesse Arg. 3 escalops B. betw. as many
         {   crescents, Or   .   .   .   .   *Ellis*
         { Nebuly Arg. & Sa. on a cheife G. 3 mullets, Or.

Thomas Ellys mercator Stapulæ et Agnes uxor eius.

Arg. a chevron betw. 10 crosse-crosselets, Sa.   .   .   .   *Haugh*

In Campanili :—
B. 3 bolles Or, jesant boares-heads couped Arg.—*bis*.   .   *Bolle*
Empaled { B. 3 bolles Or, jesant boares-heads couped Arg.   .   *Bolle*
         { B. a lyon rampant Arg.   .   .   .   .   *Mounthalle*

Fenestra Australis inferius :—
G. a cinquefoyle betw. 8 crosses botony Or   .   .   *Umframville*

Tumulus Alabastrinus :—
Hic jacet Rogerus Bardney benefactor Gildæ bēæ Mariæ in Swins-head qui obiit Año 1512, Cujus aīe &c. Obitus celebrandus in festo Scī Edw̄. Confessoris.

Campanæ :—
1. In multis annis resonet campana Johannis.
2, 3. God be our speede.
4. Ave Maria grā plena, Dñus tecum, benedicta tu in mulieribus, et benedictus fructus &c.
         (Quodlibet verbum Corona insignitum.)

[p. 225.]   Ostium Australe :—Orate pro aīa Joħis Grantham, qui istud Ostium fieri fecit.

𝕱𝖑𝖊𝖙𝖊.

In Fenestra Orientali :—
Quarterly { Or, a lyon rampant B.   .   .   .   .   .   *Percy*
         { G. 3 lucies hauriant Arg.   .   .   .   .   *Lucy*
Checquy, Or & G. a canton Erm.
Sa. a frett Arg.   .   .   .   .   *Harrington*
Barry of 8, Arg. & G.
Quarterly, *Percy* & *Lucy*, ut supra   .   .   *Comes Northumbriæ*

[p. 226.]

Biker.

In Insula Boreali :—
Orate pro aĩa Aliciæ filiæ Katherinæ et Margaretæ uxoris Walter de
Brandon.

Orate pro aĩa Thomæ Cutte, et Emmæ uxoris ejus.

In Insula Australi :—
Rogerus Atken et Margareta uxor ejus.
Thomas filius Ranulfi et Marğ. uxor ejus.

In Fenestra Australi :—
Orate pro aĩa Joħis de Wincebi Senescalli Comitis Richmondiæ.

William Procter—Sculpt. sup̃. Porticum.

Sutton Sc̃ae Mariae.

Fenestræ :—

Arg. a chevron betw. 3 billets G. . . . [*De la Laund*]
Arg. a fesse dauncy betw. 10 billets G. . . . [*De la Laund*]
B. on a bend Arg. 3 harpes G.
Arg. a saltier betw. 4 staples Sa.

Empaled { Arg. a saltier betw. 4 staples Sa.
{ Barry of 6 Arg. & Vert, over all a swan.

. . . Sprot Capellani Parochialis Sc̃i Nicħi de Lutton.

[p. 227.]

Dunnington.

Tumulus in Cancello :—
Joħes Browne Arm. obiit 3° die Januarii Año 1436 ; Katherina
uxor, Joħes et Johanna filii.

Wiłłus Hoberd, Agnes uxor ejus filia Simonis de Brighe de Pinchbeck obiit 20° Septembris Año 1453.

. . . Booth, Johanna uxor, obierunt 12° Aprił, 1524, Elizabeth
filia eorum.

Robertus Syrik, Cecilia uxor, Ric̃us Syrik—Dñus Wiłłus Syrik
Capellanus—Ranulphus Syrik.

Orate pro aĩabus Nic̃i Derman et . . . Consortis suæ.

Sculpt. in ligno : —A manch . . . 3 Feathers . . . 3 mullets
peirced . . . 3 bendlets.

Quadring.

In Fenestra Cancelli :—
Or, a lyon rampant B.—*bis.*   .   .   .   .   .   .   *Percy*

Eadem Insignia super pectus et humeros bellatoris super genua, semel super humeros fæminæ, bis Viri.

In Insula Australi :—
Joħes Hyllayltoy obiit 1° Julii 1420 Vicarius Eccłiæ, ut videtur p̄ Ornamenta.

Fenestra Superior ex parte Boreali :—
Barry of 6, Sa. & Arg. in cheife 3 annulets of the 2nd .   *Derby*

. . . Derby et Mariannæ Consortes Dñi Wiłłi Derby, et Simonis Derby, Joħ. Derby . . . Derby, Riĉi Derby, et Margaretæ Consortis, et oīm liberorum suor̄, qui istas octo Fenestras fieri fecerunt 1400.

In Insula Boreali :—
Barry of 6, Sa. & Arg. in cheife 3 annulets of the 2nd .   *Derby*

Campanæ :—
1. Sĉe Martine, ora pro nobis.   2. Sĉa Maria.   3. God blesse the Holy Church.   4. Virgo coronata, duc nos ad regna beata.

[p. 228.]

Gosberkirke.

Eꝓus Lincolñ Patronus hujus Eccłiæ.

In Fenestra Orientali Cancelli :—
G. 3 lyons pass. guard. Or, on a cheife B. the Blessed⎱   *Arma*
    Virgin embracing our Saviour, seated on a throne⎰ *Eꝓ'atus Linĉ.*
    Or.

B. a leopard's face betw. 2 barrs gemells, Or.

In utraqne Fenestra Boreali :—
B. a saltier Erm. betw. 4 Fleures de Lize, Or   .   .   *St. Hugh*

Chorus Australis juxta Cancellum :—
Hic jacet Nicholaus de Rey, Miles, et Edmundus filius ejus, quorum aīabus propitietur Deus.   Amen.

Tumulus Alabastrinus cum effigie ; super pectus, a Bend Ermyn   .
. . Item . . Bars.

In Fenestra Australi :—
Nicholaus de Ry, Margareta uxor ejus, Cecilia mater ejus, me fieri fecerunt in honore Bēæ Mariæ.

In circulis Fenestræ :—
Barry, Erm. & G.

In Insula Boreali :—
Barry of 6, Erm. & G. & 3 crescents Sa. on yᵉ 2ⁿᵈ bar a mullet,
Arg. . . . . *Waterton*

In Fenestra Australi Insulæ Australis :—
Orate pro aïa Joñis Bolls, Arm. et Catharinæ consortis suæ, Thomæ
Edmund et Julianæ consortis suæ, Wiħi Flouter et Agnetis consortis
suæ, Wiħi de Chelle et Johannæ consortis suæ, ac pro fratribus et
sororibus Gildæ Sēi Joñis Baptistæ, qui istam fenestram fieri fecerunt
A° Dñi 1465.

Empaled
{
Quarterly {
B. 3 Bolles, Or, jesants Boares heads,
    couped Arg. . . . . *Bolle*
Arg. a chevron betw. 3 crosses crosselets, Sa.*Haugh*
}
Quarterly {
B. a lyon rampant Arg. . . *Mounthalt*
Arg. 2 bars G. . . . . *Moulton*
}
}

[**p. 229.**] Subtus in muro Statua lapidea Viri (tibiis in crucem
transversis) Bolle, ut dicitur.

In Fenestra inferiori Navis :—
Orate pro aïabus Fratrum et Sororum Gildæ Sēi Joñis Baptistæ, qui
istam fenestram fieri fecerunt.

Fenestra Occidentalis :—
Party p bend, Erm. & Arg. a Bend Sa. in bast 6 martlets.
G. 2 keyes in saltiere Arg.
Sēe Petre ora pro nobis.

B. 2 swordes in saltier Arg. hilts & pomels Or.
Sēe Paule ora pro nobis.

Lapis marmoreus juxta ingressum Ecclïæ. Pars ablata.
Joñes de Ry quondam Rector hujus Ecclïæ, et Dñus hujus Villæ,
cujus aïe propitietur Deus. Amen.

[**p. 230.**]

𝕾urflet.

In Muro Boreali Cancelli :—
Statua lapidea Militis (tibiis in crucem transversis,) super pectus et
scutum depictus Leo erectus cum cauda duplici :—Cressy de Cressy
Hall ibidem.

In Fenestra Australi :—
Empaled {
G. a chevron Arg. a cheife chequy Or & B. . *Lambarte*
Sa. 2 lyons passant Arg. crowned . . . *Dymoke*
}
In Insula Boreali : —
Empaled {
Quarterly {
Party p fesse, Or & B. a demy lyon ramp.
    in cheife G. collared Arg. . *Marcham*
Arg. a lyon ramp. double-queue Sa. . *Cressy*
}
Arg. 2 Pilgrim-staves Pile in point G. piked Sa.
        Burdon of Maplebec.
}

In Fenestra Boreali predicta :—
Vir armatus super genua gestans insuper paludamenta predicta
insignia—*Marcham.*

In Fenestra Boreali :—
Arg. a lyon rampant double-queue Sa. . . . . *Cressy*

In Fenestra ex dextra Campanilis :—
Arg. on a bend Sa. 3 owles, Or . . . . . *[Savile]*

Scutum funebre :—

Empaled
{
Erm. a lyon ramp. G. crowned Or, a border Sa.
platee . . . . . *Cornwall*
G. a chevron betw. 3 escallops Arg. . . *Wolmer*
}

In Fenestra Orientali Cancelli :—
G. a frett, Or, a cheife Ermine . . . . . *Wigtoft*

Empaled
{
Sa. a fesse betw. 3 Floures-de-lize, Arg. . . *Welby*
G. a frett, Or, a cheife Ermine . . . *Wigtoft*
}

[p. 231.]

Moulton.

In Fenestra Orientali Insulæ Borealis :—
Arg. 3 bars G. . . . . *Multon*
Or, a crosse sarcely G.
Or, a plaine crosse G.

Effigies Viri gestantis super pectus—Arg. 3 barres G. et Fæminæ
ibidem gestantis—The bars & yᵉ plaine crosse in pale.

Fenestræ Boreales :—
Arg. 3 barres G. a labell of 5 pointes B. . . . . *Multon*
G. a chevron betw. 10 crosses botony, Or, a labell of 3
poyntes, Arg. . . . . *Kyme*
Arg. on a crosse Vert, 5 Eaglets displayed, Or.
Arg. 2 lyons pass. guard. G. a bend Sa.
G. 3 barres Ermine . . . . *Kirketon*

Effigies Viri gestantis super pectus :—
Arg. 3 barres G. a labell of 3 pointes, B. . . . *Multon*

Fenestræ Australes superiores :—
Arg. 3 barres G. . . . . *Multon*
Sa. a chevron betw. 3 turrets, Arg.
Sa. a fesse betw. 3 Floures de lize, Arg. . . . . *Welby*
G. a frett of 6 peices Or, a cheife Ermyn . . . *Wigtoft*
Empaled—*Welby, Wigtoft.*

Chorus Australis, vulgo the Lord's Quire.
Arg. a chevron betw. 3 turrets, Sa.

In Fenestra Australi :—
Or, a plaine crosse, G.
Arg. 3 bars, G. . . . . *Multon*
Or, a crosse sarcely, G.

Fenestra Australis inferior, juxta Ostium :—
Orate pro aïabus Dñi Thomæ | de Multon Prioris de Spalding, | et Wiłłi Denmark Monachi.

Septem sacramenta cum effigiebus Sc̃i Anthonii et Prioris cum baculo pastorali aperto capite (Quod nota).
Joñes Harcox funere dignus ampliori hic in Dño requiescit A° 1560. I.A. Ultimo testamento fundavit Scholam ibidem.

[p. 232.]

ℬincḥbecke.

In Fenestra Orientali ex dextra Cancelli :—
 A deu, et sa Mere Marie, et a Sainct Pere,
 Thomas De la Laund cest fenestre . . .
 Me tibi Christe cape Sc̃i Petri prece Papæ
 Hostis ne forte rapiat me, Papa, precor te,
 Petre, poli portæ pateant per te mihi morte,
 Portam, Petre, poli contra me claudere noli.

Arg. a fesse dauncetty betw. 10 billets, G. . . *De la Laund*
Arg. a fesse dauncetty betw. 6 billets, G. . . . *De la Laund*
Arg. a chevron betw. 3 billets, G. . . . . *De la Laund*
Chequy, Arg. & G. on a bend B. 3 water-bougets, Or.
Arg. on 2 bars Sa. 6 escalops of yᵉ first.
Empaled { Chequy Arg. & G. on a bend B. 3 water-bougets, Or.
   { Arg. a chevron betw. 3 billets, G. . *De la Laund*
Empaled { Arg. on 2 bars Sa. 6 escalops, Arg.
   { Arg. a chevron betw. 3 billets, G. . *De la Laund*

Fenestra Australis superior juxta Ostium :—
Arg. 3 dolphins naiant Sa.
Sa. a crosse engrayled Or . . . . . . *Ufford*
Or, on a fesse G. 3 plates . . . . . . *Huntingfield*

In Insula Boreali :—
Richard Ogle, Esq. deceased | yᵉ 25ᵗʰ day of November, 1555 ; | Beatrice his wife onely Sister | of Sʳ Anthony Cooke, Knt. | Thomas Ogle, Armiḡ. filius et | heres Ric̃i, Justitiarius pacis et | quorum, in Legibus peritus, obiit | 3° die Maii A° Dñi 1574 ; Et | Jana uxor ejus obiit 2° die Sep | tembris A° 1574.

Ex dextra Campanilis :—
Arg. on a bend Sa. a bezant . . . . . *Pinchbeck*

Ex sinistra :—
Arg. a saltier, on a cheife G. 3 escalops of yᵉ first   .   .   *Talboys*

Fenestra media Borealis :—
Empaled—*Pinchbeck & Talboys.*
Empaled { Arg. on a bend Sa. a bezant   .   .   .   *Pinchbeck*
{ G. 3 water-bougets, Arg.   .   .   .   .   *Ros*
[p. 233.]   Arg. on a bend Sa. a bezant—*bis.*   .   .   *Pinchbeck*
Sa. a fesse betw. 3 floures-de-lize, Arg.   .   .   .   .   *Welby*
Quarterly { Arg. a chevron betw. 3 crosse-crosselets, G.   *Copuldike*
{ Lozengy, Ermyn & G.   .   .   .   .   *Rokeley*

Orate pro aīa Riči Pinchbeck, | et Mariæ Uxoris ejus qui hanc |
Fenestram fieri fecerunt.

Super Fulchrum :—*Pinchbeck* per se, *Pinchbeck* paling *Talboys.*

Super Lignum :—
Empaled { Arg. on a bend Sa. a bezant   .   .   .   *Pinchbeck*
{ G. 3 water-bougets, Arg.   .   .   .   .   *Ros*
Empaled { *Pinchbeck.*
{ Arg. a chevron betw. 3 crosse-crosselets, G.   .   *Copuldike*

Tumulus lapideus cum multis Insigniis :—
Empaled—*Pinchbeck & Talboys.*
Empaled { B. 3 buckes trippant, Or   .   .   .   *Greene*
{ Arg. on a bend Sa. a bezant   .   .   .   *Pinchbeck*
Quarterly { G. & Sa. p pale, a lyon ramp. Arg.   .   .   *Bellers*
{ B. a bend betw. 6 mullets, Arg.   .   .   .   *Houby*

[p. 234.]

𝕮𝖆𝖍𝖆𝖕𝖑𝖔𝖉.

Campanile, a latere Australi Eccłiæ juxta Cancellum.

In Fenestra Cancelli :—
G. a fesse nebuly betw. 3 mullets of 6 poyntes, Arg.
Arg. a chevron betw. 3 crosses botony fitchy, G.

In Fenestra Orientali Insulæ Borealis :—
Or, a fesse betw. 2 chevrons, G.   .   .   .   .   *Fitz-Walter*
Sa. fretty of 6 peices, Arg.
Arg. 2 lyons passants guardants, G.   .   .   .   .   *Litlebury*
Or, 2 bars, B.
B. on a bend   .   .   3 roses, Arg.   .   .   .   .   .   *Porter*

Effigies viri gestantis super tunicam tres Rosas super Areolam
transversam :—
Orate pro aīa Joħis Porter et Amiciæ Consortis suæ.

Eadem effigies cum iisdem Insigniis in Fenestra Occidentali.

Fenestræ Boreales :—
G. a bend betw. 6 floures-de-lize, Arg.
G. a bend Ermine . . . . *Ry*
G. a crosse molyn Arg. . . . . . . *Beke*
Quarterly, Sa. & Or, over all a Bend, G.
Barry of 6, Or & B. on a bend G 3 escallops, Arg. . *Quaplod*

Effigies Viri, necnon Feminæ, gestantium super pectora Insignia eadem : —
Joħes de Quaplod fecit fieri has Fenestras in honorem beatæ Mariæ et bĕi Edmundi Martiris.

Fenestra superior Australis juxta Cancellum :—
Arg. 2 lyons passant guardant G. . . . . . *Litlebury*
B. 2 bars, Arg. . . . . *Venables*
B. on a bend . . . 3 roses, Arg. . . . . *Porter*

Fenestra Occidentalis :—
G. on a fesse betw. 3 crescents, Or, 3 escallops, B. . . *Ellys*
Quarterly { Arg. 2 lyons passant guardant G. . . *Litlebury*
{ G. 3 barres, Ermyn . . . . . *Kyrketon*
{ G. 3 crescents, Or, a canton, Erm. . . *Dalyson*
B. a chevron betw. 3 swans' heades rased, Arg.
Arg. 3 maces Sa. . . . . *Pulvertoft*

Orate pro aïabus Thomæ | Polvertoft, et Catherinæ Uxoris | suæ, et pro Gilberto Polvertoft, | et Elizabetha Uxore sua.

[p. 235.] Ermyns, 2 lozenges, Ermyn . . . *Haultoft*

Orate pro aïabus Willielmi | Haultoft, Arm̃. . . . Uxoris ejus, | et pro aïa Mr̃i Gilberti Haultoft, | et pro aïabus Wiłłi Haultoft, | et Elizabethæ, Agnetis et Aliciæ Uxorum ejus.

In Insula Boreali lapide sculpta :—
Empaled { Quarterly { Or, on a fesse betw. 2 chevrons Sa. 3 crosse-crosselets, Arg. . . *Walpole*
{ . . . 3 lozenges . . .
{ Sa. a fesse between 3 floures de lize, Arg. . *Welby*

Super Sedile :—
Empaled { . . 3 lozenges . . . . . . *Haultoft*
{ Sa. a fesse betw. 3 floures de lize, ... *Welby*

Sculpta in Ingressum Cancelli :—
Empaled { Arg. a fesse betw. 3 crescents, jesants Floures de lize, G. . . . . *Ogle*
{ . . . a fesse chequy betw. 3 cinquefoyles . .

[p. 236.]

Holbech.

Juxta Cancellum :—Tumulus lapideus cum effigie Viri super scutum gestantis binos leones ambulantes ore obverso—*Litlebury.*

Ex utraque latere quinquies *Litlebury*, et ter 3 bars, Ermyn—*Kirketon.*

In Fenestris superioribus ad Boream :—
G. 6 escallops, Arg.—*bis.* . . . . . . *Scales*
Empaled { Sa. a fesse betw. 6 escallops, Arg.—*sæpius.*
{ . . . a saltier engrayld betw. 4 crosselets fitchy.

Eadem Insignia super pectus Viri in Fenestra Orientali ad dextram Cancelli :—*Bradow.*

Fenestra Australis :—
Arg. on a bend, B. 5 crosses humets, Or . . . *Geo. Sibsay*
Arg. on a chevron betw. 3 leopards' heades, Sa. as many
    annulets of yᵉ first . . . . . . *Jo. Calow*
Barry of 6, Sa. & Arg. in cheife 3 annulets of yᵉ 2ⁿᵈ . *[Derby]*

In eadem Fenestra super pectus Viri eadem Insignia.
. . . a lyon rampant, semy of mullets, Or.
Or, on a fesse G. 3 flowers de lize of yᵉ first betw. 4 of yᵉ
    second . . . . *D'Eyvill*
B. a crosse patonce, Arg.
Orate pro aïa Dñi Roberti de Eyvill, Militis, et . . . Militis . .

Super borealem partem :—
Barry of 6, & yᵉ annulets. The fesse & floures de lize.

Duo milites super scuta genibus pronis.
Tumulus marmoreus ære fixus juxta monumentum Litlebury.

Orate pro aïa Johannæ Welby quondam uxoris Ricardi Welby. senioris, et filiæ Riĉi Leyke, militis, quæ obiit 18° die Decembris A° Dñi 1488.
Sa. a fesse betw. 3 floures de lize, Arg. . . . . *Welby*
Arg. on a cheife G. an annulet, over all a bend engrayld B. . *Leyke*
    Alter Tumulus juxta hunc Epitaphio ablato.

[p. 237.]

Gedney.

In Fenestra Orientali Insulæ Australis :—
Chequy, Arg. & G. . . . . *Vaux*
G. a fesse betw. 6 crosse-crosselets, Or . . . *Beauchamp*
Or, 3 chevrons G. . . . . *Clare*
G. 3 water-bougets, Ermyn . . . . . . *Roos*

GEDNEY.

Fenestra Australis :—
B. semy of floures de lize, a lyon ramp. Or, over all a bend
    gobony, Arg. & G. . . . . . . *Beaumont*
G. 3 water-bougets, Ermyn . . . . . . *Roos*

Fenestræ Australes Navis :—
Barry of 6, Or & G.
Or, a crosse B.
G. 3 cinquefoyles, Arg.
G. 3 water-bougets, Ermyn . . . . . . *Roos*
G. a fesse betw. 6 floures de lize, Arg.

Fenestræ Insulæ Borealis :—
Barry of 6, Or & B. a canton, Ermyn . . . . *D'Oyry*
Quarterly per fesse endented Arg. & G.
Quarterly, Sa. & Or, a bend Arg. . . . . . *Hoo*
   Tumulus ibidem Marmoreus Fulconis de Oyry cum effigie Viri
(tibiis in crucem transversis).

Fenestræ Boreales :—
Quarterly, G. & Or.
Chequy, Or & B. . . . . *Warren*
Or, a fesse betw. 2 chevrons Sa. . . . . . *L'Isle*
Barry of 6, Or & B. a quarter Ermyn . . . . *D'Oyry*
Arg. 3 lyons passants guardants, Sa.
G. 3 water-bougets, Ermine . . . . . . *Roos*
G. a crosse engrayl'd, Arg.
G. a crosse engrayl'd, Or.
G. 3 crownes, Or.

In 2ᵈᵃ Fenestra Australi Cancelli bis :—
Empaled { Quarterly Arg. & G. fretty Or, on a bend Sa. 3
       mullets of 6 pointes of yᵉ first . . *Spenser*
      Barry of 6, Or & B. a Canton, Ermyn . . *D'Oyry*

Tumulus Alabastrinus :—
Here lies Adlard Welby, & Cas | sandra his wife, daughter of Willm̄
| Aprice of Washingleys in yᵉ County | of Huntingdon, & Parish of
Lutton, | by whom he had 4 Sonnes, William, | Richard, Robert, &
John, & Susan | his daughter. He dyed Aug. 11, Ætat. | 63, 1570.
She Febr. 22, 1590, Ætat. 60.

[p. 238.] Tumulus in Cancello ex marmore super humum :—
   Ici gist . . . Roos, | Chevalier, un des Seigneurs de | Gedney,
qui mourust xj Jour de | December . . .

Ad istum Tumulum (de quo plurimum æris ablatum) adhuc fixum:—
G. 3 water-bougets, Ermyn . . . . . . *Roos*

Alter Tumulus cum iisdem Insigniis, Epitaphio ablato.

Marmorei Tumuli in Cancello super humum :—
Hic jacet Riĉus Robertson, | Vicarius hujus Eccłiæ, et Eccłiæ | de Pinchbeck, qui obiit 26° | die Maii, A° Dñi 1525, Cujus aīe &c.

Hic jacet Joħes Louterel quondam | Rector istius Eccłiæ, qui obiit . . . | die . . . A° Dñi 1435, Cujus &c.

Hic jacet Joħes Pechel quondam | Rector Eccłiæ istius, qui obiit die | Sĉi Dunstani Eṗi, A° Dñi 1404.

Involvens pannis Christum memor esto Johannis.

Super Sedulam juxta ostium australe :—
Orate pro aīa Laurentii Fros | dyke cælibis, qui obiit, et hoc opus | fieri fecit A° Dñi 1519, Cujus &c.

Idem ex opposito juxta ostium boreale :—
Idem fecit Sedulam juxta Cancellum. L.F.

In omnibus Fenestris superioribus utrinque :—
G. on a fesse B. 3 eaglets displayed betw. as many leopards-faces, Or.

[p. 239.]

Croyland.

G. 3 keyes, Or.
B. 3 crosses portate, Arg.
Lozengy, Or & G.   . . . . *Croun*
Lozengy, Sa. & Ermyn . . . . *Patten*
Empaled { Quarterly, *France & England.*
{ G. 2 barres betw. 6 martlets, Or.
G. 3 crosses botony.
G. a crosse patonce Or   . . . . . . *Latymer*
G. crosse crusilly fitchy a lyon ramp. Arg.   . . *La Warre*
G. a bend & 2 bendlets above (Or)   . . . . . *Grelle*
Lozengy, Or & G.   . . . . *Croun*
Or, a saltier engrayled Sa.   . . . . . . *Botetorte*
Quarterly { Arg. a cheife G. over all a bend B. . . . *Crumwell*
{ Chequy Or & G. a chiefe Erm.   . . . *Tateshale*
Barry of 6 pieces Arg. & B. in cheife 3 lozenges G. a mullet
difference   . . . . *Fleming*
B. a bend Or   . . . . *Scrope*
Arg. a fesse G. in cheife 3 torteaux   . . . . . *Devereux*
Arg. a chevron betw. 3 martlets Sa.
Sa. a frett Arg.   . . . . *Harington*
Quarterly { Sa. a crosse engrayled Or }
{ G. a crosse molyn Arg.   }   . . . *Willughby*
Arg. a crosse moline Sa.
Arg. a saltier G.
B. a saltier Arg.

Quarterly
{ Arg. a crosse engrayled G. betw. 4 water-bougets, Sa.
                                                Bourchier
  G. billetty Or, a fesse Arg. . . . . *Lovaine* }

Quarterly G. & Or, a mullet on yᵉ first quarter, Arg. . . *Vere*

B. an estoyle Arg.

Empaled { B. an estoyle Arg.
        Verry, Or & G. . . . . . . *Ferrers* }

Or, a chevron G. on a border B. 8 myters, Or . *Stafford Ep'us*

Arg. a fesse G. betw. 3 popinjayes, Vert. . . . . *Lumley*

B. a chevron betw. 3 garbes Or.

G. a saltier Arg. . . . . *Nevile*

Quarterly { *Bourchier*
         Lovaine } . . . . *Bourchier, Earl of Essex*

Quarterly, *France* semy & *England*, a border Arg.

Quarterly, *France* semy & *England*, a label of 3 Ermyne.

Quarterly, *France* semy & *England*, a label of 3 Arg.

Quarterly, *France* semy & *England*, on a border B.
      8 floures-de-lize, Or.

Arg. a chevron betw. 3 gryphons' heads, erased G. . . *Tilney*

G. 3 water-bougets, Ermyne . . . . *Roos*

Arg. 2 barres & a canton.

G. a crosse patonce Or, a border Arg.

[p. 240.] G. a fesse betw. 6 floures-de-lize, Arg.

G. bezanty, a canton Ermyne . . . . . . *Zouch*

    Campanæ :—

       In multis annis resonet campana Johannis.
       Sum rosa pulsata mundi Maria vocata.
       Hec campana beata Trinitati sacra.

𝔗𝔦𝔡𝔡𝔢 𝔖'𝔠'𝔞𝔢 𝔐𝔞𝔯𝔦𝔞𝔢.

Tumulus alabastrinus Chori Borealis cum effigie Mulieris juxta murum.

      Tout home que passe p icy Penses qᵈ sera en obly,
      Et altres serront en vr̄e leu, Qᵈ viendra le plaisir deu
      P'c̄ priez pour les mors, Q' sont mis en peynes fors
      Et p l' alme Wiłłm le Tidde, et sa feme dame Margaret
      Queux icy sont enterres, a queux deu done pardon
      De leurs pechez et . . . remission. Amen.

Alter Tumulus super terram cum effigie Viri.

Chorus Australis :—

Arg. 3 bars G. a bend engrayled, Sa. . . . . *Roos*

Ermyne, on a bend G. a cinquefoyle, Or.

Empaled { Arg. 3 bars G. a bend engrayled, Sa. . . *Roos*
          Arg. a fesse G. }

Empaled { Arg. 3 bars G. a bend engrayled. Sa.   .   .   *Roos*
          { G. 3 water-bougets, Ermyn   .   .   *Roos de Gedney*

Empaled { Ermyne, on a bend G. a cinquefoyle Or.
          { Arg. a lyon rampant double-queue Sa. a bend
               gobony, G. & Arg.

Monsir Richard de Ros done ceste Fenestre
Deu luy done repose en le Joy celeste.

Chequy Arg. & G. a Canton.

[p. 241.]

ḫorncastell.

Tumulus marmoreus gratus (?) super solum :—
      Leonis fossa nunc hæc Dymoke capit ossa,
      Miles erat Regis, cui parce Deus prece matris.
      Es testis, Christe, quod non jacet hic lapis iste
      Corpus ut ornetur, sed spiritus ut memoretur.
      Hinc tu qui transis, senex, medius, puer an sis,
      Pro me funde preces, quia sic mihi fit veniæ spes.

Juxta in muro boreali :—
In honore sc̃e et individue Trinitatis : Orate pro aĩa Leonis
Dymmoke, qui obiit 17° die mensis Augusti, A° Dñi 1519, Cujus &c.

Effigies super tumulum, necnon Filii duo, et tres Filiæ : Insignia
etiam sequentia, vizt :—

Quarterly { Sa. 2 lyons passants Arg. crowned Or, a crescent
            difference   .   .   .   .   .   *Dymoke*
           Quarterly G. & Arg. a crosse engr. counter-changed.
           Ermyn, 5 fusills in fesse G.   .   .   .   *Hebden*
           Barry of 6, Erm. & G. 3 crescents Sa.   .   .   *Waterton*
           Verry, a fesse G.   .   .   .   .   .   *Marmyon*

In Fenestra Insulæ Borealis :—
      Orate pro aĩa Thomæ Coppuldike Armiğ. et Dñæ
      Margaretæ consortis suæ, fundatoris Gildæ Cantar̃.
      . . . fenestram fieri fecit Año Dñi 1526.

In superiori Fenestra Boreali Cancelli :—
G. a lyon passant guardant, Arg.
Sa. 3 flowres de lize betw. 6 crosses botony fitchy Arg.
G. a crosse sarcely, Arg.   .   .   .   .   .   .   *Beke*

In Fenestra Orientali Insulæ Australis :—
Orate pro benefactoribus artis Sutorum qui istam Fenestram fieri
fecerunt. Sc̃e Neniane cum sera et catena. Item Sc̃i Crispinus et
Crispinianus cum instrumentis Calceariis.

[p. 240.]   Fenestræ boreales, superius :—

Empaled { Sa. 2 lyons passants Arg. crowned Or   .   .   *Dymoke*
         { Or, a lyon rampant, double-queue Sa.   .   .   .   *Holles*

Empaled { Quarterly { Arg. a chevron betw. 3 bulls pass Sa.   *Tournay*
         {   { B. a fesse betw. 3 goates-heades erased Arg.
         { Quarterly { Arg. a chevron gobony, Sa.
         {   { Arg. on a bend G. 3 roses Arg.

Quarterly { Arg. a chevron betw. 3 griphons' heads erased G.   *Tilney*
          { Arg. 3 bars G. over all a bend engr. Sa.   .   .   *Ros*

Quarterly { Quarterly, Or & G. a border Sa. bezanty   .   *Rochford*
          { Arg. 3 crosses botony fitchy B. semy of flowres de lize.

Quarterly, Ermine & Chequy, Or & G.   .   .   .   *Gipthorpe*
Arg. a chevron between 3 roses G.
Taylboys, &c.

Fenestra Australis superior :—
G. a fesse between 3 water-bougets Ermyne   .   .   .   *Meres*

Empaled { Merchants Marke.
         { Arg. on a bend G 3 Ferniers* of yᵉ first.

Hic jacet Francisca filia primogenita Petri Freschville de Staveley in Cõm. Derb. Arm̃. (ex priore uxore sua Elizabetha filia Gervasii Clifton in Cõm. Nott. Militis) quondam uxor Gervasii Holles de Burgh in Cõm. Lincolñ. Militis, cui peperit Freschevillum Holles, et Margaretam gemellos, et Franciscum Holles filium juniorem. Obiit Horncastell . .

[p. 243.]

𝕷angton juⱦta 𝔓artney.

Ecclesia Sanctorum Petri et Pauli Apostolorum.

In Insulæ borealis Fenestra :-
Falconem tibi do, pia Virgo, mei memor esto.
Effigies Viri gestantis Falconem.

Tumulus lapideus :—
Hic jacet Elizabetha uxor Joħis Langton, Arm̃. et filia Wiħi Quadring, Arm̃. quæ obiit 4° die Maii, Aº Dñi 1524.

Fenestra Australis :—Effigies Scõrum Petri et Pauli Apłorum.

Super Crucem in Cemiterio :—
A plaine crosse.

Quarterly (Sa. & Arg.) a bend (Or)   .   .   .   .   *Langton*

Empaled { 3 floures de lize, in cheife a lyon passant.
         { A fesse nebuly between 3 roses.

---

* *Ferniers.*—Holles has already used this term, p. 55, but it is not found in any ordinary Heraldic Dictionary, nor are ferniers figured in the tricking of either coat.
—*Ed.*

In Insula Boreali :—
Hic jacet Riĉus Ligh generosus, servus Dñi Regis Hen. 8 . . .
Hic jacet Johannes Wortes Rector istius Ecclesiæ, qui obiit 6° die
Septembr' A° 1582.

Thimbleby.

Hic jacet Johes Gedney Rector hujus Eccłiæ qui obiit 2° die
Novembris, A° Dñi 1461, Cujus aīæ &c.

Hic jacet Wiłłus Brakynburgh et Emmota uxor ejus ; obiit ille 6°
die Januarii A° Dñi 1496, Quoĩ aīaƀ, &c.

[p. 244.]
Langton juxta Horncastell.

Boreales Fenestræ in Cancello :—
Arg. crosse crusilly, a lyon rampant double-queue, G.
G. a lyon ramp. Verry, crowned Or   .   .   .   *Everingham*
Arg. billetty, a lyon double-queue, G.
          Rob : de : Leyrt : me : fecit : fieri.
B. a bende betw. 6 mullets of 6 pointes, Or.

Fenestra Australis :—
Barry of 6, Arg. & G. in cheife a greyhound cursant Sa. collared Or,
                                                                        Skipwith

In Campanili :—
Quarterly { G. a crosse sarcely, Arg. . *Beke* }
          { Sa. a crosse engrayled, Or, *Ufford* } . . *Willoughby*

Merton.

Roughton.

Fenestræ Australes Cancelli :—
G. 3 lyons passants guardants, Or   .   .   .   .   *England*
Verry, a fesse Or, fretty G.   .   .   .   .   .   *Marmyon*
Or, a lyon rampant, Purpure   .   .   .   .   .   *Lacy*
Chequy, Or & G. a cheife Ermyne   .   .   .   .   *Tateshale*

In Campanili :—
Arg. a sword sheathed Proper, a buckle appᵗ wᵗʰ Girdle wrapped,
          hiltes, pomel, & neuf, Or.

[p. 245.]

ᕼ𝔞𝔩𝔱𝔥𝔞𝔪.

In Fenestris Cancelli :—

Verry, a fesse G. fretty Or	*Marmion*
G. a crosse sarcely, Arg.	*Beke*
Sa. 2 lyons passant Arg. crowned Or	*Dymoke*
Or, a lyon rampant double-queue, Sa.	*Welles*
Sa. 3 flowres de lize betw. 6 crosse-crosselets fitchy, Arg.	
G. 3 bars Ermyne	*Kirketon*
Barry of 6, Or & Sa.	

Fenestræ Boreales :—

B. a lyons head erased betw. 6 crosses botony Arg.	*Touthby*
Arg. 3 bars G. a border, Sa.	
Dymoke, each lyon charged sur l' epaule wth an annulet.	
Ermyne, on a bend G. a cinquefoyle Or.	
G. a crosse crusilly fitchy, a lyon ramp. Arg.	*La Warre*
Or, a lyon rampant double-queue, Sa.	*Welles*

Fenestræ Australes :—

G. 3 water-bougets, Arg.	*Ros*
Or, on a fesse G. 3 plates	*Huntingfield*
Quarterly, Or & G. a border Sa. bezanty	*Rochford*
Rochford, with a garbe in ye 2nd quarter, Arg.	
Rochford, with an annulet in ye 2nd quarter, Arg.	
Or, a manch, G.	*Hastings*
G. a bende Ermyne	*Ry*
Rochford, with an eagle displayed in ye 2nd quarter, Arg.	
Arg. fretty of 6 peices G. a canton Ermyne.	

In Fenestra Boreali Navis :—

G. crosse crusilly fitchy, a lyon rampant, Arg.	*La Warre*
Arg. on a bend G. 3 gryphons-heads erased Or.	

In Campanili :—Joħes Staines—W. Io.

[p. 246.]

𝔎𝔦𝔯𝔨𝔢𝔟𝔶.

Or, 2 barres G. in cheife 3 torteauxes	*Wake*

𝔅𝔦𝔩𝔩𝔦𝔫𝔤𝔞𝔶 𝔠𝔲𝔪 𝔚𝔞𝔩𝔠𝔬𝔱.

Tumuli in Cancello :—

Hic jacet Joħes Foster quondam Vicarius istius	Ecclesiæ,

qui obiit 14° die Maii, A° Dñi 1497, Cujus &c.

Hic jacet Thomas Wilkinson, Vicarius . . . rector . . . qui obiit . . .

Of yᵣ charity pray for the Sowle of Sʳ William Tupholme Parson of Waydingham, & Chauntrey Preist of Dogdike, wᶜʰ departed this life yᵉ 7 day of January 1530.

Helpringham.

Fenestræ Boreales :—
G. 3 chevrons Or, a label of 5 pointes B.
Arg. 2 bars G. in cheife 3 torteaux, over all a bend Sa.

Threkingham.

G. 3 water-bougets Arg.	.	.	.	.	.	.	.	*Ros*
Dñus Lambert de Threkingham me fecit.
Or, a bend G.
Or, a bend Sa.
Arg. a cheife G.
Sa. a crosse engrayled Or, a label of 3 pointes Arg.	.	.	*Ufford*
G. a crosse patonce, Or	.	.	.	.	.	.	*Latymer*
G. a chevron betw. 10 crosses botony, Or .	.	.	.	*Kyme*

[p. 247.]
South Kyme.

Tumulus marmoreus ære fixus :—
Gilbert Lord Tailboys, Lord of Kyme, married Elizabeth the daughter of Sʳ John Blount of Kinlet in Shropshire Knt. & died 15° April', A° 1530.

Arg. a saltier, on a cheife G. 3 escallops of yᵉ first	.	*Tailboys*
Nebuly of 6 peices, Or & Sa.	.	.	.	.	.	*Blount*
Tailboys Crest—a Bulles head couped.
Party p pale, G. & B. a bulle passant, Arg.

Tumuli lapidei cum ære :—
Mary the wife of Thomas Whichcoote gentleman died 16° Febr. Anno 1591.

		Ermyne 2 seingliers trippant G. . *Whichcote*
	Quarterly	G. 3 lapwings Or . . . . *Tirwhit*
		G. a cheife endented Or . . *Grovall*
Empaled		Arg. on a bend Sa. 3 owles of yᵉ 1ˢᵗ *Savile of*
	Quarterly	. . an escocheon & orle of martlets. *Newton*
		. . a bend, in cheife an eagle displayed.
		. . on a bend . . 3 escallops.

John the Sonne of Thomas Whichcote & Mary deceased 15° Sept'. Anno 1588, Ætat 8°.

G. a chevron between 10 crosses botony, Or . . . *Kyme*

Effigies Viri et Mulieris in Fenestra Occidentali gestantium manibus arma predicta et super tunicas.

Thomas Weston pincerna (ut dicitur) Prioratus cum clave sculptus in introitu porticus.

Robertus Cressi.

[p. 248.]

ℌowell.

In Fenestra Orientali Cancelli :—
Effigies genuflexa Hugonis de Claypol Rectoris Eccłiæ de Howell : Superius ex dextra Beata Virgo, ex sinistra Sc̃us Andreas.

In summa :—
Ermyne, 5 fusills in fesse, G. . . . . . *Hebden*
Ad dextram :—
Ermyne, 2 barres G. a bend Sa.

Ad sinistram :—
Arg. on a chevron betw. 3 chaplets G. as many crosses botony fitchy, Or.

Fenestra Australis 1ᵐᵃ :—
Hoc lucis munus dedit J. Spenser pius Unus.

Ejus effigies in veste rubra sub qua Inscriptio modo ablata, continens (ut dicitur) Benefica Dñæ Catherinæ Hebden.

Superius—Virgo Virginum et Sc̃us Andreas.

Fenestra Australis 2ᵈᵃ :—
Alme Deus celi Spenser nunc parce Johanni.

Effigies veste purpurea : Superius Sc̃us Antonius et Sc̃us Michael.

Fenestra Australis 3ᵃ :—
O Rex celestis Spenser miserere Johannis :—
Juxta Sc̃a . . . dextra tenens plumam, sinistra claves, catenam et corollam ; Superius Sc̃a Catherina et Sc̃a Margareta.
Arg. a sword Sa. hilt, pomell, & neuf, Or.

Tumulus lapideus juxta Altare :—
Hic jacet Magister Johannes Croxby, quondam Rector istius Eccłiæ, qui obiit . . . die . . . A° Dñi M°CCCC°, Cujus &c.

Tumuli lapidei :—
Hic jacet Ric̃us de Hebden, miles, qui obiit 25° die Aprilis, A° Dñi 1373, Cujus &c. . . . quondam Uxor Ric̃i de Hebden, militis, quæ obiit 15° die . . . A° Dñi 1353, Cujus aĩe &c.

[p. 249.] Super tumulum dicti Ricardi quinque Scuta, viz. in medio:—
Ermyne, 5 fusills in fesse G.   .   .   .   .   .   *Hebden*

Ad caput ex dextra :—
B. a bend between 6 martlets, Arg.   .   .   .   .   *Lutterell*

Ex sinistra :—
Empaled { Ermyne, 5 fusills in fesse, G.   .   .   .   *Hebden*
         { G. a bend Ermyne   .   .   .   .   .   .   *Ry*

Ad pedes in dextra :—
Arg. on a chevron betw. 3 chaplets G. as many crosses botony fitchy,
    Or.

Ex sinistra : —
Ermyne, 2 bars G. a bend Sa.

Hic jacet Wiłłus filius Nicholai de Hebden, militis, et Catherinæ
uxoris suæ, qui obiit A° 1386.

Hic jacent Nicholaus de Hebden, miles, qui obiit . . . A° 1416,
et Katherina uxor ejus, quæ obiit . . . A° 1427.

Sculptum in superiori gradu ascensionis ad Altare—Hic Deum adora.

In Choro Boreali :—
Hic jacet Riõus Spenser } Conjuges } Anno 8ᵛᵒ
Hic jacet Em'ota Spenser} qui obierunt } H. VI.

Horum effigies in Fenestra Boreali cum Inscriptione . . . bēæ
Mariæ huic Altari dederunt.

Arg. a sword Sa. hilt, pomell & neuf, Or—*bis*.

Hic jacet Riõus Whitead . . . qui obiit 27° die mensis Septembris A° Dñi 1508, Cujus aīe propítietur Deus. Amen. Sc̄us Petrus—
Sc̄us Andreas.

Super Baptisterium :—The chevron wᵗʰ chaplets & crosses botony
fitchy.

Hebden per se.
In pale, *Hebden* & *Ry*.
A bend between 6 martlets   .   .   .   .   .   *Lutterell*
In pale, *Hebden* & *Ry*.

Juxta Ingressum Eccłiæ :—
Hic jacent Ric̄us Boteler de Howell qui obiit primo die Januarii A°
Dñi 1457, et Matilda uxor ejus quæ obiit 6° die Augusti A° Dñi 1457,
Quorum aīabus &c.

Hic jacet Joħes Spenser . . .

In Fenestra Australi Navis :—
Ermyne, 2 barres G. a bend Sa.

In Fenestra Campanilis :—
Nicholaus Rector . . .
Effigies mulieris et viri.
Salutatio Gabrielis ad Virginem.—Sc̄a Trinitas.

Super Crucem in Cemiterio :—
Orate pro aïa Johannis Spenser Rectoris Eccłiæ istius.　I.H.C.

[p. 251.]

Hale.

Fenestra Borealis :—

Or, 3 chevrons G.	*Clare*
Chequy, Or & B.	*Warren*
Barry of 6, Or & B. a bend G.	*Gant*
B. semy of floures-de-lize, Or, a lyon rampant debruised wᵗʰ a bend gobony, Or & G.	*Beaumont*
Quarterly, G. & Or, a mullet in the first, Arg. . . .	*Vere*
B. a fesse dauncee between 10 billets, Or . . .	*Deyncourt*

Fenestræ Australes :—

B. semy of floures-de-lize, Or	*France*
G. 3 lyons passants guardants, Or	*England*

> Vox in deserto clamantis parce Roberto,
> Virgo tibi do me, fac Natum parcere Thomæ,
> Agneti bina da gaudia, tu Katherina.

Barry of 6, Or & B. a bend G.	*Gant*
B. semy of floures-de-lize, a lyon rampant, Or, a bend gobony Arg. & G.	*Beaumont*
G. a crosse patonce, Or	*Latimer*
B. a crosse patonce, Arg.	*Goldesburgh*

Billingborrow.

Fenestræ Orientales in Choro Australi :—

England, on a label of 3, B. 9 floures-de-lize, Or . .	*Lancaster*
B. semy of floures-de-lize, a lyon rampant, Or, a border gobony, Arg. & G.	*Beaumont*
Verrey, on a fesse G. 3 cinquefoyles Or.	
Arg. on a fesse dauncy Sa. 3 besantes	*Burgh*
G. a lyon rampant Verry, crowned Or	*Everingham*
Arg. 3 barres G. over all a bend engrayl'd Sa. . . .	*Ros*
Or, a lyon rampant, Purpure	*Lacy*

Tumulus in Cancello :—
Orate pro aïa Joħis Phelippe qui fieri fecit pavimentum totius
Cancelli . . . obiit . . . A° Dñi 1461.

Sempringham.

Fenestræ Boreales :—
Quarterly G. & Or, in yᵉ first Quarter a mullet, Arg. . . *Vere*
Or, on a chevron G. 3 crescents of yᵉ first between as many
     annulets, of yᵉ second . . . . . . *Sutton*
Party per fesse, Or & B. a demy-lyon rampant in cheife G. *Markham*

Fenestra Occidentalis :—
G. 3 lucies hauriant, Arg. . . . . . . *Lucy*

Hic jacet Rogerus Laurance, qui obiit 2° die Jañ'. Anno 1602.

[p. 253.]

Swaton.

Ecclesia de Swaton, appropriacio Abbathiæ de Barlinges.

Fenestra Occidentalis, magna . . .
B. 3 garbes, Or . . . . *Meschines*
Chequy, Or & B. . . . . *Warren*
Or, 3 chevrons, G. . . . . *Clare*
Or, a lyon rampant Purpure . . . . . . *Lacy*

Fenestra ad dextram :—
G. 2 barres, Or, in cheife 3 bezantes . . . . *Gobaud*
Chequy, Or & B. . . . . *Warren*

Fenestra Borealis :—
Chequy, Or & B. . . . . *Warren*
Or, a lyon rampant, Purpure . . . . . . *Lacy*
B. a bend Arg. cotised betw. 6 lyons rampant Or . . *Bohun*
G. a fesse between 6 crosse-crosselets, Or . . *Beauchamp*
G. 3 water-bougets, Arg. . . . . *Ros*
Quarterly, G. & Or, in yᵉ 1ˢᵗ quarter a mullet of 6 poynts Arg. *Vere*

Fenestra Australis :—
Or, a lyon rampant, Purpure . . . . . . *Lacy*
Barry bendy, Or & G. . . . . *Holland*
Arg. a lyon rampant G. crowned Or, a border Sa. bezanty
             Rich' Erle of Cornwall'
G. 3 water-bougets Arg. a labell of 3 poyntes, B. . . . *Ros*

Tumulus in Cancello :—
Hic jacet Dñus Wiłłus Gregge, quondam Vicarius istius Eccłiæ, qui obiit 14° die Februarii A° Dñi 1488, Cujus aīe &c.

Chorus Sċi Joħis, ad Austrum :—
Effigies Viri, tibiis in crucem transversis, Arthuri de Spanby, ut dicitur.

Chorus Bēæ Mariæ ad Boream.

In Capella Spanby :—
Hic jacet Joħes de Spanby, qui obiit . . . A° Dñi 1417, Cujus aīe propitietur Deus. Amen.

[p. 254.]

Heckington.

Fenestra Orientalis Cancelli :—
B. semy of floures-de-lize, a lyon rampant, Or, a bend gobony,
Arg. & G. . . . . *Beaumont*
Or, a plaine crosse, Sa. . . . . *Vesey*

Effigies Militis et Mulieris, gestantium insignia predicta.

Ermyne, on a crosse G. a crowne Or—Sæpius.
G. 3 crownes, Or.

Riĉus de Potesgrave . . . istius Eccłiæ hoc Cancellum fecit in honore bēæ Mariæ et Sĉi Andreæ, et oīm Sĉorum, A° Dñi MCCC° . .

Effigies lapidea in muro boreali cujusdam Religiosi—Potesgrave, ut dicitur.

Fenestra Australis :—
B. semy of floures-de-lize, a lyon ramp. Or . . *Beaumont*
Or, a plaine crosse Sa. . . . . *Vesey*

Tumuleus marmoreus :—
Hic jacet Henricus Asty, miles, qui obiit x° Kl. Junii, Anno Dñi 1383, Cujus aīe &c.

Juxta quem Tumulus lapideus :—
Hæc Asty fossa nunc Aliciæ tenet ossa,
Propter eam stantes hic vos estote precantes.

Tumuli juxta Cancellum :—
Hic jacet Dñus Joħes Dogson, qui obiit 14° die Septembris A° Dñi 1510. M.Y.Kye.

3 water-bougets sculpt' super Sedulam.
Hic jacet Joħes Cawdron qui obiit 28° die Novembris, Anno 1488, &c.

Hic jacet Henricus Cawdron qui obiit 20° die Julii Anno Dñi 1503, Cujus aīe &c.

[p. 255.] Hic jacet Wiħus Cawdron, Ballivus de Heckington, qui obiit ultimo die Aprilis, A° Dñi 1544, et Margeria (Meres) uxor ejus, quæ obiit 10° die Martii A° 1509, et Elizabetha uxor ejus, quæ obiit 29° die Octobris, A° Dñi 1556, Quorum aīabus &c.

Tumulus alterius Elizabethæ Cawdron (uxoris Henrici, ut autumo).

Hic jacet Robertus Thornburgh, generosus (filius) qui obiit 8° die Julii, A° Dñi 1457, Cujus &c.

Riby Quire—Insula Borealis :—
A fesse between 3 water-bougets—super Sedulam.

Fenestra Orientalis :—
B. semy of floures-de-lize a lyon rampant Or .   .   .   *Beaumont*
  Ex dono Dñi Simonis de Radston, quondam Rectoris hujus Ecctiæ.
B. 3 crownes Or—Sæpius in vitro.

  Fenestra Australis infra ostium :—
  Ex dono Dñæ Loræ de Gant, cum effigie sua.
      Winkhill Isle.
  Dñus Robertus Marshal.
  Stephanus Boston, clericus, quondam   .   .   .
  Willus Lyndsey.

[p. 256.]

Horbling.

Fenestra Occidentalis :—
B. a bend between 6 martlets, Arg.   .   .   .   .   *Lutterell*
G. 2 bars Or, in cheife 3 bezantes   .   .   .   .   *Gobaud*
Ermyne, on a fesse G. 3 crosses botony fitchy Or   .   .   .   *Wyke*
  Joñes Wyke, Dñus de Horbling, Anno 17° Hen. 6.
Or, a fesse G.   .   .   .   .   *Colvill*
Ermyne, on a fesse G. 3 bezantes.

Tumulus Alabastrinus in Choro Boreali :—
Arg. a fesse daunce between 6 billets, G.   .   .   *De la Laund*

Quarterly {
  Arg. a fesse daunce betw. 6 billets G.   .   *De la Laund*
  .   .   a lyon rampant, Arg.
  Erm. on a fesse G. 3 crosses botony fitchy, Or.   .   *Wyke*
  Arg. a crosse betw. 4 falcons-heads erased G.   *Tey de North Witham*
}

De la Laund per se, supported by a man & a woman.

Fenestra Borealis :—
Ermyne, on a fesse G. 3 bezantes.

Fenestra Australis :—
Arg. a fesse daunce between 8 billets, G.   .   .   *De la Laund*

  Tumuleus lapideus :—Johannis Tempest, militis (ut dicitur) fugientibus literis.

[p. 257.]

Dowsby.

In Fenestra Orientali Capellæ Australis :—
G. a fesse Verry between 3 water-bougets, Or.

Fenestra inferior Borealis :—
G. 3 water-bougets, Or   .   .   .   .   *Roos*

Fenestra Australis superior :—
G. 3 bendlets, Or.
Quarterly, Arg. & Sa. a bend lozengy G. . . . *Cheney*
G. 3 lyons passants Or . . . . . . *Pedwardyn*
Fenestra Borealis Navis :—
G. a fesse Verry between 3 water-bougets, Or.
Fenestra Occidentalis :—
Verry, a fesse Or, fretty G. . . . . . . *Marmyon*
Fenestra Orientalis :—
G. 3 lyons passants guardants, Or, on a labell of 3, B. 9
    floures-de-lize of yᵉ 2ᵈ . . . . . *Lancaster*
Effigies Principis gestantis in Scuto et Vestimento eadem Insignia.

Tumulus lapideus super solum :—
Hic jacet . . . Roos, armiğ. filius Thomæ Roos, militis, Dñus
istius Villæ, et patronus Ecctiæ, qui obiit 9° die Maii, A° Dñi 1452,
Cujus aïe &c.

Super Tumulum :—3 water-bougets.

Effigies Etheldredæ, relictæ . . . Ashton, Arm̃. uxor Witti
Rigdon, militis, cum octo liberis.

[p. 258.]

Rippingale.

Fenestra Orientalis :—
G. 3 barrs, Or, in cheife 3 bezauntes . . . . *Gobaud*

Empaled	Quarterly	B. a cheife endented, Or . . . *Dunham*	
		Arg. a cinquefoyle pierced betw. 3 Rayne-deers heads, cabused & attired Sa. *Bowet*	
		G. bezanty, a canton, Erm. *Zouch of Kirtlington*	
		Arg. on a fesse dauncey Sa. 3 bezaunts *Burgh*	
		Sa. a frett, Or . . . . *Bellow*	
		B. a cheife endented, Or . . *Dunham*	
	Sa. a bend between 6 escallops, Or . . *Fouljambe*		

Fenestra Australis :—
Chequy, Or & B. . . . . *Warren*
    In spe decessit John de Thorpe, hic requiescit,
    Corpus putrescit, animæ precor ut requiescit.

Tumulus marmoreus ære fixus, juxta murum in choro boreali :—
Pray for the soules of Mawncere Marmyon of Ringstone, Esqre. &
Edith his wife, one of the daughters of Sir Thomas Barkeley, Knight :
Mawncere deceased the 25ᵗʰ day of February Anno 1505, Edith
deceased the 23 day of October 1538, on whose soules Jhesus have
mercy.

Lapideus Tumulus insculptus :—
Issy gyst dame Jane Bowet, Iadis feme au Sr Nicholas Bowet, Chivaler, et file de Sr Laurence Barkeley, que trespassa cest mortel vie en le fest du Conversion St Pol, l' an de grace 1471.

Effigies Viri cum duabus hinc inde Consortibus, diversis insigniis utrinque superius et inferius depictis, Vizt. sæpius :—

Empaled { G. 7 mascles, Or . . . . . [*Quincy*]
{ G. bezanty, a canton Ermine . . . . *Zouch*

Empaled { G. 7 mascles, Or . . . . . [*Quincy*]
{ Arg. a lyon rampant, Sa.

G. bezanty, a canton Erm. a crescent for difference . . *Zouch*

[p. 259.]   In muro Australi :—
Sire Richard de Gobaud me fist fere
En le honor de sa mere.
Ecce coronata sedet Annæ fulgida Nata,
Agmine laudata cæli, quoque turrificata.   Amen.

Obiit dña Margareta uxor Dñi Rogeri de Colleville, et postea uxor Dñi Joñis Gobaud . . . Ep̄i Linc'. . . . penitent . . .

Juxta statua dictæ dñæ barbatæ, ad cujus caput duo armati support-antes G. a fesse Or (*Colvile*), Altera statua viri armati sub pedibus.

Thurlby.

Or, a fesse betw. 2 bars gemells, B. a labell of 5 poynts, G.
Arg. a cheife G. over all a bend B. . . . . *Crumwell*
Barry of 6, Arg. & G. on a bend B. 3 lyons passants, Or.
G. a chevron between 3 goates passants, Arg.
Or, a fesse betw. 2 barrs gemells, B. a labell of 5 poynts, G.
[*De la Mare*]
Or, a lyon rampant double-queue, G. . . . . [*Mallory*]
Empaled { Or, a lyon rampant double-queue G. . [*Mallory*]
{ Arg. 3 cinquefoyles & a canton G. . . *Driby*
Verry, Arg. & G.
Empaled { Verry, Arg. & G.
{ G. 3 cinquefoyles, Arg.

[p. 260.]

Downesby.

Fenestra Borealis Cancelli :—
Or, 2 barrs G. in cheife 3 torteaux . . . . . *Wake*
Fenestra Australis inferior :—
B. 3 cinquefoyles betw. 8 crosses botony, Or . [*Darcy*]

Fenestra Australis superior :—
Or, on 2 barrs G. 3 water-bougets, Arg. . . *Willughby of Wollaton*

Fenestra Borealis superior :—
Or, a chevron G. . . . . *Stafford*
Or, 2 barrs G. in cheife 3 torteaux . . . . . *Wake*

Tumulus lapideus ex ære :—
Here lyeth the body of John Tyngyll, who dyed the 23rd day of Aprill 1515, on whose soule &c.

Super humum in saxo sculptum :—
Hic jacet Johes Atwike de Dounesby.

Super Lavacrum :-
Vous qui passez per ici, Priez pur Robt. de . . . Baptista :
IHS : XRS : MARIA.

𝔐orton.

Fenestra Borealis Cancelli :—
Or, 2 bars G. in cheife 3 torteaux . . . . . *Wake*

Depict' in laquear' Campanilis :—
Arg. a chevron G.
G. a crosse Arg.

[p. 261.]

𝔥aconby.

Fenestra Orientalis :—
B. a fesse daunce betw. 3 falcons, Or.

Fenestra Borealis :—
Or, a maunch G. . . . . *Hastings*

Capella Borealis :—
Sa. 2 keyes in saltier, Arg. . . . . . . *S. Peter*
Sa. 2 swordes in saltier, Arg. . . . . . *S. Paul*

Orate pro aïabus Radi Oudeby, Arm. et Elizabethæ uxoris ejus, et Willi Rothwell, Arm. et Elizabethæ uxoris ejus, qui hanc capellam fieri fecerunt.

In duabus Fenestris Navis borealis :—
Orate pro aïabus Radi Oudeby, Arm. et Elizabethæ uxoris ejus, et Willi Rothwell, Arm. et Elizabethæ uxoris ejus, qui hanc ecclesiam fieri fecerunt.

Alibi—W. Rothwell.

Boothby Paynell.

Fenestra Occident'. et Borealis :—

Or, 2 bars G. in cheife 3 torteaux .   .   .   .   .   *Wake*

B. semy of flowers-de-lize, a lyon ramp. Or, a bendlet . *Beaumont*

G. 3 water-bougets, Arg. .   .   .   .   .   .   *Ros*

Quarterly { Or, 3 chess-rooks.
{ B. a lyon ramp. & a labell of 3, Arg. . . *Monthalt*

G. a fesse between 3 escalops, Arg. .   .   .   . *Saint Low*

Party per fesse endented G. & Or, a labell of 5 poynts, a cross patonce.

Bis ex utraque parte Sedulæ cum apice.

Empaled { . . 2 chevrons . . . . *Paynell*
{ . . a chevron between 2 roses . . . . *Barkeley*

The Crest a Swan's head couped.

[p. 262.]

Burne.

Fenestra Australis Navis :—

G. 2 barrs, in cheife 3 mullets of 6 poynts, Or . . *Brunne*

Effigies Viri gestantis manibus et super pectus eadem insignia.

Or, 2 barrs G in cheife 3 torteaux . . . . . *Wake*

G. 2 barrs, in cheife 3 mullets of 6 poynts, Or . . *Brunne*

The window embordered interchangeably wth y[e] last escocheon, & wth a lyon rampant Arg.

Fenestra Campanilis :—

Or, 2 barrs G. in cheife 3 torteaux . . . . . *Wake*

Empaled { Or, 2 barrs G. in cheife 3 torteaux . . *Wake*
{ G. 3 lyons pass. guard. Or, a border, Arg. . *Holland*

Or, 2 barrs G. in cheife 3 torteaux . . . . *Wake*

In Fenestra Boreali superiori 2[da] : —

Sa. 3 thistles, Proper.

Arg a fesse betw. 3 crescents G. a border engr. Sa.

Arg. on a crosse patonce G. 5 escalops of y[e] first.

In Fenestra Boreali superiori 1[a] :—

Empaled { G. 2 barrs, in cheife 3 mullets of 6 poynts, Or . *Brunne*
{ Arg. a chevron betw. 3 talbots' heads erased Sa.

Subscript' :—Walterus Brunne.

G. 2 barrs, in cheife 3 mullets of 6 poynts, Or.

Subscript' :—Egidius Brunne.

Utrinque juxta Cancellum :—

Empaled { G. 3 lyons pass. guard. Or, a labell of 3, Arg. *Brotherton*

{ G. a chevron Or.

In Fenestra Boreali inferiori :—Effigies Regis gestantis in scuto—
Or, a crosse fleury.

Reginaldus de Berford—Juliana de Berford.

In Fenestra Orientali Cancelli :—

Quarterly, *France & England*, on a border B. 8 martlets, Or.

Jasper Dux Bedfordiæ

B. semy of fleures-de-lize, a lyon rampant, Or, debruised with

a bend gobony, Arg. & G. a labell of 3, Ermine . *Beaumont*

Arg. on a chevron between 3 brushes Sa. a crescent.

Tumulus super humum :—
Hic jacet Galfridus Abbas.

[p. 263.]

Deping Markett.

In Capella juxta Campanile :—

Or, 2 barrs G. in cheife 3 torteaux . . . . . *Wake*

G. 2 barrs Arg. in cheife 3 plates.

Or, 3 chevronels, G. . . . . *Clare*

Or, an eagle displayed Sa.

Or, a lyon rampant.

Fenestra Campanilis :—

Or, 2 barrs G. in cheife 3 torteaux . . . . . *Wake*

Cancellum :—

Simulacrum ligneum militis, tibiis in crucem transversis, in scuto
gestantis.

. . . 2 barrs, in cheife 3 roundlets . . . . *Wake*

Baldwinus Wake, ut dicitur.

In Fenestra Orientali :—

Orate pro aïa Johis Swarby, quondam Rectoris hujus loci, qui hanc
fenestram fieri fecit, ad laudem Dei et Sči Guthlaci, A° Dñi 1438.

In Fenestra Australi :—

G. a crosse patonce Or, on a border B, 8 crosses botony, Arg.

G. a payre of wings supporting a crosse botony, Or.

B. 3 pillars arched Arg.

Quarterly, *France* & *England*, a border gobony, Arg. & B.

Beaufort Dux Somerset

Quarterly, *France* & *England*, a labell G. bezanty.

G. 3 lozenges, Arg.

Orate pro aïa Johis Swarby, quondam Rectoris hujus loci, qui hanc
fenestram fieri fecit &c. ut supra.

Willus Colsell Rector April 8, 1605.

[p. 264.]

Deping Sci Jacobi.

In Fenestra Insulæ Australis :—
Or, 2 barrs G. in cheife 3 torteaux . . . . . *Wake*
Chequy, Or & B. . . . . *Warren*
G. 3 lyons passants guardants Or, a border Arg. . . *Holland*
Or, 2 barrs, in cheife 3 torteaux, a border engrayled G.
Sa. a lyon double-queue, Arg. collared G. . . . *Wastneys*
G. 3 roses between 7 crosses botony, Arg.
Or, 2 barrs G. in cheife 3 torteaux . , . . . *Wake*
Or, a fesse between 2 barrs gemels B. . . . *[De la Mare]*

Fenestra Borealis :—
Orate pro aīa Dñi Thomæ Berham, quondam Vicarii hujus Eccłiæ
qui has tres fenestras fieri fecit Aº Dñi 1408.—*Bis.*

In quarta Fenestra quaternis vicibus :—
Or, 2 barrs G. in cheife 3 torteaux . . . . . *Wake*

Deping Occidentalis.

Fenestra Cancelli :—
B. a bend Arg. cotised betw. 6 lyons ramp. Or . . *Bohun*
Chequy, Or & B. a fesse G. . . . . . . *Clifford*
Or, 2 barrs G. in cheife 3 torteaux . . . . . *Wake*
B. semy of fleurs-de-lize, Or . . . . . . *France*
Quarterly, *France* semy & *England*, a labell of 3 Erm. . *Lancaster*
Fenestra Navis :—
Ermine, on a cheife endented Or, a lyon passant G.
Arg. 3 trefoyles, Vert.
Wake in Campanili.
Super Baptisterium :—
Verry . . *Wake* . . *Clifford.*
Or, a fret betw. . . fleurs-de-lise.
. . a chevron . .
. . a fesse . . in cheife 2 bars betw. 3 sisefoyles.
. . a fesse between 5 crosses formy.
. . a fesse between 3 chevrons.

[p. 265.]

Braisburgh.

In Fenestra Orientali Cancelli : —
Sa. 3 cinquefoyles Arg.
Verry, Arg. & G.
Sa. a lyon rampant Arg. collared Or . . . . *Wasteneys*
Et e converso cum effigie feminæ gestantis Templum.

Fenestra Borealis Cancelli :—
Sa. 3 cinquefoyles Arg.
Verry, Arg. & G.
Sa. a lyon rampant Arg. collared Or . . . . *Wasteneys*

Fenestra Australis Cancelli :—
Sa. 3 cinquefoyles Arg.
Verry. Arg. & G.
Wasteneys.

Marmoreus Tumulus cum statuis æreis :—
Icy gysont enterres Monsieur Thomas de Wasteneys et Johanna sa femme, le quel . . . morust en la grande pestilence l' an de grace 1349, Que pour leur almes prient.

In superiori Fenestra Australi Navis Eccłiæ :—
Sa. 3 cinquefoyles Arg.
Verry, Arg. & G.
Wasteneys.

Eadem in Fenestra Australi inferiori.

Fenestra Borealis superior :—
Effigies militis gestantis—Arg. a crosse formy G.
Effigies militis gestantis—Arg. 3 barrs B. a baston G.

Fenestra Borealis inferior :—
Barry of 6, Arg. & B. a labell of 5 pointes, G. . . . *Grey*
Wasteneys.
Arg. 3 escalops.

[p. 266.]

Carl.

Fenestra Australis Cancelli :—
Empaled { G. a plaine crosse & crescent, Arg.
{ G. a crosse patonce, Or . . . . *Latimer*
Empaled { G. a chevron betw. 3 leopards-faces, Arg.
{ G. a crosse patonce, Or . . . . *Latimer*
Quarterly, Or & G. a border Sa. bezanty . . . . *Rochford*
Empaled { Sa. 3 pick-axes, Arg. . . . . . *[Pigot]*
{ G. a crosse patonce, Or . . . . *Latimer*

Fenestra Orientalis Navis :—
G. 3 herons Arg. a mullet difference . . . . *Heron*
G. a chevron between 3 leopards-faces, Arg. . . *[Monke]*

Fenestra Orientalis Cancelli :—
G. a chevron between 3 leopards-faces, Arg. . . *[Monke]*
The Crest—a Heron proper.

Fenestra Orientalis ad dextram Navis :—
Arg. a fesse between 3 crescents, a border engr. G.
G. a chevron between 3 leopards-faces, Arg. . . *[Monke]*

Fenestra Australis :—
Sa. 3 herons, Arg. . . . . [*Heron*]
Vairè, Arg. & G.

Fenestra Borealis :—
G. a chevron between 3 leopards-faces, Arg. . . . *Monke*
Sa. 3 boares-heades couped, a border engr. Arg.

Bis depict' super muros Cancelli :—
Sa. a chevron between 3 leopards-faces, a border, Arg . *Monke*

[p. 267.]

Stamford.

ECCLIA SCI GEORGII.

In Cancello :—
Empaled ⎰ Ermine, a crosse peirced, Ermyns.
      ⎱ Sa a chevron between 3 wolfes-heads, couped, Arg.
         collared, Or.

In Fenestra Orientali Insulæ Australis :—
Sa. 3 dove-cotes, Arg. . . . . *Sapcote*
Empaled—*Sapcote*, & Arg. 3 turnepikes, Sa.
Orate pro aĩabus Ricardi Sapcote et Johannæ uxoris ejus.

Adhuc in fenestris : —
Or, a chevron B. betw. 3 sisefoyles, G.

Or, 2 barrs G. in cheife 3 torteaux . . . . . *Wake*
G. 3 water-bougets, Ermyn . . . . *Roos*
Or, 3 chevrons, G. . . . . *Clare*
Or, a plaine crosse, G. . . . . *Bigot*
Chequy, Or & B. . . . . *Warren*
G. a crosse patonce, Arg.
Or, a chevron B. between 3 sisefoyles, G.

Ex bibliotheca in Coll. Magd. Oxon. Pag. 336 :—
Joanna mater Ricardi Regis ob mærorem Joñis Holland filii sui obiit
et apud Stamford sepulta est A° 1384.*

[p. 268.]

ECCLIA SCÆ MARIÆ.

Cancellum Boreale :—
Tumulus alabastrinus in muro boreali cum simulachro Militis gestantis super pectus 3 lyons pawes couped—*Broun.*

---

* Joan, the Fair Maid of Kent, widow of the Black Prince, was buried in the
Chapel of the Grey Friars at Stamford, in which her first husband Sir Thomas
Holand, in her right Earl of Kent, had been buried in 1361. She died 8 July, 1385,
it is said of grief because her son Richard II refused to pardon his half-brother, Sir
John Holand, for the murder of the son of the Earl of Stafford, and by her will she
directed that she should be buried in the same chapel near her first husband.—*Ed.*

In Fenestra Orientali—bis :—
G. 3 lyons pawes couped Arg.   .   .   .   .   .   *Broun*
In Fenestra Boreali—bis :—
Broun.
Sa. 3 hammers, Arg.
Hic jacent Wiłłus Hikham Aldermannus, et Alicia uxor ejus : obiit
ille . . . illa . . . 1484 . . . testudinem* fieri fecerunt.
Quarterly, Or & G. a border Sa. bezanty   .   .   .   *Rochfort*
Rochfort sæpius in Fenestris.

[p. 269.]

ALHALLOWES CHURCH.

Hic jacet Arthurus Walpole qui obiit 3° die Augusti A° Dñi 1583.
Fenestra Australis :—
Empaled { Party p bend Sa. & Arg. 3 lozenges counterchanged.
{ Arg. on a bend Sa. a bezant   .   .   .   *Pinchbecke*
Eadem insignia sculpta super trochleam† Baptisterii.

Epitaphium ex ære deaurato :—
Hic jacet Joħes Broune, Mercator Stapulæ Calesiæ, et Benefactor
hujus Eccłiæ, qui obiit 26° die Julii, A° Dñi 1545, Cujus aïe &c.
Hoc in muro boreali.

[p. 270.]

Somerby juxta Roppesley.

In muro boreali :—
Statua lapidea, tibiis in crucem transversis, innixa equo fræno et
ephippio ornato ab homine ducto.   Super scutum :—
(Or) A chevron between 10 crosses botony, (Sa.)

Juxta super humum lapis marmoreus ablato Epitaphio et tribus
Evangelistis, remanente Mathæo.
A bend engrayled betw. 3 conies-heads erased   .   [*Conisholme ?*]
Aliud scutum ablatum.

Fenestra Borealis Navis :—
Arg. 2 barrs, in cheife 3 torteaux, over all a bend Sa.   *Threkingham*
Arg. a pale B. a fesse G.

Ter in superioribus Fenestris :—
Quarterly, in the 2ⁿᵈ quarter an estoyle, Sa.

Juxta Cancellum super solum in ære :—
Hic jacet Robertus Bawde de Somerby, Arm. et Justitiarius Pacis ac
Quorum in partibus de Kesteven in Com. Linc. qui obiit   .   die
Februar' A° Dñi 1509, Cujus aïe &c.   Jhesu mercy—Lady helpe.

---

* *Testudo*, a vaulted roof.—*Ed.*
† *Trochlea*, a pulley, probably to raise the font cover.—*Ed.*

𝔥umby 𝔐agna.

No entry.

[p. 271.]

Castle Bitham.

Fenestra Australis :—
Arg. a plaine crosse G.

Empaled { Barry of 6, Arg. & B. . . . . *Grey of Codnor*
Verry . . . . . . *Beauchamp of Hache*

Empaled—*Grey*, & Or, 3 piles G. . . . . . *Basset*

Empaled { Or, a lyon ramp. double-queue, G. . . . *Mallory*
Arg. 2 roses, & a canton, G.

Or, a fesse, G. . . . . *Colvill*

Bitham Parva.

Fenestra Orientalis Cancelli :—
Or, a plaine crosse, Vert . . . . *Hussey*
Barry of 6, Erm. & G. . . . . *Hussey*

The crest—a Hinde Trippant Arg. collared & chayned, in a Hawthorn bush.

Orate pro aīa Humfridi Polard Rectoris hujus Eccłiæ, qui hanc fenestram fieri fecit.

Sčus Medardus. Sčus Gildardus.

Fenestra Orientalis ad Austrum :—
Hugo Wayn fecit istam fenestram in honore Sčæ Mariæ et Sči Nicholai.

[p. 272.]

Kirke Stoke alias Stoke Rochford.

Fenestra Orientalis Cancelli :—
Barry of 6, Arg. & B. . . . . *Grey*
Quarterly, Or & G. a border Sa. bezanty . . . *Rochford*

Empaled { *Rochford* with a fleur-de-lize in 1ˢᵗ quarter.
Arg. 3 floures-de-lize betw. 9 crosses botony fitchy,
Sa. a border G. . . . . . *Hillary*

Hillary per se.

Prima Fenestra Orientalis in Capella Australi :—

Quarterly { Arg. a cheife G. over all a bend, B. . . *Crumwell*
Chequy, Or & G. a cheife Ermine . . *Tateshall*

Arg. a cross moline Sa.
Quarterly, Or & G. a border Sa. bezanty . . . *Rochford*

Secunda Fenestra Australis in Capella Boreali :—

Empaled { *Rochford.*
Quarterly { Or, a manch. G. . . . . *Hastings*
Arg. a chevron betw. 3 crosses botony
    fitchy Sa. . . . . *Russell*

Rochford, with a crosse botony fitchy in the 1st quarter.

Tertia Fenestra Australis in Capella Boreali :—
Rochford, with an annulet, Arg. in the 1st quarter.
Arg. a chevron between 3 griphons heads erased Sa. . *Tilney*
Arg. a cheife G. over all a bend engr. B. charged with a martlet, Sa. *Leek*

Orate specialiter et devote pro aīa Raďi Rochford et . . . uxoris
suæ, . . . qui hanc capellam et has tres fenestras fieri fecit A° Dñi
1448.

Fenestra Orientalis in Capella Boreali :—
Quarterly, *Rochford*, & G. an eagle displayed, Or.
Empaled, *Rochford*, & B. a bend, Or . . . . *Scrope*

Crest—On a chapperon Sa. doubled Arg. upon a Torce a Saracen's
head couped, Proper.

Crest—A hande supporting on a staffe a Flag, G. therein a Greyhounde cursant Arg. collared with pikes, chayned Or.
. . . 3 Estrich feathers, B.

Secunda Fenestra in Capella Boreali :—
Orate pro aīa Henrici Rochford et Elizabethæ uxoris suæ et Joħæ
uxoris suæ primæ . . .

[p. 273.] Tumulus ex ære marmore fixo, super quem :—
Empaled, *Rochford* & *Scrope.*
Sa. 3 garbes, Arg.
Hic jacet Henricus de Rochford, qui obiit 22° die Octobris A° Dñi
1470, Cujus &c.

Fenestra Borealis superior :—
Empaled—*Rochford*, & Erm. on a cheife Arg. 3 crosses Tau, Arg.

Fenestra Borealis inferior :—
Empaled—*Rochford* & *Scrope.*

Fenestra Borealis Navis Prima :—
Rochford. Sa. 3 garbes, Arg.

Fenestra Borealis Navis 2da :—
Arg. 3 horse-leaches, Sa.
Quarterly, *Rochford*, & an Eagle displayed, Or.
Quarterly, B. & Or, a border Sa. bezanty.
Arg. a cheife G. over all a bend engr. B. charged with a martlet, Or *Leek*

Fenestra Australis :—
Quarterly, *Scrope*, & Arg. a saltier engr. G. . . . *Tiptoft*
G. 3 floures-de-lize parted Arg.

Tumuli in Cancello ex marmore et ære :—
Here lyeth the body enterred of Oliver Saint John, sometymes
Squier to the Duchesse of Somersett, grandame to King Henry the
Seaventh, which Oliver died the 12th day of June, 1503, on whose
soule &c.   Eliz. Bigod uxor Olivī Sᵗ John.*

Hic jacet Sibilla quondam filia Oliveri Sᵗ John, Arm. quæ obiit
primo die Junii A° Dñi 1493, Cujus aīæ &c.

Arg. a bend, on a cheife G. 2 mullets, Or, an annulet on bend *St. John*

[p. 274]   In Capella Boreali in muro Tumulus lapideus ; Juxta super
humum effigies Viri et Mulieris lapide sculptæ.

In Capella Australi Tumulus lapideus cum scutis, insigniis fugientibus, circumsculptus.

Alter Tumulus ex opposito juxta Capellam.

In Sedula Cancelli Australi ligno sculpt', *Rochford*, & an Eagle
displayed, & 2 greyhoundes addorsed, collared Or.

𝔍𝔫𝔤𝔬𝔩𝔡𝔰𝔟𝔶.

Ex utraque parte ostii—a saltier—a crosse.

Super Fontem— . .   on a chevron   . .   3 crosses botony.

Fenestra Orientalis ad dextram Cancelli :—
Arg. a fesse G. between 3 Borages B.
Arg. a cheife endented B. .   .   .   .   .   .   *Nevile*

[p. 275.]

𝔈𝔡𝔢𝔫𝔥𝔞𝔪 𝔠𝔲𝔪 𝔊𝔯𝔦𝔪𝔰𝔱𝔥𝔬𝔯𝔭, 𝔖𝔬𝔲𝔱𝔥𝔬𝔯𝔭, 𝔖𝔠𝔬𝔱𝔱𝔢𝔩𝔱𝔥𝔬𝔯𝔫 & 𝔄𝔦𝔩𝔰𝔱𝔥𝔬𝔯𝔭.

In Fenestra Orientali Cancelli :—
Barry of 6 peices, Or & B. a bend G. .   .   .   .   *Gant*
B. semy of floures-de-lize, a lyon ramp. Or   .   .   .   *Beaumont*

Fenestra Borealis :—
B. a bend between 6 martlets, Arg. .   .   .   .   *Luttrell*
Arg. 3 dolphins naiant, Sa. .   .   .   .   .   .   *Simeon*

---

* This inscription is wrongly given.   It should be " Pray for the soll of Mastyr
Olyv Sentjohn squire sonne unto yᵉ right excellent hye & mighty princes duchess of
Som'sete, gr'dame unto oʳ sovey'n Lord Kynge Herre the VII, & for the soll of
Dame Elizabeth Bygod his wiffe whoo dep'ted frome this t'nsitore liffe yᵉ XII day of
June in yᵉ yeer of oʳ Lord MCCCCC & III."   Sir Oliver St. John married Mar-
garet, sister and heir of John de Beauchamp of Bletsoe ; she afterwards married John
Beaufort, Duke of Somerset, and was mother of the Lady Margaret Beaufort, mother
of Henry VII.—*Ed.*

Juxta Tumulus lapideus cum statuis Viri et Mulieris, vir gestans in scuto—a cheife endented—*Nevile* ut opinor.

A latere Tumuli :—

. . on a fesse . . 3 crosses botony fitchy . . *Colville*
. . a bend between 6 martlets . . . . . *Luttrell*
Quarterly, *Nevile* & *Simeon.*

Fenestra Australis superior :—*Beaumont.*

Super Porticum sculpt'—Empaled *Beaumont* & 3 garbes.

Ex opposito :—Crusilly botony fitchy, a lyon rampant.

Effigies ærea (Episcopi, ut autumo) super Campanile ex parte occidentali.

Effigies erecta fæminæ cum inscriptione juxta ostium boreale.
Grimsthorp dudum sedes Ernisii de Nevile, modo Comitis de Lindsey.

[p. 276.]

Swinhamsted vulgo Swinstead.

Appropriatio Prioratus de Drax, Ebor.

In Cancello statua Viri tibiis in crucem transversis.

Fenestra Borealis *bis* :—
Or, on a fesse G. 3 crosses botony, Arg. . . . *Colville*

Superius et inferius duo Milites genibus flexis gestantes super tunicas et manibus supportantes insignia dicta. Ille ad dextram—The crosses botony fitchy. *Colvile.* Eadem arma in proxima Fenestra. Item in Capella Scæ Annæ.

Fenestra Occidentalis :—
Or, a fesse, G. . . . . *Colvile*
Or, on a fesse G. 3 crosses botony, Arg. . . . . *Colvile*
Or, on a fesse G. 3 crosses botony fitchy, Arg. . . *Colvile*

Fenestra Australis :—
Or, a fesse G. . . . . *Colvile*
Or, on a fesse G. 3 crosses botony Arg. . . . . *Colvile*
Or, on a fesse G. 3 crosses botony fitchy, Arg. . . *Colvile*

Depicta in muro Insulæ Australis :—Catherina, uxor Johis Elmes dñi villæ, obiit 4ᵗᵒ die Februarii, Aᵒ Dñi 1593.

Of yᵉ Lord Zouch her father Richard upstood,
To hir mother Lord Stanley Monteagle gave breath
By Duke Brandon's daughter & named Elizabeth,
Catherine Duchess of Suffolke hir godmother.*

---

* That is, Catherine, wife of John Elmes, was daughter of Richard, Lord Zouch, by Elizabeth, who was daughter of Sir Edward Stanley, Lord Monteagle, by Elizabeth, daughter of Charles Brandon, Duke of Suffolk, and Ann, daughter of Sir Anthony Browne. The Duchess Catherine, who was her godmother, was the Duke's fourth wife, Catherine daughter and heiress of William, Lord Willoughby.—*Ed.*

Empaled { Ermyn, on 2 barrs Sa. 10 elme leaves, Or . *Elmes*
{ G. 10 bezants, with a crescent difference . . *Zouch*

In pale—*Stanley & Brandon.*

In pale—*Elmes & Mordant.*

Empaled { *Elmes,* &
{ Ermyn, a saltier ; on a cheife Sa. 2 mullets, Arg. *Ewarby*

Empaled { *Elmes* (Sr John Elmes) &
{ Sa. 3 hammers Arg. . . . *Broune of Stamford*

Zouch paleth *Stanley.* *Elmes* paleth *Zouch,* ut supra.

Empaled { Sir John Ewarby.
{ Er, a crosse engr. G. a Cornish chough Ppr. in 1st Qr.
Mussenden

Empaled { Sa. 3 hammers, Arg. . . . . *W. Broune*
{ Quarterly { Or, on a fesse G. 3 crosses botony, Arg. *Colvile*
{ { Erm. 3 stockes Sa. charged . *Sr. Wm. Stockes*

[p. 277.]

Corby.

Fenestra Australis Cancelli :—
Barry of 6 peices, Arg. & B. . . . . *Grey of Codnor*
Barry of 6 peices, Arg. & B. a bend, Or.

Hic jacent Joħes Armstrong quondam Mercator Stapulæ Calesiæ et Johanna uxor ejus, qui quidem Joħes obiit penultimo die Julii A° Dñi 1515, Cujus aīæ &c.

Fenestra Borealis Navis :—
Arg. a fesse between 2 chevrons, G.—*bis* . . . . *Peche*
Or, a manch, G. . . . . *Hastings*

Fenestra Borealis ad sinistram Cancelli :—*Grey.*

Fenestra Borealis Insulæ Borealis :—
Arg. a fesse in cheife 3 mullets of 6 pointes, in bast a crosse paty, Sa.
Arg. a chevron, ex dextra a crosse paty, ex sinistra a crescent Sa.
Arg. a chevron, & crescent in ye sinister point Sa. . [*Ricard*]

Subscriptio :—Orate pro aīabus Johannis Ricard, Roħti, et Nicholai Ricard qui istam fenestram fieri fecerunt.

Depicta ad ingressum Cancelli :—

Orate pro aīabus Joħis Colston et Agnetis uxoris ejus.

Orate pro aīabus Joħis Spenser et Johannæ uxoris ejus.

[p. 278.]

𝔍𝔯𝔫𝔥𝔞𝔪.

Tumulus lapideus juxta Capellam in Cancello :—

Empaled
{
  Quarterly
  {
    Sa. a saltier, Or . . . . *Belesby*
    Arg. on a chevron Sa. 3 boares heads
    couped, Or . . . . *Swinford*
  }
  . . . a bend between 6 martlets . . . *Luttrell*
}

Empaled
{
  Quarterly
  {
    3 pallets & 4 mullets in bend . *Thimelby*
    . . . a saltier . . . . . *Belesby*
    Swinford & *Luttrell.*
  }
  a lyon rampant.
}

Tumulus in Navi :—
Hic jacet Andreas Luttrell, Dñus de Irnham, qui obiit 6° die Septembris, A° Dñi 1390, Cujus aĩæ &c.

Ejus statua ærea marmore fixa, et Fenestra boreali superius :—
B. a bend between 6 martlets, Arg. . . . . *Luttrell*

In summo quatuor fenestrarum Capellæ Borealis :—
B. a bend between 6 martlets, Arg. . . . . *Luttrell*
Arg. on a chevron Sa. 3 boares heads couped, Or . *Swinford*
Sa. a saltier, Or . . . . *Belesby*
Arg. 3 pallets, & 4 mullets in bend, a crescent difference *Thimelby*

Subtus :—Orate pro aĩabus Ricardi Thymelby & Elizabethæ uxoris ejus, quondam dñi de Irnham, et Benefactoribus hujus Capellæ, A° Dñi 1531.

[p. 279.]

𝔏𝔞𝔟𝔦𝔫𝔤𝔱𝔬𝔫 𝔠𝔲𝔪 𝔒𝔰𝔤𝔬𝔡𝔟𝔶 𝔢𝔱 𝔎𝔶𝔰𝔢𝔟𝔶.

In Australibus Fenestris Eccĩæ Sc͠i Petri de Lavington :—
Arg. an escocheon between 8 cinquefoyles, G.
Arg. an escocheon Sa. betw. 8 cinquefoyles, G.
G. a fesse between 3 escalops Arg. . . . *De Sc̃o Laudo*

Tumulus cum statua et epitaphio æreis ablatis insigniis :—
Here lyeth the body of Richard Quadringe, Esq. who deceased yᵉ 29ᵗʰ day of Septembᵣ Anno 1511, on whose soule &c.

Fenestra borealis :—
G. a lyon tampant Verry, crowned Or . . . . *Marmyon*
Subscript :—Orate pro aĩa Wiłłi Marmyon, Militis.
Ermyne, a saltier engrayled, on a cheife G. a lyon passant,
guardant, Or . . . . *Ayremyn*
Orate pro aĩa Wiłłi Ayremyn de Osgodby, Militis.
The same, the saltier not engrayled . . . . *Ayremyn*
Subscript :—Orate pro aĩa Thomæ Ayremyn, Arm. de Osgodby.

Braisby.

No entry.

[p. 280.]

Pickworth.

Fenestra Borealis :—
Arg. a saltier between 4 cuppes covered, Sa.
  . . . Alicia . . . Joħis de Pickworth.

Sapurton.

Fenestra Australis Cancelli :—
Ermyn, a chevron, G.   .   .   .   .   *Tuchet*

Fenestra Australis Navis :—
B. a fesse daunce between 10 billets Or   .   .   .   *Deincourt*

Welby.

Fenestra Borealis Navis :—

Empaled { Ranged* { Arg. a cheife G. over all a bend, B.   *Crumwell*
         {   { Chequy, Or & G. a cheife, Ermyn   *Tateshale*
         { B. a fesse daunce between 10 billets, Or   .   *Deincourt*

In Fenestra boreali Insulæ in unoquoque rhombulo marsupium† et dictum, vizt :—N'ay Je droit.

Tumulus lapideus in Cancello :—
    De Billesfeild natus jacet hic Robert tumulatus
    Hujus ecclesiæ quondam Rector fuit ille.
    Qui obiit 5° Kl mensis Martii A° 1467.

[p. 281.]

Roppesley cum Humby parva.

Super Porticum :—
Hac non vade via nisi dicas Ave Maria.

Fenestra Borealis Cancelli :—
Thomas de Veston me fecit.
Or, 2 chevrons, on a canton G. a crosse patonce Arg.
Or, 2 chevrons, on a canton G. a mullet, Arg.

---

* *Ranged*, i.e. the two coats are placed one above the other, not quartered.— *Ea.*
† *Marsupium*, the Purse or Pouch for the Lord Treasurer Cromwell, see Tattershall, pp. 139-42.—*Ed.*

Fenestra Australis Navis :—

Empaled { G. 3 water-bougets, Arg. . . . . . *Ros*
{ G. a fesse between 6 crosses botony, Or . *Beauchamp*
Or, 2 chevrons G. on a canton Arg. a lyon pass. Sa.

Fenestra Orientalis ex sinistra Cancelli :—
Willus de Colby.—Alex. de Houringe.

Fenestra Australis :—
Subscript' :—Orate pro aīabus Joħis Colby et uxoris ejus, 1427.

Ex dextra Cancelli Borealis :—
Joħes de Colby.—Joħes de Welby.

Vir armatus gestans super pectus :—
Sa. a fesse double dauncee charged with 3 Scalops.

Columna prima :—Ista columna facta fuit ad festum Sc̄i Michaelis, A° 1380, et nomen factoris Thomas Bale de Corby.

Juxta ostium Eccłiæ :—Año Dñi M°CCCC°LXXX°VI° ista porta facta fuit.

Effigies Fæminæ in muro boreali Cancelli.

[p. 282.]

𝔥𝔞𝔱𝔥𝔢𝔯.

Prebenda de Lincoln.

Fenestra Borealis Navis :—
B. a bend Or, a labell of 3 points, G. & Arg. . . . *Scrope*
The same—a labell of 3 pointes Ermyn—*bis* . . . *Scrope*
Henry le Scrope, Chivaler.

Altera Fenestra Borealis :—
Orate pro aīa Galfridi le Scrop, Prebendarii hujus Eccłiæ, et pro aīa Beatricis Leonthrell sororis ejus. Hic Galfridus fuit Canonicus Eccłiæ Bēæ Mariæ Linc̄. A° 6° R. 2.
Arg. 6 annulets G. a bend, B. . . . . . . *Plessy*
Or, 2 barrs G. in cheife 3 torteaux . . . . . *Wake*
Arg. 2 barrs, Sa.—*bis* . . . . *Bussy*
The same—crescent difference . . . . *Edmund Bussy*

In Cancello :—G. 3 crownes in pale, Or.

In Insula Boreali :—
Arg. a chevron betw. 3 crosses botony Sa. a border Sa. bezanty
Fitzwilliam
Edwardus Beetson de Calverthorp filius Thomæ Beatson de Swarby, obiit 6° die Febr. 1593.

[p. 283.]

𝔠𝔞𝔩𝔳𝔢𝔯𝔱𝔥𝔬𝔯𝔭𝔢.

Or, a cross patonce.

Kelby.

No entry.

Ounesby.

Priez pur l' alme Wauter de Ounesby q̃ dona.

In muro ære sculpt':—Orate pro aïa Christopheri Hogekinson, quondam dñi manerii de Ounesby, qui obiit 20° die Decembr' A° Dñi 1544.
Subtus Tumulus lapideus ex sinistra Cancelli.

Tumulus in Cancello :—
Joħes Colthrist (pater Joħis, qui vixit 1600).

Swarby.

Appropriat' Priorat' de Kyme.

Ex parte occidentali Campanilis :—
John Thursbe . . . of thy Soule God have mercy.   Vicarius ibidem, ut dicitur.

[p. 284.]

Alwarby.*

In Cancello :—
G. a cinquefoyle peirced betw. an orle of crosses botony, Or *Umfravile*

Depicta super Sedulam :—
Arg. 3 escocheons B
G. 3 lucies hauriant, Arg. . . . . *Lucy*

Fenestra Occidentalis :—*Umfravile.*

Tumulus lapideus :—
Hic jacet Dñus Robertus Dawnce, quondam Rector istiue Eccłiæ, qui obiit 28° die Januarii Anno Dñi 1460, Cujus aïæ &c.

Depicta super ingressum Cancelli :—
G. a chevron between 10 crosse-crosseletts. Or . . . *Kyme*
Arg. a saltier ; on a cheife G. escalops of the 1st . . *Tailboys*

Fenestra Australis :—
Orate pro aïabus Roberti Daunce, Joħis Daunce et Johannæ uxoris ejus.

---

* *Sic*, but meant for Aswardby.—*Ed.*

Tumulus in Choro Boreali :—
Hic jacet corpus Wiłłi Jones qui obiit 9° die Octobr. 1580.
Vana, Deum, requiem, sprevit, amavit, habet.
. . a crosse batune between 4 . . .

Juxta Ostium :
Hic jacet Wiłłus Dymson et Johanna uxor ejus, qui obiit 5° die
Augusti A° Dñi 1558, Cujus aīæ &c.

[p. 285.]

Burton Pedwardyn.

Fenestra Orientalis Cancelli :—
G. 2 lyons passants, Or . . . . . . *Pedwardyn*
Lozengy, Or & G. . . . . *Creoun*

Fenestra Borealis superior :—
G. 2 lyons passant, hors del champ, a labell of 5, Arg.
G. 2 lyons passant, hors del champ, Or.
Out of a crown a lyon pass. Or—*Bis* . . *Pedwardyn's Crest*

Fenestra Australis :—
G. 2 lyons passant, Or . . . . . . *Pedwardyn*
Or, 3 crescents G. each charged with a plate . . *Longchamp*

Fenestra Chori Borealis :—
Fæmina, genu flexo, super vestem—*Pedwardyn*; dextra tenens
insigne oneratum—*Longchamp*. Altera Fæmina itidem supportans
insigne, super vestem—*Longchamp*, in insigni *Creoun*.

Sub muro in marmore sculpt' :—
Dame : Alis : de : Pedwardyn : gist ici :
File : de : Longchampe : S : Henri :
Deu : de : sa : alme : eyt : merci.

Ex antiquo manuscripto collecta tempore R. 2.

Alicia de Longcampo, filia et hæres Henrici de Longchamp, obiit
15° die Mensis Maii A° Dñi 1330, et jacet in boreali parte Capellæ
Bēæ Mariæ in Ecclesia de Burton Pedwardyne.

Ex eodem :—Henricus de Longchamp filius et hæres Wiłłi de Longchamp et Dñæ Petronillæ de Croun obiit die Martis proxima post
festum Nativitatis Bēæ Mariæ Virginis A° Gīæ 1274, et legavit corpus
suum Abbīæ de Swinsheved, et cor suum Eccłiæ de Burton ad sepeliendum in Capella ante altare Bēæ Mariæ Virginis.

Ex eodem :—Rogerus de Pedwardyn duxit Aliciam filiam et hæredem
Henrici de Longchamp ; Qui quidem Rogerus Eccłiam de Burton
Pedwardyn cum Capella Bēæ Mariæ integerrimam construxit, excepto
le South Isle, cum Capella Sēi Nicholai Eþi, constructis per parochianos
ejusdem Villæ.

[p. 286.] Ex eodem :—Rogerus de Pedwardyn, filius et hæres Rogeri et Aliciæ de Longchamp obiit 10° die Februarii Anno Dñi 1368, qui perquisivit bullam continentem 500 et 20 dies Indulgentiæ Benefactoribus Eccłiæ et Capellæ de Burton, ut in dca bulla conspicientibus plenius apparebit.

Ex eodem :—Walterus de Pedwardyn, filius et hæres Rogeri et Agnetis filiæ Philippi Dñi Darcy obiit 11° die Junii A° Dñi 1405.

Ex eodem :- Walterus de Pedwardyn, filius et hæres Roberti obiit 14° die Augusti, A° Dñi 1429.

Scredington cum Northbeck.

Hic jacet Wiłłus Pylet de Scredington, qui obiit 28° die Junii, A° Dñi 1408, cujus aĩæ &c.

Statua in muro boreali :—

<blockquote>
Ma . . . a re Thomæ Wyke rector p
Gaudia de p me tumulus que car . . . II.
</blockquote>

Thomas Wyke de Scredington Rector Eccłiæ de Manchester vixit año 7° Ric. 2.

Ric. Skarlet.

[p. 287.]

Kirkby-Lathorp.

In Cancello :—

B. 3 lyons rampants, Or	*Dacres*
Erm. on a fesse G. 3 crosses botony, Or	*Aunsell*

Fenestra Australis Navis :—

Chequy, Or & B.	*Warren*
G. 3 lyons passants, guardants, Or	*England*
Quarterly, Or & G. a bendlet Sa. a labell of 5 points, Arg.	*Lacy*

Fenestra Orientalis ad sinistram Cancelli :—

Arg. a chevron, Or, betw. 3 trefoyles Vert . . . *Sleford*

(*Note in margin.* Where in windows I fynde Or in *Arg.* I beleave it is but a decay of yᵉ colour Gules.)

Barry of 6, G. & Arg. a Cross portate in bend sinister, B. *S. Gilbert*

Barry of 6, G. & Arg. in cheife 3 mullets peirced Arg. . [*Brunne*]

Fenestra borealis inferior :—

Ermyn, a saltier engr. on a cheife G. a lyon passant, guardant, Or.

Ayrmyn

In Campanili :—G. 3 barrs, Arg.

Super Sedulam :—2 keys in saltier, wards downwards.

The three Carrs, Robert, William, & Edward, neatly painted above the pillars.

[p. 288.]

Sleford alias Lafford cum Haldingham.

In pariete extra eccliam sub fenestra Orientali Cancelli :—
Orate pro aĩa Riči Cokke, Johannæ uxoris ejus, Johis filii eorum, et oĩm benefactorum, quorum aĩabus propitietur Deus. A° 1403.

Tumulati in Cancello :—
Here lyeth yᵉ body of Richard Buller Preist, who deceased the 21ˢᵗ day of August 1540.

Hic jacet Robertus Bayl, Vicarius, qui obiit 30° die Maii A° Dñi 1553.

Hic jacet Johes Godfray, Vicarius, qui obiit 25° die Julii Anno Dñi 1539, cujus aĩæ &c.

In tabulis tecti Cancelli—sæpius—G. 3 bendlets, Or.
G. a lyon rampant regardant Arg.
G. 3 goates heads erased, Arg.

Fenestræ Navis :—

Empaled { Or, a plaine crosse, Vert . . . . *Hussey*
{ G. a chevron betw. 10 cinquefoyles, Arg. . . *Barkely*
B. on a cheife Or, a demy-lyon ramp. G. a border, Arg. . *Marcham*
Quarterly, B. 3 crownes, Or, & Arg. a crosse patonce, Sa.
Sa. 3 shuttles, Or.
G. a crosse patonce, Arg.
G. a crosse patonce, Erm.
B. 2 chevrons Or, betw. 3 roses, Arg. . . *Russel, Epᵘs Linc.*

Here lyeth Robert Tymberland, butcher, & Alianor his wife, wᶜʰ Robert deceased yᵘ 11ᵗʰ day of May, 1552.

Here lyeth Gilbert Hanson, fishmonger, who dyed 27 January, 1556.

Here lyeth James Clyfton, draper, & Alice his wife, which James deceased yᵉ 10ᵗʰ day of July, 1528.

[p. 289.] Tumulus super solum :—
Hic jacet Georgius Carre et Anna uxor ejus, qui quidem Georgius obiit A° Dñi 1521.

Tumulus alabastrinus juxta Cancellum :—
Hic jacet Robtus Carre, filius Georgii Carre, qui obiit 16° die Sept. A° Dñi 1590 ; Elizabetha prima conjux, filia Willi Cawdron, per quam Georgius, Robtus, Willus, et Edwardus masculi—Elizabetha, Anna, et Brigida fæminæ.

Anna 2ᵈᵃ uxor, filia Georgii Tailboys, Militis, relicta Edri Dymoke, Militis, per quam nulla soboles.

Anna 3^{tia} uxor, filia Caroli Knivet, relicta . . . Robinson et Leonardi Irby.

Georgius, Roƀti filius, duxit Mariam filiam Ambrosii Sutton, per quam Robƈus et Elizabetha.

Roƀtus, filius Roƀti, duxit primo Elizabetham filiam Henrici Comitis Wigorniensis, relictam Dñi Grey de Wilton—secundo Cassandram filiam Wiłłi Aprice, Huntingdoñ.

Wiłłus filius Roƀti duxit Brigidam filiam Joħis Chaworth, Militis.

Edouardus filius Roƀti duxit Catherinam filiam Caroli Bolle.

Elizabetha filia Roƀti nupta primo Wiłło Fairfax—2do Christophero Kelke.

Anna 2da filia nupta primo Roƀto Whichcote—2^{du} Roƀto Legard.

Brigida 3^{tia} filia Roƀti Carre Ricardo Rosseter desponsata.

Insignia super Tumulum predictum :—

Quarterly { G. on a chevron Arg. 3 mullets, Sa. . . *Carre*
{ Or, an orle, B. . . . . *Balliol*

Carre's Crest :—a Stag's head couped Arg. attired Or, about his neck 2 barrs gemeux G.

Arg. a chevron betw. 3 martlets ; on a cheif Sa. 3 crosse-crosselets, Or . . . . *Cawdron*

[p. 290.] Arg. a saltier, on a cheife G. escalops of ye first *Tailboys*

Arg. a bend & a border engrayled, Sa. . . . . *Knyvet*

Or, on a chevron betw. 3 annulets G. 3 crescents of ye 1st . *Sutton*

Arg. in fesse France & England, a border gobony Arg. & B.
Somerset, Comes Wigarn

14 Closets* Arg. & B. 3 martlets in triangle, Sa. . . *Chaworth*

B. 3 bolles Or, jesants boares heads, Arg. . . . *Bolle*

Sa. a bend betw. 2 cottises fleury, Arg. . . . . . *Kelke*

Ermine, 2 sangliers trippants G. . . . . . *Whichcote*

Arg on a bend Sa. 3 chaplets of ye first . . . *Rosseter*

Super Crucem hinc inde :—
A saltier betw. 4 Roundels, 1575.

[p. 291.]

Ebedon.

Super Baptisterium :—
Arg. a fess dauncy betw. 3 lyons heads erased Sa.
. . . a fess dauncy betw. 10 billets—*Bis.* . . [*Herdeby*]
. . . a chevron betw. 3 escallops.

In Fenestra Chori australis : —
Or, 3 griphons passants, B. 2 & 1.
Sa. a fesse betw. 3 griphons passants, Arg.

---

* *i.e.* Barry of 14, see p. 91.—*Ed.*

Effigies Viri et Mulieris gestantium eadem bis super vestimenta. Tumulus Thomæ Herby, Domini et Patroni de Evedon, super quem insculpta quatuor scuta, Viz*t*. a fesse dauncy betw. 10 billets ; a fesse dauncey betw. 3 lyons' heads erased ; Empaled, a fesse dauncy betw. 10 billets.

Empaled { a fesse betw. 3 griphons passants.
{ a chevron betw. 3 escalops.

Riskinton.

In fenestris :—

Empaled { Arg. a fesse B. a labell of 5 pointes, G. . *Everingham*
{ B. a crosse patonce voyded, Arg. . . . *Melton*

Empaled { B. a crosse patonce voyded, Arg. . . . *Melton*
{ Arg. a fesse B. a labell of 5 pointes, G. . *Everingham*

Arg. a fesse B. a labell of 5 pointes, G. . . . *Everingham*
  This last under a mantle & Crest defaced.

G. a chevron between 10 crosse-crosselets, Or . . . *Kyme*
B. 3 cinquefoyles, Or . . . . . . *Bardolfe*

[p. 292.]

Jwarby.

Fenestra orientalis Chori borealis :—
Erm. 2 barrs G. over all a bend, Sa.
Arg. 2 barrs G. in cheife 3 torteaux ; over all a bend, Sa. *Threkingham*
Or, 2 chevrons & a border G. a labell of 5, B.
  Stephanus Capellanus . . . de Iwarby me fecit.

Fenestra borealis Chori :—
  Effigies Viri, genu flexo, super vestem et manu gestans :—Erm. 2 barrs G. a bend, Sa.

Fenestra borealis Navis :—
  Effigies Viri, genu flexo, gestans veste et manibus :—Barry of 6, Or & B. a bend G.—*Gant.*

Fenestra occidentalis ad sinistram Campanilis :—
Arg. 2 chevrons G. a labell of 5 pointes, B.
Barry of 6, Arg. & G. 3 torteaux in cheife ; over all a bend, B.
                                    Threkingham

Fenestra Campanilis :—
Or, 2 chevrons G. a labell of 5, B.
G. 2 chevrons Or, a labell of 5, B.

Fenestra australis Cancelli :—
Arg. 2 barres G. in cheife 3 torteauxes, over all a Bend, Sa.—*bis.*
                                      Threkingham

In choro boreali :—
Tumulus marmoreus cum effigie Alexandri Aunsell, Militis, ut dicitur, qui obiit sine exitu.

Super tumulum hæc insignia, vizt :—
Erm. on a fesse G. 3 crosses botony, Or   .   .   .   *Aunsell*

Super ingressum Cancelli : —
Pray for the welfare of M^{rs}. Joane Gibson.

Tumuli in Cancello :—
Hic jacet Ricardus de Owningham, quondam Rector istius Eccɫiæ, qui obiit 10° die Aprilis, A° Dñi 1396, Cujus &c.

Ricͯus Typler, Rector.

Tumuli in Navi :—
Hic jacet Wiɫɫus Broun, qui obiit 16° die Augusti, A° Dñi 1464, Cujus aïæ &c.

Hic jacet . . . Glover, qui obiit 20° die Februarii, A° Dñi 1505, Cujus &c.

[**p. 293.**]   Hic jacet G. Broun.

Hic jacet Joħes Boulle, qui obiit 2° die Octobris, Anno Dñi 1505, Cujus aïæ &c.

Super Crucem in Cœmeterio :—
    Sumptu Rectoris fuit hæc Crux facta Johannis
    Hasebrugh, mæroris expers sit in omnibus annis.
3 lyons passants.
A lyon rampant   .   .   .   .   *Percy*
3 lucies hauriants.
A cinquefoyle between 8 crosse-crosselets   .   .   [*Umfraville*]

Ex opposito Crucifixi :—
Virgo Maria inter Divos Petrum et Paulum.

Osbournby.

Sedulis speciosa.

Fenestræ australes :—
Or, a lyon ramp. B.   .   .   .   .   *Percy*
Or, a fesse, Sa.
Or, a bend, Sa.   .   .   .   .   *Mawley*

Fenestra orientalis ad dextram :—
Arg. 3 barrs, Sa.   .   .   .   .   *Bussy*
G. a chevron betw. 10 crosses botony, Or   .   .   .   *Kyme*
Arg. 3 cinquefoyles peirced, G.   .   .   .   .   *Limbury*
Verry, a fesse G. fretty Or   .   .   .   .   .   *Marmyon*

[p. 294.]

Threkingham.

In Fenestra boreali :—
Arg. 3 barrs G. in cheife 3 torteaux ; over all a bend Sa. *Threkingham*
Or, 2 chevrons & a border G.
G. 3 water-bougets, Arg. . . . . . . *Ros*
Barry of 6, Arg. & B. . . . . *Grey*

Tumulus lapideus cum statua Lamberti de Threkingham, tibiis in crucem transversis, gestantis in scuto :—
2 barrs with 3 roundles in cheife, over all a bend, Sa. *Threkingham*
 Juxta Consors ejus.

Fenestra occidentalis :—
Arg. a fesse between 3 cootes Sa. . . . . *W. Coote*

In Cancello :—
Empaled { Arg. a fesse between 3 cootes, Sa. . . . *Coote*
{ Arg. a fesse dauncy betw. 3 talbots' heads erased Sa. *Spayne*

Nuper depict' :—G. a chevron betw. 3 floures de lize, Arg. *Pickering*

Quarington.

A chevron between 3 turrets :—Sæpissime super tumulum juxta solum in Cancello.

[p. 295.]

Algerby.*

Ecclia Sci Andreæ—Fenestra occidentalis Cancelli :—
Arg. a saltier, on a cheife G. 3 escalops of the 1st . . *Taylboys*
G. a cinquefoyle peirced betw. 8 crosses botony Or . *Umfravile*

Fenestra australis :—
G. 3 livery pottes, Arg. . . . . . . *Blande*
Orate pro aĩa Stephi Muston et Agnetis uxoris ejus.

Fenestra borealis :—
Sa. a chevron between 3 estoyles, Arg.
 Vir gestans in tunica eadem insignia.
 Orate pro aĩa Willi Kingsman et Elizabethæ consortis suæ.

In laqueari :—Omnia dicta insignia depicta ; Item
G. a chevron betw. 10 crosses botony, Or . . . *Kyme*

---

* *i.e.* Asgarby.—*Ed.*

Tumulus lapideus in Choro :—

> Es testis, Christe, quod non jacet hic lapis iste,
> Corpus ut ornetur, sed spiritus ut memoretur.
> Istuc qui graderis, senex, medius, puer an sis,
> Pro me funde preces, quia sic mihi fit veniæ spes.

Sepultus sub lapide vixit in hoc beneficio . . . annis . . .
qui obiit . . . die . . . A° Gr̄æ M°CCCC°LX°, Cujus aīæ &c.

Dn̄e dilexi decorem domus tuæ.

Orate pro aīa Wiłłi Fish et Johannæ uxoris ejus.

In muro australis Capellæ :—
Carolus primogenitus Johannis Butler de Baketon obiit 17° die Maii
1603, ætatis 8.
Arg. on a chevron B. 3 cups covered Or, betw. as many demy-
lions pass. guard. G. crowned Or . . . . *Butler*

Fenestra Campanilis :—
Joħes More et Margar. uxor ejus.
Campanæ in honore Sc̄i Johannis, Sc̄i Jacobi, Sc̄i Andreæ.

[**p.** 296.]

𝕎illougȟby 𝔑ortȟ alias 𝔖ilke 𝕎illougȟby.

Fenestra Orientalis Cancelli :—
Or, a bend B.

| Empaled | G. 2 chevrons, Arg. . . . . *Geffrey Paynell* |
| | Arg. a fesse, B. a labell of 5, G. . . *Everingham* |

| Empaled | G. a fesse betw. 3 water-bougets, Erm. . *Tho. Meres* |
| | *Everingham.* |

Empaled	Erm. a saltier engrayled, on a cheife G. a *Wiłł'us Ayrmyn*
	lyon passant guardant Or . . . *Junr. Miles*
	Everingham.

Empaled	Arg. on 2 chevrons G. 10 mullets, Or ; on a cheife
	of yᵉ 2ⁿᵈ 3 falcons volant of yᵉ 3ʳᵈ . *W. Stanlow*
	Arg. 3 barrs Sa. . . . . . . *Bussey*

Hic jacet Wiłłus Ayrmyn, Junior, Miles, qui obiit 16° die Octobris,
A° Dn̄i 1468, Cujus aīæ &c.

Hic jacet Thom. Ermyn, filius et hæres Wiłłi Ermyn de Osgodby,
qui obiit . . . die . . . A° Dn̄i 1498, Cujus aīæ &c.

Hic jacet Margareta, uxor Wiłłi Ermyn de Osgodby, Dn̄i de North
Willoughby, quæ obiit 20° die Septembr. A° Dn̄i 1506, Cujus &c.

Hic jacet Wiłłus Armyn, Dn̄us de Osgodby, qui obiit 23° die Septembris, A° Dn̄i 1532 Cujus aīæ &c.

Super Tumulum antedictæ Margaretæ hæc arma, Viz᷒ :—
Sa. 3 conies' heads erased, Arg. . . *Conisholme* for *Langholme*

Hic jacet Joħes Stanlow de Silkeby, Arm. ac Dñus Villæ, qui obiit 27° die Junii, A° Dñi 1409.

Hic jacet Johanna uxor Wiħi Stanlow, et quondam filia Joħis Bussy Militis, qui obiit . . .

[p. 297.]

ffolkingham.

In Fenestra Campanilis :—

B. semy of floures de lize, a lyon ramp. Or, debruised with a
   bend gobony Arg. & G. . . . . . *Beaumont*
B. 3 cinquefoyles peirced Or . . . . . *Bardolfe*
Quarterly { *Beaumont*, with the bend gobony.
          { B. 3 garbes, Or . . . . . *Comes Boghan*
Clinton & *Say*, quarterly within the Garter . *Edw. Erle of Lincoln*

In Cancello :—*Beaumont.*
Fenestra borealis Navis :—*Beaumont.*

Fenestra orientalis Navis :—
Quarterly, *Jerusalem* & *Beaumont*, with yᵉ bend—*Bis.*
Arg. a plaine crosse, Sa. . . *Vesey, uxor Henrici Beaumont*
Effigies Joħis de la Novel Kastel,

In Porticu hinc inde Ostii :—3 garbes, *Beaumont.*

Effigies Religiosi juxta Fontem :—
Hic jacet Emot Gilson . . obiit . . die . . A° Dñi . .
Hic jacet Thomas Beverley.

[p. 298.]

Aslackby.

In Fenestra orientali Cancelli :—
G. a plaine crosse, Arg.
G. a lyon ramp. debruised with a bend, Sa.

Fenestra orientalis Navis, ad dextram :—
G. a bend fusilly, Or.
. . . 3 lyons passants . . . over all a Bend, B.
Arg. a lyon ramp. Sa. crowned, Or.
   Tria predicta insignia recta serie collocata in duabus fenestris australibus.

Fenestra orientalis Navis, ad sinistram :—
   Virgo Dei nutrix, Willelmi sis pia tutrix.
   Virgo tu vis, Diva potes, Regina teneris.
   Ne salus miseris mei juvamen eris.
   Radix Jesse pulchrum.

Tumulus lapideus :—
Orate pro aīa Dñi Joħis Saunderson, quondam Capellani Sc̃i Joħis
de Aslackby, qui obiit 23° die Martii, A° Dñi 1514, Cujus aīæ &c.

Upon this monument is the Epitaph of one Richard Serle, thrice
Ensigne bearer to a Generall of yᵉ Field, who deceased yᵉ first day of
March, 1587.

[p. 299.]

ඕXxalcot.

Priez pur Nicholas Mayster et . . .   sa femme.

Fenestra borealis Navis :—
Effigies Viri et Mulieris—Wiħus de Wareville.

In Choro australi :—

Empaled $\Big\{$ Quarterly $\Big\{$ Arg. a chevron betw. 3 chesse rooks, Sa.   *Walcot*
G. a fesse betw. 6 floures-de-lize, Arg.
G. on a fesse Or, 3 crosses formy of yᵉ 1ˢᵗ.

Empaled $\Big\{$ *Walcot*,
Arg. on a bend Sa. an annulet, Or . .   [*Pinchbeck*]

Empaled $\Big\{$ Quarterly, *Walcot* & a fesse betw. 6 floures-de-lize.
a cheife & bend, & 2 barrs & a crosse botony in base, ranged
Empaled, *Walcot*, & the 2 ranged coats.*

In Choro boreali :—
Tumulus lapideus fugientibus literis et insigniis *Walcot* pene obliteratis
Alter Tumulus.

[p. 300.]

ħaceby.

In Fenestra australi Cancelli :—
Arg. a chevron betw. 3 chesse rooks, Sa.   .   .   .   *Walcot*
Quartereth G. a fesse betw. 6 floures-de-lize, Arg.
Paleth Or, a cheife G. over all a bend B.   .   .   .   *Harrington*
Rangeth* with B. 2 barrulets, a crosse botony fitchy in base, Or.
                                      Walcot bis
Fenestra australis superior :—
Arg. a chevron between 3 chesse rooks, Sa.

Tumulus super humum Cancelli :—
Hic jacet Thomas Jarcocke, quondam Rector Eccħæ de Haceby,
qui obiit . . .

Per nullam sortem poteris excludere mortem.

---

     * *Ranged*, i.e., the two coats are placed one above the other, not quartered—*Ed.*

[p. 301.]

Newton.

In Fenestra boreali Cancelli :—
Anno Dñi millesimo tricentesimo octavo Will . . . .
Helmswell Rector Ecctiæ de Newton . . . .

In Fenestra orientali Insulæ australis :—
Roy Edward de Carnarvon prie deu merci & socl . . . .
Effigies Regis cum insigniis Angliæ.

Fenestra Insulæ australis :—

Empaled { Arg. a chevron between 3 chesse rookes . *Walcot*
{ Or, a cheife G. over all a bend, B. . . *Harrington*
B. a crosse botony fitchy, & 3 barrulets above, Or, ranged.

Fenestra borealis superior : —
Arg. a fesse dauncy betw. 10 billets G. reversed . *De la Launde*

Fenestra borealis inferior :—
Erm. 2 barrs, G. . . . . *[Kirketon]*
Erm. a chevron, G.

Juxta Ostium boreale :—
Erm. a chevron G. . . . . *[Tucket]*
Robert Lovet alias Fitz-Marie.

[p. 302.]

Grantham.

ECCLIA SCI WULFRANI.

In Fenestra orientali Cancelli :—
Chequy, B. & Or, a border, Sa. semy de trefoyles, Arg. in cheife the
letter G. . . *Insignia Burgi, ex dono Com. Warenne*
Chequy, Or & B. . . . . *Warren*
G. a saltier, Arg. . . . . *Nevile*
Quarterly { Or, a lyon rampant, B. . . . . . *Percy*
{ G. 3 lucies hauriant, Arg. . . . . . *Lucy*
Quarterly { G. a crosse sarcely, Arg. . . *Beke* }
{ Sa. a crosse engrayled, Or . . *Ufford* } *Willoughby*
Quarterly, *France & England*, a labell of 3 with 9 torteaux.
Edm. D. of York
G. 3 lyons passants guardants Or, a labell of 3, Arg. . *Brotherton*
Quarterly, *France* & *England*, a border gobony, Arg. & B.
Beaufort, D. of Somerset
B. semy of flowers de lize, a lyon ramp. Or . . . *Beaumont*
G. crusilly botony fitchy, a lyon ramp. Arg. . . *La Warre*
Quarterly { G. 3 water-bougets, Arg. . . . . . *Ros*
{ Arg. a fesse betw. 2 barrs gemeux, G. . . *Badlesmere*
Paly of 6 peices, Arg. & Vert, a mullet upon ye 2nd pallet, of ye first.

In Fenestra australi :—
Arg. on a plaine crosse Sa. a floure de lize, Or, between 4 keys
    of the 2nd . . . . . . *Mercator Stapulæ*

Tumulus lapideus in muro australi :—
    Baldwin Harington icy gist
    Dieu luy done Joy perfict
    Qui al terre dona sa rent
    L'an dieu mile ter cent
    Sessant quater sans delay
    4 Kalends Moys de Maye.
Upon this monument are insculpt two escocheons, Vizt., Three lyons
heads erased & crowned, wth ye Crest, a lyons head erased & crowned
& ex opposito—A cheife, over all a bend, which is *Harington*.

Hic jacent Ricus Saltby et Margareta uxor ejus qui obierunt . . .
Anno Dñi 1362.

Upon this last monument these 2 coates empaled, Vizt. [p. 303.]
Arg. a fesse dauncy betw. 3 mullets, Sa. & . . . 3 bendlets sinister,
on a cheife 3 pallets.

Hic jacet Joñes Saltby qui . . . Año Dñi 1429, Cujus aīæ &c.

In Fenestra :—
Ermines, a cinquefoyle, Ermine . . . . . *Flower*

Fenestra borealis :—
Or, a cheife G. over all a bend, B. . . . . *Harrington*
B. a crosse botony fitchy, & 2 barrulets above, Or.
Arg. a chevron betw. 3 lyons heads erased, Sa. . . . *Hall*

Qui capellam ibidem ex parte boreali Cancelli construxit.

In hac Ecclesia sepulti jacent (ut ex collectaneis Joñis Lelandi tomo
primo accepimus) Scus Wolfranus Epus, Scus Symphorianus Martyr, et
Sca Editha Virgo.

[p. 304.]

Binnington.

B. a bend cotised Arg. betw. 6 lyons rampant, Or . . *Bohun*
Diabolus :—
Hanc animam posco quia plenam crimine nosco.

Anima :—
O spes in morte, succurre Maria precor te.

In cœmeterio effigies Viri et Fæminæ lapide quadrato co-operta :
Inscriptio :—
    Henri et Isabell gisont icy,
    Deu de leur almes aiet mercy.

ffoston.

In Fenestra orientali Cancelli :—
B. a crosse between 4 lyons rampants, Arg.

Super Crucem in cœmeterio :—
Orate pro aïa Gilb'ti Esin.

[p. 305.]

Barrowby.

In Fenestra orientali Cancelli :—
Arg. a lyon rampant G. crowned Or, a border Sa. bezantee.

Comes Cornubiæ

In Fenestra boreali :—

Empaled { Arg. 3 birdbolts G.   .   .   .   .   .   *Bozon*
{ Sa. 3 roses (cinquefoyles) a border engr. Arg.   *Sembes*

Simulachrum Fæminæ gestantis :—
Sa. 3 cinquefoyles, a border engrailed, Arg.   .   .   .   *Sembes*
Quarterly, *Bozon & Sembes.*
G. a chevron Or, 6 crosses botony . . .

Superius Simulachrum Viri eadem insignia gestantis.

Empaled { Arg. 3 birdbolts, G.   .   .   .   .   .   *Bozon*
{ G. on a chevron Or, 6 crosses botony . . .

Simulachrum Fæminæ eadem gestantis insignia in veste.

In Fenestræ australi :—
Sa. 3 cinquefoyles, a border engr. Arg.   .   .   .   .   *Sembes*
Arg. semy of floures-de-lize, a lyon ramp. Sa.   .   *Buckminster*

Tumulus juxta suggestum* ex marmore et ære :—
Under this monument lye buryed the bodyes of Nicholas Deen &
Catharine his wife (daughter & heyre of Walter Pedwardyn) who died
the eleventh day of Oct. Anno Dñi 1479.

Three escocheons of Brasse are torn away from this monument,
that one wch remayneth hath 4 coates quarterly, Viz^t :—

Quarterly { Arg. 2 barrs, Sa. a border G.   .   .   .   .   *Deen*
{ G. 2 chevrons, Arg.   .   .   .   .   .   *Paynel*
{ Sa. 3 cinquefoyles, a border engr. Arg.   .   .   *Sembes*
{ Arg. 3 bird-bolts G.   .   .   .   .   .   *Bozon*

Alter Tumulus juxta :—
Hic jacet Jacobus Deen, de Barrowby, Armig. et Margareta uxor
ejus ; Obiit ille 29° die Aprilis, A° Dñi 1498, Illa 19° die Januarii, A°
Dñi 1508. Quorum aïabus &c.

---

* *Juxta suggestum,* i.e., near the Reading Desk.—*Ed.*

[p. 306.]   Super hunc Tumulum Effigies Fæminæ cum insigniis *Ayrmyn* in veste, necnon hoc scutum, Viz^t :—

Empaled ⎰ B. on a cheife Or, a demy-lyon rampant, G.   *Markham*
        ⎱ Erm a saltier engr. on a cheife G. a lyon pass. Or *Ayrmyn*

Item *Ayrmyn* per se in scuto æreo circumscriptio cujus :—Agnus Dei, qui tollis peccata mundi, miserere nobis.

Tumulus lapideus :—
Orate pro aīabus Robīi Sharpe et Isabellæ uxoris ejus, qui quidem Robertus obiit 13° die Aprilis, Año Dñi 1504, et Isabella obiit die Sĉi Petri et Pauli proximo præterito.

Campanæ :—
     1-2. In multis annis resonet campana Johannis.
     3. Cælorum, Christe, placeat tibi, Rex, sonus iste.   4.

Allington.

Ecclesiæ binæ cum campanilibus dupliciter arcuatis.
Occidentalis Ecclia Sĉe Trinitatis :—
Orientalis Capella Sĉi Jacobi infra decimationem de Segbrooke.

[p. 307.]

Segbrooke.

Sæpissime in Fenestris totius Ecclie :—
Party p fesse, Or & B. in cheife a demy-lyon ramp. Or, a border,
     Arg.   .   .   .   .   .   *Markham*
Tumulus marmoreus cum effigie et insigniis ex ære ablatis.
In one of them—*Markham*, with the border, empaled :—
Arg. on a saltier engrayled, Sa. 9 annulets, Or   .   .   .   *Leake*
This (they say) is the Judges tombe.*

In Fenestra orientali :—
Chequy, Arg. & G. a bend Sa.   .   .   .   .   *Bekering*

Empaled ⎰ *Bekering*, an annulet in cheife Sa. for difference.
        ⎱ Arg. on a chevron Sa. 3 escalops Or, a mullet,
              peirced, for difference   .   .   .   *Mering*
Sa. a lyon rampant, a border gobony, Arg. & Sa.
Arg. 3 crescents G.
B. a chevron betw. 3   .   .   .   Arg.
Effigies Judicis.   Item in Fenestra orientali Cancelli, et alibi.

---

* This is Sir John Markham, knt., Chief Justice of England, 1461-9, a son of John Markham, of Markham, co. Notts., who was also a Judge. He married Margaret, d. and co-h. of Sir Simon Leke of Cotham, co. Notts., and was the founder of the branch of the Markham family settled at Sedgebrook, where he was buried in 1479. He seems to have adopted the border to his arms as a difference. His father's first wife was Elizabeth, d. of Sir Hugh Cressy, his second wife was Millicent, widow of Sir Nicholas Burdon, and d. and co-h. of Sir John Beckeringe; she re-married Sir William Mering. which accounts for the arms of these two families being in Sedgebrook church.—*Ed.*

Tumulus marmoreus ære fixus in area :—

Orate pro aĩabus Wiłłmi Markham et Joħis Markham filiorum Joħis Markham, Militis, et Margaretæ uxoris suæ, qui obierunt 18° die Martii, A° Dñi 1458, &c.

Hic jacet Simon filius Joħis Markham, Militis, qui obiit 17° die Febr. A° 1455.

Tumulus lapideus :—

Hic jacet Dorothea, filia Joħis Markham, Armig. et Aliciæ uxoris ejus, que obiit 20° die Januarii, A° Dñi 1494, Cujus aĩæ propicietur Deus, Amen.

[p. 308.] In Fenestra boreali Chori borealis :—
Arg. 3 crosses botony fitchy betw. 3 flowers-de-lize, G.

Empaled { *Markham*, with the border, &
{ *Bekering*, with an annulet Sa. for difference.

Empaled { Or, on 2 barrs G. 3 water-bougets, Arg.
{   *Willoughby of Wollaton*
{ Arg. on a saltier, Engr. Sa. 9 annulets, Or . *Leake*

Empaled { Arg. a cheife G. . . . . *Hercy*
{ The Saltier & Annulets . . . . *Leake*

In eadem Fenestra :—

Roħtus Markham, Miles, filius Roħti Markham, Militis. Elizabetha, soror Johannis Markham Armig. et uxor Roħti Markham, Militis, patris Roħti.

In Fenestra orientali :—
Vaire, Arg. & Sa. . . . . . *Staunton*
Chequy, Arg. & G. a Bend, Sa. an annulet . . *Beckering*

In Fenestra Campanilis :—
B. on a cheife, Or, a demy-lyon rampant, G. a border Arg. *Markham*
Arg. 6 crosses, botony, fitchy, G.

In Fenestra boreali : —
Tho. Palmer, Rector medietatis Eccłiæ.

Wiłłus Porter, Senior Clericus Joħis Markham, Militis, et Elizabethæ uxoris suæ.

[p. 309.]

Cleypole.

In Fenestra orientali Cancelli :—
Orate pro aĩabus Nicħi de Howell et . . qui hanc fenestram fieri fecerunt.

Fenestræ australes :—
1. Arg. a lyon rampant, double queued, Sa. . . *Cressy*
 Arg. 3 dolphins, naiant, Sa. . . . . *Simeon*
 Ermyn, 5 fusills in fesse, G. . . . . *Hebden*
2. *Cressy. Simeon. Hebden.*

Fenestra borealis :—

Ermyn, 5 fusills in fesse G. a labell of 3 B. . . . *Hebden*

Ermyn, 5 fusills in fesse G. . . . . . . *Hebden*

Ermyn, 2 barrs G. over all a bend Sa.

Ermyn, 5 fusills in fesse G. . . . . . . *Hebden*

In muro australi :—
Tumulus lapideus excelsus cum insigniis *Hebden* in medio bis, et a latere Delphini et Leones bis, ut supra.

In Insula boreali :—
Hic jacet Nicħus de Howell, Rector medietatis Eccħiæ de Cleypole, qui obiit . . . A° Dñi M°CCC° . . .

G. a fesse between 6 escalops, Arg. . . . . *Seint-low*

Eadem insignia in sex fenestris superioribus.

In Fenestra australi :—Effigies fæminæ, super ejus tunicam *Cressy*, with a bend G. over all, et in manibus *Bekering*.

Ex altera parte Vir, gestans manibus et in tunica *Cressy*.

[p. 310.]

ffenton.

Fenestra orientalis ad austrum :—

Quarterly, *Beke & Ufford* . . . . . . *Willughby*

Stubton.

Orate pro aīa Maḡri Thomæ Marson . . . Baccalaurei . . .

Rectoris . . . qui hoc opus fieri fecit A° Dñi . . . XXX . . .

Beckingham.

In Fenestra Cancelli :—

Or, a bend between 6 martlets, G. *bis* . . . *Furnivall*

G. fretty of 6 peices, Ermine.

Tumulus marmoreus quondam ære fixus, Simonis Yates ibidem Rectoris (ut dicitur) et super sedulam Rectoris extra Cancellum Ys bis sculpt'.

In Fenestra boreali Navis :—
Thomas de Sibthorp p'sona istius Eccħiæ fecit et fundavit istam Capellam.

[p. 311.]

Brant Broughton.

In Fenestris Cancelli sæpius :—

G. 4 fusills in fesse Arg. in cheife 3 mullets pierced, Or. *Daubeney*

G. 4 fusills in fesse, Erm. in cheife 3 mullets pierced, Or. *Daubeney*

Venerabile monumentum Vıri (tibiis in crucem transversis) gestantis super pectus et in parma *Daubeny*.

Item, circumsculpt' *Daubeny* with a border engrayled.
Item, the Fusils charged with mullets.
Item, the Fusils with a border bezanty.
Item, the Fusils with a labell of 4 points.
Effigies quatuor Evangelistarum.

Aliud Monumentum :—super hoc monumentum Scutum with 4 fusils in fesse & 3 martlets in cheife, et hoc Epitaphium,
> Johan de Aubigne gist icy ;
> Deu de sa alme ait mercy.

Aliud :—Upon this monument are engraven in severall escocheons— First, 4 fusills in fesse ; Item, 4 fusills in fesse Ermine ; Item, 4 fusills charged with mullets ; Item, 4 fusills with martlets, & this inscription, Viz^t :—
> Jamys de Aubeney gist icy ;
> Deu de sa alme ayt mercy.

Aliud in muro boreali :—Upon which are severall escocheons, Viz^t : 4 fusills, Ermine ; Item, 4 fusills in fesse, each charged with a mullet ; Item, 4 fusills in fesse, in cheife 3 crescents ; Item, on 4 fusills in fesse as many crosse crosselets fitchy.

In Fenestra :—
G. 4 fusills in fesse, Ermine, in cheife 3 mullets of 6 points,
    peirced, Or . . . . *Daubeney*

Tumulus in Cancello ex marmore et ære :—
Hic jacet corpus Venerabilis Viri Maḡri Joħis Thorold, utriusque juris Baccalaurei, quondam Canonici Collegii de Southwell, necnon Rectoris et benefactoris hujus Eccłiæ, qui obiit 29° Septembris, A° Dñi 1468, Cujus &c.

[p. 312.] In Fenestra australi inferiori :—
G. 4 fusills in fesse, Arg.—*Bis.* . . . . . *Daubeney*
Chequy, Or & B. a quarter Erm.
Party per pale, Arg. & G. . . . . . . *Walgrave*

Ex utraque parte Campanilis :—
Arg. 3 bendlets G. a labell of 5 pointes, B.
G. 4 fusills in fesse, Erm. 3 mullets in cheife, Or . *Daubeney*
G. 3 fusills in fesse, Arg. . . . . . . *le même*

Fenestræ boreales :—
Quarterly { Quarterly { B. 3 floures de lize, Arg. . . *Burgh*
                { Or, a lyon rampant, B. . . . *Percy*
       { Or, 3 Pallets, B. . . . . . . *Athole*
Hæc prædicta infra Periscelidem.*

---

* This coat of arms, within the Garter, is that of Sir Thomas Burgh, knt., created K.G. and Baron Burgh of Gainsborough in 1487. He quartered the arms of Percy and Athol in right of his mother Elizabeth, daughter and co-heiress of Sir Henry Percy, knt., whose mother was daughter and heiress of David de Strabolgi, Earl of Athol. See under Gainsborough, p. 151.—*Ed.*

Quarterly { Sa. a fesse between 3 cinquefoyles, Arg.   *Villiers*
Party per pale, Arg. & Sa. a lyon ramp.   *Belers*

Quarterly { Quarterly, Arg. & Sa. over all a bend lozengy G.   *Cheney*
Arg. a chevron. in y⁵ dexter quarter a cinquefoyle,
peirced, Sa. . . . . . *Remston*

Empaled { Quarterly { Quarterly, Arg. & Sa. over all a bend
{ . . a fesse dauncy between 6 crosses . .
lozengy, G. . . . . *Cheney*
Sa. fretty of 8 peices, Or.

G. a fesse between 2 chevrons, Ermine . . . *Charnells*

Orate pro aīa Joħis Gosse, qui hanc fenestram vitriari fecit.
Hic jacet Johanna, quondam uxor Joħis Gosse, quæ obiit . .

[p. 313.]

Leddenham.

ECCLĪA SCĪ SWITHUNI.

Super Porticum australem :—. . a fesse . . .

In Fenestra borealis Insulæ :—
G. on a fesse B. 3 lyons pass. Or, betw. 8 billets, Arg.

Fenestra australis Navis :—
Paly wavy of 6 peices, Arg. & Sa.

In Cancello :—
Hic jacet Johannes Dykenson, quondam Rector istius Ecclesiæ, et
Capellanus Reginæ Mariæ, qui obiit primo die Octobr. A° 1557.

Hic jacet Joħes Barnaby, quondam Rector istius Ecclesiæ, et Capellanus Ducis Clarentiæ . . .

Tumulus Christopheri Berisford, Armig. Dñi et Patroni de Ledden-
ham et Fulbecke, qui obiit 12° die Octobris, A° Dñi 1590.

Upon y⁵ Monument this Escocheon, Vizᵗ :—

Quarterly { Arg. a beare saliant Sa. collared & chayned, Or. *Berisford*
Party per chevron . . . & 3 Pheons counter-changed,
a crescent difference.

[p. 314.]

Fulbecke cum Southorp.

ECCLĪA SCĪ NICHOLAI.

In Fenestra orientali Cancelli :—
England.
Chequy, Or & B. . . . . *Warren*
Chequy, Or & B. a border G. enurnee of lyons passants . *Dreux*
guardants, Or, a quarter, Ermine . . *Comes Richmundiæ*

In Fenestra australi Insulæ australis :—

G. a lyon rampant, Arg. over all a bend, B. charged with 3
  martlets, Or . . . . . . , *Mydelton*

In Campanili :—

G. a lyon rampant, Arg. on a bend, B. 3 escalops Or.

On a fayre wrought Pinacle on the South side of the Church is
engraven in Stone an escocheon with helmet crest & supporters accurately. The coate is a Lyon rampant, over all a bend charged with 3
escalops. The crest—a Saracen's head, & the supporters a Wiverne &
a Hyena.* All about the verge of the Fount, which is a most curious
one, are escallops carved. Likewise upon the Crosse in the Church-
yard is the Lyon with the bende & escallops.

In a high window :—Orate pro aīabus . . . Quinting et Johannæ
uxoris ejus . . .

On a flat gravestone :—

> Enclosed here Miles Garthwaites corps doe rest ;
> His spirit Heaven hath for ever blest.
> He loving Pastor like Christ's sheep susteyned
> With sacred writ, Soules food by Christ ordeyned.
> All Pastors preach Gods worde, all People heare,
> That you may rest with Christ our Saviour deare.

Obiit 4to die Januarii, Anno Dñi 1616, Ætatis suæ 40.

Posuit Helena Garthwaite.

[p. 315.]

Welburne.

Prior de Eye, Norwic. Dioces. Patronus ab antiquo.

In Fenestra boreali superiori :—

B. semy of fleurs-de-lize, a lyon rampant, Or . . *Beaumont*
Quarterly, *Beaumont*, & B. 3 garbes, Or *Boghan. quondam D'nus Villæ*

Hic jacet Willus Worthington, qui obiit 4to die . . . embris, A°
Dñi 1550, et Johanna uxor ejus, quæ obiit 4to die Septembris, 1557.

Hic jacet Dñus Willelmus Mike Eccłiæ Eboracensis Præbendarius,
et etiam Rector istius Eccłiæ, qui obiit 30° die Martii, A° Dñi 1545,
Cujus aīæ &c.

Hic jacet Nicholaus Baily, qui obiit 14° die Octobr. A° 1557.

---

* *Hyena* is written in the text, but in the marginal illustration a *Harpy* is
represented, which is no doubt correct.—*Ed.*

In **Fenestra** orientali Cancelli :—
Orate pro bono statu Wiłłi Clerke, Rectoris Eccłiæ de Welburne, et
Capellani . . .

Fenestra australis Cancelli :—
Arg. on a chevron Sa. 3 mullets, Or. *Bis.*

[p. 316.]

Carlton Scrope.

Fenestra orientalis Cancelli :—
Effigies Viri et Fæminæ gestantium in manibus et super vestes :—
G. a fesse fusilly, Or.
B. 3 crownes, Or, 2 & 1.
Or, on a bend Sa. 3 eaglets displayed, Arg.
Arg. 2 barrs B. in cheife 3 mullets, G.

Fenestra australis :—
Effigies Militis, flexis genibus, super pectus gestantis—B. a bend
Or, a labell of 3 poyntes, Arg. . . . . . *Scrope*

Eadem insignia bis in australi Fenestra Navis.

Ex australi parte Campanilis :—
B. a bend Or, a labell of 3 Arg. *ter.* . . . . . *Scrope*

Tumuli :—
Isabell wife of Robert Palmer died 1590.
Reignold Palmer deceased 1° die Februarii 1602.
John Porter yeoman died 8ᵛᵒ Aprilis, 1554.
Effigies cum epitaphiis ex ære.
Alii duo ejusdem nominis.

[p. 317.]

Hougham.

Fenestra orientalis Cancelli :—
Effigies Viri et Fæminæ, ille gestans super pectus—Arg. 3 bars S. *Bussy*
Illa—G. 4 fusills in fesse Arg. a border engr. Or . . [*Nevile*]

. . . quondam Rector istius Eccłiæ, qui istam Fenestram fieri
fecit 1405.

Fenestra australis Cancelli :—
Arg. 3 barrs Sa.
Arg. 3 lyons passant in pale barways, G. . . . *Amundeville*
Empaled { Chequy, G. & Or. on a cheife Arg. a lyon pass. Sa.
{ Arg. 2 chevrons B. *Comberworth*
Empaled, *Comberworth*, & Arg. 2 barrs engr. Sa. . . *Staynes*

Fenestræ boreales :—

Arg. 3 barrs Sa. . . . . *Bussy*

G. a crosse sarcely, Arg. . . . . *Beke*

Empaled ⎰ Quarterly, G. a castle, Or, *Castile* & Arg. a lyon
⎱   ramp. Sa. . . . . . . *Leon*
⎱ Quarterly, *France* semy & England, a labell of 3
        points, Erm. . . . . . *Lancaster*

G. a crosse botony, Or.

G. 2 chevrons a Border, Arg. . . . . . *Paynell*

Quarterly, Or & G. a border Sa. bezantee . . . *Rochford*

Æs marmore fixum versus Boream :—

Of your Charity pray for the soules of Hugh Bussy & Jane his wife, which Hugh deceased . . . 1479, & Jane departed this life yᵉ 25° day of July, 1508, on whose soules &c.

On this Monument this empalement, Viz^t :—

Empaled ⎰ Arg. 3 bars Sa. . . . . . . *Bussy*
⎱ Erm. 2 sengliers trippant, G. . . . *Whichcote*

Ex parte australi :—

Statua marmorea, tibiis in crucem transversis—in parma gestantis 3 barrs, *Bussy*.

Juxta Tumulus marmoreus cum effigiebus ex ære et scutis armorum ablatis dempto uno, Viz^t : a cheife indented, a labell of 3.

[p. 318.] Fenestræ inferiores :—

Or, a lyon rampant G.

B. 6 lyons ramp. Arg. 3, 2, 1, a canton, Erm.

Effigies duorum bellatorum gestantium super tunicas.

Arg. 3 barrs Sa. . . . . *Bussy*

Alter Vir in fenestra superiori consimiliter.

Fenestræ australes superiores :—

Empaled ⎰ Verry, a fesse G. fretty Or . . . *Marmyon*
⎱ Erm. a fesse fusilly G. . . . . *Hebden*

Empaled ⎰ Arg. on a bend G. 3 mullets, Or.
⎱ Erm. a fesse fusilly, G. . . . . *Hebden*

Quarterly ⎰ Arg. 3 barrs Sa. . . . . . *Bussy*
⎱ G. 4 fusills in fesse, Arg. a border engr. Or.

Arg. a plaine crosse Sa.

In Campanili :—

Empaled ⎰ Quarterly ⎰ Arg. 3 barrs, Sa. . . . . *Bussy*
⎱ ⎱ G. 4 fusills in fesse, Arg. a border engr. Or.
⎱ Chequy, G. & Or, on a cheife Arg. a lyon pass. Sa.
                              Comberworth

Super portum Domus Villæ :—

3 Barrs . . . . [*Bussy*]

2 chevrons & a border [*Paynell*] 3 barrs with a labell of 3.

Normanton.

No entry.

[p. 319.]

Calthorp.*

In Fenestra australi :—
Chequy, Or & B.   .   .   .   .   *Warren*
Or, a plain crosse, Sa.   .   .   .   .   *Vescy*

Fenestra orientalis Insulæ borealis :—
Arg. a saltier, Sa.
Arg. a chevron G. between 3 boares heades couped Sa.   .   [*Agard*]
Orate pro aïa Riĉi Agard.

Fenestra borealis Navis :—
B. 3 cinquefoyles, Or   .   .   .   .   *Bardolfe*

Fenestra australis :—
Orate pro aïa Johannis Walkwood Rectoris qui hanc fenestram fieri fecit.
3 cinquefoyles peirced—*Bardolfe*— super portam occidentalem exterius: Item super clibanum in villa.†

Super Crucem in cœmeterio :—
Empaled { Semy of fleurs-de-lize, a lyon rampant   .   *Beaumont*
         { 2 lyons passant crowned   .   .   .   .   *Dymoke*

Hough cum Brandon et Gelston.

Appropriatio Prioratus de Moultg've,‡ Ebor. Dioc.

Campanæ :—
Sĉa Helena ora pro nobis.
Protege prece pia quos convoco Sĉ Maria.
Cælorum Xp̄e placeat tibi, Rex, sonus iste.

[p. 320.]

Merston.

Fenestra orientalis Cancelli :—
Arg. 2 barrs, G.
Empaled { Arg. 2 barrs G.
         { G. 2 chevrons & a border, Arg.   .   .   .   *Paynell*
Empaled { Arg. 2 barrs, G.
         { Arg. 3 barrs Sa. a labell of 3 points, G.   .   .   *Bussy*
Or, 3 chevrons, G.   .   .   .   .   *Clare*

---

* *Sic*, but meant for Caythorpe.—*Ed.*
† *Clibanus*, a stove, furnace, or oven, perhaps a public oven for the use of the tenants.—*Ed.*
‡ *i.e.* Mulgrave Priory, near Whitby, a small alien house.—*Ed.*

Fenestra orientalis Navis :—

Empaled { Sa. 3 goats saliant, Arg. . . . . *Thorold*
Arg. 3 barrs G. on a canton B. a martlet, Or, on
y⁰ middle barr a mullet . . . *Hough*

In Choro australi :—
Tumulus totaliter marmoreus Wiłłmi Thorold, filii et hæredis Joħis
Thorold, primi Vice-comitis Com. Lincolñ regnante regina Elizabetha
qui obiit 20° die Novembris Año Dñi 1569. Super hunc tumulum hæc
insignia :—

Empaled { Sa. 3 goats saliant, Arg. . . . . *Thorold*
Arg. on a saltier engrayled, Sa. 9 annulets, Or, a
trefoyle in cheife . . . *Leake* 1ᵐᵃ conjux

Empaled { Sa. 3 goats saliant, Arg. . . . . *Thorold*
Or, a plain crosse, Vert. . . *Hussey,* 2ᵈᵃ conjux

Ex opposito juxta Cancellum :—
Tumulus alabastrinus Antonii Thorold, Militis, filii p'dči Wiłłi, qui
obiit 26° die Junii, A° Dñi 1594. Ambrosii Sutton filia prima conjux ;
Anna filia Joħis Constable de Kinolton in Com. Nott. conjux secunda.
Per primam conjugem tres filii et duo filiæ . . . imus filius duxit
. . . filiam Pierpoint, 2ᵈᵘˢ filius duxit . . . filiam Tyrwhit de
Kettleby. Joħes Thorold, Miles, 3ᵗⁱᵘˢ filius duxit . . . filiam
Cranmer. 1ᵐᵃ filia nupta Joħi Markham de Segbrooke ; Martha, 2ᵈᵃ
filia desponsata Philippo Tyrwhit de Stanfield, Militi. Per 2ᵈᵃᵐ uxorem
unica filia Winefreda nupta Georgio Clifton de Clifton in Com. Nott.
Armig. postea . . . Carvill de Norfolc'.
Or, on a chevron betw. 3 annulets G. 3 crescents of y⁰ first . *Sutton*
Quarterly, G. & Verry, over all a bend, Or. . . . *Constable*
Arg. semy of cinquefoyles G. a lyon ramp. Sa. . . *Pierpoint*
G. 3 lapwings, Or . . . . *Tyrwhit*
Or, on a chevron G. 3 cinquefoyles, Arg. betw. 3 pellicans, Sa *Cranmer*
B. on a cheife Or, a demy-lyon ramp. G. a border Arg. . *Markham*
Sa. semy of cinquefoyles, a lyon ramp. Arg. . . . *Clyfton*

[p. 321.]

Brancewell.

Henricus de Roucebi.

Bloxham, Amwicke, Dirrington.

No entries.

[p. 322.]

Timberland.

In Fenestra australi Cancelli :—
B. a fesse dauncè betw. 10 billets, Or . . . . *Deincourt*

Scaupwicke.

No entry.

Kirkby Greene.

In Fenestra australi :—
Barry of 6, Arg. & B. on a bend G. 3 lozenges, Or.
B. a fesse dauncè between 7 billets, Or   .   .   *Deincourt*
Or, 3 griphons passants in transverse, B.

Siston.

No entry.

[p. 323.]

Gunwardby.

In Fenestra australi :—
Quarterly, *France* (semy) & *England*   .   .   .   .   *England*
Quarterly, *France* (semy) & *England*, a labell, Erm.   .   *Lancaster*
Chequy, Or & B.   .   .   .   .   *Warren*

Tumulus in muro :—Hic jacet Roḃtus Tiling, qui obiit . . . 1536.
In cœmeterio :—Roḃtus Sharpe . . . Midilton.

Barkeston.

Insculpt' super Porticum :—
Me Thomam Pacy post mundi flebile funus
Jungas veraci vitæ tu trinus et unus.
Dñe Deus vere Thomæ Pacy miserere.

Fenestra borealis 1ma :—
Orate pro aïabus Thomæ Pacy et Aliciæ uxoris ejus, qui hanc
fenestram fieri fecerunt.

Fenestra borealis 2da :—
Orate pro aïabus Ricardi Bullen et Johæ uxoris ejus qui hanc
fenestram fieri fecerunt.

Fenestra orientalis :—
Orate pro aïabus Roḃti Pacy et Aliciæ uxoris ejus.

Fenestra australis :—
G. 3 lyons passants guardants, Or, a border B. semy of fleurs de lize of
yᵉ second   .   .   .   .   .   *Holland, Dux Exoniæ*

[p. 324.]

Ancaster cum Wylughby and Sudbrooke.

In Fenestra boreali :—
Effigies bellatoris gestantis super scutum et hastam, Viz^t :—
Arg. a bend G. a border chequy Or & B. . . . *Trehamton*

Lapis super humum :—
Hic jacet Joħes Seman de Wylughby.

Cranwell.

Fenestra orientalis Cancelli :—
Barry of 8, Arg. & G. a crosse portate in bend, B. . *Sc'us Gilbertus*
Empaled { G. 3 barrs Arg. a labell of 4 points, B.
{ G. 3 cranes, Arg. . . . . . *Cranwell*

Orate specialiter pro aĩabus Witħi Cranwell Armig. et Margaretæ consortis suæ.

Fenestra australis Navis :—
Arg. a crosse patonce, Sa.
Arg. a cheife G. over all a bend B. a border, Sa. . . *Cromwell*

Tu mihi nate, pater, et tu mihi filia mater,
Virgo Virginum et Rex Regum.

[p. 325.]

Welsford cum Hambeck.

Fenestra borealis :—
G. a lyon ramp. Arg. a border gobony B. & Arg.

In Fenestra orientali Cancelli :—
Dñus Hugo de Darley, Rector istius Ecctiæ fecit hanc fenestram in honorem Bēæ Mariæ Virginis, Año Dñi 1383.

Tumulus in Cancello :—
Hic jacet Dñus Rogerus Warde quondam Rector istius Ecctiæ qui fieri fecit Cancellariam in honorem Nativitatis Bēæ Mariæ Virginis . . obiit . . . 1479, &c.

Insula borealis :—
Thomas frater Dñi Rogeri Ward obiit 1484. Edmundus Ward obiit . . .

Tumuli in Cancello :—
Hic jacent Joħes Seman de Ancaster ex parochia de Welsford, qui obiit 1° Kl. Martii, Año Dñi 1466, Cujus aïæ &c.

Hic jacet Thomas Seman de Ancaster paroch. de Welsford, qui obiit 11° die Julii, Año Dñi 1480, &c.

Hic jacent Roħtus Seman et Joanna uxor ejus, obierunt 3° Kl. Octobris, Año Dñi 1521, Quorum, &c.

Statuæ exterius in muro boreali Sči Petri Sčæ Katharinæ, et Sči Joħis Baptistæ.

[p. 326.]

Rouceby, North.

Fenestra borealis superior :—
Paly of 6, Arg. & B. in cheife a cinquefoyle, G.   .   .   *Strelley*
Orate pro aïa Wiħi Styrlay Vicarii qui hanc fenestram fieri fecit.

Fenestra borealis inferior :—
G. 3 mullets Arg. a labell of 3 pointes, Or.
G. 2 barrs Arg. in cheife 3 roundlets Ermyn.
Arg. on a bend Sa. double cottised G. a chevron betw. 7 crosses
     botony of yᵉ first.
Arg. on a chevron Sa. 3 crosses botony of the first.
Sa. a chevron betw. 10 crosses botony, Arg.
Arg. 2 barrs G. in cheife 3 torteaux, a bend Sa.   .   *Threkingham*
Arg. a chevron G. between 3   .   .   .
Arg. a fesse betw. 3 cinquefoyles G.   .   .   .   .   *Powtrell*

Juxta Cancellum :—
Hic jacet Wiħus Powtrel de Rousby, qui obiit   .   .   .

Hic jacet Elizabetha quondam uxor Riči Pinchbeck, quæ obiit 18° die Septembris 1505, Cujus &c.

In Cancello Tumulus ex marmore et ære : —
Hic jacet Wiħus Styrlay, quondam Vicarius istius Ecctiæ et Canonicus de Shelford, qui obiit 4ᵗᵒ die Decembris, Año Dñi 1536, &c.

Hic jacet Heñr. Edward, curatus de Rausby, qui obiit XI° die Julii, Año Dñi 1552, &c.

The cleristory builded in the tyme of Sir William Styrlay, Vicar and Parish Preist, and Sir Henry Edward. The charge £44 8. 8.

In Cœmiterio :—Hic jacet Dñus Wiħus   .   .   .

[p. 327.]

Rouceby, South.

Hæc Ecclesia diruta.

Lesingham cum Roxham.

Fenestra orientalis ad dextram Cancelli :—

Chequy, Or & B. . . . . *Warren*
Arg. 2 lyons passants, Sa. . . . . . . *Fletewick*
Or, 3 chevrons G. . . . . *Clare*

Fenestra borealis :—

Arg. 2 lyons passants, Sa. . . . . . . *Fletewicke*
David de . . . vere me fecit in honore Bëæ Mariæ.

Digby.

Ecctia appropriata Prioratui de Catley.

Fenestra orientalis Navis :—
Priez pur Johan Elmere et Loue sa femme. Joħes Aylmer et . . . uxor sua me fecerunt.

Fenestræ superiores australes Campanis conjunctis decoratæ, et plures ejus nominis benefactores. *Cooke* & *Beeche.*

[p. 328.]

Rowston.

Fenestra australis Cancelli :—

Empaled {
Or. on a crosse Sa. 5 bulles' heads couped Arg.
Sa. on a chevron Arg. 3 mullets peirced G. betw. as many pheons of yᵉ 2ⁿᵈ, a cheife over all extended. G. charged with a crosse, Arg.* . . *Knights Hospitallers*
}

Fenestra borealis Navis :—
Arg. on a bend Sa. 3 owles crowned of yᵉ first . . . *Savile*
. . . Savyle et Agnetis uxoris . . .

Fenestræ boreales Insulæ borealis :—
Orate pro bono statu Roħti Hodleston et Emmotæ consortis suæ.
Orate pro bono statu Joħis Inman et Joħæ consortis suæ.
Orate pro aïa Wiħmi Grege et Aliciæ consortis suæ.

Effigies Sĉi Egidii, et subtus Vir orans.
Tu fotus a cerva repellas cuncta proterva.†

---

* These coats belong to the Knights of St. John, who succeeded the Templars of Temple Bruer, to whom Rowston was given by Matilda de Cauz, the chief being the manner in which the arms of their order were borne. The two coats are those of Boynton and Newport. Sir Thomas Newport was Bailiff of Eagle in 1522 and 1528, in the former year he was wrecked in an endeavour to bring succour to the Knights at Rhodes, then besieged by the Turks. The same two coats are repeated at Navenby and Temple Bruer.—*Ed.*

† *Fotus,* the past participle of *Foveor, i.e.,* Nourished. though with its first syllable improperly shortened. An allusion to the legend of St. Giles who, as an aged hermit, is said to have been nourished by the milk of a hind, which visited him daily in his cave.--*Ed.*

[p. 329.]

Blankney.

Fenestræ : —

Quarterly { B. a fesse daunce betw. 7 billets d' Or . *Deyncourt*
Barry of 6, Arg. & B. a bend, G. . *Grey of Rotherfield*

Quarterly { Nebuly, Or & G. . . . . . *Lovell*
B. semy of flowers de Lize, a lion ramp. Or . *Beaumont*

Empaled { Quarterly, *Cromwell* & *Tateshale*.
B. a fesse daunce between 11 billets, Or . *Deyncourt*

Quarterly { Sa. a cross engrayled, Or . . *Ufford* } *Willughby*
Gu. a crosse sarcely, Arg. . . *Beke* }

B. semy of Flowers de lize, a lion ramp. d' Or . . [*Beaumont*]

Empaled { Arg. a fesse daunce betw. 10 billets, Sa. . *Deyncourt*
Arg. on a chevron G. 5 bezantes . . [*Erdeswike*]

Arg. a fesse daunce betw. 10 billets. Sa.

B. a fesse daunce betw. 10 billets, Or . . subscribed *Deyncourt*

Empaled { B. a fesse daunce between 6 billets, Or . *Deyncourt*
G. a saltier Arg. . . . . . *Nevile*

Empaled { B. a fesse daunce between 6 billets, Or . *Deyncourt*
Barry of 6, Arg. & B. a bend G. . . . *Grey*

B. a crosse patonce voyded Arg.

Lozengy, Arg. & G. a mullet difference . . . *Fitz-William*

Tumulus in muro Australi : Epitaphium ære sculptum : —
Hic jacet Roḃtus Husee | de Lintwood, Miles, tertius filius | Wiḣi
Husee, Militis, qui duxit | in uxorem Annam, unam hæredem | duarum
filiarum Thomæ Say de Lyſton, | Militis, qui obiit 20° die M. Maii, |
Año Dñi 1544.

Or, a plaine crosse, Vert. . . . . *Hussy*

Quarterly { Party p pale, B. & G. 3 chevronels humets counter-
changed, purfled, Arg. . . . . *Say*
G. on 3 fusills Arg. as many escalops, B.

[p. 330.]

Metheringham.

Ecclesia de Metheringham combusta 9° die Julii 1599. Instaurata
18° die Augusti, 1602, Riͨo Wilson Vicario.

Eccłia appropriata Prioratui de Kyme.

Fenestræ antiquæ : —
G. a cinquefoyle pierced, an orle of crosses botony, Or . *Umfreville*
B. a fesse daunce between 10 billets, Or . . . *Deyncourt*
B. on a bend Sa. 3 escallops, Arg . . . *Meesy. Wigorn*

Insignia depicta super muros :—

Quarterly
- Arg. on a peele, Sa. 3 white loaves . *Pistor*
- G. a chevron betw. 3 pheons, Arg.
- Arg. a chevron betw. 3 escalops, G. .
- Arg. a chevron betw. 3 hutchets,* Sa. .

Dñi Villæ.

Arg. 2 barrs dauncee Sa. a pallet in cheife Erm. *Enderby*
Arg. a chevron betw. 3 roses, Arg. . . . *Smith, Medicus*
Or, a crosse Sa. 5 crescents, Arg. . . . . *Ellys, Legista*

Statuæ australes :—

Or, fretty, B. . . . . *Willughby*
G. 3 lapwings, Or . . . . *Tirwhit*
G. on a chevron, Arg. 3 mullets, Sa. . . . . *Carre*
Ermyn, a griphon, segreant . . . . . *Grantham*

Statuæ boreales :—

Sa. 2 lyons pass. Arg. crowned, Or . . . . *Dymoke*
B. 3 bolles, Or, jesants boares' heads couped Arg. . . *Bolle*
Or, 2 chevrons, G. . . . . *Munson*
G. a fesse betw. 3 water-bougets, Erm. . . . . *Meres*

Juxta Campanile :—

Sa. on a chevron engr. Arg. 3 escalops of yᵉ 1ˢᵗ . *King, of Ashby*
G. a chevron betw. 3 escalops, Arg. . . *Wolmer, of Bloxham*

Cancellum :—Est commune mori, mors nulli parcit honori.

Sedula :—Enderby elevata ex . . .

[p. 331.]

Bardney.

In Fenestra boreali :—

Quarterly
- Arg. 3 six-foyles pierced G. . . . . *Darcy*
- Sanguine, a lyon ramp. double-queued, Arg. *Wimbish*

Tumuli :—

Hic jacet Joħes Parker quondam Vicarius . . .
Hic jacet Wiħus Marton quondam Abbas† . . .

---

* *Hutchet*, a hunter's horn or bugle. French, *Hucher*, to call or summon. The charge is not figured in the tricking of this coat.—*Ed.*

† William Marton was elected Abbot of Bardney, 31 Aug., 1507, in succession to Richard Horncastel, whose fine sepulcral slab has lately been discovered during the excavations on the site of the Abbey. He was the last Abbot, and on 1 Nov., 1539, he with thirteen of his monks surrendered the Abbey to the King's use. This accounts for his burial in the Parish Church, the Abbey having been already dismantled.—*Ed.*

Harmston.

Empaled { Arg. a bend Sa. . . . . . . *Paynell*
{ Ermyn . . .

Fenestra australis :—
. . . Et pur les almes Huberd de Marcham et Margerie sa feme
priete Pater et Ave . . .

Fenestra super ostium Australe :—
Orate pro aīa Roƀti H . . . et Isabellæ uxoris ejus . . .

Ermyn, on an escocheon Sa. a rose Arg.

[p. 332.]

Nocton.

Empaled { Sanguine, a lyon rampant, Arg. . . *Wimbish, John*
{ Arg. a chevron betw. 3 mullets peirced.
Chequy, Arg. & B. a cheife, Or.
Arg. a pale, on a cheife Sa. a fillet wavee of yᵉ 1ˢᵗ.
Party per pale, G. & Vert, an eagle displayed Arg.

Empaled { Quarterly { Sanguine, a lyon ramp. Arg. . *Wimbish*
{ Arg. 3 six-foyles peirced G. . . *Darcy*
{ B. a fesse dauncey betw.6 escallops, Arg.[*Engaine*]
{ Quarterly, Arg. & Sa. a bend G. . . [*Everingham*]

Tumuli :—
Hic jacet Christopherus Wimbishe, Arm. Dñus de Nocton, qui obiit
primo die Aprilis Año Dñi 1530, Cujus &c.

Hic jacet Joñes Wimbish, Arm. Dñus de Nocton, qui obiit ultimo
die Septembris, Año Dñi 1536, Cujus &c.

Orate pro aīa Graciæ quondam uxoris Nicħi Wimbishe, quæ obiit
27° die Aprilis, 1504, &c.

Nicholaus Wimbishe residentiarius Eccłiæ Cathedralis bēæ Mariæ
Linc'.*

[p. 333.]

Colby.

No entry.

Botheby.

Arg. a cross molyn, G.

---

* Nicholas Wimbishe was collated to the Prebend of Ketton in Lincoln Cathedral
in 1427. He died in 1460, being then also Archdeacon of Nottingham and Prebendary of Bole in York Cathedral.—*Ed.*

Thurlby juxta Auburgh.

Fenestra orientalis Cancelli :—
Johes de Herdeby. Effigies Viri et Fæminæ gestantium manibus et super tunicas, Arg. a fesse between 10 billets—coloribus fugientibus.

Skinnand.

No entry.

Carlton in Moreland.

No entry.

[p. 334.]

Navenby.

Super statuas Navis :—
Arg. 10 torteaux, a labell of 3 pointes, B. . . . *Babington*

Quarterly
{
Babington.
Arg. a fesse vaire Or & G.betw. 3 water-bougets, Sa. *Dethicke*
Arg. a cheife G. on a bend B. 3 escutcheons of y[e]
1st charged of cheifs as y[e] second . *Allestree*
}

Empaled
{
Or, on a crosse Sa. 5 bulls-heads couped Arg. [*Boynton*]
Sa. on a chevron Arg. 3 mullets peirced G. betw.
as many pheons of ye 2nd ; a cheife extended
over all G. charged with a crosse Arg. [*Newport*]
}

Empaled
{
. . . 3 piles in pointe . . . a cheife, Ermyne.
. . . a crosse.
}

Campanæ :—
1. Richard Dorwean gave me To the Church of Naneby, 1598.
2. In nomine Jesu Maria.
3. Sce Edmunde, ora pro nobis.
Campanile prostratum Año 1598.

Ashby-De-la-Laund.

Fenestra orientalis Cancelli :—
B. 3 dartes, Or.
G. a bende Ermyn . . . . *Ry*
Arg. a fesse daunce betw. (14) billets, G. . . . *De la Laund*

Tumuli :—
Simon de la Laund.
Isabell de la Laund.
Denuo instaurata per Edw̃. King, 1605.

Empaled {
Sa. on a chevron engr. Arg. 3 escallops of ye 1st . *King*
Sa. a bend Arg. betw. 2 cottises daunce, Or, a
    mullet difference . . . *Clopton*, uxor 1ma
}

King paleth—Arg. 2 barrs nebuly Sa. on a canton . *Keble*, uxor 2da
G. a bend Or.

[**p. 335.**]

Temple Bruer.

Præceptoria S͠ci Jo͠his Jerusalem in Anglia.

Empaled { Quarterly {
Arg. a chief G. over all a bend. B. . *Cromwell*
Chequy, Or & G. a cheife, Erm. . *Tateshale*
}
B. a fesse daunce between 10 billets, Or . *Deincourt* }

Raͩus Baro Cromwell Angliæ Thesaurarius tempore Hen. VI.

G. a lyon ramp. Arg. on a bend B. 3 escalops, Or.

Quarterly {
Sa. a crosse engrayled, Or . *Ufford*
G. a crosse sarcely, Arg. . . *Beke*
} *Willoughby*

G. a lyon rampant, Arg. . . . . . *Moubray*

Quarterly {
B. semy of floures de lize, a lyon ramp. Or . *Beaumont*
3 cinquefoyles, Or . . . . . *Bardolfe*
}

Ermyn, a chevron, Sa

Empaled {
Or, on a crosse Sa. 5 bulls-heads couped, Arg. [*Boynton*]
Sa. on a chevron, Arg. 3 mullets, G. between 3
    pheons of ye 2nd; over both a cheife extended
    G. charged with a crosse, Arg. . . [*Newport*]
}

Tumulus Dorotheæ uxoris Rogeri Roleton, quæ obiit 18° die Januarii, 1529, &c.

On this monument this empalement, Viz^t :—

Empaled {
Quarterly {
Party p fesse, G. & Arg. a lyon pass. in chiefe.
Arg. in bast a cinquefoyle peirced, B. *Roleton*
. . . a chevron betw. 10 martlets, Sa.
}
Arg. 10 torteauxes, a labell of 3, B. . . *Babington*
}

Arg. a chevron between 3 eaglets, Sa.
G. a chevron Erm. a border engrayled, B —*Bis*.
B. 3 cinquefoyles, Or . . . . . . *Bardolfe*

Quarterly {
B. 3 leopards-heads jesants floures de lize, Or *Cantelupe*
G. crusilly botony fitchy, a lyon rampant, Arg. *La Warre*
}

Or, a lyon rampant, double queue, Sa. . . . *Welles*
G. bezanty, a canton Ermine . . . . . *Zouch*
Chequy, Or & B. a fesse G. an annulet difference . . *Clifford*
Barry of 6, Arg. & B. . . . . *Grey*
Arg. on a bend Sa. 3 owles of the 1st, a mullet difference . *Savile*
B. 2 raynardes passants, Or.
G. a lyon ramp. Arg. over all a bend, B. charged with 3 escalops, Or.

[p. 336.]

Wellinghoue,

Tumulus :—
Simulachra Viri et Fæminæ ex alabastro et ex australi latere tria
Scuta :—

Sa. 2 lyons pass. Arg. crowned, Or . . . . *Dymoke*
Sa. 3 barrs, Arg.
Arg. on a fesse G. 3 floures-de-lize, Or . . . . *Disney*

Tumulus :—
Carolus Wingfield de Temple Bruer obiit 15° die Aprilis, Año 1575.
Tumulus Joñis filii Joñis Boys.
Alter tumulus cujusdam Boys . . .
Johannes Hervell.

[p. 337.]

Basingham.

Fenestræ :—

G. a crosse sarcely, Arg. . . . . . . *Beke*
G. a chevron betw. 10 crosse-crosselets, Or . . . *Kyme*
Or, 3 pallets, G.
Arg. 2 chevrons, Sa. . . . . . . [*Staunton*]
B. 2 chevrons & a border, Or.
Chequy, Arg. & G.
G. 3 barrs, Arg.

Dunston.

Dunston appropriatio Prioratus de Nocton-Parke.

Fenestra australis Cancelli :—
Arg. 3 six-foyles G. a border gobony, Vert, & Eagles displayed, Or.

Campana 3ᵗⁱᵃ :—
Cælorum Christe placeat tibi Rex sonus iste.

Hanworth, Potter.

Fenestra australis Cancelli :—

B. a fesse daunce betw. 10 billets, Or . . . *Deyncourt*
G. a crosse sarcely, Arg. . . . . . . *Beke*
B. a crosse patonce, Arg.
Sa. 3 leopards-faces jesants fleur de lis, Arg.
Or, a lyon rampant, B. . . . . . . *Percy*

[p. 338.]

Braunceton.

Fenestra orientalis Cancelli :—
Deyncourt. Beke.
Arg. a fesse daunce between 10 billets, Sa.
G. 8 bezants, a canton Ermine   .   .   .   .   .   *Zouch*

Fenestra australis :—
G. a crosse-crosselet, Or.
Arg. 2 barrs nebuly, in cheife 3 martlets Sa.

Fenestra orientalis Navis :—
B. a fesse daunce betw. 7 billets, Or   .   .   .   *Deyncourt*
Orate pro aïa Dñi Henrici de Brauncewel, Rectoris Eccłiæ de Braunceton, qui istam fenestram fieri fecit.

Fenestra borealis 1ma :—
B. a fesse daunce betw. 10 billets, Or   .   .   .   *Deyncourt*
Effigies Militis gestantis manibus, tunica, et in tergo—*Deyncourt.*

Fæmina gestans in veste *Deyncourt*, et in manibus *Zouch.*

Fenestra borealis 2da :—
Vir gestans in tunica, Arg. a fesse daunce betw. 10 billets, Sa.
Sčus Georgius gestans crucem rubram in clipeo argenteo :—Ora pro nobis, beate Georgi.

[p. 339.]

Belton.

Fenestra borealis superior :—
Sa. 3 belles, Arg.   .   .   .   .   *Porter*
Empaled { Arg. 3 bendlets . . on a canton a lyon passant   . .
         { Sa. 3 belles Arg. a canton Erm.   .   .   .   *Porter*
Empaled { Or, on a crosse Vert, a mullet Arg. difference   .   *Hussey*
         { Arg. 4 barrs Sa.

Fenestra orientalis Insulæ borealis :—
Arg. on a chevron G. 3 crescents, Or.
         { Quarterly Or & G. in yͤ 1ˢᵗ quarter an
         {   eagle displayed, Vert   .   .   *Pakenham*
         { Quarterly { G. a chevron betw. 10 cinquefoyles,Arg. *Berkeley*
Empaled {   { Arg. a fesse daunce betw. 6 billets, G. *De la Laund*
         {   { Or, a lyon ramp. double-queue Sa.   .   *Welles*
         { Or, a chevron betw. 3 cinquefoyles, G.   .   .   *Chicheley*
         { Quarterly, Or & G. an eagle displayed in the 1ˢᵗ
Empaled {   quarter, Vert   .   .   .   .   *Pakenham*
         { Sa. a chevron engr. Arg. betw. 3 plates, each charged
         {   with a pallet, G.   .   .   .   .   *Dochwray*

Tumulus marmoreus cum Epitaphio æreo :—

Hic jacet Augustinus Porter, de Belton, Arm., qui obiit 17° die Junii, Año Dñi 1554, et Helena uxor ejus, quæ obiit 2° die Julii 1569, Quorum aïæ per misericordiam Dei omnipotentis requiescant cum Abraham, Isaac, et Jacob in regno cælorum.

[p. 340]

Norton Disney.

Fenestræ Cancelli :—

Arg. a plaine crosse, G. . . . . . *S͞c us Georgius*
Barry of 6 peices, Arg. & G. over all a cross portate in bend B.*
                                          S͞c us Gilbertus
Arg. on a saltier engrayled Sa. 9 annulets, Or . . . *Leake*
Arg. on a fesse G. 3 flowers de lize, Or . . . . *Disney*
Empaled—*Disney* & *Leake.*
Barry of 6 peices, Arg. & B. . . . . . *Grey*

Fenestra borealis Capellæ :—

Empaled { Quarterly { Arg. on a fesse G. 3 flowres de lize . *Disney*
              { Arg. 3 lyons pass. guard. G. . [*Amundeville*]
         { Party p chevron, Vert & Erm. in cheife a pelican, Or *Joyner*
Empaled { Quarterly, *Disney*, ut supra.
         { G. a chevron between 10 roses, Arg.

Sufferance doth ease—Disney's word.

Capella borealis :—

Tumuli lapidei quatuor, marmorei duo, Effigies hominis in scuto gestantis—3 lyons passants.

Ici gist Joan que fust la feme Gillam Disnie et file Sire Nichol de Langford, deux eit merci de sa alme. Amen.

Super hunc lapidem insculpta :—3 lyons passants . *Disney*†
Item :—3 pallets, over all a bende . . . . *Langford*

Hic jacet Hantascia‡ (Anastacia forsan) filia Wi͞lli Disnie de Nortun. Super hunc tumulum hæc scuta, Viz͡t :—

. . 3 lyons rampant . . .
3 pallets with a bend & Barry of 8 peices.

Effigies sub muro boreali gestans tres Leones—*bis.*

---

* The Rectory of Norton Disney was appropriated to the Gilbertine Priory of Sempringham, hence St. Gilbert's arms.—*Ed.*

† Arg. 3 lions passants G. was the coat of Amundeville, whose arms Disney assumed for a time on marriage with the heiress, see Kingerby, pp. 68, 69.—*Ed.*

‡ This peculiar name was long retained in the Disney family. As late as 21 Nov., 1651, there is an entry in the Parish Register of Norton Disney of the baptism of "Hantasia the daughter of Coll. Moleneux Disney, Esq., & Marie his wife." She was buried 28 November.—*Ed.*

Plurimæ effigies in fenestris et super tunicas :—
Arg. on a fesse G. 3 flowers de lize, Or . . . . *Disney*

These two following both in one plate :—Willus Disney et Margareta Joyner uxor ejus. Filii Ricus, Willus, Thomas, Franciscus ; Filiæ Anna, Maria, Margareta, Catharina, Brigida.

[p. 341.]

Empaled { Arg. on a fesse G. 3 flowers de lize, Or . *Disney*
{ Party p chevron Vert & Erm. in chief a pelican, Or *Joyner*

Ricus Disney et Nele uxor ejus, filia Willi Hussey,* Militis, ex qua procreavit Willum, Humfridum, Johem, Danielem, Ciriacum, Zachariam et Isaac filios, et Saram, Esther, Judith, Judeh et Susannam filias.

Jana uxor altera, filia Gulielmi Aiscough, Militis, per quam nulla soboles.

Empaled { Arg. on a fesse G. 3 flowers de lize, Or . . *Disney*
{ Or, a plaine crosse, Vert . . . . *Hussey*

Empaled { Arg. on a fesse G. 3 flowers de lize, Or . . *Disney*
{ Sa a fesse Or, betw. 3 asses pass. Arg. . . *Ayscough*

𝔖tapleford.

Rectoria appropriata Prioratui Scæ Catharinæ extra muros civitatis Lincoln'.

𝔏onderthorp.

Statua lapidea sub muro boreali tibiis in crucem transversis.

In Fenestra australi effigies Sci Wolfrani et Sci Egidii, et subtus, Orate pro bono statu Rici Andrew, Prebendarii de Grantham.

[p. 342.]

𝔄shby, 𝔚est.

Fenestra borealis Cancelli :—
Sa. a crosse between 4 cinquefoyles, Arg.

Campanæ :—
1. Sit nomen Domini benedictum.
2. Intonat e cælis vox campanæ Michaelis.
3. Sum rosa pulsata mundi Maria vocata.

---

* This marriage of Richard Disney with Nele, d. and h. of Sir William Hussey, son and heir of John, Lord Hussey, brought into the Disney family a claim to the Barony of Hussey of Sleaford, which had been forfeited by the attainder of John, Lord Hussey, in 1536. Col. Molyneux Disney presented a petition for the restoration of the Barony in 1680, but did not proceed with it, probably owing to the execution of his only surviving son, William Disney, for complicity in Monmouth's rebellion in 1685.—*Ed.*

Reston.

Fenestra australis :—
G. a fesse between 3 escallops, Or .   .   .   . *Chamberlaine*

Hic jacet Thomas North et Elizabetha uxor ejus qui obierunt 10°
die .   .   .   M°CCCC°LX° .   .   .   quorum &c.

Legbourne.

Sa. 2 lyons pawes erased, in saltier, Ermyne .   . *Legbourne*

Hoc scutum quater in Cancello, quater in Navi Ecclesiæ, et semel
in Campanili.

In Cancello :—
Hic jacet Mary Kyngerbe quæ obiit . . Año Dñi 1500, &c.

Hic jacet .   .   . Palmer, Capellanus, qui obiit .   .   . Año Dñi
1460, cujus aīe &c.

Hic jacet .   .   . Harrington, Capellanus, qui obiit .   .   .

[p. 343.]

Conisholme.

Fenestra orientalis Cancelli :—
Or, a lyon rampant double-queue, Sa. .   .   .   . *Welles*
Empaled { Or, a lyon rampant double queue, Sa. .   .   . *Welles*
{ Barry of 6, Erm. & G. 3 crescents, Sa. .   . *Waterton*
Empaled { Or, a lyon rampant double queue, Sa. .   .   . *Welles*
{ G. a lyon rampant, Arg. .   .   .   .   . *Mowbray*
Empaled { Or, a lyon rampant double queue Sa. .   .   . *Welles*
{ Quarterly, *Ufford* & *Beke* .   .   .   . *Willughby*
Welles, with a labell of 5, Arg.

Tumulus marmoreus ære fixus :—
Hic jacent Joħes Langholme de Conisholme, Arm. et Anna uxor
ejus, qui quidem Joħes obiit X .   .   .

Super tumulum effigies quinque filiorum et novem filiarum. Tria
scuta ablata, unum permanens, Viz^t :—
Empaled { Arg. on 2 barrs . . 6 bezants, a border . .
{ A bend engrayled.

Fenestra borealis :—
Sa. 3 conyes heads erased, Arg. .   .   .   . *Conisholme*
Arg. a chevron betw. 3 Pine-apple trees, Vert.

Fenestra australis :—
Empaled { Or, a lyon ramp. double queue, Sa. .   . *Welles*
{ G. a lyon rampant, Arg. .   .   .   . *Mowbray*

[p. 344.]

Burton en les Coggles.

Fenestra orientalis Insulæ australis :—

Empaled { Arg. a fesse between 3 cootes, Sa.   .   .   . *Coote*
{ Arg. a fesse daunce betw. 3 talbots-heads, erased, Sa. *Spayne*

Or, 3 chevrons, Vert   .   .   .   .   .   . *Corville*

Arg. 3 barrs G. in bend a crosse portate, B.   . *Sc'us Gilbertus*
Hæc sunt arma Divi Gilberti.

Fenestra australis :—

Or, 3 chevrons, Vert, *bis*   .   .   .   .   . *Corville*

Fenestra occidentalis :—

Or, 2 barrs G. in cheife 3 torteaux   .   .   .   . *Wake*

In muro australi Insulæ prædictæ, Duo milites tibiis in crucem transversis.

Tumulus in Cancello :—

Robertus Cholmeley, Arm. obiit 4ᵗᵒ Idus Jun. 1590, Ætat. 64.

G. in cheife 2 helmets Arg. in bast a garbe, Or   .   . *Cholmeley*

Empaled { Quarterly { G. in cheife 2 helmets, Arg. in bast a
garbe, Or   .   .   .   . *Cholemeley*
{ Fusilly & bendy, Arg. & B. a bend G. fretty, Or.
{ Arg. 3 cockes Sa. over all a martlet difference.
{ Arg. a manche, Sa.   .   .   .   .   . *Hastings*

Thomas Bell, Rector.

[p. 345.]

Scampton.

Frances, wife of Henry Fitzwilliam of Scampton, daughter of Sir James Fuljambe of Walton, Knt., dyed 10° die Decemb. 1581, Año 24° Eliz.*

Per pale { Lozengy, Arg. & G. (a mullet within a crescent) *Fitzwilliam*
{ Sa. a bend between 6 escalops, Or   .   . *Fuljamb*

---

* Illingworth gives the atchievement on this monument as quartering 12 coats for Fitzwilliam, and four for Foljambe ; Viz : 1. Lozengy, Arg. and Gules (*Fitzwilliam*) ; 2. Chequy (*Warren*) ; 3. Or, a chief Azure (*Lizeurs*) ; 4. Quarterly, Or and G. a bend Sa. a label of 5, Arg. (*Fitz-eustace*) ; 5. G. an orle, Arg. (*Baliol*) ; 6. Arg a chief G. and a bend. Az. (*Cromwell*) ; 7. Erm. a fesse G. (*Bernake*) ; 8. Arg. 2 cinquefoyles in base, and a canton, G. (*Driby*) ; 9. Chequy, Or and G. a chief. Erm. (*Tateshale*) ; 10. G. a lion ramp. Or (*Albini, Earl of Arundel*) ; 11. Az. 3 garbes Or (*Blundeville*) ; 12. Az. a wolf's head, erased, Arg. (*Lupus*). Empaling : 1. Sa. a bend between 6 escalops, Or (*Foljambe*) ; Arg. a bend Az. semee of crosscrosslets Or (*Loudham*) ; 3. Arg. a chevron between 3 escalops G. (*Bretton*) ; 4. Erm. a fesse .   .   . (*Bernake ?*).—*Ed.*

Kirkeby, East.

In Fenestris :—

G. 3 lyoncells passants gardants Or, a labell of 3, Ermyn.

G. 3 crosse crosselets fitchy, Arg.

Barry wavy Arg. & Sa. on a cheife G. a lyon ramp. Or *Mercatores Siapulæ*
Arg. on a chevron B. 3 crescents Or, betw 3 trefoyles, Sa.

In Fenestra orientali Capellæ australis :—

Effigies bellatoris, super cujus humerum parma aurea in qua depingitur Leo rubeus, erectus, nec non super paludamentum talis Leo rubeus et erectus ; subter pedes in Fenestra hæc inscriptio :—

> Silkeston Miles hic Robertus tumulatus,
> Hanc qui Cantariam fecit et Ecclesiam.

[p. 346.]

Staveley.[*]

Juxta ostium aquilonar' Cancelli :—

Upon a grey ashlar ye effigies in brasse of one in complete armour, saving y^t his head is uncovered, his feete resting upon a greyhounde, his sword hanging crosse along his belly, ye hilt towards ye right side ; on his surcoate on either shoulder a Bend betw. 6 escalops ; ye same over his belly In a scrowle on ye right side of his face this—Sancta Trinitas, unus Deus, miserere nobis. On the other side this—Deus propitius esto mihi peccatori. Over his head ye picture of ye Trinity in Brasse. At ye 4 corners of the stone 4 escocheons :—

1. A bende between 6 escalops . . . . *Frescheville*
2. Empaled—*Frescheville*, & on a bende betw. 6 martlets 3 lozenges voyded . . . . . . *Wortley*
3. Empaled—*Frescheville*, & a lyon rampant guardant . *Musard*
4. *Frescheville* alone.

About ye verge this inscription :—Orate pro aīabus Petri Frechwell, Arm. Dñi de Staley in Com. Derb. qui obiit . . die mensis . . Año Dñi M^{o}CCCC^o . . . et Matildæ uxoris ejus, Quorum aīabus propitietur Deus. Amen.

---

* Staveley is near Chesterfield in Derbyshire, but is here included by G. Holles on account of his own descent from the Frescheville family. Sir Piers, or Peter Frescheville, whose monument is first mentioned, died in 1503, having married Maud, d. of Thomas Wortley, who died in 1482. Their son, John Frescheville, Esq., married Elizabeth, d. of Henry Sothill, Esq., and died in 1509, as is also recorded above. Their son, Sir Peter, knighted at Leith in 1544, married Elizabeth, d. of Richard Tempest, Esq., and died in 1588 ; and it was their son, another Peter Frescheville, who married Elizabeth, d. of Sir Gervase Clifton, Knt., and left two daughters coheiresses, one of whom, Frances, married Sir Gervase Holles, of Burgh, Knt., and was the mother of Frescheville Holles, Esq., who died in 1630, and the grandmother of Col. Gervase Holles, our author.—*Ed.*

Upon ye wall close to itt ye effigies in brasse of a man in armour kneeling, his wife over agaynst him standing, behinde him eight sonnes kneeling. In a scrowle before his face this—Sancta Maria, ora pro nobis. Before hirs this—O mater Dei, memento mei. Above ye Virgin with Christ in hir armes. Under, this inscription—" Here under foote lyeth ye bodyes of Peyrs Freychwell & Mawde his wife, & sometyme Squier unto ye noble & excellent Prince King Henry ye Sixth, & Lord & Patron of this church, & grete benefactor to the seyd chirch, which Peyrs decessyd the 25th day of Marche in y^e [p. 347] yere of our Lord 1503, on whose soulys Jhesu have mercy Amen."

On ye south side of ye Chancell :—

Upon a flatt white stone of Alabaster raysed some halfe a yard from ye floore is ye pourtrayture of a man armed, his sword hanging on his left side, even downeward, his feete upon a greyhounde, over his head a Bend betw. 6 Escallops . . . About ye stone this inscription :—

Hic jacet Joħes Fretchwell, Armig. qui diem suum clausit extremum vicesimo . . . mensis Januarii, Año Dñi 1509, Cujus aïæ propitietur Deus. Amen.

On a grave-stone :—

Hic jacet Dñus Joħes Warton, quondam Rector istius Eccħæ, cujus aïæ propitietur Deus. Amen.

In ye East window :—
Arg. 5 fusills in fesse, G. . . . . . . *Hebden*
Arg. a bend between 6 martlets, Sa. . . . . . *Tempest*

Underneath—Orate pro bono statu Thomæ Tempest, Armig., et . . . uxoris ejus qui istam fenestram fieri fecit.

In ye next window South :—
B. a bend between 6 escallops, Arg. . . . . *Frescheville*
Arg. on a saltier engrailed Sa. 9 annulets, Or . . . *Leake*

At ye bottom of ye window under ye first coate one in armour kneeling, upon his surcoate the Bend & 6 Escallops ; his hayre yellow, his hands closed & erect. Underneath, this inscription :—

Orate pro aïa Johannis Fretchvile, Armigeri, et pro aïabus oïm antecessorum.

In the next pane his wife kneeling at an Altar (as likewise hir husband) hir hands erect, upon hir gowne ye saltoyre [p. 348] & annulets ; underwritten :—

Orate pro bono statu Elizabethæ uxoris ejus, unius benefactorum.

In ye same pane behinde him his sonne kneeling at an altar, in a red robe, yellow haired ; underwritten :—

Orate pro bono statu Petri Freschevile filii dči Joħis.

Behinde hir a daughter kneeling, in a red gowne.

In the next window :—
Arg. 3 magpies, Proper . . . . . . *Bakewell*
Underwritten :—Orate pro aïa Joħis Bakewell, Capellani, qui istam fenestram fieri fecit.

In a south window :—
B. a bend between 6 escallops, Arg. . . . . *Frescheville*
Written in old characters—𝕽𝖆𝖉𝖚𝖑𝖕𝖍𝖚𝖘 𝕱𝖗𝖊𝖈𝖍𝖊𝖇𝖎𝖑𝖊.*

In yᵉ south window :—
Sa. 6 annulets, Or, 3, 2, 1 . . . . . . [*Leeke*]
Arg. 3 Livery potts, G. a border, Sa. bezanty . [*Monboucher*]
Paly of 6, Or & G. on a bend Sa. 3 water-bougets, Arg. . [*Birton*]
Or, on a fesse G. 3 water-bougets, Arg. over all a bend, Sa. [*Bingham*]
Barry of 6, Or & G. a canton, Erm. . . . . *Gousla*

[p. 349.]

ᵂ̴alesby.

Sa. a bend between 6 crosses crosselets, Arg. . . *Lungvilliers*
B. a crosse chequy, Arg. & G. . . . . . *Cokefeld*

Faldingworth.

G. a chevron between 10 crosse-crosselets, Or . . . *Kyme*
G. a cinquefoyle peirced betw. 8 crosses patonce, Or . *Umfravile*
G. a cinquefoyle pierced betw. 5 crosses patonce, Or . *Umfravile*
Or, a cheife endented. Vert, over all a bend, G. *Nevile, of Faldingworth*

Effigies bellatoris, super cujus paludamentum p̄dca insignia de *Nevile*, necnon præ manibus—*Nevile*.

Effigies fæminæ gestantis præ manibus eadem insignia de *Nevile*, et super tunicam hæe, Vizᵗ :—B. fretty Arg.

On a grave-stone :—
Icy gist . . . omas de Nevile patrone de cest eglise, qui morust . . .

---

* Probably Ralph Frescheville, grandfather of the first Sir Peter, who acquired Staveley by his marriage with Margaret, daughter and heir of Nicholas Musard, lord of Staveley, 7 Edw. III (1333).—*Ed.*

General Index.

NAMES AND PLACES.

N.B.—This index does not include the names and places on pages 17 and 18.

Bard, Hugh, 20.
—— Thomas, 106.
Bardney, 239.
—— John, 162.
—— Roger, 170.
Barioneis, Richard, 20.
Barkeley, Sir Laurence, 194.
—— Sir Thomas, 193.
Barkeston, 234.
Barley, Thomas, 31.
Barlings Abbey, 155, 190.
Barnabe, —, 80.
—— Margaret, 80.
Barnaby, John, 12, 228.
Barnardiston, Elizabeth, 71.
—— Isabella, 72.
—— Joan, 72.
—— John, 72.
—— Roger, 72.
—— Thomas, 71.
Barnetby, 117-8.
—— John, 81.
—— Robert, 80.
Barrowby, 223.
Barton, co. Nott., 19.
—— on Humber, 78-81.
—— —— St. Mary's, 78-80.
—— —— St. Peter's, 80, 81.
Bary, Hugh, 41.
Basford, 44.
Bassingham, 243.
Baumber, 135-6.
Batelay, Robert, 12.
Bawde, Robert, 201.
Bawtry, 48.
Bayl, Robert, 213.
Beatrice, Nun of Grimsby, 12.
Beatson, Edward, 209.
—— Thomas, 209.
Beauchamp, John de, 204.
—— Margaret, 204.
Beaufort, John, Duke of Somerset,204
—— Lady Margaret, 204.
Beaumont, Francis, 49, 50.
Becket, St. Thomas, 110, 114, 124.
Beckingham, 226.
Bek, Sir Walter, 164.
Bekering, Sir John, 224n.
Bekingham, Elias, 22, 30.
Beelsby, 132-3.
Bel, Hugh de, 22.
Belchford, 44.
Belesby, William de, 16, 132.

Bell, Thomas, 248.
Bells at Asgarby, 218.
—— Barrowby, 224.
—— Croyland, 181.
—— Digby, 237.
—— Dunston, 243.
—— Hough, 232.
—— Navenby, 241.
—— Quadring, 172.
—— West Ashby, 246.
Belton, 244, 245.
Benington, 159.
Beningworth, 134.
Bennington, 222.
Bereford, Juliana de, 197
—— Reginald de, 197.
—— William de, 22, 30.
Beresford, Christopher, 228.
Berham, Thomas, 198.
Berkeley, Edward, ix, *Ped.*
—— Elizabeth, ix, xii, *Ped.*
—— Gervase, ix, xii.
Bertie, Sir Peregrine, 87.
—— Richard, 86.
Bestwood, 36.
Bevercotes, Richard, 44, 66.
Beverley, Thomas, 219.
Bicker, 171.
Bigby, 118-20.
Bigod, Elizabeth, 204.
Billesfield, Robert de, 208.
Billingay, 185-6.
Billingborough, 189.
Binbroke, John, 6.
Binbrooke, St Gabriel, 133-4.
—— St. Mary, 133.
Bingham, Thomas, 39.
—— Wapentake, 25.
Biron, Richard de, 44.
Bissa, a Hind, 21.
Bitham Castle, 202.
—— Parva, 202.
Blackewall, —, 103.
Blankney, 238.
Blount, Agnes, 136.
—— Elizabeth, 186.
—— Sir John, 186.
—— Thomas, 136.
Bloxham, 233.
Blund, Richard le, 21, 22.
Blythe, co. Nott., 47, 48, 49.
—— Hosp. of St. John Evang., 49.
Blyton, 148.

Clement, presbyter, 14.
Clibanus, 232.
Clifford, Roger de, 28.
Clifton, co. Nott., 19-51 *passim*, 183, 233.
—— Church, 42-3, 46, 48.
—— College, 36, 37, 42, 45, 46, 47.
—— St. Mary, 36, 37.
—— St. Nicholas de, 37.
Clifton, Clyfton, Agnes, 47.
—— Alice, 36, 42, 213.
—— Aluared, 19, 20.
—— Amflisia, 25.
—— Anthony, 43.
—— Catherine, 29.
—— Elizabeth, 43, 183, 249.
—— Frances, 43.
—— Gervase, Sir Gervase, vi, *Ped.*, 20-51 *passim*, 140, 183, 249.
—— George, 42, 50, 233.
—— Hugh, 47.
—— Isabella, 27, 28, 45, 46.
—— Ismania, 20.
—— James, 213.
—— Jane, 48.
—— Joan, 45.
—— John, 22, 26, 29, 42, 48.
—— Margaret, 23, 28, 45.
—— Mary, 43.
—— Matilda, 38, 44
—— Ralph, 26, 28.
—— Richard, 48, 49.
—— Robert, 20, 23, 26, 27, 32, 34, 36, 37, 41, 42, 43.
—— Robert, Archdeacon, 46, 47.
—— Roger, 26.
—— William, 49.
—— Winifred, 42, 43, 49, 233.
Clipstone in Shirewood, co.Nott.,35,36.
Cnut, 19.
Cobham, Anne, 151.
—— Reginald, Lord, 151.
—— Sir Thomas, 151.
Cockerington, 91.
Cock, John, 134.
Coke, Frances, 74.
—— Sir Francis, 74.
Cokke, Joan, 213.
—— John, 213.
—— Richard, 213.
Colby, John de, 209.
—— William, 209.
Coleby, 240.

Colsell, William, 197.
Colston, Agnes, 206.
—— John, 206.
Colthirst, John, 210.
Colville, Margaret, 194.
—— Roger, 194.
Coningsby, 136-9.
—— Gild of St. Mary, 138.
Conisholme, 247.
Constable, Agnes, 42.
—— Anne, 65, 233.
—— Sir John, 42, 233.
—— Sir Robert, 42, 65.
Cooke, Sir Anthony, 175.
Copledike, Francis, 131.
—— John, 129, 130, 131.
—— Sir John, 129.
—— Margaret, 129, 182.
—— Thomas, 182.
Corbrig, Thomas de, 65.
Corby, 209.
Cornwall, Edmund, Earl of, 28.
—— Duke of, 118.
Corringham, Magna, 149.
—— Parva, 149.
Cosdre, 141.
Cosson, Agnes, 132.
—— Margaret, 132.
—— Robert, 132.
Cotes, Little, 11-13.
—— Ch. of St. Michael, 12.
—— Magna, 71, 72.
—— by Stow, 145.
Cotes, John, will of, 12, 13.
—— Elizabeth, 12.
—— Peter, 12.
Cotham, co. Nott., 224n.
Cotton, John, 35.
Cracroft, Leonard, 154.
Cressy, Catherine de, 29, 29.
—— Cecilia, 30, 31.
—— Edmund, 30.
—— Elizabeth, 29, 224.
—— Geoffrey, 30.
—— Hugh, 29, 31, 224.
—— Joan, 30.
—— John, 29.
—— Robert, 49, 187.
—— Roger, 30, 31.
—— William, 30, 31.
Cranemere, Hugh de, 168.
Cranmer, daughter of, 233.
Creoun, Petronilla de, 211.

Wingfield, Charles, 243.
Winkhill Aisle (Heckington), 192.
Wirkesworth, co. Derby, 40.
Witham, 102.
Withcall, 105.
Witherwicke, John, 99, 100.
—— Judith, 99.
—— Matilda, 100.
Wivelsby, 82.
Wivelsby, Philip de, 15.
Woodhouse, co. Nott., 35, 46, 49, 50.
Woodroffe, Walter, 156.
Woodthorpe, Thomas, 100.
Worcester, Henry, Earl of, 214.
Worsley, Seth, 36.
Wortes, John, 184.
Worthington, Joan, 229.
—— William, 209.
Wortley, Maud, 249.
—— Thomas, 249.
Wowe, Amabilla, 26.
—— Richard de, 26.
Wrangle, 160-1.
Wray, Sir Christopher, 146-7.
—— Sir John, 64.
—— Lucy, 63, 64.
—— Sir William, 63, 64.

Wren, John, 92.
Wright, Thomas, 64.
Wyche, Margaret de, 116.
Wydevile, Anthony, 44.
Wyga, John, 106.
Wykes (Wekes), 31, 44.
Wyke, John, 192, 212.
Wyld, Thomas, 133.

Yarborough, Charles, 94.
Yates, Anne, 93.
—— Simon, 226.
—— William, 93.
Yawthorpe, 149.
Yaxley, Anthony, 71.
Yerburgh, Edmund, 66.
—— Margaret, 66.
York, St. Mary's Abbey, 41.
York, Prebendary of, 229.
York, Henry, Duke of, 41.
—— Richard, Duke of, 50.
—— William of, 22
Yorke, Elizabeth, 145.
—— George, 145.

Zouch, Richard, Lord, 205n.

Index of Coats of Arms.